VILLAGE IN VIETNAM

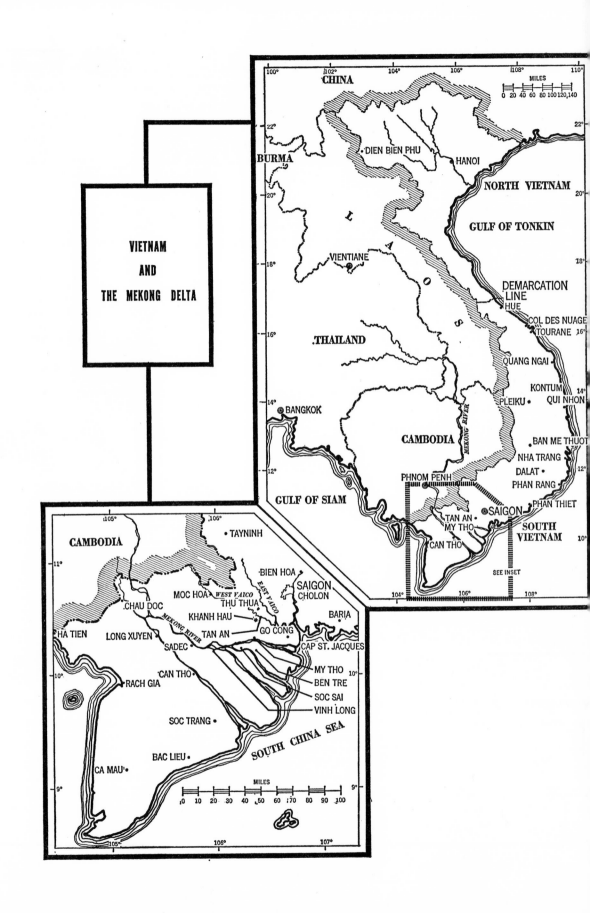

VIETNAM
AND
THE MEKONG DELTA

VILLAGE IN VIETNAM

by Gerald Cannon Hickey

New Haven and London, Yale University Press, 1964

To my parents

Contents

PLATES

FIGURES

TABLES

Foreword

BY PAUL MUS

THERE WAS A TIME, in what soon was to cease to be French Indochina, when, secure in our long experience, we French looked with some shade of self-complacency on the well-intentioned endeavors of the first American observers, later styled advisers, to assess the situation for themselves. Those of us still on the scene, mainly in private business or as educators, would have little occasion to do so now that the collection and sorting of information, of which the present volume is a valuable sample, is developing on a scale and with motivations undreamt of in our day. In the United States, specialized departments in several major universities act as rear bases. With the help of Eastern and Western instructors and native informants, plus up-to-date audiovisual centers, they have given the lie, for instance, to our settled belief that Vietnamese was too difficult a language to be learned by the average European adult. Our specialists (usually only cum interpreter) now face a growing team of American opposite numbers who are fully aware, although the niceties of the variotonic pronunciation remain a serious difficulty, that once mastered, they afford unique help in memorizing terms, distinguishing the overtones, and feeling the drive, balance, and semantic contour of a sentence. *Le mouvement se prouve en marchant.*

This throws no discredit on previous accomplishments, which were, of course, in keeping with earlier and very different circumstances. Father Léopold Cadière's contributions in so many fields to our intimate knowledge of Vietnam and the Vietnamese and Professor Pierre Gourou's masterwork, *Les Paysans du Delta Tonkinois,* are likely to remain long unequaled.

However, comparing Mr. Hickey's study with standard productions of the French Colonial period, such as Kresser's *La Commune Annamite en Cochinchine,*[1] Ory's *La Commune Annamite au Tonkin,*[2] or Rouilly's *La Com-*

1. *La Commune Annamite au Cochinchine; Le Recrutement des Notables,* Preface by J. Krautheimer, Paris, Les Editions Domat-Montchrestien, 1935.
2. Paris, Challamel, 1894.

mune Annamite,[3] we soon discern that, although one may gather a great deal of direct, coherent information on such matters as the organization, the customs and behavior, the social and moral values, as well as the historical background of Vietnamese rural communities, yet what we usually miss is the *tempo,* the color of the scene, as it must have appeared to those who lived and enacted it on such diverse and sometimes sharply differentiated occasions. On them, much; of them on themselves, not enough.

By welcome contrast, lively and highly informative illustrations and episodic accounts will be found throughout Mr. Hickey's well-organized and substantial chapters. The meaning to be read in these short documentary films far exceeds, sociologically, the mere picturesque. A good instance of this is the seemingly odd way some experienced members of the Village Council will arbitrate a difference between two of their fellow villagers in order to avoid embittering the dispute, a danger no one having any familiarity with Vietnamese country life will underestimate: "Part of the pattern is for the arbitrator to appear somewhat disinterested, often continuing to read a document or carry on business with another villager or with the village clerk" (p. 197). This should by no means be construed as a slight deliberately put upon the disputing parties by a self-assertive petty official; it is part of a formal procedure reminiscent of the behavioral injunctions (there again essentially symbolic) of ancient Roman law. Should one coin such a phrase as *manus retentio,* to match the classic *manus injectio?* The scenario dramatizes and publishes a repugnance to take the case into one's hands—the reverse of an eagerness to step in that would portend some personal angle or leaning.

In social circles where "face" values play so dominant a role, meeting with such a reception, or rather absence of reception, cannot but impress, especially on the plaintiff, a strong feeling of having become parenthetic in a community the eyes and ears of which should be, *par excellence,* the notables. It must seem like being relegated to a world apart, a world of no standing, where one remains unperceived, a barely less acute, if much shorter, experience of what it means, institutionally, for an Indian to be "untouchable." The author continues:

> The village chief employs two techniques. One is to invoke a moral message, the other is to treat the situation lightly; sometimes he combines them. For example when Ong Ke Hien brought action against a tenant farmer for cutting down a banana tree on his property, the village

3. Paris, Les Presses Modernes, 1929.

chief advised him to be lenient, noting that he already had abundant worldly goods, and mercy would befit the highest venerable. Ong Ke Hien was moved by the argument and dropped the case.

The seeming facetiousness of the second technique appears to be a mechanism for preventing discussion from becoming too heated.

A woman from Ap Cau and her sister appeared at the Council House with a complaint against their neighbor who, in the course of an argument, struck her on the face. . . . Since she would require medical treatment, she wanted her assailant to pay the bills. The village chief agreed to give her a medical certificate to visit the clinic in Tan An but was reluctant to pass judgment on the man's conduct. Another member of the Village Council advised her to forget it, saying that he would receive his punishment "according to the principles of justice." . . . The woman, however, was not placated. . . . She also added that having one side of her face swollen as it was made her ugly, whereupon the village chief suggested that she let her neighbor strike her on the other side of the face so as to restore the balance. This brought laughter even from the woman and she agreed to drop her charges and accept the certificate for medical treatment [pp. 197–98].

More is meant here than meets the eye—probably more than a mere mechanism for preventing the discussion from becoming too heated. The process proved to be curative as well as preventive. In the previous instance the village chief had skillfully included the rich and influential Ke Hien in the circle from which emanate the moral and social pronouncements on right and wrong commonly endorsed by the consensus of the villagers as a whole. From that comprehensive standpoint and as a moral message from the sacred precincts, an appeal to the plaintiff's sense of mercy evoked Buddhistic rather than Confucian values—more personal, in the eyes of the community, though urging duties toward the others; worldwide values, in short, but fitting the local conditions. Parochial would perhaps be an acceptable approximation, with purely laudative implications.

At close examination, subtle local concerns and stresses appear to be at work behind the alleged motive. For if the village chief indisputably represents the face and mouthpiece of the administration, being the specific intermediary between the village and the higher authorities, on the other hand the Ke Hien, the "highest venerable" of the Cult Committee, stands for wider religious and moral beliefs and motivations, including a deeply ingrained if not always very active reverence for the Buddhistic ideals.

It was, in fact, *ex officio in officium,* each in his statutory capacity, that the village chief was addressing the Ke Hien publicly. One could easily frame his argument in a quasi-syllogistic form: The circle of the people whose opinions matter to the mind of the villagers believe that mercy befits a man; the Ke Hien is the soul and center of such a circle; the Ke Hien consequently will admit that to forgive his tenant befits him—and will drop the case. The old man, a devout Buddhist, as a matter of fact (a circumstance neither the village chief nor the bystanders ignored), had no escape left: he was cornered into forgiveness.

In the second instance, no Vietnamese will fail to sense a change of atmosphere, the key to which might well be that the parties, instead of being inhabitants of the central portion of the settlement near the *dinh,* come from a distant hamlet, Ap Cau, "The Hamlet of the Bridge" on the Rach Ong Dao, "favored by celestial forces," with its houses "comfortably shaded beneath coconut and areca palms," but for all that still just a hamlet; though integrated in the community, its denizens could not be considered full-time participants in the social circle centering on the Council House.

In many rural societies, and particularly among the Vietnamese, who are endowed with a keen sense of humor, such slight inequalities usually develop a hilarious tone, the effect of which is to mark the sociological threshhold without overstressing it; in fact, rather ameliorating it: a position closely akin, in that respect, to Marcel Mauss' *Parentés à plaisanteries.*[4] Relativity is the deep lesson implied: "You will ever find a rustic's rustic!"

In that light, the second anecdote evidently hinges on the artless way in which the plaintiff betrays her feminine concern regarding the effect of the blow. With a woman of the inner circle, the chances are that conventional modesty would have prevented so candid a statement; moreover, she would have been aware that the sight of a familiar face thus altered would have been more eloquent than words. But who knew if such was not the ordinary appearance of that one from Ap Cau? She manifestly wanted to make the point clear—and there the village chief found his cue.

All considered, then, this pattern does not deviate so flagrantly from the former one. In both cases the reference is to the same basic circle. The highest venerable did not dare to step out of it. In her turn, the lady from Ap Cau, by joining in the general laughter, reintegrated it. She thus concurred in erasing, or in "putting between brackets," to use Husserl's favorite phrase, her previous assertion of herself.

4. Marcel Mauss, *Parentés à plaisanteries, Ann.* de l'Ecole Pratique des Hautes Etudes . . . , 1927–28, Paris, 1928.

When the time comes, and it may not be so distant, for a general and in-
tensive elaboration and interpretation of the material collected by Mr.
Hickey and his fellow-workers in the project initiated by the Michigan State
University Vietnamese Advisory Group, my guess is that Mr. Hickey's contribution will rank high for its sharp and penetrating accommodation not,
as so often in such matters, *of* but *to* facts. In this field of the Southeast Asian
humanities there has been, in my opinion, so much honorable work accomplished by my compatriots in close cultural contact with the Vietnamese
(the latter being, however, significantly unaware that we would some day
refer to them under that name) that we should not now begrudge our appro-
bation and often our admiration to a handful of enterprising young American scholars and to an incipient Vietnamese–American cooperation. They
are indubitably adding to our own contribution much that is new and much
that is true, as a confirmation of the simple, usually unobserved, yet at times
deadly circumstance that *the question conditions the answer*—and even
more, what the questioner makes out of it.

The French were in charge, and too often what they finally gathered mir-
rored their preoccupations and prejudices, so apparent to the observant Vietnamese, in the way we had put our questions. This, however, was not without
some compensation. It is a feature of the Vietnamese character that an official investigation brought to them through regular channels will elicit from
them readier and more explicit answers than will any unfamiliar private inquirer. This remains from their long experience of Chinese and Sino–Vietnamese officialdom and administrative techniques. Inquiring into the common weal and woe should be the strict prerogative of the sovereign, his dele-
gates, and his advisers. Knowledge is power. All information concerning the
realm should accordingly be kept "classified," as we might put it ourselves—
made aware as we have been, thanks to the spirit and experience of the Cold
War, of the possible use and misuse of a restrictive discipline.

A Vietnamese peasant being asked a question, futile as it may seem at
first sight, by one whose bearings are not clear to him, more often than not
will fear that a naive and open answer might later be charged upon him as a
serious offense; and so, "Who cares to speak the truth?" as one of Kipling's
characters asks.

Under such conditions, all question and answer processes (except in familiar intercourse between equals—the "sociability level" of Gurvitch's
differential sociology) have to be presented as "on duty": official purpose on
one side and discharge of a subject's obligations on the other. Moreover, part
of those very obligations was to provide the authorities with answers that

were satisfactory. The inquirer was supposed to be experienced and clever enough to take due account of such a disposition in his informers, careful, above all, not to make him lose face.

The colonial administration, of course, had no eye for such niceties. On the spot, or more usually through the collected and processed answers accumulated in its files, it went straight to "facts," in the belief that knowledge of the facts would solve any problem, whereas, in that setting at least, *the* problem was to reach them.

Yet for the reason already stated, the official inquirer gathered more basic information, though biased, than the average private one, with the exception perhaps of a few technicians of the humanities, usually educators or priests, like Gourou or Cadière, who were content to invest long years of their lives in their studies.

The official results may be checked at their best, for instance, in a work like Yves Henry's *L'Economie Agricole de l'Indochine,* whose concrete information compares with *Les Paysans du Delta Tonkinois* or *Anthropologie populaire annamite.*[5] Its weaker point remains the heterogeneity of its sources, carrying with them unknown coefficients of deformation, unchecked on the spot by the same observer.

This sets off, by contrast, the advantages of the monographic method, of which Mr. Hickey has taken full benefit, laying hold, as it were, of life itself, with all it meant and means for the participants. Other tools, other products; and this method also has its limitations. In times of transition, however, not to speak of disintegration, local focus and immediacy becomes a must, if only to keep clear of theoretical, wishful thinking.

Indirectly approached in books and memoirs, official or semiofficial documents, statistics and census tables, the first half of the twentieth century in Vietnam would appear to be marked primarily by the conflict, the attempts at adjustment, and the final rupture between the colonial enterprise and a nation made aware of its qualifications by a long and often bloody, though culturally fruitful, intercourse with its gigantic neighbor, the most absorptive and assimilative of all the colonial powers the world has known—China. From Paul Doumer, organizer of the Indochinese Federation, to Dien Bien Phu, the whole affair would then document the struggle between Western and Eastern ideals and techniques, which now leaves that critically situated part of the world and its final choice halfway between.

5. Léopold Cadière, "Anthropologie populaire annamite," *Bulletin de l'École Française d'Extrême Orient, 15* (1915), 1–103.

Such an interpretation, objective as it claims to be, depends in fact on too many slogans and set judgments—"West is West . . ." and the like—to offer an accurate idea of the story as lived at ground level by 90 per cent of the interested parties, in the rice fields and sheltered villages of the rural areas. Constructing history on that elusive foundation, or rather on what of it did not escape us, two modes of generalization are permissible and should be complementary. The first would relate any limited area, such as Vietnam or French Indochina, to a continental or even intercontinental perspective, at the level of world affairs, wars and alliances, crises, and recoveries. Vietnam would thus be brought into line with what happened during the same period in the Philippines, Indonesia, Burma, and India, or in African territories and by contrast in independent Thailand, in Japan, or China, following the ups and downs of the colonial or colonialist adventure.

But a diachronic rather than synchronic study—taking into account time rather than geographical extension, for the first method pays more attention to the rhythm of development than to the clash and balance of factors, forces, and situations—emphasizes uniformities and changes, stagnation and acceleration, hysteresis and compensation, permanence and recurrence. It thus remains closer to the basic story, balanced between what made it what it is and what it will in turn make of the future; the broad synchronic synthesis of panoramic history seems risky, by comparison, if insufficiently supported by these ground-level considerations.

Once thus brought down to earth—to the "Good Earth" of the Far Eastern countryside—the long and eventful French episode appears to have been just an episode, a tool in the hands of history, rather than the creator of history. Seen from that standpoint, the real conflict, still continuing, might be said to have occurred less between French and Vietnamese colonizers, or colonialists and colonized, in a counterpoint of mutual but unequal interest and curiosity—adhesion, assimilation, contention, rebellion, and sporadic guerrilla resistance—than between town and village, new values and options having been introduced by the former element as against what the latter traditionally stood for.

In the light of my own limited but immediate experience, which began in 1907–08, the last echoes of the rebellions once spearheaded in the interior by the literati, and even the semipiratical guerrilla warfare doggedly carried on by the famous De Tham, entrenched in his long-impregnable den in the rough Yen The region, at that time no longer deeply affected life in towns like Hanoi, Haiphong, or Saigon, centers of the Colonial Administration and of the bulk of the European population. Order reigned in Warsaw—though from our house on the outskirts of Hanoi, halfway between the so-called Pagoda of the Great Buddha and the colorful Pigsty Village (let us remember that the pig is an emblem not of uncleanliness but of prosperity: *Schwein haben*), I listened as a child to the stray volleys of musketry from De Tham's guerrilleros on the other side of the peaceful Western Lake, on the day of the finally unsuccessful attempt to poison the French garrison (June 27, 1908).

To mark another significant stage in a somewhat agitated span of events, four years later I had become old enough to piece out, from bits of talk between adults and from what our servants had to say, some idea of a marked improvement in the tactics of the revolutionaries, such being the new appellation applied to them instead of rebels or pirates. It was the time of the Hanoi Hotel terrace "terrorist" bombing, in which two distinguished French senior officers, Majors Montgrand and Chapuis, lost their lives:[6] a new type of argument, visibly having more to do with us than the literati's conspiracies, screened by the bamboo curtain of back-country villages, or De Tham's vain dream some day to storm our urban strongholds.

Compensatorily, however, the new brand of conspirators—most of them trained and indoctrinated in Southern China or in Japan—did not at first enjoy the sympathy and extensive support granted by the rural masses to the traditional leaders of the previous period. It took time to adjust the two factors—time and costly experiences, like the premature and ill-fated "nationalist" action (nationalist in the terminology of the time meant non-Marxist) of Nguyen Thai Hoc, a noble figure in the history of his country who was guillotined in Thai Nguyen in the early thirties with a group of fellow-conspirators. They were by no means merely "agitators" back from a period of instruction in foreign countries, but students or former university students whose last word on the scaffold was "Vietnam!"

Meanwhile the more positively calculating Nguyen Ai Quoc, now President Ho Chi Minh, was establishing his underground network of communications, never completely eradicated by the active French Sûreté; which was destined to play a major role in the following years, bringing town and village into closer cooperation on doctrine and program. This was the key to all further successes and, distasteful as it may be to us, there is no denying that in such matters the Marxist line proved most effective, starting as it did from such depressed areas as Nghe Tinh or Thai Binh.

6. By an unfortunate coincidence, both, and especially Major Chapuis, happened to be what some colonial circles of the period called "annamitophiles," i.e. "friends of the Annamites."

One of the distinctive features of the 1930–31 "unrest" was thus a cleavage between the programs put forward by the more (and prematurely) active political leaders of the new generation and the dissatisfactions and sporadic uprisings in the rural areas; in other words, between the modernized ideas and approaches of the former and the traditional tempo of the latter.

North Vietnam seems—at least officially—to have outgrown most of these conflicting factors, but a cleavage of nearly the same order is still a disquieting element in the South Vietnamese situation. Who among the local leaders can safely foretell the impact on rural circles of what may or may not be planned and decided in Saigon? It is precisely this recurrent question, to which the colonial authorities in their day more than once gave unsatisfactory—when not utterly disastrous—answers, that so validly introduces Mr. Hickey's study at the village level.

Let us not lose sight of George Santayana's warning that "Those who do not remember the past are condemned to repeat it." There is still a good deal to be learned from the French endeavors to innovate as well as to preserve; but the last and essential lesson should be *wherein they failed*. We might here define this, in the light of Mr. Hickey's researches, as a failure to introduce harmony and understanding between leadership, as assumed by urban circles, and basic productivity and political support at the village level, with its implied sets and patterns of public opinion.

We are thus brought back to the rough sketch of a sociological syllogism, drawn from Mr. Hickey's vivid and thorough account of the inner story of *his* village. The major premise presents itself neither as a circle of things nor of persons but as the balanced total of the opinions professed on the things that matter by the persons who count in the eyes of the community as a whole. No person, no thing, stands any chance to be accepted locally (that is to say, throughout the country) that has not been thus filtered. An immediate consequence is that, for all the care with which administrative previsions and predictions may have been worked out by the most competent experts, they are not likely to be brought into being if sufficient account has not been taken of that collective condition and if adequate means to implement them have not been provided.

In his instructive study, *La Commune Annamite en Cochinchine: Le Recrutement des Notables,* Kresser sums up as follows the opinions that prevailed in the years 1925–26, in French administrative circles, concerning the organic structure of the village councils in South Vietnam (i.e. Cochinchina), as defined and established by a decree of the Governor General dated August 27, 1904:

The communal structure . . . had ceased to be in keeping with local circumstances. It had fallen behind the new needs resulting from a soaring economy and from the extension of a network of thoroughfares permitting fast and easy connexions with the remotest villages of the interior. It had moreover become psychologically ill-adapted to the evolution of a people which although its solidity has long been in the cohesion of its families, nevertheless evinces nowadays an ever increasing leaning towards individualism.[7]

Khanh Hau provided an ideal setting to test the soundness of such views. Far enough from Saigon to be truly rural (34 miles), it is by no means a remote village of the interior; furthermore it is situated along the national highway connecting Saigon with the Cambodian border. Better still, "a spur road capable of accommodating any kind of vehicle runs through the agglomeration, connecting at both ends with the national highway" (p. 19).

For all that can thus be observed at first sight, no rural community ever adapted itself more unreservedly to a neighboring system of communication. Along the spur road, "a number of shops and many farmsteads are located . . . which gives it something of a 'main street' function" (p. 19). Local records show that this spur road, a deliberate attempt to connect the village with the outer world, was built in 1925, in perfect timing with the considerations quoted by Kresser.

Yet, thirty-five years later—more than the span of a generation—Khanh Hau baffles the experts' expectations. Individualism did *not* carry the day after all and, instead of achieving closer communication with an outer, modernized world, the village as Mr. Hickey sees and describes it is still a solid, self-reliant rural community, aware of what may be going on at a higher level but on its guard and alert to strain through its own social and political syllogisms whatever it decides to accept from it.

Of this, good evidence is at hand either here or in Hendry's earlier *Study of a Vietnamese Rural Community: Economic Activities* (Saigon, 1959). In fact, some inhabitants of Khanh Hau have proved successful in commercial enterprises, but all such ventures appear to have been mainly connected with the ancestral way of life, comprising chiefly attempts to modernize the traditional rice-milling process. Prior to 1950, most of the rice mills in Southern Vietnam were in Cholon, the prosperous and extensive Chinese establishment close to Saigon, but by 1959 Khanh Hau possessed two ma-

7. Kresser, p. 62.

chine-powered rice mills, "one of the most advanced technical innovations in the village" (p. 170). To quote Mr. Hickey's comment:

> In spite of the fact that the commercial people have traditionally been ranked low in Vietnamese society [the traditional Chinese and Sino–Vietnamese listing was scholar, peasant, artisan, merchant] these entrepreneurs are not regarded with disdain, and among them are members of the Village Council and high-ranking members of the Cult Committee [p. 173].

That such should remain the natural and final criterion in evaluating even innovations, as reflected in social values, speaks well for the persistent loyalty of the community to customary standards. The rural village stands its ground and tailors modern initiative to its own measure.

This does not mean that individualism and free enterprise, though not triumphant as prematurely predicted, are done with at that level. At times they will find limited but striking expression, as for instance in Ong Lam's motto: "The home of the truly big man, the clever man, is everywhere" (p. 173). This philosophy of "the most venturesome businessman" in Khanh Hau runs directly counter to the outlook of most of the village. It corresponds to a larger market economy, not to the subsistence system.[8]

Is Khanh Hau in transition then? The changes are bound to come. Yet, for the time being, Mr. Hickey's evaluation would point to a side-of-the-road rather than middle-of-the-road position. He emphasizes the Ngo Dinh Diem government's meritorious endeavors to break through an unspoken, intangible, and, up to now, invincible reticence, the center of which, reminiscent of Blaise Pascal's famous definition of infinitude, is everywhere, the contour that would permit taking hold of it, nowhere; for, as already observed, it is neither a circle of things nor of people but an elusive and tenacious, though not officially assumed, body of opinions. I feel inclined to believe that awareness of this central value and supreme source of valuation constitutes, in Mr. Hickey's monograph, the most precious contribution to our understanding not only of South Vietnamese rural communities but by and large of the whole situation in the area. No prejudice, no subservience to any biased propaganda, obscures his vision. Here, for a change, we meet things and men as they are and as they manifest themselves on the spot:

> Support of the central government is the major theme of the National Revolutionary Movement, which is the only official political

8. Hendry, pp. 198, 230.

party in the village. . . . During 1958 and 1959, at some of the large village-sponsored gatherings, speakers emphasized the necessity for villagers to join the party to demonstrate their loyalty to the government and their will to fight the Viet Cong [the Communist resistance movement]. On these occasions the villagers appeared impassive [pp. 202–03]. . . . One of the primary propaganda vehicles in the village is the Communist Denunciation Committee, which consists of 24 members who, according to the village chief, are drawn from the "elite" of the village (including all members of the Council and some high venerables) [members of the Cult Committee]. . . . Villagers dutifully assist at these meetings but most do not appear particularly attentive. Some squat outside the dinh chattering in low tones while a few read newspapers. After one denunciation meeting, a young farmer regaled his friends in one of the nearby shops by imitating the speaker of the evening [p. 205].

Who could ask for a clearer and more convincing instance, not of just a scoffing attitude, even less of clownish levity, but in true rural style of a conventional quasi-ritual action of the people as such, "putting into brackets" as in a world apart an institution or a behavioral pattern of which sociologically—one may go so far as to say semantically—the village did not approve?

This, by the way, disposes of any politically biased interpretation that would induce us to read in such an attitude a concealed preference for the "other side": rebels, agitators, conspirators, revolutionaries are old names for something not entirely new. Even when sheltering some activities of this kind, the village remains marginal, bracketing them provisionally with the rest.

In his parallel *Study of a Vietnamese Rural Community: Administrative Activities* (Saigon, 1960), Woodruff gives the following sample of the kind of speech current in these meetings:

> Myself, when I popularize the governmental policies, I directly participate in the political life of our country. Why not you? Why are you somewhat afraid of politics? Comfort yourselves, I would say. Since the top leader of our organization—the National Revolutionary Movement [disbanded after the coup of Nov. 1, 1963]—is our President himself, any of you who fails to join shows evidence of his indifference and could be regarded as guilty [p. 203, n. 20].

After such unequivocal apologia of the Führer's principle, the villagers dutifully come to the gatherings—and quietly read the papers.

What they want is an ideal wherein they can find more that concerns them.

In considering how far one's manner in putting questions goes in influencing and conditioning the answers, especially at the rural level where the inquiry had to be carried through, it is highly to the credit of Mr. Hickey and his co-workers that their reports should survive without needing recasting the dramatic turn recently taken after President Ngo Dinh Diem's assassination. One imagines easily how confusing would have been the publication and perusal of out-of-date themes of propaganda and governmental self-eulogy in the teeth of what has ensued.

Several of my own students at Yale are now at work in the field or just back from it and though, to my regret, Mr. Hickey does not happen to be one of them, I feel direct sympathy for his exertions and accomplishments. His country has shouldered a heavy burden and done much—not perhaps without some unavoidable misconceptions—but this alone would add up to a net profit: no one ever improved by experience his understanding of his fellow men who did not in the process improve his knowledge of himself.

Vaux-sur-Seine
June 1964

Preface

THE OBJECTIVES of this study are manifold. There is primarily the intention of making an ethnological contribution by adding a description of southern Vietnamese village society to the growing body of information about peoples of the world. As a village study, the broad conceptual base is rooted in the interlocking ideas of Henry Maine, Fustel de Coulanges, Lewis H. Morgan, Emile Durkheim, Ferdinand Tönnies, and Robert Redfield, whose discussion of the little community as an entity of human society was particularly influential. I have attempted to present the village as a whole—to unfold the fabric of interrelated social institutions that have to do with all aspects of village life, not from a flat, two-dimensional view but to show the changes that have been occurring and continue to occur—and relate it to the greater society of which it is a part. Finally, the village is analyzed in its own terms —as a little community.

Certain parts of the study speak to some specific social science theories, concepts, and techniques. Criteria for the existence of social classes as outlined by Max Weber and Frank Lynch are favored in discussing socioeconomic differentiation. The analysis of kinship has something to say about ideas of kin group solidarity as expressed by Edmund Leach and Maurice Freedman. Han Chi Fen's technique for analyzing Chinese kin terms was used in describing Vietnamese kin terms. William Davenport suggested a way of presenting household composition which facilitated numerical determination of adherence to the residence rule, and Moni Nag provided formulae for expressing fertility ratios. The technique of using profiles to illustrate socioeconomic variations and mobility patterns was modeled on the method employed by W. Lloyd Warner in his studies of American class structure.

Another purpose of this study is to furnish information that may be of use in fields related to anthropology. Those interested in economic development, for example, may find the changes in livelihood patterns (especially in relation to other social changes) to be of particular significance. There are data of use to the cultural geographer. The political scientist may focus on changes in village administration as they relate to other changes both within the village and in the greater society; and the historian might find interesting the microscopic view of a society in flux.

Research on the village of Khanh Hau was sponsored by the Michigan State University Vietnam Advisory Group, and the study was sanctioned by the Government of the Republic of South Vietnam through its local officials—the Province Chief of Long An province and the District Chief of Thu Thua district. The research team consisted of James Hendry, an economist, who was assisted by Nguyen Van Thuan; Lloyd Woodruff, a specialist in government, assisted by Nguyen Ngoc Yen; and myself, an anthropologist, assisted by Bui Quang Da, who in addition to collecting field data reliably extricated me from periodic linguistic entanglements. Rather than agreeing on common problems to study, we simply agreed to work in the same village, pursuing our separate disciplinary paths, discussing our findings, and sharing our data. The result was stimulating cooperation, some pooling of information, and increased sensitivity to the tools and interests of one another's approach to the study of society. After several months of planning and visiting villages of the Mekong River delta, we settled on Khanh Hau, and field research began in March 1958.

In gathering anthropological data, I used a wide variety of techniques. Besides the actual observation and incessant note-taking, I was able to participate, owing to the kind hospitality of the villagers, in weddings, funerals, ancestors' death anniversaries, and lunar new year observances, and to attend rituals in the village communal temple, the Buddhist pagodas, and the Cao Daist temples. The Village Council also invited me to attend various meetings and village celebrations, which provided ample opportunity to construct patterns of behavior and to note deviations from these patterns. In the course of visiting almost every household in the village, vast numbers of genealogies and some personal case histories were collected. Chatting with villagers on the roads and footpaths, in the shops and houses, observing the workers in the fields, and periodically posing questions yielded a great deal of information on all aspects of village life; at the same time it enabled me to obtain some degree of consensus on information already collected, particularly on reports of recent changes.

Specific informants were sought for certain kinds of information; for example, older women for descriptions of birth practices, former council members for data on organization and past functions of the Village Council, Buddhist monks, nuns, and adherents for information concerning Buddhism in the village, and members of the Village Council and hamlet chiefs for data on all aspects of government. Visits were made to Cao Daist holy sees at Ben Tre, Soc Sai, and Tay Ninh to obtain material on hierarchical organization and its relations with village congregations. Leaders of the Buddhist Association of South Vietnam at the Xa Loi pagoda in Saigon supplied information on the Buddhist hierarchy.

There was inevitable overlapping in the team's informal divisions of labor. Examination of village legal and administrative records was primarily Woodruff's function, but in the course of visiting the Council House I observed some of the administrative activities as well as arbitration of villagers' conflicts. Hendry analyzed land records and population figures, but since he also visited all parts of the village and participated in the activities of the villagers, there was considerable overlapping in our field notes, which permitted cross-checking and construction of common patterns for such things as agricultural techniques.

Cooperation among the team members continued, as did fieldwork, during the preparation of the preliminary reports that were intended primarily for the American Aid agencies in Saigon. Vietnamese language versions of these reports were presented to the Vietnamese Government. Some of the material from my colleagues' reports has, with their permission, been used in this book.*

Fieldwork ended in December 1959, but subsequent visits to Vietnam in 1962 and 1964, made possible by the RAND Corporation of Santa Monica, California, gave me the opportunity to return to Khanh Hau a number of times and permitted me to check specific information and update some of the field notes.

Some of those who helped make possible this work already have been mentioned, and to them I would like to express my gratitude. I also would like to extend my thanks to others who contributed directly or indirectly. Father Emmanuel Jacques and members of the Vietnamese Students' Association (then in Chicago) first stimulated my interest in Vietnam, and the faculty of the University of Chicago, particularly Fred Eggan, Robert Redfield, and Norton Ginsberg, imparted the professional skills necessary to the social scientist. Sally Cassidy and the Groom Foundation of Chicago provided a fellowship that made it possible for me to spend a year in Paris doing research on Indochina and attending lectures given by Claude Levi-Strauss, Paul Levi, and Georges Condominas.

Wesley Fischel offered me the research position with the Michigan State University Vietnam Advisory Group, and David Cole encouraged the Viet-

* Hendry (1959) and Woodruff (1960).

namese Government to approve the village study. Nguyen Van Mung, an old friend and former member of the Vietnamese Students' Association, helped me in making initial contacts with the villagers of Khanh Hau and generally provided valuable assistance in the field research. Here I would like to reiterate my gratitude to my Vietnamese and American fellow field-workers.

A postdoctoral fellowship from the Southeast Asia Studies Program of Yale University enabled me to spend several years in New Haven working on the manuscript and teaching. Adrienne Suddard, Ruth McVey, John Musgrave, and Huynh Sanh Thong read parts of the manuscript and offered valuable suggestions. The manuscript was typed by Ella Gibson, Helen Reed, and Gladys Page. Nguyen Van Tam did the sketches of village houses, construction features, artifacts, and decorative Vietnamese motifs used throughout the book. Richard Thompson drafted the maps. The professional guidance of Jane V. Olson and Anne Wilde at Yale University Press has been invaluable in producing the final product—the book.

Finally, I would like to offer my most heartfelt thanks to the Village Council and the good people of Khanh Hau for their kindness and cooperation, and for the things I learned from them.

Saigon, Vietnam   G.C.H.
March 1964

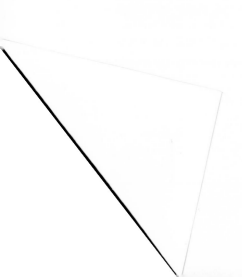

for data on all aspects of government. Visits were made to Cao Daist holy sees at Ben Tre, Soc Sai, and Tay Ninh to obtain material on hierarchical organization and its relations with village congregations. Leaders of the Buddhist Association of South Vietnam at the Xa Loi pagoda in Saigon supplied information on the Buddhist hierarchy.

There was inevitable overlapping in the team's informal divisions of labor. Examination of village legal and administrative records was primarily Woodruff's function, but in the course of visiting the Council House I observed some of the administrative activities as well as arbitration of villagers' conflicts. Hendry analyzed land records and population figures, but since he also visited all parts of the village and participated in the activities of the villagers, there was considerable overlapping in our field notes, which permitted cross-checking and construction of common patterns for such things as agricultural techniques.

Cooperation among the team members continued, as did fieldwork, during the preparation of the preliminary reports that were intended primarily for the American Aid agencies in Saigon. Vietnamese language versions of these reports were presented to the Vietnamese Government. Some of the material from my colleagues' reports has, with their permission, been used in this book.*

Fieldwork ended in December 1959, but subsequent visits to Vietnam in 1962 and 1964, made possible by the RAND Corporation of Santa Monica, California, gave me the opportunity to return to Khanh Hau a number of times and permitted me to check specific information and update some of the field notes.

Some of those who helped make possible this work already have been mentioned, and to them I would like to express my gratitude. I also would like to extend my thanks to others who contributed directly or indirectly. Father Emmanuel Jacques and members of the Vietnamese Students' Association (then in Chicago) first stimulated my interest in Vietnam, and the faculty of the University of Chicago, particularly Fred Eggan, Robert Redfield, and Norton Ginsberg, imparted the professional skills necessary to the social scientist. Sally Cassidy and the Groom Foundation of Chicago provided a fellowship that made it possible for me to spend a year in Paris doing research on Indochina and attending lectures given by Claude Levi-Strauss, Paul Levi, and Georges Condominas.

Wesley Fischel offered me the research position with the Michigan State University Vietnam Advisory Group, and David Cole encouraged the Viet-

* Hendry (1959) and Woodruff (1960).

namese Government to approve the village study. Nguyen Van Mung, an old friend and former member of the Vietnamese Students' Association, helped me in making initial contacts with the villagers of Khanh Hau and generally provided valuable assistance in the field research. Here I would like to reiterate my gratitude to my Vietnamese and American fellow field-workers.

A postdoctoral fellowship from the Southeast Asia Studies Program of Yale University enabled me to spend several years in New Haven working on the manuscript and teaching. Adrienne Suddard, Ruth McVey, John Musgrave, and Huynh Sanh Thong read parts of the manuscript and offered valuable suggestions. The manuscript was typed by Ella Gibson, Helen Reed, and Gladys Page. Nguyen Van Tam did the sketches of village houses, construction features, artifacts, and decorative Vietnamese motifs used throughout the book. Richard Thompson drafted the maps. The professional guidance of Jane V. Olson and Anne Wilde at Yale University Press has been invaluable in producing the final product—the book.

Finally, I would like to offer my most heartfelt thanks to the Village Council and the good people of Khanh Hau for their kindness and cooperation, and for the things I learned from them.

Saigon, Vietnam   G.C.H.
March 1964

CHAPTER 1

History of the Village

To REACH THE VILLAGE of Khanh Hau from Saigon, one must travel southwest by vehicle through the clamorous Chinese city of Cholon into the delta of the Mekong River. Without a buffer of suburbs, the delta begins at the very edge of Cholon, and the scene changes from urban to rural with startling suddenness. Paddy fields stretch from the highway in a monotonous expanse, broken here and there by great clumps of tropical greenery that obscure the hamlets which form the villages of the delta. As the road continues southward there are several large bridges. One of these traverses the West Vaico River, and on the south bank the road swings past the town of Tan An, a market center and chief town of Long An province, an administrative area extending from the Cambodian border to the South China Sea. (Late in 1963 a new province called Hau Nghia was formed of the northern portion of Long An province.) Four kilometers south of Tan An and some 55 kilometers from Saigon, the road passes through the village of Khanh Hau.

Unlike the agglomerative villages of northern and central Vietnam, the Mekong River delta village is comprised of a number of dispersed hamlets. Khanh Hau has six administrative hamlets. To the west of the highway one collection of farmsteads is divided into two hamlets—Ap Dinh-A, the "center of the village," and Ap Dinh-B—and scattered groupings of farmsteads make up the hamlet of Ap Moi. To the east of the highway are the hamlets of Ap Thu Tuu, set amid the paddy fields, and the string settlements of Ap Nhon Hau and Ap Cau (see Fig. 1). Prior to 1917, Ap Dinh A and B, Ap Moi, and Ap Thu Tuu had formed the village of Tuong Khanh; Ap Nhon Hau and Ap Cau had been the village of Nhon Hau.

HISTORICAL SETTING

The Mekong River delta is the only place in Southeast Asia where the great traditions of China and India meet. Diffusing eastward, the Indian

1

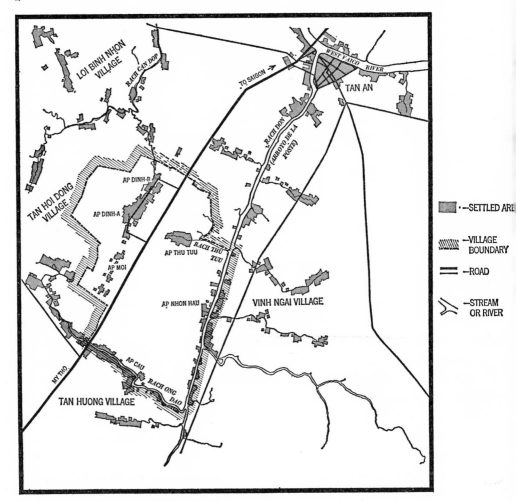

1. Settlement Pattern of Khanh Hau.

tradition molded the civilizations which flourished in Burma, Thailand, Laos, and Cambodia, but remained west of the Annamite Cordillera; the Vietnamese in their southward migration along the coastal plain of the Indochinese peninsula carried the Chinese tradition to the delta of the Mekong River, then occupied by a Cambodian population. To understand the place of Khanh Hau in this historical drama, it is essential to review briefly some Vietnamese history, particularly certain aspects of the period of Chinese domination and the *nam tien* or "movement southward."

In 221 B.C. the Chinese emperor Ch'in Shih Huang-ti sent an army into the Red River delta to conquer the population and incorporate the area into his growing kingdom. By 218 B.C. this conquest was complete, and the delta became part of a military command that included much of southeastern China. The death of Ch'in Shih Huang-ti in 210 plunged China into anarchy, during which the kingdom of Nam Viet—encompassing the Red River delta and coastal areas of southeastern China—was formed. The independence of this kingdom was relatively brief, however, for when the armies of the Emperor Han Wu-ti swept southward, they overran Nam Viet in 110 and organized it as the province of Giao Chi, under a military governor.

In keeping with the Chinese pattern of sinicizing conquered peoples, the governors sought to implant sinitic cultural institutions among the ethnic groups of Giao Chi. During the governorship of Hsi Kuang at the beginning of the Christian era, a flood of Chinese settlers—farmers, artisans, shop-keepers, deportees, and fugitives as well as literati and civil servants seeking refuge from the Wang Mang usurpation—moved into Giao Chi. They were encouraged by Governor Hsi Kuang who also founded schools and intro-duced Chinese methods of animal husbandry and agriculture to the arable delta. In addition, he made it compulsory for the inhabitants to observe Chinese marriage rituals and wear Chinese garb, particularly shoes and hats.[1]

According to Le Thanh Khoi, the introduction of Chinese agricultural techniques, notably the iron plow, revolutionized Vietnamese society. It permitted them to abandon their previous subsistence pattern of hunting, fishing, and swidden cultivation with a stone hoe, which precipitated an increase in the population and a new way of life. He also subscribes to Maspero's view that when the Chinese conqueror Ma Yuan in A.D. 44 replaced the ancient feudal structure (localized rule by aristocratic Vietnam-ese families) with a Chinese type of administration (initially consisting of Chinese administrators), he gave the Vietnamese the means to resist later Chinese attempts to dominate them. The centralized administration gen-erated internal cohesion, permitting concerted action when the threat of invasion arose:

> Jusque-là traité en simple protectorat, gardant ses institutions et ses moeurs, il devint une véritable province chinoise. Si l'Annam après s'être libéré, a pu pendant des siècles résister à la puissance de la Chine, alors que tous les autres Etats voisins, Ye Lang, Tien, Nan Tchao, ont peu à peu succombé soumis à l'administration régulière chinoise, et que celle-ci, brisant les institutions particularistes et les

1. Le Thanh Khoi, *Le Viet Nam,* pp. 99–103. Maspero, "Études d'histoire d'Annam," pp. 1–55.

groupements locaux, et introduisant les idées et les formes sociales chinoises lui donna une cohésion et une force qui manqua toujours à ses voisins. Le conquérant en detruisant les vieilles institutions politiques du Tonkin a jeté ce pays définitivement dans le sillage de la civilisation chinoise, commençant par là à lui donner cette forte armature qui lui a permis de jouer depuis le Xe siècle le premier rôle dans l'histoire de l'Indochine orientale.[2]

Numerous material benefits resulted from the Chinese-dominated administration of this period. Roads and bridges were constructed to improve communication with China, extensive irrigation projects were undertaken in the delta, and harbors were improved. In addition, Chinese cultural influence increased and spread among the Vietnamese. The Chinese literary tradition provided a basis for the emerging Vietnamese literature and poetry, written in *chu nom,* a demotic script based on Chinese calligraphy.[3] Legal codes were modeled after those in China. Chinese classical opera, painting, and architecture were implanted in Vietnamese society as were traditional Chinese medical practices and pharmacy.

In the first centuries of the Christian era, Confucianism and Taoism slowly penetrated into Giao Chi, largely confined at first to the elite because, according to Le Thanh Khoi,[4] "Neither the rationalism of the one nor the individualistic mysticism of the other could inspire a still primitive population." On the other hand, Indian Buddhism with its "aura of tenderness, the consolation of its ethics, and the marvelous legends of its bodhisattvas," had strong appeal among the population, and by the end of the second century, Giao Chi already was a "seat of Buddhist culture." Cadière[5] notes that by the seventh century there were Buddhist communities in the Red River delta, and he also points out that evidence indicates that Chinese Buddhism was introduced by civil servants and merchants during the period of Chinese rule. Examining numerous documents, Tran Van Giap[6] found Indian Buddhism predominant among the Vietnamese between the third and eleventh centuries, with Chinese Buddhism manifestly spreading by the ninth century. By the eleventh century, Buddhism flourished at all levels of Vietnamese society.

2. Le Thanh Khoi, pp. 103, 132–33. Masper, "L'expêdition de Ma Yuan," p. 11.

3. *Chu nom* has remained the scholarly script in spite of the fact that a romanized script introduced by the French missionary Alexandre de Rhodes in the 17th century, became the popular script and is now the national script.

4. Op. cit., p. 105. (Translations by the present author.)

5. *Croyances et Pratiques Religieuses des Vietnamiens,* 1958, pp. 1–6.

6. "Le Bouddhisme en Annam," pp. 191–268.

Although some investigators contend that when the Vietnamese gained their independence from the Chinese in A.D. 939, pre-Han Vietnamese culture persisted at the village level,[7] there is considerable evidence indicating that during the long period of domination, Chinese influence permeated all levels of Vietnamese society. It would be difficult to believe that village society was unaffected by the introduction of sinitic cultural institutions ranging from rice-planting techniques to the Buddhist–Taoist–Confucianist religious ideology. Since this influence is apparent in southern Vietnamese villages, it certainly must have been rooted in Vietnamese village society of the tenth century. Even the kinship system (and kinship is considered a relatively conservative cultural institution) reflects strong Chinese influence. In his linguistic analysis of the Vietnamese system, Benedict[8] finds many terms with Chinese affinities and concludes,

> It will be observed that the Annamese nomenclature has incorporated precisely those features of the Chinese terminology which are essential for the maintenance of distinctions in lines of ascent, which in turn are tied in with the generalized patriarchal family system absorbed by Annamese culture as a trait-complex from the same source.

Also, comparison of material on the structure and function of the Vietnamese kinship system (such as is found in this study) with the Chinese system as presented in works by Han Chi Feng, Hsien Chin Hu, Francis Hsu, or Maurice Freedman[9] would reveal a great many similarities.

According to Le Thanh Khoi,[10] Vietnamese southward expansion began in earnest after independence had been gained. Initially it was a peaceful infiltration of settlers occupying land left by the Cham who had occupied the coastal plain of the peninsula. Villages sent groups of pioneers—landless

7. For example:

After a millennium of Sinization aimed at assimilating another tribe into the great family of the Chinese, the villages of the Red River valley and those three hundred miles down the coast were still inhabited by a people essentially unchanged since the Chinese subjected them to their domination. Chinese culture had not penetrated into the masses of the Vietnamese. [Buttinger, *The Smaller Dragon*, p. 108.]

Ancré au sol à l'aube de l'histoire, le village vietnamien auquel les conquérants n'ont pas touché a constitué derrière sa haie de bambous le réduit anonyme et insaisissable où s'est concentré l'esprit de la nation. [Le Thanh Khoi, op. cit., p. 133.]

8. "An Analysis of Annamese Kinship Terms."

9. Feng, *The Chinese Kinship System.* Hu, *The Common Descent Group in China and Its Functions.* Hsu, *Under the Ancestor's Shadow.* Freedman, *Lineage Organization in Southeastern China.*

10. Op. cit., pp. 163–69; 268–74.

young people, adventurers, and undesirables—to form new settlements and clear the surrounding area for paddy cultivation. When a new settlement became self-sufficient, it achieved the status of a *xa* (village) by receiving a name from the emperor who also appointed a guardian spirit or spirits to watch over the village and bring it peace and prosperity. On its part, the village was expected to construct a *dinh* or communal temple as a repository for the imperial document naming the guardian spirit. The dinh also houses the altars honoring the guardian spirit and, in effect, it is a symbolic bond between the village and the emperor.

Encouraged by the central government and supported by the army, the Vietnamese settlers continued migrating southward, and conflict with the kingdom of Champa was inevitable. In the eleventh century a series of wars between the Cham and Vietnamese began, and during the next two centuries the Cham continually lost territory to the Vietnamese, sometimes by conquest and sometimes by ransom such as that paid for the release of the Cham king Che Cu (Rudravarman III). His freedom was obtained in 1069 by conceding to the Vietnamese the present-day territories of Quang Binh and the northern part of Quang Tri province. At other times political alliances resulted in territorial gains by the Vietnamese, as in 1307 when the Cham emperor gave the Vietnamese princess Huyen Tran on the occasion of her marriage the two districts of O and Ri.[11] Resistance to Vietnamese expansion came to an end in 1471 when the Vietnamese army overran the Cham capital of Vijaya, assuming control of the entire central coastal plain with the exception of three districts in the vicinity of Phan Rang which remained under Cham authority until the end of the seventeenth century.[12]

The final phase of Vietnamese expansion occurred under the Nguyen emperors. At the end of the seventeenth century, in addition to annexing the last Cham territory, the Nguyen encouraged settlement of the northern delta, then sparsely occupied by Cambodians. Colonies were established at Bien Hoa and Ba-ria (now Phuoc Le), and they were rapidly settled by pioneers, many of whom were refugees from the Trinh-Nguyen wars.[13] Between 1698 and 1757 the Nguyen extended their control southward to a point below the Bassac River, and by 1780 they had annexed the remaining part of the Mekong River delta west to Ha Tien and Chau Doc, the present border of Cambodia. The delta was being settled during the nineteenth

11. Le Thanh Khoi, pp. 163–69.

12. Ibid., pp. 230–31.

13. The Trinh family, ruling northern Vietnam, and the Nguyen family who dominated southern Vietnam, engaged in intermittent wars between 1620 and 1787; ibid., pp. 251–96.

century when the French occupied the area and organized it as the colony of Cochinchina.

Some of the Khanh Hau villagers relate that their ancestors came to the south from central Vietnam either because of the dynastic wars between the Trinh and the Nguyen or during the Tay Son rebellion at the end of the eighteenth century. The only written document that sheds light on the early days of Khanh Hau is the life history of Marshal Nguyen Huynh Duc, compiled by his descendants from letters, personal notes, and information contained in the *gia pho,* the family genealogy book. (See Appendix A for the Duc family genealogy.)

In 1748 Huynh Cong Duc, as Marshal Duc was known before receiving imperial sanction to use Nguyen (the surname of the emperor), was born in Tuong Khanh village. His paternal grandfather, commander of the third fleet under one of the Le emperors, had come to the Mekong delta from central Vietnam in the early eighteenth century. According to oral family history, Nguyen Huynh Duc's father was born in Tuong Khanh which at the time was supposed to have been a wooded area filled with wild animals. He also became a military officer in the army during the Le dynasty, and he instructed his son Duc in the military arts.

During the Tay Son rebellion, Nguyen Anh, the royal prince, was encamped in the area of Gia Dinh, and while hunting in the West Forest, he encountered Duc, who was known locally as the "tiger officer." They viewed their meeting as heavenly ordained, and Duc joined Nguyen Anh in his struggle to arrest the Tay Son expansion. Huynh Duc's military prowess soon earned him a high place in Nguyen Anh's army, and he distinguished himself by acts of loyalty to his leader. For example, at one point Huynh Duc was captured by the Tay Son and rejected their attempts to bribe him into joining them. On his escape, he journeyed to Thailand where Nguyen Anh had fled, only to find that the prince had returned to Vietnam to resume his fight against the Tay Son. In spite of great difficulties Huynh Duc rejoined Nguyen Anh, and they fought together until the final defeat of the Tay Son in 1802. Nguyen Anh proclaimed himself emperor, taking the name Gia Long, the first of the Nguyen dynasty.

As a reward for his valuable service, Gia Long permitted Huynh Duc to adopt the name Nguyen, and he bestowed on him the title of marshal. Nguyen Huynh Duc continued in the service of the emperor, and in 1815 he was appointed governor of the Gia Dinh region. During this period his protégé, Le Van Duyet, entered the military service of Gia Long, and eventually his military achievements won him a generalship and lasting reputation as the most famous hero of southern Vietnam. In 1819, because of ill health, Nguyen Huynh Duc returned to Tuong Khanh and in that same year died. His tomb was constructed in the village, and Emperor Gia Long sent special envoys to assist at the funeral and award posthumous honors to the family.

The guardian spirits in both the Ap Dinh-A and the Ap Nhon Hau dinh were awarded by Gia Long, indicating that Tuong Khanh and Nhon Hau had been sufficiently settled to warrant village status some time in the early nineteenth century. Village history, however, tells us nothing of events following the arrival of the French until 1917 when the villages of Tuong Khanh and Nhon Hau were fused to form Khanh Hau. The Council House in Ap Dinh, one hamlet of Tuong Khanh, became the administrative center of the new village, and the Ap Dinh dinh became the official village temple, although the dinh in Ap Nhon Hau continued to function as a center of ritual activity for the surrounding hamlets. The task of selecting a new Village Council rested with a committee of venerables, property owners, and men of good repute from all hamlets. The candidates, all of whom were members of the recently dissolved councils, were voted upon, and six members of each former council were elected.

The economic crisis of the early 1930s affected the village severely. Farmers recall that rice prices fell drastically and remained low until the beginning of World War II. With the war, the French instituted a military conscription that drew some male villagers into the army, and the colonial administration solicited cash contributions to aid the war effort. After the fall of France in 1940, the Vichy government assumed control over the colony and collaborated with the Japanese when they occupied Indochina in 1940. Villagers say that they saw the Japanese only occasionally when troops moved along the main highway. In the spring of 1945, however, when the Japanese took complete control of Indochina, a concentration of troops was stationed in nearby Tan An, and a small detachment was sent to guard the bridge at Ap Cau. During this period the villagers experienced an ever-increasing number of shortages, particularly of cloth, fuel for lamps, gasoline, bicycle parts, and manufactured goods.

During the Japanese occupation, the Viet Minh movement spread to the vicinity of Khanh Hau, and a cadre was organized in the village. When the Japanese quit Vietnam after their surrender in August 1945, the Viet Minh organized their own administration in each village, replacing the traditional Village Council. In Khanh Hau the Viet Minh party members elected six members to their Uy Ban Hanh Chanh (Administrative Committee). The committee chairman and his assistant were brothers from a relatively well-to-do family; the other four members were tenant farmers. When the French reoccupied Indochina in January 1946 and re-established the colonial administration, the Viet Minh committee disbanded and the traditional Village Council was reinstated.

The return of the French and the beginning of Viet Minh guerrilla activities marked the advent of the Indochina War. In Ap Dinh-A the French constructed a small stockade and garrisoned it with Vietnamese and Cambodian troops under French officers. By day the French claimed control of most of the village, but as the sun descended, this area contracted to the barbed wire enclosure that encompassed the stockade, Council House, and dinh. The village was split in its sympathies, and accusations of being pro-French or pro-Viet Minh were common. Those identified as pro-French—usually big landowners and members of the Village Council—were likely victims of periodic punitive Viet Minh raids on the village at night. During one such nocturnal raid, for example, the Viet Minh demanded a large sum of money from Ong Ke Hien, the highest venerable in Khanh Hau and its wealthiest resident landlord. He refused and with the aid of his sons fought off the raiders until they retreated. He and his family then sought refuge in the military outpost at the bridge on the main highway, and when the raiders later returned to the hamlet, they burned his sumptuous house. On the other hand, those accused of being pro-Viet Minh often were apprehended by the French, and more than one villager was arrested. In 1946 the Council House was burned by the Viet Minh, and French troops destroyed the Ap Nhon Hau dinh when they learned it was being used as a Viet Minh meeting place. Villagers also contend they looted the dinh of valuables, including the imperial document of Emperor Gia Long naming the guardian spirit.

Several well-to-do villagers were kidnapped by the Viet Minh, although none suffered death at their hands. The only victim of these troubled times was a daughter of the Ap Moi hamlet chief. Hearing that a Viet Minh meeting was taking place in the hamlet, the French officers at the stockade dispatched a squad which was erroneously directed to the hamlet chief's house. As they approached, several soldiers opened fire, killing the chief's twelve-year-old daughter who was sleeping in the main room.

When the debacle at Dien Bien Phu in May 1954 made it clear that French control was coming to an end, Viet Minh activities became bolder. Again the Council House was burned by night raiders who also burned some landowners' houses. The Village Council and a number of landowners

fled into Tan An. After the Geneva Truce Agreement in July, relative order
was restored and the refugees returned to the village. The political events
of the period that followed affected Khanh Hau society deeply. The Republic of South Vietnam was proclaimed after the election on October 23,
1955, of Ngo Dinh Diem. In Khanh Hau the initial effect was the establishment of President Diem's Phong Trao Cach Mang Quoc Gia (National
Revolutionary Movement) as the only official political party in the village.
By 1958 administration reform and agrarian reform programs began to
reach Khanh Hau. In that year the UNESCO-sponsored School of Fundamental Education, which had launched its Khanh Hau program in 1956,
completed new buildings next to the national highway and promised improvements in agricultural production.

By 1958, Khanh Hau also for the first time experienced the activities of
a relatively new political movement—the Mat Tran Dan Toc Giai Phong
Mien Nam Viet Nam (National Front for the Liberation of South Vietnam),
referred to by the South Vietnamese government as the Viet Cong or Vietnamese Communists (Viet Cong will be the designation used in the present
study) and invariably called the Viet Minh by the villagers. In the vicinity
of Khanh Hau the initial efforts of the Viet Cong were largely confined to
antigovernment propaganda. Early in 1958 Nguyen Van Mung, the director
of the UNESCO School of Fundamental Education awoke one morning to
find a Viet Cong flag stuck in the ground before the entrance to his house.
Several months later, banners bearing antigovernment slogans were strung
across the spur road in Ap Dinh-A. There were guarded comments by
villagers of Viet Cong patrols coming into Khanh Hau and neighboring
villages at night to spread propaganda either orally or by tracts. The Dan
De or Self-Defense Guards, numbering around 15, were stationed in the
military stockade, and the Hamlet Guard maintained watch posts throughout the village, but after dark the area of security dwindled as it did during
the Indochina War to the barbed wire enclosure around the Council House,
dinh, and stockade.

By the end of 1958 the ever-increasing number of assassinations throughout South Vietnam, of which most victims were public servants, was attributed by the government to the Viet Cong. Several of the Self-Defense
Guards were suddenly arrested, accused of being Viet Cong, and the father
of one of the guards was apprehended when some of his neighbors reported
that he fed Viet Cong nocturnal patrols. The villagers were shocked at this
sudden action, and the village chief protested directly to the province chief,
vouching for the good character and loyalty of the three accused. The older

man was released subsequently, but the guards were detained six months before being allowed to return to the village.

Viet Cong activities increased in Khanh Hau through 1959, and when the annual Cau An ritual was held at the Ap Nhon Hau dinh, the village chief and deputy chief were unable to attend because security was lacking. Government control of some surrounding villages such as Loi Binh Nhon and Tan Hoi Dong, both close to the Dong Thap Muoi (Plaine des Joncs), had greatly weakened by the end of 1959, and three hamlets in Khanh Hau —Ap Nhon Hau, Ap Cau, and Ap Thu Tuu—were considered insecure even in daytime. The situation worsened steadily in 1960 and, as in the Indochina War, the village chief and some landowners took up residence in Tan An, returning to the village only during the day. Villagers either voluntarily or because of threats paid the Viet Cong taxes in paddy or cash, and according to some villagers young men responded favorably to Viet Cong recruitment efforts, particularly when the appeal was to their sentimental attachment to the village: if the young man joined the Viet Cong he would remain in the vicinity of the village; if he joined the National Army he would be sent far away.

In July 1961 while attempting to ambush a Viet Cong night patrol the police chief was killed, and by November the Viet Cong patrols could move through any hamlet of the village at any time. On several occasions residents of Ap Thu Tuu and Ap Cau were compelled by Viet Cong armed with machetes to halt traffic on the main highway in order to distribute anti-government leaflets to passengers of buses, taxis, and private vehicles. Another Viet Cong patrol, led by a young student known as Co Dep (literally Miss Beautiful) from the secondary school in Tan An, rounded up residents of Ap Dinh A–B to lecture to them on the evils of the government. During one of these gatherings several villagers accused of being supporters of the Diem-My (Diem-American) "gang" were brought forward to be executed, but when the gun misfired, the prisoners were able to escape. By the end of the year two more villagers had been killed in clashes between the Viet Cong and the Self-Defense Guards.

In January 1962 the Self-Defense Guard was increased to over 100 members, and the National Army began patrolling the main highway more frequently. Viet Cong activities consequently were less manifest. Late in February, the Self-Defense Guards captured several Viet Cong cadremen, and one of them had a membership list of a Viet Cong "committee" in the village. The primary function of the committee was to collect taxes, and the chairman was the hamlet chief of Ap Cau, a relatively well-to-do farmer.

All members were arrested, but by April, having convinced the authorities that they were forced to cooperate with the Viet Cong, most of the accused, including the hamlet chief, had been released. Early in March the provincial authorities decided to implement the newly launched Ap Chien Luoc (Strategic Hamlet Program) in four villages, one of which was Khanh Hau. The plan called for a fortification around the Ap Dinh A–B agglomeration, to be financed with contributions from villagers and constructed with corvée labor—a maximum of three days by every able-bodied male. By May 1962 Khanh Hau was on the way to becoming a fortified village.

Within six months, the Strategic Hamlet Program was implemented, and the settlement pattern of the village was altered somewhat by the relocation of some families from isolated farmsteads into the enclosed settlements and by the creation of a small settlement between Ap Thu Tuu and the highway. The fortifications failed to halt Viet Cong incursions, however, and often their nocturnal patrols entered the hamlets; in October 1963, they kidnapped the village chief, but released him several days later.

The Strategic Hamlet Program began to dissolve after the fall of the Ngo Dinh Diem regime with the coup d'etat of November 1, 1963, and the relocated families began moving back to their original farmstead sites. Viet Cong activities in and around Khanh Hau increased during December 1963 and January 1964, sometimes provoking extreme action by the National Army. In mid-February 1964, armored units of the National Army entered Ap Moi, and villagers paused in their harvest activities to watch artillery and tanks shell the neighboring village of Cu Chi, where a contingent of Viet Cong had been reported to be.

KHANH HAU IN SOUTHERN VIETNAM

Upon arriving in Khanh Hau, the only things that immediately distinguish it from other villages of the vicinity are a somewhat faded sign announcing that the tomb of Marshal Nguyen Huynh Duc, the nineteenth-century Vietnamese hero, is in Khanh Hau, and beside the highway there are the newly constructed buildings of the UNESCO-sponsored School of Fundamental Education. Further acquaintance with the village reveals several other distinctions. With a population of 3,241 at the time of the study, Khanh Hau is smaller than the estimated average of 4,300 for villages of Long An province, and with around 1,000 hectares it is smaller in size than the provincial average of 2,300. Although most Vietnamese villages have only one dinh or communal temple, Khanh Hau has two, because it was two villages before 1917. Consequently it also has two cult committees, whose major responsibility is to maintain the Cult of the Guardian Spirit associated with the dinh. Finally, although it is not unusual, it should be pointed out that Khanh Hau has no market.

Whether considered separately or cumulatively, these characteristics do not render Khanh Hau alien to villages in the surrounding area nor, indeed, to villages of southern Vietnam. This is not to say that Khanh Hau is typical of southern Vietnamese villages, but then—given variation in physical surroundings and consequent differences in livelihood patterns as well as the different impact of historical events (particularly such things as the uneven spread of the Hoa Hao and Cao Daist religious movements)—no village could claim the distinction of being typical.

Brief research in other villages throughout southern Vietnam as well as research done by other investigators makes it possible to learn from Khanh Hau a good deal about the rural society of this region. Two aspects of Khanh Hau society that reflect the more general regional picture are kinship and the formal political structure. The structure and terminology of the kinship system in Khanh Hau as well as certain family functions—the form and mode of marriage, birth practices, such family cults as the Cult of the Ancestors, and funeral practices—are found in all Vietnamese villages south of the coastal plain and the Annamite Cordillera. Since 1904, administrative legislation has dictated the formal structure and functions of village councils in what was the colony of Cochinchina, resulting in a high degree of uniformity throughout the area. Prerogatives and responsibilities of councillors derived from their roles as leaders in village society, however, cannot be generalized beyond Khanh Hau.

For most other aspects of village society, areal qualifications must be made. Generally speaking, Khanh Hau shares more socioeconomic features with villages north of the Mekong River, south of Cholon, and east of the Dong Thap Muoi (Plaine des Joncs)—an area that can be designated the northern delta—than it does with villages in other parts of the delta or the transitional zone between the northern fringe of the delta and the Annamite Cordillera. As already indicated, the northern delta was settled during the late eighteenth and early nineteenth centuries and, outside of the immediate vicinity of My Tho and the Gia Dinh area where military land grants were given,[14] the prevailing pattern was for individual pioneer families to claim and clear the land. Excluding one holding of 235 hectares, the average Khanh Hau landowner has around 7 hectares, and in this vicinity it is considered about average. Also, all villages of the northern delta have *cong dien*

14. Deschaseaux, "Notes sur les anciens *don dien* Annamites," pp. 133-36.

and/or *cong tho* types of communal land, although the amount varies; for example, Khanh Hau has less communal land than other villages of Long An province.

Paddy cultivation is the predominant economic activity in the northern delta, and the *cay* (transplanting) method is used by most farmers. Also since most villages are located away from the Mekong there is general reliance on the rains to flush brackish tidal water from the watercourses so that farmers can irrigate their seedbeds and paddy fields. Chemical fertilizer is used extensively throughout the area. Most families have a few fruit trees, and some cultivate fruit groves to produce an ancillary cash crop. Kitchen gardens are common but not universal. The usual draft animals are cattle and water buffalo; pigs, chickens, and ducks are raised for food and sometimes for sale. Fishing is a widespread activity, and numerous families engage in fish raising.

Village-sponsored Mahayana Buddhist pagodas are ubiquitous in the northern delta, and all villages have dinh. The cult committees associated with the dinh, however, vary in composition from village to village. By and large the same popular beliefs and practices are found throughout the area, although in some villages specific cults receive more attention; for example, villages near large rivers have more cults venerating water deities, and in heavily forested areas villagers are more likely to honor the tiger in a cult. Khanh Hau has few Catholic families, and the Catholic population of the northern delta is relatively small. Since its inception in 1925 Cao Daism, a reformed Buddhist religious movement, has spread through this part of the delta. In most villages there are adherents to one of the seven Cao Daist sects, and in some there also are Cao Daist temples (there are two in Khanh Hau, representing two different sects).

Moving southward from the northern delta, the ethnic composition changes with scattered groupings of Khmers amid the predominant Vietnamese population. In My Thuan village, Vinh Long province, for example, one of the ten hamlets of the village is predominantly Khmer.[15] Associated with the Khmers is Theravada Buddhism, characterized by Khmer-style pagodas and monks in saffron robes. Even in large river ports such as Can Tho, the sight of Theravada monks accepting food offerings in the morning market is not uncommon. Vietnamese villages have their Mahayana pagodas and dinh and, although Cao Daism is found in the southern delta, large areas, particularly the trans-Bassac between the Bassac and Mekong Rivers,

15. This and other information on My Thuan is from J. D. Donoghue and Vo Hong Phuc, *My-Thuan: The Study of a Delta Village in South Viet Nam.*

have been swept by Hoa Hao, another reformed Buddhist movement. In My Thuan between 85 and 90 per cent of the villagers were reported to be members of this sect; in Binh Tien, Vinh Long province, an estimated 75 per cent of the population was of the Hoa Hao religion.

Much of the territory south of the Mekong River was opened to settlement after the arrival of the French, and large areas were claimed by Vietnamese and French landlords who organized rice estates. Gittinger points out that prior to 1880 the total cultivated area in Cochinchina was estimated at 552,000 hectares, and between 1880 and 1937, irrigation increased this to 2,200,000 hectares, some 250,000 of which were held by French landowners.[16] The traditional cong dien and cong tho communal lands are not found in many villages in the southern delta.

The transitional area also varies somewhat more from the northern delta in economic than other aspects. In addition to Mahayana Buddhism and other traditional cults, Cao Daism is widespread in the transitional area. Although the pattern of settling the area resembled that of the northern delta, paddy cultivation is restricted to certain zones because of topography, soil conditions, and lack of water. Landholdings tend to be small in most villages; for example, farmers in Tan An Hoi and Trung Lap, both villages in Binh Duong province, report that most landowners have one or two hectares. Much of the transitional area is forested, so that woodcutting is the occupation of many people, and there are extensive rubber estates belonging to individual families and French companies.

The transitional area is considered poor for rice cultivation. Away from the larger rivers, the farmers rely on rainfall for their paddy cultivation and the rice is inferior. The result is that secondary crops often are more important for cash income. In the vicinity of Tan An Hoi, for example, tobacco is

16. The opening of extensive new ricelands, whether to foreign or to individual settlers, tended to give rise to villages where the community spirit was less pronounced than in older villages to the north. Local organization was quickly and firmly established, but under the new system few of the villages acquired any communal land. Nonetheless, the concept of communal land embedded in the cultural tradition remained very much alive, and even in these new villages the attitudes toward land continued to reflect the strong feeling that land was a resource essentially at the command of the society over which the individual had something in the nature of a heritable usufruct right. (From Gittinger, "Communal Land Concepts in Recent Vietnamese Policy," p. 10.)

During the Indochina War a land reform program instituted by the Viet Minh in areas under its control resulted in a redistribution of much of these landholdings. Also between 600,000 and 800,000 hectares were "abandoned" by the owners and, since the implementation of the 1956 land reform program, holdings over 100 hectares were redistributed to tenants. (Ibid., p. 11.)

widely grown in the paddy fields after the harvest, and farther west in the area of Trung Lap peanuts are the most important cash crop. Corn and kapok also are widely cultivated in the transitional area, and because of the precariousness of their livelihood many villagers grow stands of bamboo as "cushion crops" which they cut and sell in times of need.

CHAPTER 2

Physiographic Setting and Settlement Pattern

Physiographic Setting

THE MEKONG DELTA is a geologically recent region built up by alluvial deposits carried on the waters of the Mekong and lesser rivers, including the Saigon and the East and West Vaico Rivers. The village of Khanh Hau lies on the edge of an area with predominantly undifferentiated alluvial soils, but immediately to the east, soils range from acid alluvial (acid sulfate soils) to very acid alluvial, associated with the Dong Thap Muoi (Plaine des Joncs). At one time a stream coursed through what are now Ap Moi, Ap Dinh-A, and Ap Dinh-B, resulting in a vein of sandy soil. Villagers consider this the best place for vegetable cultivation, although during part of the year it tends to be very dry. To the west there is highly acidic heavy black clay which necessitates liming the fields; to the east the acid content diminishes as diverse alluvial soils with little or no acidity or salinity commence.[1]

Monotonously flat, the delta has required extensive drainage projects to make it habitable, and tidal action, carrying brackish water a considerable distance inland, creates irrigation problems in most parts of the region, particularly those away from the Mekong River. This is the case in Khanh Hau which, although it has connections with the Mekong River, is most affected by the West Vaico. This river brings sediment and fresh water in the rainy season, but during the dry months it is subject to tidal action, and brackish sea water gushes into the streams, canals, and irrigation channels of the village. The major watercourse in Khanh Hau is the Rach Don, formerly known as the Arroyo de la Poste, a stream connecting the West Vaico at Tan An with the Mekong at My Tho, some 20 kilometers to the south. The Rach Don forms the western boundary of the village, and its tributary, the Rach

---

1. Moorman, *The Soils of the Republic of Viet Nam,* pp. 1–12.

Ong Dao, borders the village on the south. A third stream, a branch of the West Vaico known as the Can Dop (the Vietnamese deformation of a Khmer name), flows into Ap Dinh A–B at the northwestern end of the village. In 1957 the Tuong Khanh canal was constructed to connect the Can Dop with the Rach Ong Dao, and a year later another canal was dug within the limits of Ap Thu Tuu to bring water to the paddy fields near the national highway. These two canals provided Khanh Hau for the first time with an interrelated water system which, although it is navigable only in sections, has improved internal communications and permits a more extensive use of its water resources.

With the exception of the highlands, the southern portion of the Indochinese peninsula is tropical, and the area of Khanh Hau has a climate similar to that of Saigon, with greater humidity.[2] The rains, coming first from the southwest and then from the northwest, commence in May or June and subside in November. Khanh Hau, however, is on the border of two precipitation zones and therefore has a somewhat unpredictable and occasionally precarious rainfall pattern. Since the watercourses continue to be brackish early in the rice-planting cycle, rainfall is needed for the seedbeds. Moreover, if the rains are delayed or insufficient, the watercourses may not be flushed of brackish water when the time for transplanting arrives. This occurred in 1958, and in desperation some farmers began irrigating with the saline water at hand, though they knew it would have a deleterious effect on the soil.

The village similarly is dependent on rainfall for potable water. There are few wells.[3] Rainwater draining from the roofs is stored in earthen jars—and more recently in concrete tanks—to provide water for drinking, cooking, laundering, and bathing. At the end of the dry season, as the supply of potable water diminishes, the villagers tend to become fearful of cholera which they believe is caused by an evil spirit associated with "bad water."

2. Saigon monthly average temperatures recorded between 1947 and 1956 ranged from 77.9° in December to 83.7° F in April. Temperatures during the growing season, from June to January, averaged from 79° to 80° with a high of 81° in April and a low of 77.0° in December. Average relative humidity varied from a low of 72.2 in March, the middle of the dry season, to a high of 87.1 in September, the peak of the rainy season. (Gittinger, *Vietnamese Agricultural Statistics*, p. 5.)

3. Technicians from the Ministry of Public Health and the American Aid Mission estimated that there were fresh water sources some 150 meters below the surface of the Khanh Hau area, and they dug several wells in the village. All of them, however, dried up within a short time. The villagers did not consider the experiment successful, pointing out that the wells were costly and furthermore were only 100 meters deep and dried up when the rains subsided.

When there is a drought such as that in 1958, the water problem becomes so critical that the Village Council must ask for assistance from the district. Some villagers resort to stream or canal water, pouring it into a jar containing rock alum which is supposed to draw out impurities; although this water is considered good for most household purposes, many villagers are reluctant to drink it.

THE SETTLEMENTS

The six dispersed administrative hamlets that constitute the village of Khanh Hau encompass a variety of settlement types, all of which can be found throughout the Mekong River delta. They include clustered settlements, string settlements along systems of communication such as streams, canals, roads, and footpaths, and isolated farmsteads.[4] A general view of Khanh Hau is provided in Figure 1 (p. 2), and the following hamlet-by-hamlet description will isolate the various settlement forms.

Ap Dinh-A and Ap Dinh-B, which until 1957 constituted one administrative unit, form the largest as well as the densest agglomeration in Khanh Hau. Ap Dinh-A is considered something of a focal center, since it contains the public buildings of the village. A spur road capable of accommodating any type of vehicle runs through the agglomeration, connecting at both ends with the national highway. A number of shops and many farmsteads are located along this road, which gives it something of a "main street" function. According to village records, the spur road was constructed in 1925 as a result of the efforts of a local district chief who advocated making the tomb of Marshal Duc more accessible to the national highway in the hope of encouraging pilgrimages and stimulating a nationwide interest in this rather neglected hero of the south.

Most of the 226 farmsteads in Ap Dinh A–B lie along footpaths which branch from the spur road and often extend into the expanse of paddy fields beyond the residential area. These footpaths are in effect minute lines of communication for clusters of farmsteads which usually contain families of the same kin grouping and, in some instances, members of the same religious sect. Along the western edge of the agglomeration most of the farmsteads are constructed along the bank of the Can Dop, a small stream that drains into the West Vaico River.

4. Information on settlement forms was taken from available topographic sheets of the Tan An area, issued by the Service Géographique de l'Indochine, 1950 series, in scales of 1/100,000, 1/50,000, and 1/25,000.

There are no constant sources of water in the eastern part of Ap Dinh A–B. Accordingly, that side is considerably drier, especially in the hot season, and the dominant growths are thick stands of bamboo that obscure the houses. There is considerable open space, however, and kitchen gardens flourish with the fresh water available during the rainy season. The western side is well watered, and with its many coconut trees and great leafy backdrop of latania palms, it has a lush, fluvial air, but it is too shady for extensive garden cultivation. Channels from the Can Dop course along and around the farmsteads, and pirogues are a necessity for the residents in this part of the hamlet.

Ap Dinh-A contains the primary school, the Council House, an information hall, and the century-old dinh. The hamlet also boasts a twenty-bed maternity center, constructed next to the primary school in 1962. In Ap Dinh-A there also is a Cao Daist temple of the Tien Thien sect. Another temple, belonging to the Ban Chin Dao sect of Cao Dai, is located near the spur road in Ap Dinh-B. Near it is the tomb of Marshal Nguyen Huynh Duc, its weathered gray stone contrasting sharply with the newly constructed shrine honoring this hero. Ap Dinh-B has the only rice mill in Khanh Hau and is the site of two Chinese cemeteries—one Hakka, the other Fukienese. Both were established by merchants' associations in the nearby town of Tan An to provide a temporary burial place for members until they could be transported to ancestral villages in China.

According to some of its elderly residents, Ap Moi (New Hamlet) was founded by families who moved out of the Ap Dinh A–B agglomeration in the latter part of the nineteenth century in order to be near their paddy fields in the southern area of the village. Kin tended to form residence groupings, and eventually the hamlet encompassed 73 farmsteads. An extension of the Ap Dinh A–B spur road runs several hundred feet into the hamlet. The northernmost cluster of farmsteads is oriented along this extension, and might properly be considered part of Ap Dinh A–B, since they are separated only by an arbitrary administrative border. The village Buddhist pagoda is located in this part of Ap Moi, as is the village nurse's dispensary and the only shop in the hamlet. Since there were no roads or streams along which they might have constructed their farmsteads, settlers in the other three clusters of the hamlet are grouped haphazardly. The canal built in 1957, however, provided a new line of communication, and several farmsteads were established along its banks.

When the staff of the School of Fundamental Education prepared a base map of Ap Dinh A–B and Ap Moi, a discerning villager pointed out that the pattern of the residential area strongly suggests the shape of a dragon. The clusters of farmsteads in Ap Moi form the head and neck, and the Ap Dinh A–B agglomeration forms the body. The Can Dop traces the arched back of the dragon; the farmsteads along its bank emerge as dorsal protuberances. This observation met with enthusiasm among the villagers; it was a felicitous portent, an omen of good luck for Khanh Hau.

Ap Cau (Hamlet of the Bridge) is so named for its proximity to the highway bridge over the Rach Ong Dao. The 85 farmsteads that make up this hamlet stretch for several kilometers along the north bank of the river, forming an almost continuous string settlement with intermittent clusters of farmsteads. Because the farmsteads are relatively large, the density of the settlement is low. There is a privately supported pagoda near the highway, and several small shops lie along the footpath that winds the entire length of the hamlet and serves all farmsteads.

Ap Cau is considered a hamlet favored by celestial forces; it has good water resources, and its fields are relatively low, so that even in years of poor rainfall they are well watered. The flora is thick and varied, and groves and gardens flourish in every farmstead. The houses are comfortably shaded beneath coconut and areca palms, and the Rach Ong Dao is hidden by a thick screen of latania palms. At high tide the water rises, and the stream presses in around all the houses lining the bank, giving the impression that Ap Cau is a floating hamlet.

Most of the 115 farmsteads of the hamlet of Ap Nhon Hau are on or near the west bank of the Rach Don. At the confluence of this stream and the Rach Ong Dao, the hamlets of Ap Cau, and Ap Nhon Hau meet, forming the southeast corner of the village. Like Ap Cau, Ap Nhon Hau is a riverine hamlet set in a profusion of tropical growth. It is very similar in appearance to its sister hamlet, although its farmsteads are smaller. The second village dinh is in Ap Nhon Hau, and it also contains a privately supported pagoda dedicated to the deity Quan Cong, an ancient warrior of China. Between the main body of the settlement and the national highway, isolated farmsteads are scattered among the paddy fields.

The 92 farmsteads of Ap Thu Tuu form one relatively dense cluster which looks like a large green island in the midst of the paddy fields. Many farmsteads within it are located along the Rach Thu Tuu, a branch of the Rach Don. The stream is too narrow to constitute any kind of natural dividing line within the hamlet, but it is a fair source of water and thus has invited settlement. Like Ap Moi, Ap Thu Tuu is primarily residential; it has several small shops but no public buildings or religious edifices.

Systems of Communication

The dispersed character of the settlements that make up the village of Khanh Hau presents a greater problem of internal than external communication. The national highway segmenting the village is a major line of communication from Saigon to the south, and no farmstead in Khanh Hau is more than 3 kilometers from it. One can always leave the village by any one of the many public carriers that use this highway. On the other hand, to go from far-removed parts of Ap Cau or Ap Nhon Hau to the Council House in Ap Dinh-A necessitates a trip of at least 5 kilometers. Within the village the best way to get about is on foot, which is arduous in the mud of the rainy season and uncomfortable under the brazen sun of the dry months.

There are no automobiles in Khanh Hau. Several years ago Ong Ke Hien, the highest venerable, possessed a large black Citroen which he kept in his Tan An house; but because its upkeep proved too costly, he sold it. Two relatively wealthy villagers own motor scooters, and there are 15 motor bicycles registered. A man in Ap Dinh-B has a motorcycle transport, one family has a horse and cart, and another family has a team of oxen and a large, heavily built cart with great solid wood wheels. Finally, there are an estimated 200 bicycles and an unreported number of pirogues and sampans.

Within Khanh Hau the two major means of communication are by footpath and water. The entire village is interlaced with footpaths that serve all farmsteads and traverse the paddy fields on the bundings connecting the hamlets; in the dry season it is possible to take short cuts across the desiccated paddy fields. The national highway functions as a means of north–south communication within the village, and the spur road facilitates travel into Ap Dinh A–B and part of Ap Moi. Transport to hamlets not served by these roads is restricted to two-wheeled conveyances such as bicycles, motor bicycles, and motor scooters. Even these are difficult to maneuver over the narrow, bumpy paths, most of which are virtually impassable by vehicle in the rainy season.

Since the completion of the canal through Ap Dinh A–B and Ap Moi in 1957, the watercourses in the village form one system that serves all hamlets. This offers a feasible, although somewhat circuitous route for transport by sampans and pirogues from one hamlet to another. Water cargo transport within the village is restricted to such things as paddy cultivated in fields distant from the farmstead and water-palm (latania) fronds for house construction. For example, if a resident of Ap Dinh-A purchases several hundred of the fronds grown around Ap Thu Tuu—considered the best in the village—he must transport them by laborers or by sampan, and the latter is less costly. In Nhon Hau and Ap Cau where the streams are wide, transportation by pirogues is easy as well as pleasant.

In addition to boats for transporting paddy at harvest time, the villagers hire a number of land vehicles for this purpose. Farmers who live in Ap Dinh A–B and who have fields on the other side of the national highway have horse carts, motorcycle transports, and even small buses to pick up sacks of paddy along the road and carry them to the point nearest their farmsteads. Motorized transport, however, is a luxury in Khanh Hau, rarely used outside the harvest period. One of the most common sights continues to be the man or woman rhythmically padding along a path, balancing a shoulder board to which are attached baskets containing paddy, polished rice, seedlings, fertilizer, firewood, fruit, vegetables, or anything else that must be taken from one place to another.

The national highway makes Khanh Hau accessible to most parts of the delta. Until July 1958 a railroad running from Saigon to My Tho flanked the highway; the nearest station was in Tan An, some 4 kilometers from Khanh Hau. Removal of this means of communication does not appear to have affected access to the village, however, since the national highway has been widened and the number of buses and other public carriers using it has increased accordingly. The variety of public vehicles plying the highway is almost staggering. There are relatively large interurban buses, most of which do not stop at Khanh Hau but concentrate on transporting passengers and goods between the larger market towns and cities. In addition, there is an array of small buses, converted truck-buses, motorcycles, motor-scooter transports, taxis, jitneys, and horse carts, all of which can be flagged down along the highway. These carriers also are the major means of transporting produce to and from the local markets. Livestock, baskets of fowl, garden and grove produce, luggage, bicycles, furniture, lumber, and more than likely a few spare passengers are piled high, and is not uncommon to see one of these top-heavy vehicles tipped over in a paddy field. Among the conveyances crowding the highway there also are large, relatively new delivery trucks that belong to big Saigon–Cholon firms and clanking, hybrid trucks of small transporters, carrying bulk goods from Saigon to the market towns in the delta.

Since Khanh Hau has no market, there is a daily movement of villagers to and from the markets in neighboring Tan An and Tan Huong. A resident of Ap Dinh-B has a motorcycle transport that makes daily trips be-

tween that hamlet and the Tan An market, and the son of a family in Ap
Moi, which has the only horse and cart in the village, operates a transport
service to and from the neighboring markets.[5] Small scooter and motorcycle
transports as well as occasional small buses enter Ap Dinh A–B on the spur
road to bring villagers and their purchases from the market at Tan An.
These carriers as well as pickup trucks and small Citroen trucks also deliver
to local shops a variety of goods distributed by Tan An branches of firms in
Saigon or Cholon. Individual suppliers, their goods in cans strapped to the
rear fenders of their bicycles, can enter any hamlet by the paths on the
bunds in favorable weather. Most of them purchase tobacco, cookies, candy,
and other small items from wholesalers in Tan An and sell them to clients
in the surrounding area. These delivery men carry out their work in a
leisurely fashion, stopping to have tea with their clients and to pass on news
from the market towns and other villages.

Motor vehicles also enter the village to pick up produce or livestock purchased by Tan An merchants, and paddy sold to merchants in Tan An and
My Tho is transported by barge as well as by truck. The network of streams
and canals in and around Khanh Hau is a microcosmic part of a vast water-
way system dissecting the Mekong delta, rendering practically every village
and town in the region accessible by water transport. Khanh Hau, therefore,
has relatively good external communication by water; barges are restricted
to the Rach Ong Dao and the Rach Don, but smaller sampans and pirogues
can manage the canals and narrow streams, particularly at high tide. Vendors from Tan An move down the larger streams selling food items and manufactured goods to villagers along the banks of Ap Nhon Hau and Ap Cau.
Other vendors come into the village from the area south of Khanh Hau,
known for its fruit groves and extensive gardens. They paddle their prod-
uce-laden pirogues through the ever-narrowing streams and canals, stopping periodically to lift the log footbridges in order to reach farmsteads deep
in the hamlets.[6]

Since there are no postal facilities in Khanh Hau, letters must be posted
in the nearby town of Tan An. Receiving mail is somewhat more compli-

5. During September and October 1958 he transported about 1,000 sacks of chemical
fertilizer from Tan An to the village at the rate of 2$ VN per sack (in 1958, as now, the
exchange in plasters, i.e. $VN, is about 72 to $1.00 U.S.).

6. One vendor selling earthen water jars, green ceramic pots, dishes, and cheap blue
and white rice bowls, came from Thu Dau Mot, a pottery-producing center north of the
delta. He started by transporting his wares in a barge, subsequently transferring part of
them to a pirogue which navigates the shallow waterways more easily.

cated. Letters addressed to anyone in Khanh Hau are delivered to the post office in Tan An and from there are sent to the district headquarters at Thu Thua, in the opposite direction; they are then brought to the village by the courier who brings administrative documents daily from Thu Thua to Khanh Hau. From there word is sent out to the recipients who are expected to come and claim their mail at the Council House. At one time a messenger was sent from the village each day to collect incoming mail, but lack of funds forced the discontinuation of this service.

There are six battery-operated radios in Khanh Hau, all owned by wealthy villagers. For the most part they are used only for short periods each day, mostly for news broadcasts. Villagers going into the market at Tan An often purchase Saigon morning newspapers either for themselves or for neighbors. In addition, the man who operates the daily motorcycle transport between the village and Tan An usually purchases several newspapers on his first trip. About twenty villagers take newspapers regularly, but the number of readers increases considerably each week when the results of the national lottery are published.

News of interest to the villagers is disseminated orally by a highly effective gossip system which centers in the Council House. The deputy chief, who lives nearby, has a radio, and usually there is a copy of one of the Saigon newspapers available for the Village Council and any visitors who might care to read it. Each day people from all parts of the village visit the Council House, carrying back outside news of interest as well as local gossip which they pass on to whomever they meet en route. In addition, each hamlet has shops that serve as gathering places for both men and women and, as one might expect, a good deal of news and gossip is exchanged in the course of making purchases or drinking with friends.

HOUSE TYPES

Farmsteads in Khanh Hau have the same basic characteristics. There is the house and, for those who store paddy, the granary, which is always part of the dwelling. If the owner has livestock there will be a stable, which usually is abutted to the house and also may serve as a place to store tools, fish traps, and farm implements. A few farmsteads in the village have chicken coops and/or pigsties. Houses are surrounded by plots of land varying in size, commonly enclosed by a hedge growth consisting of tangled cacti, assorted bushes, clumps of bamboo, and prickly tropical plants, intended to deter man and beast. If, however, there are kin living next door or if relations with close neighbors are particularly amicable, the hedge is apt to be trimmed low enough for anyone to skip over it.

The area immediately in front of the house is used for sunning paddy or drying weaving reeds, and for storing rice stalks (kindling) and coconut shells (fuel). In farmsteads of the well-to-do, part of this area is given over to a garden of flowering plants and bushes, many of which are set in colored ceramic pots placed on stands in the Chinese fashion. A kitchen garden commonly is found to one side of the house, and most villagers cultivate a variety of fruit trees. If there is sufficient space the fruit trees may be planted in a grove, but in most instances they grow in pleasantly disorganized profusion. Many farmsteads have ponds fed by channels from the nearest watercourse. In addition to being a source of fish, they also provide water for household uses when the brackish water has been flushed away after the outset of the rainy season. Women do their washing in the ponds, children amuse themselves in them, and in recent years the villagers have been encouraged to build wooden latrines over them. By February 1964, however, the few latrines that had been constructed in 1958–59 had disappeared.

In house construction the first step is to build an earth mound a foot high and, on an auspicious day (by the lunar calendar), a small altar dedicated to Ong Linh Than Tho Vo, the Spirit of the Soil, is arranged in the middle of the mound. Candles, a container for joss sticks, and a dish heaped with fruit, cooked rice, and other food offerings are placed on the altar, after which the head of the family performs a ritual consisting of kowtowing three times while he requests permission of Ong Linh Than Tho Vo to use the plot of land for a house. Construction of the frame can then begin, and the altar remains in place until the roof is added and the family begins to move in.

In Khanh Hau there are four major types of houses, distinguished according to the materials employed in their construction: thatch houses with wooden frames, wooden houses with thatched roofs, wooden houses with tile roofs, and houses with masonry walls, wooden frames, and tile roofs.[7] The style of the house depends largely on the building material used, and village dwellings consequently show some variety of architectural form. The interior arrangement, however, is dictated by custom so that floor plans tend to be similar regardless of the style and size of the house.

Most villagers live in the thatched houses so typical of rural southern Vietnam. Two types are distinguishable—a small thatched house, usually of

7. Figure 2 gives the distribution of house types in the hamlets of Ap Dinh A–B and Ap Moi as well as the number and percentage of each house type in these three hamlets.

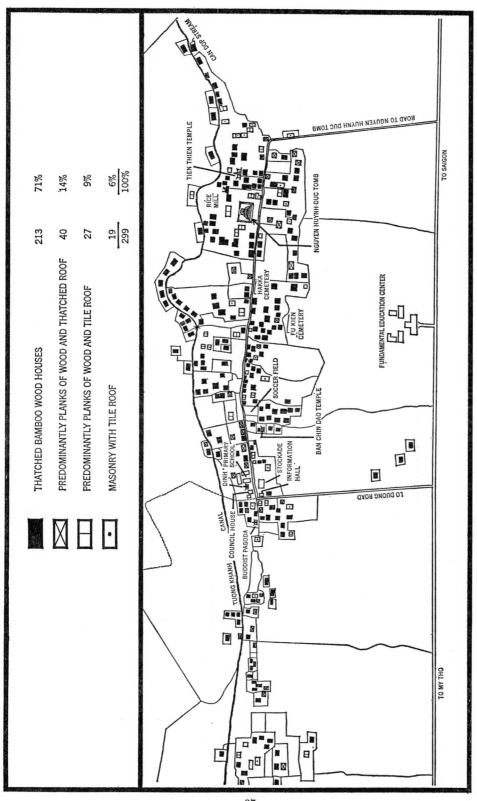

THATCHED BAMBOO WOOD HOUSES 213 71%

PREDOMINANTLY PLANKS OF WOOD AND THATCHED ROOF 40 14%

PREDOMINANTLY PLANKS OF WOOD AND TILE ROOF 27 9%

MASONRY WITH TILE ROOF 19 6%
299 100%

CAN DOP STREAM

TIEN THIEN TEMPLE

RICE MILL

NGUYEN HUYNH DUC TOMB

ROAD TO NGUYEN HUYNH DUC TOMB

TO SAIGON

HAKKA CEMETERY

FU KIEN CEMETERY

FUNDAMENTAL EDUCATION CENTER

SOCCER FIELD

BAN CHIN DAO TEMPLE

DINH · PRIMARY SCHOOL

STOCKADE

INFORMATION HALL ·

LO DUONG ROAD

CANAL

TUONG KHANH COUNCIL HOUSE

BUDDIST PAGODA

TO MY THO

27

2. Distribution of House Types in Ap Moi, Ap Dinh-A, and Ap Dinh-B.

rudimentary construction, and a larger house which often requires the
services of a specialist.

The first type is illustrated in Figure 3. Its framework, made from un-
planed logs, sticks, and bamboo, is fastened by cord produced from the
rough fibrous stem of the latania palm frond. This structure is rectangular
and rather low, with a straight-sloped, saddle, or ridge-style roof (Fig. 4),
and it usually has a small addition to one side. Some of these houses have
only one entrance, invariably at one side of the front, but most have two

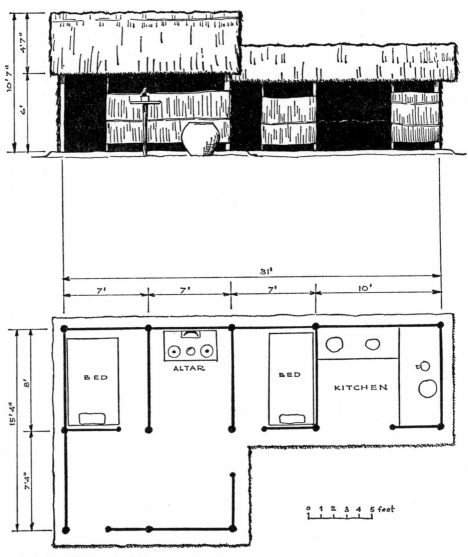

3. A Small Thatched House.

doorways separated by a flimsy partition. Generally there are no windows in dwellings of this type. The construction of small thatched houses does not require special skills, and the bamboo, sticks, and small logs needed for the frame are found in the patches of forest around the village and in the hedge growths surrounding the farmsteads.

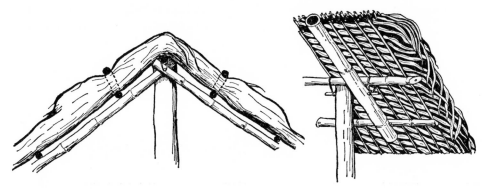

4. Structural Detail of a Small Thatched House.

Larger thatched houses, such as that illustrated in Figure 5, require sturdier frames of squared wooden posts or round pillars resting on stone bases (Fig. 6). Larger logs for such houses are brought into either Tan An or My Tho by boat or truck from the heavily wooded areas north of the delta and are transported to Khanh Hau where local carpenters cut, trim, and plane them before fitting the framework together. One of the carpenters in Ap Dinh-B learned his trade working for a shipbuilder on the coast, and he employs some of the same fitting techniques in house construction.

Fronds for the roofs, walls, and partitions of both types of thatched houses are from a type of latania water palm known as *cay dua nuoc,* which grows in great profusion along the edges of watercourses in the village. These plants produce large segmented nuts which are planted by the villagers in the soft mud and then left to grow themselves. The fronds sprout directly out of the water, reaching a mature height of 20 feet or more. They are then cut, dried, and used in house construction. The water palms grown in Ap Thu Tuu are more highly valued than those in other hamlets because, according to the villagers, the water in Ap Thu Tuu is less brackish and the palms therefore have thicker fronds.

A well-thatched roof is a matter of pride to the residents of Khanh Hau, and every man is expected to know how to thatch. Figure 7 illustrates the two local methods of thatching. In the *la xe* method (A) the fronds are split

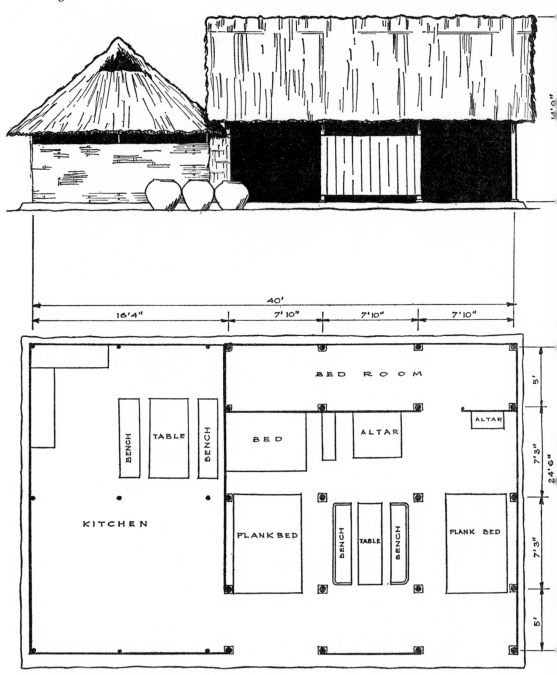

5. A Large Thatched House.

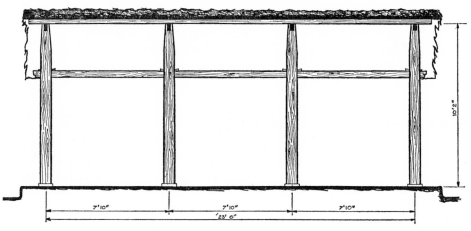

6. Structural Detail of a Large Thatched House.

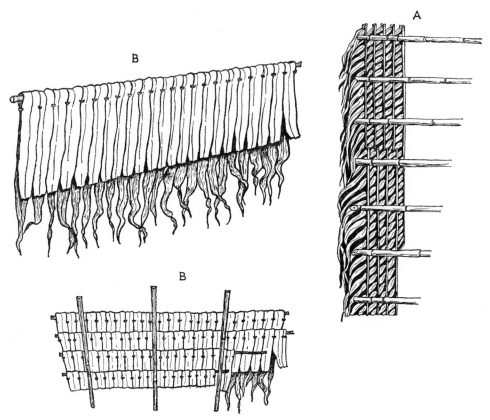

7. Thatching Methods: A, *la xe*; B, *la cham*.

in half and laid vertically on the frame, one upon the other, and are held in place by the overall weight. The *la cham* method (B) is somewhat more complicated. The leaves are cut from the stem and are then folded over it one at a time and sewed into place; the sections thus produced are imbricated horizontally on the frame. La cham is less popular than la xe and is said by villagers to have been adopted from the indigenous Khmers.[8] According to villagers, it takes fifteen men one day to thatch a medium-sized roof, 7 by 9 meters, by the la xe method. A thatched roof should last a minimum of three years, providing a sturdy rainproof shelter that insulates the house as well. Thatched houses, however, have a tendency to be damp, particularly in the rainy season when the pounded-earth floors become wet from water seeping in under the front door and through cracks in the walls.

Most thatched houses consist of a main room that contains at least one altar which in most instances is dedicated to the ancestors (Buddhist, Cao Daist, or Catholic deities also are honored, depending on the religion of the household). A table with stools or benches invariably is placed before the altar, and here guests are invited to sit and drink tea with their host. There are wooden plank beds in this room, sometimes set apart by a flimsy partition. The kitchen usually is a rudimentary shelter abutted to the rear of the house. Paddy is stored in the main room; tools, traps, and implements are attached to the beams or placed on bamboo shelves suspended from the roof frame. Larger thatched houses are essentially an elaboration of the smaller type. The material and construction are better, but there is no difference in the thatching. The interior, particularly the main room, is larger, and in some such houses there are several small rooms in the rear that serve as bedrooms. These dwellings usually have an addition of somewhat ruder construction than the main part of the house, which is used as a general workroom, kitchen, bedroom, and storeroom for tools, traps, implements, and paddy. The kitchen is in one corner of this room and generally consists of an open hearth of three stones (representing the three spirits of the hearth), perhaps several earthen braziers, and a table on which pots, dishes, bowls, chopsticks, and other culinary equipment are kept.

The house in Figure 8 is typical of the wood-thatch type; its front and rear walls are of wood, the side walls and roof are thatched. Roofs in this sort of house may have two slopes, as illustrated, or a gabled four-slope hip

8. The la cham type of thatching is found throughout Cambodia, Thailand, and Malaya. The Vietnamese name for it raises the question of whether it actually was adopted from the Khmers or from the Cham of the central Vietnam coastal plain.

roof. The framework of the wood-thatch house resembles that of the larger thatched house but is constructed of better wood with a more elaborate fitting of crossbeams and roof supports (see Fig. 9). The walls and interior partitions are of wooden planks fitted together and fastened by nails. The front of the house is indented so that the overhanging eaves form a small veranda. Front doors are louvered, and most houses of this type have several windows fitted with wooden bars.

Like most thatched houses, these dwellings usually have pounded earth floors, although in recent years some of the more prosperous villagers have installed floors of flat brick squares set with mortar. The arrangement of

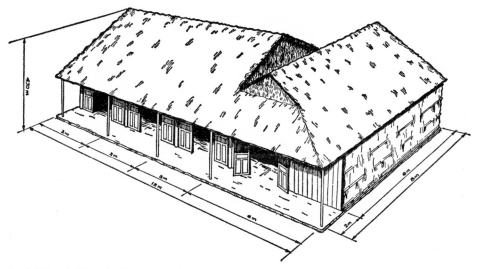

8. A Wood-Thatch House.

the interior is very similar to that of the larger thatched houses; altars line the rear wall of the main room, there are the table and chairs for receiving guests, the inevitable wooden beds and cabinets, and the multipurpose addition abutted to the main building.

Although the house with wooden walls and tile roof shares many features with the wood-thatch house, it is more elegant, has greater prestige, and is therefore a more substantially constructed dwelling. The wood-tile house (Fig. 10) was the traditional residence of the elite before masonry houses became fashionable, and considerable sums of money were lavished on fine wood for the framework and pillars as well as for carvings to grace the front doors and the altars (Fig. 11). These dwellings were intended to become

9. Structural Details of a Wood-Thatch House.

ancestral houses—places where the Cult of the Ancestors would be maintained in succeeding generations.

The house in Figure 10, constructed some 45 years ago, typifies the wood-tile houses of Khanh Hau. They usually are large, and all have the stylized roof considered to be traditionally Vietnamese. Pillars in this type of house are of polished dark hardwood; the crossbeams and supports are stylized and

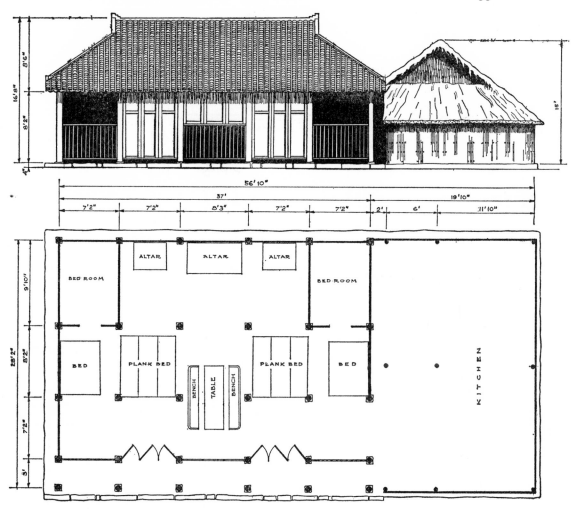

10. A Wood-Tile House.

carefully fitted. The roof is of semicylindrical tiles arranged in interlocking, alternating concave–convex rows (see Fig. 12). The tiles rest on a wooden framework and are held in place by a masonry border along the apex, sides, and eaves.

Most wood-tile houses have pounded dirt floors, although some brick floors have been installed in recent years. Their interior plan resembles that of the wood-thatch and larger thatched houses, though there always are additional rooms used for sleeping and/or storage. The main rooms of the wood-tile houses are large and seem cavernous because of the high roof and the

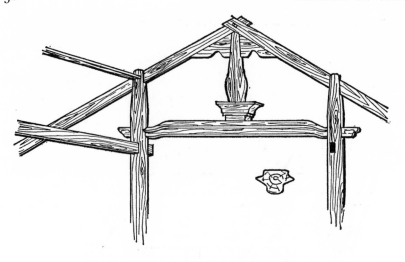

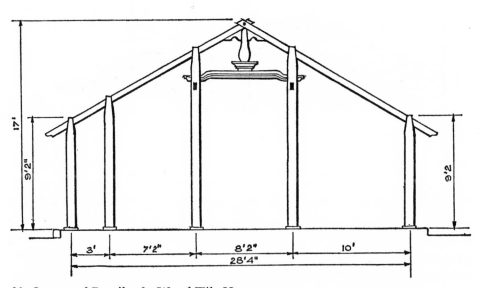

11. Structural Details of a Wood-Tile House.

fact that the partitions usually reach only to the crossbeams. All houses of this type have the combination workroom, storeroom, bedroom, and kitchen, which is invariably of wood with thatched walls and roof and adjoins the main building. Villagers manifest a definite penchant for thatched additions, and they explain this by pointing out that money and effort are concentrated on the main part of the structure because that is where the altars are housed and the rituals associated with the Cult of the Ancestors performed. Another practical reason for thatching the roof of the addition is to permit smoke from cooking to dissipate easily.

Prior to World War II there were few masonry and tile houses in Khanh Hau. One of these, and probably the most elaborate house ever constructed

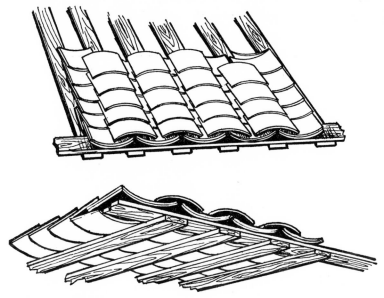

12. Traditional Roof Tiling.

in the village, belonged to Ong Ke Hien, the highest venerable and wealthiest resident. This house, on the banks of the Rach Ong Dao in Ap Cau, was a sizable structure, substantially constructed of thick masonry walls and wood of the finest quality. The rococo stone veranda was supported by fluted columns, and the elegance of the house was further enhanced by an exquisite garden, a fish pool, and a high iron fence with stylized wrought-iron gate. In one of their nocturnal raids on the village during the Indochina War, the Viet Minh burned this house, leaving a charred ruin—a mute reminder to those who might consider constructing a similarly elegant dwelling.

With the end of the Indochina War and the return of relative stability to the village, wealthy residents began constructing masonry-tile houses in increasing numbers. It was now safe to do so and, in addition, a brick factory had been established on the national highway near the village, making bricks available at lower cost. Masonry houses vary somewhat in architectural style; Figure 13 illustrates two relatively new large houses, both of which have the straight roofs currently the mode in the village. They also have the wide verandas and louvered doors typical of new masonry houses in market towns such as My Tho. Roof tiles in these houses are an innovation—they are flat, with either squared or rounded ends. Imbricated on the wooden roof frame, the tiles are held in place by notches on the bottom that catch on the frame's edge (see Fig. 13), and thus they require a more complicated lattice frame than do the more traditional tiles. Another innovation is the use of colors on the exterior walls and doors; front doors may be bright blue or green, and the walls often are painted buff, beige, or saffron yellow.

The main rooms in masonry houses are high and cavernous, although they tend to be brighter than in wood-tile houses, probably owing to the current preference for lighter-colored woods. Bedrooms are to one side of the main room or to the rear. Most masonry houses have floors of brick squares, a few have a costly type of red tile floor, and two recently constructed residences have floors of concrete. Metal gutters to collect rainwater are popular features on new houses, and several have large concrete water tanks attached to the main part of the structure. With all their innovations, however, even these houses have the wood-and-thatch multifunctional addition. In six new houses cooking is done on a new type of brick stove in which paddy husks are the principal fuel. In spite of their requiring flues and chimneys, owners of these stoves retain thatched roofs on the kitchens.

Geomancy and Settlement Pattern

Geomancy is deeply rooted in rural Vietnamese society and is akin to the Chinese beliefs on this subject. In the following passage, Soothill [9] briefly states some geomantic beliefs found in China, which also are found in Vietnam:

> Seeing that spirits exist everywhere, and take up their abode in anything, it is of vital importance that every new line of action should be taken only after the assurance that the spirits will not be disturbed. For the spirits have the power and the will to wreak vengeance on any disturber of their peace. Consequently, no man dares to dig up the long-undisturbed ground to build a house, or even a pigsty, until he has appealed to the geomancer to know whether the feng-shui will be disturbed. No grave can be built until the site has been carefully chosen

9. *The Three Religions of China*, p. 164.

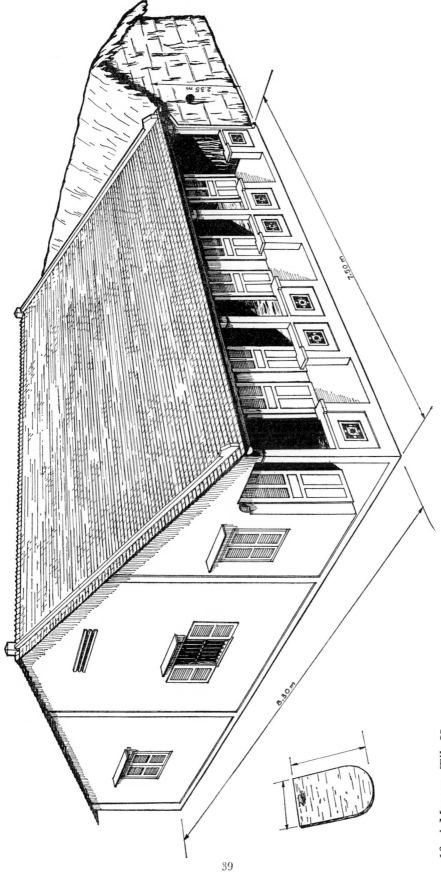

2.35 m

7.50 m

8.30 m

39

13. A Masonry-Tile House.

in a position where the feng-shui, or geomantic conditions have been
discussed, and shown to make for the repose of the soul of the deceased;
otherwise the yin part of the deceased, being unable to find rest, might
turn into a peculiarly truculent form of demon and bring woe upon
the family; for the prosperity of a family is dependent not more upon
the efforts of the living than upon the goodwill of the dead.

In addition to placating spirits, geomancy enables the individual to interpret
the portents of nature and thereby so to orient himself toward his physical
surroundings as to attract favorable cosmological influences. All these things
become important in constructing a house, planning the layout of the kitchen, and selecting the site for the family tombs.

Well-to-do villagers retain the services of a geomancer whose proficiency
lies in his ability to select the most harmonious orientation for structures
and tombs. Although there is no geomancer in Khanh Hau proper, there
are several in the vicinity, all of whom learned the secret techniques from
their fathers. The five physical signs which are the basic considerations in
making geomantic decisions are metal, wood, water, fire, and earth or soil.
The geomancer visits the intended site of the house or tomb and looks for
manifestations of these elements in the physical surroundings. For example,
a low row of pointed trees might be a manifestation of fire, while a low
mound might be earth or metal. The geomancer alone is qualified to interpret these signs, and when he has determined what they are and what their
relationships may be, he decides which location on the site would be most
propitious. A location between manifestations of fire and water would not
be advisable, since these are incompatible elements, whereas one between
wood and fire would most likely be harmonious.[10]

Those who can afford it often employ more than one geomancer in order
to increase the possibility of an optimum selection. The choice of an unfavorable tomb site, for example, would stir the wrath of the deceased and
result in misfortunes for the family. There have been several village families
who had difficulties attributed to the unhappy spirits of recently deceased
kin, and this necessitated consultation with a new geomancer and relocation
of the tombs.

For the ordinary villager who cannot afford the services of a geomancer,

10. Ong Ke Hien, the highest venerable in Khanh Hau, recently hired a geomancer
to select the sites for his and his wife's tombs. One site is next to the Ap Cau pagoda
supported by Ong Ke Hien, and the other is nearby on the edge of the paddy fields.

there is a basic set of taboos and sanctions concerning house construction (but not applicable to the selection of tomb or grave sites). If possible, a house should face east, northeast, or southeast. Two directions to avoid are west and northwest, both of which are associated with the "five demons." A house never should face the side of the house next door, nor should it face the trifurcation of a road or a watercourse. If the plot of ground is such that one of the taboo arrangements cannot be avoided, the villager purchases a *thuong luong* (an octagonal talisman with a mirror in the center) which is hung from the crossbeam at the entrance to ward off evil spirits attracted by the unfavorable position of the house.

In planning a kitchen, the western and northwestern sides of the room are the most favorable locations for the hearth because the fire will bar entrance to the five demons associated with these directions. Villagers consider it wise to hire a geomancer to plan the kitchen, since Ong Tao, the Spirit of the Hearth, is likely to be upset if the position of the hearth is inauspicious and might cause endless difficulties for the family.

Most villagers make an effort to orient their houses and kitchens in the prescribed manner, and those who cannot avoid violation of a taboo do not hesitate to obtain the counteracting talisman. The 1957 construction of the Tuong Khanh canal brought out the local credence in geomantic principles. During the Indochina War, French troops had commandeered one of the village chief's houses in Ap Dinh-B and converted it into a temporary slaughterhouse. This shocked the villagers, who believed that such desecration of a house would surely drive the good spirits from the vicinity. Subsequent misfortunes in the hamlet were attributed to this and, when the canal was proposed, some villagers immediately asked whether it would have any effect on the persistent bad luck. Ong Ke Hien and other high venerables approved of the canal; given the dragon shape suggested by Ap Moi and the Ap Dinh A–B agglomeration, they felt that the canal would provide a vein through which good fortune might flow. Since its completion, villagers contend that the good spirits have been restored to that part of the village. The manifestations are many, and the most outstanding has been the large sum of money collected for the construction of a new shrine honoring Marshal Nguyen Huynh Duc.

LAND USE

According to village records, Khanh Hau encompasses an area of approximately 1,000 hectares, making it somewhat smaller in size than most villages of Long An province.[11] Approximately 926 hectares are classified as paddy land, 31 are village land, and 45 hectares are devoted to farmsteads, garden plots, and burial places which include the scattered tomb sites as well as the small Catholic, Hakka, and Fukienese cemeteries.

Of the 31 hectares owned by the village, 17 are classified as cong dien, communal paddy land which usually is parceled out to needy villagers. This is a relatively small amount even for southern Vietnam,[12] and when in 1958 five hectares were leased to the School of Fundamental Education there was considerable dissatisfaction among the villagers. Some expressed the opinion that the school should have been located in a village with much more cong dien. With the 1959 distribution, the available cong dien was divided into 19 lots, the largest of which was 1.2 hectares.

Two and a half hectares of village-owned paddy land is classified as pagoda land and is rented by the Buddhist monk; the income is used to maintain the pagoda. Another 1.5 hectares are dinh land, cultivated by the guardian of the dinh. Some 4 hectares of village land are divided into 19 garden plots, all of which are rented to village needy for an indefinite period. The remaining village land is occupied by public buildings and the spur road, considered the property of the village.

The pattern of land ownership in Khanh Hau is constantly changing. In southern Vietnam, both males and females inherit, and inheritance is the primary cause of landholding fragmentation. In most sales the buyer is the tenant, but some sales also are made to big landowners who prefer to acquire pieces of land adjacent to fields they already own. Finally, the landholding pattern has been altered somewhat by the recent government program of land redistribution under the Agrarian Reform Program (Vietnamese Government Ordinance no. 57, October 22, 1956).

Prior to the implementation of the land reform program in 1958, all paddy land in Khanh Hau (with the exception of cong dien, pagoda, and dinh land) was held by 130 landowners of whom 31 were nonresidents and 99 residents of the village. One nonresident held the largest amount (323 hectares or 35 per cent) of the total privately owned paddy land. Excluding

11. Provincial records indicate that the average size of the 101 villages in Long An province is 2,300 hectares.

12. The 17 hectares would be approximately 1.8% of the total 926 hectares of cultivated paddy land. In his *Économie Agricole de l'Indochine Française* (p. 109) Yves Henry estimates the cong dien in Cochinchina (southern Vietnam) at 3% of the total as contrasted with 21% in Tonkin (northern Vietnam) and 25% in Annam (central Vietnam).

this landowner, there was no basic difference between the ownership pattern of residents and nonresidents. The average holding was 7 hectares. Slightly more than three fourths of all the landowners possessed about one fifth of the paddy land and owned less than 6 hectares each. A little over one fourth owned less than one hectare each, and only 14 landowners (10.8 per cent) owned more than 10 hectares[13] (see Table 1).

TABLE 1. Ownership of Paddy Land in Khanh Hau, 1958

Area of Holding (hectares)	Number of Land- owners*	Percentage of Land- owners	Cumulative Percentage, Land- owners	Number of Hectares	Percentage of Hectares	Cumulative Percentage, Hectares	Percentage of Hectares Excluding Largest	Cumulative Percentage of Hectares Excluding Largest
Less than 2	60	46.2	46.2	52.23	5.6	5.6	8.7	8.7
2–3.9	25	19.2	65.4	70.82	7.6	13.2	11.8	20.5
4–5.9	14	10.8	76.2	69.71	7.5	20.7	11.6	32.1
6–7.9	11	8.5	84.7	75.71	8.2	28.9	12.6	44.7
8–9.9	6	4.6	89.3	54.03	5.8	34.7	9.0	53.7
10 or more	14	10.8	100.1	603.41	65.2	99.9	46.4	100.1
TOTAL	130	100.1		925.91	99.9		100.1	

* Includes communal and pagoda land.

Most nonresident landlords live in neighboring villages or in the town of Tan An, and their lands are worked by tenants. Some of this nonresident land ownership results from the southern Vietnamese custom of extending property inheritance rights to females. A woman born in Khanh Hau and residing with her husband in another village may inherit local land, which she usually leases to kin. Some nonresidents hold land in the village as an investment; for example, a retired schoolteacher living in Tan An owns a few small parcels in Khanh Hau as does a minor official in the provincial administration. These nonresident owners, however, have little impact on the village for nearly two thirds of them own less than 6 hectares, and together they hold only 6 per cent of the paddy land in Khanh Hau.[14]

13. Hendry, *The Study of a Vietnamese Rural Community*, pp. 16–31.
    Reference also will be made to a stratified survey conducted in the village by Hendry. The sample included 100 families stratified into an upper level of those owning more than 4 hectares or renting more than 5 hectares, a middle level of those who own between 2 and 4 or rent between 2.5 and 5, and a lower level of those who own or rent less than the previous minimum or have no land at all.
14. Ibid., pp. 16–18.

The Agrarian Reform Program limited ownership of paddy land to a maximum of 100 hectares per owner; the excess was sold to the government which redistributed it to former tenants, each of whom could purchase up to 5 hectares.[15] Of the 38 landowners in Long An province holding more than 100 hectares, only one, the aforementioned owner of 323 hectares, had land in Khanh Hau and, under the program, holdings over the maximum were distributed among his former tenants. Applications were filed in November 1957 and temporary titles were distributed during the annual Cau An celebration at the Ap Dinh-A dinh. Recipients emerged from the Council House beaming with delight. In spite of a rumor in the village that the maximum eventually would be reduced to 15 hectares, landowners with less than the minimum 100 hectares seemed unconcerned.

Before agrarian reform in Khanh Hau, 642 hectares of land (including paddy land, cong dien, and farmstead land) were rented to tenants. Normally land was rented from only one landowner, but 15.7 per cent of the tenants had two or more landlords, and one had four. When reckoned on a village-wide basis, the average amount of land rented came to 2.4 hectares, but this included some relatively large leaseholds, and the median tenant actually rented only 1.7 hectares (see Table 2). Similarly, the village-wide average of land leased out came to 12.6 hectares per landlord, but if the two largest (Ong Hue and the village itself) were excluded, this figure would drop to 7.2 hectares.[16]

The villagers reckon value of land according to productivity, which includes both its past record of crop production and factors that determine

15. Owners compelled to sell land to the government under the terms of the land reform law were reimbursed with 10% of its value in cash, the balance being paid either in 12-year redeemable government bonds or in shares in government enterprises. An amendment to the law permits landowners to retain, in addition to the original 100 hectares, up to 15 hectares of *huong hoa* (family land), the income from which supports the Cult of the Ancestors. The landowner has the right to select which 100 hectares of paddy land, however scattered, he wishes to retain.   .

Whereas only former tenants of large landowners were beneficiaries of the land reform program in Khanh Hau, the ordinance does provide that refugees, unemployed persons, and landowners with less than 3 hectares and more than five children are eligible to apply for land if enough is available. When an application is approved, the tenant receives a temporary title which becomes permanent when payments have been completed; during the interim, final ownership rests with the government. Land values are estimated by the government and range from 12,000 to 15,000$ VN per hectare; payments are spread over a 6-year period, the first falling due at the end of the first year in which crops are harvested.

16. Hendry, pp. 31–36.

its potential capacity. Land near good sources of water is highly valued and, although there probably is only 7 or 8 inches' difference in elevation throughout the village, "high" land is valued less than "low" land because it tends to drain too easily. Thus Ap Cau land is highly valued because it is low, near good sources of water, and consequently can be double-cropped, whereas land in Ap Moi is high and until the construction of the Tuong Khanh canal was without available water. High land is the first to be affected by drought or unsteady rainfall, restricting cultivation to "hasty" (three-month) rice.

TABLE 2. Size of Tenant Holdings in Khanh Hau, 1958

Size of Holding (hectares)	Number of Tenants	Cumulative Percentage of Tenants	Number of Hectares	Cumulative Percentage of Hectares
0–1	47	17.60	31.94	5.1
1–2	93	52.43	115.19	22.9
2–3	48	70.41	109.63	40.0
3–4	25	79.77	83.66	53.0
4–5	22	88.05	93.45	67.6
5–6	14	93.25	73.03	79.0
6–7	11	97.37	70.00	89.9
7–8	2	98.12	14.60	92.2
8–9	1	98.87	8.68	93.6
9–10	3	99.62	28.20	98.0
10 or more	1	100.00	13.75	100.1
	267		642.13	

Source: Rent contract records, village of Khanh Hau.

Villagers' estimates of land values in Khanh Hau range from 12,000 to 30,000$ VN per hectare;[17] however, under the Agrarian Reform Program, prices paid by the government varied between 12,000$ and 15,000$ per hectare. This would indicate that the best of the redistributed land brought the owner only 50 per cent of its value, while the poorest went for anywhere from 70 per cent to full market value.

Prior to World War II, rents were reported to have been as high as 40

17. There are no reliable figures on land values in Khanh Hau. These and the following figures are approximations worked out by Hendry in 1959 on the basis of villagers' recollections of past sales and from estimations of land values collected from a stratified sample of owners and tenants (pp. 36–40).

per cent of the main crop in delta villages. The Indochina War, however, disrupted the tenancy pattern; large landowners fled to Saigon, and many smaller landlords went to provincial towns, leaving their lands in the hands of tenants who for the most part paid no rent. In some villages the Viet Minh confiscated land to implement their agrarian reform program. This did not occur in Khanh Hau, but many of its landlords periodically sought refuge in Tan An or My Tho; Ong Hue, the largest landowner and a resident of Saigon, was cut off from his rent revenues from time to time.

The agrarian reform law required that every plot of land as well as the expected main crop be recorded, and it set the rent at 25 per cent of the expected crop to be paid in kind. Previous legislation had established the same rate, although rent had been payable either in kind or in cash at the current market value of rice. The effect of these regulations has been to reduce the landlords' leverage on their tenants. Nonetheless, the landlords have retained an important advantage in being able to terminate the current five-year rental contracts under certain conditions. For example, if the landlord himself or a direct dependent aged 18 or more wishes to cultivate the land, or if the tenant delays paying his rent or can be proved to have damaged the property, the tenancy may be terminated with as little as six months' notice.[18] Actually, the recorded leases do not give a completely accurate reflection of land rental arrangements, for it is not uncommon for landlords and tenants to reach private agreements different from those in the formal contract.[19]

18. Hendry, pp. 39–40.

19. This resulted in rent estimates that ranged from 15 to 25% of total yield (not just the main crop), fully as often as it did in estimates above 25%. To illustrate this, a few farmers were able to grow vegetables on paddy land before or after the rice crop, but paid rent only on the normal yield of the main paddy crop. Tenants renting land from nonresident landlords frequently reported themselves particularly fortunate because such landlords were generally less well informed on actual yields and accepted lower rents than resident landlords would accept. It was also the practice of some resident landlords to fix rents at 30–35% of the first crop, but to exact no payment from a second crop if the tenant raised one. Thus tenants who reported paying rents of 35% of the main crop may have actually paid 25% or less of the total yield for the crop year. Finally, over one third of the tenants rented land from relatives, and since some in this group actually received the use of the land rent free, the average rent paid by this group is probably somewhat below the legal maximum of 25% of the main crop. To complicate matters further, the paddy harvest of 1958–59, the period during which field work for this study was carried out, was badly hit by drought and plant disease, with the result that many landlords reduced rents by 25–40% for tenants who had lost a large portion of the harvest. The foregoing comments on rents, therefore, reflect the recollections of village residents of conditions during previous periods. (Hendry, pp. 36–41.)

POPULATION PATTERNS

In 1958 the population of Khanh Hau was 3,241.[20] The Ap Dinh A–B agglomeration contained the largest number of residents—38 per cent of the total village population; Ap Moi was the smallest with 11.5 per cent. This would mean that almost half (49.5 per cent) of the village population lived west of the national highway. A slight majority (51 per cent) of the population were females, but of the 54 per cent under 18 years of age, a little more than half were males (see Table 3). The average household had 5.5 persons with a range of variation from 5.1 in Ap Dinh-A to 5.9 in Ap Dinh-B. The village median was 6 persons. One household had 16 members; 35 households had 10 or more members; 26 households consisted of one person.[21]

TABLE 3. Population of Khanh Hau, by Hamlets, 1958

Hamlet	Men over 18 Years	Women over 18 Years	Boys 18 Years and Under	Girls 18 Years and Under	Total
Ap Dinh-A Ap Dinh-B	258	309	363	309	1,239
Ap Moi	82	97	87	107	373
Ap Cau	101	110	129	124	464
Ap Nhan Hau	137	150	161	188	636
Ap Thu Tuu	112	132	156	129	529
TOTAL	690	798	896	857	3,241

Source: Census of Khanh Hau village, September 1958.

The population pyramid for the village (see Fig. 14) sharply indents at the 11–12 age group, indicating a sudden drop in the village birth rate around 1946 and 1947. This was a period of great unrest as the Viet Minh activities against the French intensified, and numerous males left the village to fight with the French or the Viet Minh. Disruption of normal village life also is reflected in the noticeable narrowing, particularly on the male side, beginning with the age 20 group. Expressed numerically, the 41–48 age group with 166 persons was larger than the 31–40 group which had 154, or the 21–30 age level with 158 persons. Given the pattern of life expectancy

20. Data on village population were collected by village officials and staff members of the School of Fundamental Education in a house-to-house survey conducted in September 1958.

21. Household composition is discussed in Chapter 5.

in Southeast Asian societies, one would expect a decrease of population in
the higher categories. This also is attributable to the Indochina War. In
addition to those who joined the army or Viet Minh, some villagers departed
to find security in Saigon or one of the larger towns. There also appears
to have been a greater outward migration of males in the past twenty years.
Villagers contend that, because of fragmentation of landholdings during
this period, increasing numbers of young men were unable to buy or rent
land, and since other sources of work were scarce they had to quit the village.
This loss of males is reflected on the female side of the pyramid. To avoid
incest in marrying consanguineal kin, many villagers prefer to take wives
from other villages, and residence prescriptively is patrilocal.

The national highway provides a convenient means of leaving the village,
and from time to time most villagers make trips, although few go beyond a
50-kilometer radius. Visits to neighboring villages for family celebrations are
common, and many villagers make frequent trips to the markets in Tan
An and the neighboring village of Tan Huong. The market in My Tho
occasionally attracts Khanh Hau people. The farthest most villagers travel
is to Saigon.[22] In spite of the fact that it is a costly trip, villagers feel that
at least one visit to the capital city is part of one's life experience. More
extensive travel is rare. Several brothers were engaged in a business venture
that took them to Ban Me Thuot in the southern highlands, and several well-
to-do villagers had visited the highland resort of Dalat or the seaside resort
of Cap St. Jacques. The only villagers who have visited central Vietnam are
some members of the Duc family[23] and some young men doing military
service.

Despite the fact that the Vietnamese villager traditionally has had strong
attachments to his village, particularly to his farmstead and the tombs of his
ancestors, emigration has been an outstanding feature of Vietnamese history.
In a period of approximately a thousand years, the Vietnamese population
has expanded from the Red River delta to the delta of the Mekong River,
and more recently—in 1955—over 800,000 northern Vietnamese entered
southern Vietnam as refugees. The situation in Khanh Hau indicates some
of the reasons for emigration: with increasing population and continual

22. In Hendry's survey, 16% of the 100 household heads interviewed had never been
to Saigon; 59% reported that they had been to the city once or twice in the previous
year. Pleasure, business, and visits to relatives constituted 90% of the reasons given for
the trip (pp. 79–80).

23. The Duc family claims revenues from land in central Vietnam through a document given by Emperor Gia Long to Marshal Nguyen Huynh Duc. This is discussed in
Chapter 10.

fragmentation of existing landholdings, the time comes when young men must leave the village to find opportunities elsewhere.[24]

According to the villagers, those emigrants with skills prefer finding employment in Tan An or My Tho, enabling them to return to the village frequently. Those without skills have less choice, and most go to Saigon. For the most part they find work as laborers or cyclo (pedicab) drivers, eventually with good fortune moving up to become taxi drivers. Since the cost of moving a family to a new place is prohibitive, most emigrants leave their families in the village, hoping eventually to send for them, and villagers cite several examples of emigrants who have failed to return, leaving dependents to fend for themselves.

For those who quit the village to seek land, the only area open for homesteading is west of the village in the Plaine des Joncs, an extensive marshy area near the Cambodian border. In 1956 the government launched a program encouraging settlement of this area. Settlers would be allowed to claim 5 hectares of cleared land (it was stipulated that only land cleared by a settler could be claimed), and for the first years (unspecified how many), settlers would be exempt from land tax. In addition, loans up to 500$ VN per hectare would be granted and, although they were described as "longterm" with "low interest," some settlers reported that they were expected to repay after the first harvest (which presumably would be the second year of settlement) at 10 per cent rate of interest.

In 1957 a tenant farmer from Ap Cau and his son immigrated to the Plaine des Joncs area. He constructed a rudimentary house of wild swamp reed near a new settlement that had just completed its Buddhist pagoda and dinh (with a newly formed Cult Committee). Clearing for paddy cultivation proved difficult—in places the water is waist deep, and there are thick growths of grasses, reeds, and roots. The government brought in some mechanical equipment but it was ineffective in the mud, and the settlers relied on water buffalo which were costly to rent because of the demand. The settler requested 2,500$ VN and, although he received it late in the year, he could clear only 2 hectares which he planted to a variety of floating rice.[25] In 1959 he realized his first harvest, selling some of the paddy to

24. In his survey of 100 households, Hendry found that 44% had kin who had emigrated, and they numbered 67 persons. Saigon drew the largest group (40%), followed by Tan An (28%) and other parts of southern Vietnam (22%). It should be pointed out, however, that given kin ties in the village, some of the responses may be overlaps (p. 80).

25. He estimated that clearing and cultivating 1 hectare would cost around 2,000$. The clearing cost 800$, and two plowings around 400$ each, while labor and seed cost around 400$.

merchants who entered the area in boats.[26] By this time, however, he had to repay 1,000$ VN of the loan with an added 100$ interest. He requested additional funds to clear the remaining 3 hectares, but rather than rent buffalo from local farmers, he returned to Khanh Hau to rent them from friends (specifying that it would be less costly, and he preferred dealing with people he knew). This involved riding the buffalo for two days over the paddy fields westward into the Plaine des Joncs and returning them afterward.

Late in 1959 a group of three farmers (two tenant farmers and one landowner who wished to expand his holdings) immigrated to the Plaine des Joncs, leaving their families in Khanh Hau. At first they were discouraged by conditions there, but after they received government loans and had realized one crop, they decided to bring their families and remain (one settler's son married a girl in the new settlement). Other villagers talked about emigrating, but by late 1960 government control in the Plaine had diminished considerably, and between 1961 and 1963 it was the scene of large-scale military operations.

Population Characteristics

Three of the five fertility measures suggested by Nag[27] can be applied to the random fertility sample of 40 women between the ages of 20 and 45 collected in Khanh Hau. For the total maternity ratio, the total number of women 45 years and over in the sample is 20 and the total number of live births to women of the same age category is 106, giving an average of 5.3. Applying the formula for maternity ratio, the total sample includes 40 women with a total of 235 live births, giving an arithmetic mean of 5.9. Referring to the pyramid on total village population in Figure 14 for the child–woman ratio, there are 525 children under age 5 while there are 681 women in the 15–44 age group, giving a ratio of 771.

In 1948 the village began keeping records of births and deaths (see Table 4). The ratio of births to deaths has averaged 5.2 to 1 over the ten-year (1948–57) period. Since 1953, however, the births per year in the village

26. Most farmers in the area harvested between 150 and 200 *gia* (40 liters) which they sold from prices ranging between 45 and 50$ VN per gia.

27. *Total maternity ratio:* average (arithmetic mean) number of live births per woman when all living women (unmarried and ever-married) of age 45 and over are considered. *Maternity ratio:* average (arithmetic mean) number of live births per woman when all living women (unmarried or ever-married) of all ages are considered. *Child–woman ratio:* ratio of the number of living children of age 0–4 years (under 5 years) to the number of living women of age 15–44 (less than 45 years). (*Factors Affecting Human Fertility*, pp. 15–16.)

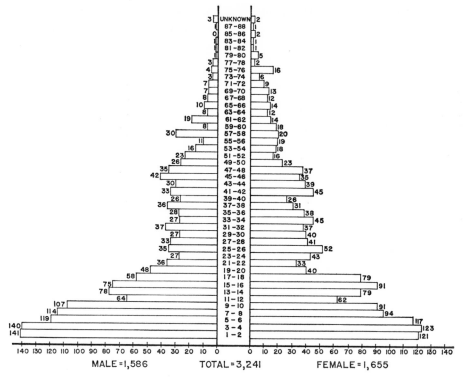

14. Population Pyramid, Khanh Hau, 1958.

have been about double those of 1948, and while the ratio of births to deaths has been relatively consistent the excess of births over deaths has shown a similarly proportionate increase[28] (see Fig. 15).

Only ten villagers are able to read and write the traditional Sino–Vietnamese script. Some had learned when they were young at a school started by a railroad employee who had retired in the village. In 1958 the staff of the School of Fundamental Education conducted a survey on illiteracy in the Ap Dinh A–B agglomeration where the primary school is located. Giving a sample test in ability to read and write the romanized national script, they found that 13 males and 76 females between the ages of 15 and 45 were illiterate. Broadening the age sample to include everyone over the age of 15, they found that 43 males and 168 females were illiterate. Matching this with the village census figures on this section of the village, the survey showed that of the 692 villagers over 15 years of age, some 30.5

28. In noting this, Hendry points out that, based on the village population in 1958, the net increase measured by the excess of births over deaths is proceeding at the rate of about 44 persons per thousand per year. All other things being equal, this promises an increase of nearly 1,500 persons over the 1958–68 period.

TABLE 4. Births, Deaths, and Marriages in Khanh Hau, 1948–1957

Year	Number of Births	Number of Deaths	Excess of Births over Deaths	Number of Marriages	Ratio of Births to Deaths
1948	83	18	65	22	4.6:1
1949	94	20	74	14	4.7:1
1950	90	17	73	25	5.3:1
1951	98	21	77	22	4.7:1
1952	99	16	83	17	6.2:1
1953	180	35	145	34	5.1:1
1954	123	37	86	28	3.3:1
1955	166	27	139	41	6.1:1
1956	176	26	150	17	6.8:1
1957	177	33	144	17	5.4:1

per cent were illiterate; of the 479 between the ages of 15 and 45, some 18.6 per cent were illiterate.

The greater number of illiterates among females reflects the past pattern of providing education only for males while females learned household arts. This has diminished as educational facilities have expanded, and more villagers have come to accept the notion that it also is well to give females a basic formal education. Expansion of facilities too accounts for the diminishing illiteracy among younger villagers. In spite of the increasing number of villagers who can read and write, there is little opportunity to use either skill. Few take Saigon newspapers, and there is a marked absence of books in

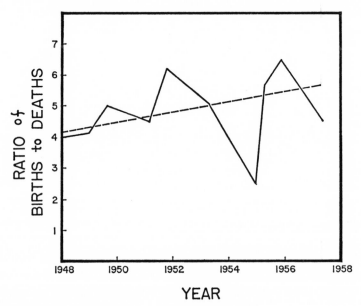

15. Ratio of Births to Deaths, Khanh Hau, 1948–1957.

village houses. For pupils who wish to study there is no place to do so—houses lack privacy and most are poorly lit after dark.

FORTIFIED HAMLETS

In February 1962 the Strategic Hamlet Program was launched by the government as a means of creating greater security in the rural areas. In essence this program provided that fortifications be constructed around existing settlements, in this case hamlets, and that a number of new organizations, most of them paramilitary, be established at the village level to maintain better control and communication among the villagers. In Long An province three villages, one of which was Khanh Hau, were selected as models for the program. It was decided that Ap Dinh-A, Ap Dinh-B, and Ap Moi would be the first hamlets so fortified. Provincial military authorities estimated that this would entail the construction of ditches and earthworks some 4,000 meters in length, enclosing an area of 80,000 square meters.

By May 1962 a ditch had been dug around the perimeter of Ap Dinh A–B, and in some sections the earthworks had been completed. To avoid sacrificing valuable paddy land, the fortification was constructed close to the farmsteads, and some villagers already were speculating about using the ditch for irrigation. Gates were constructed at the spur road, and several tall watch towers were built on the edge of Ap Dinh-B. According to the plan, barbed wire supported by concrete posts would be strung along the top of the earthworks, and both the earthworks and ditch would be studded with bamboo spikes. Isolated farmsteads were to be relocated within this enclosure.

The province was to supply the barbed wire, but the village was held responsible for providing other construction materials and labor. All able-bodied males between the ages of 18 and 60 were required to labor one day on the fortification and a second day if that should prove necessary. Well-to-do families were asked to donate cash while poorer ones contributed material and labor for the concrete posts. In January 1962 the police agent found a list of tax contributors on a captured Viet Cong cadreman. Taking the list, the Village Council visited each family and, noting the amount the family had paid the Viet Cong, the village chief advised its members to match that sum for the construction of the fortification which would protect them from further nocturnal collections.

By the end of June 1962, a fortification consisting of barbed wire fencing (about 4½ feet high) and shallow ditches had been arranged around Ap

Dinh-A and Ap Dinh-B (the earthworks had not been extended and the bamboo spikes were not used). In the months that followed, similar defenses were erected in the other hamlets of the village. Isolated families were brought within the fortifications and a small new settlement grew up between the highway and Ap Thu Tuu. Relocated families were supposed to receive 2,000$ VN, but some complained that they received no compensation and others reported that they received only part of the expected amount.

The fortification presented no barrier to the Viet Cong, however, and their patrols simply cut through the barbed wire to enter the hamlets. Sometimes they demanded food and cash tribute, and often they moved through the hamlet, cutting the wire on the other side to make their exit. There were no reports of clashes between these patrols and village defense units. No deaths occurred during this period, and the only unusual incident was the kidnapping of the village chief.

By February 1964 those who had been relocated had begun to move back to their former farmstead sites, leaving the new settlement in Ap Thu Tuu partially abandoned. Some declared preference for the old sites because they were closer to their paddy fields and had shade trees. Also, the Viet Cong had warned villagers that those who relocated within the strategic hamlet would be considered pro-Government, and Village Council members saw this as one reason for abandoning the new location. Council members also pointed out that owners of the land on which the new settlement had been constructed were urging the relocated families to return to their own land. There was general agreement that the Strategic Hamlet Program was a failure, and one elderly villager summed up the situation by stating, "It was a waste of Vietnamese labor and American money."

CHAPTER 3

Religions and Popular Beliefs

IN THE DRAMA of Southeast Asian history, the Mekong River delta has been the meeting place of great traditions, all of which continue to be identifiable in the traces of their religions. Once predominant, Theravada Buddhism survives among the fragmented Khmer population, superseded by the Mahayana Buddhist–Taoist–Confucianist ideology brought southward by the expanding Vietnamese. Catholicism was established in the delta by the French during the nineteenth century, and Protestantism more recently has found followers in some of the larger delta towns.

During the past four decades, several religious movements indigenous to the delta have made their appearance. Founded in 1925, Cao Daism has become widespread in the delta (see Appendix B). This religion, which describes itself as reformed Buddhism, is a mixture of Buddhism, Taoism, and Confucianism with lesser amounts of Catholicism, Indian mysticism, and a variety of popular beliefs and practices. Another type of reformed Buddhism known as Hoa Hao is of recent emergence. It is not syncretic as is Cao Daism, nor is it so widespread, being largely concentrated in the trans-Bassac (the area between the Bassac and Mekong Rivers).

In writing on Vietnamese religion, Cadière[1] explicitly used the singular in characterizing it as an omnipresent thing, enveloping all the individual's daily acts. At the little-tradition level of Khanh Hau there is an amalgamation of the Mahayana Buddhist–Taoist–Confucianist ideology with the popular beliefs and practices of the oral tradition, and it affects practically all aspects of village society. The Buddhist–Taoist–Confucianist tradition is part of the Chinese heritage, but popular beliefs and practices have myriad origins. Some can be traced to Chinese sources while others are uniquely Vietnamese, and some have been borrowed from the Cham, Khmers, and

---

1. *Croyances et Pratiques Religieuses des Vietnamiens,* 1958, pp. 1–23.

55

highland groups with whom the Vietnamese have been in contact. Some cults of this genre, such as the Cult of the Guardian Spirit of the Village, are found in all villages whereas the occurrence of other cults is regional. The result is that while the religious amalgam is universal among the Vietnamese, its content varies somewhat from place to place.

In Khanh Hau the syncretism has been enriched by the coming of Cao Daism. Although this religious movement is of relatively recent establishment there, it contains so many elements of the existing amalgam that it simply became part of it. It also has made some hitherto alien additions, such as deities from the Judeo–Christian tradition and principles of karma. The few Catholic families in the village do not participate in rituals of either the traditional formal religions or those associated with the popular cults, and in a sense Catholicism does not constitute a real presence in village society. Nonetheless, the Catholics retain much of the cosmological view that is an intrinsic part of village religion.[2]

COSMOLOGICAL VIEW

Although few could articulate it, villagers share a cosmological view that is daily manifest in behavior and expressed attitudes. It is a notion about the universe deeply rooted in the Chinese philosophical tradition taken over by the Vietnamese during the long period of Chinese domination. Universal order is the essence of this cosmology and from it spring other concepts, one of which is individual destiny. Villagers believe that one's destiny is guided by a particular star—the lucid manifestation of a cosmic force—that shone brightly at the time of the individual's birth. The relationship of this star to other stars affects the cosmic force, augmenting or diminishing it, thus boding good or evil for the individual, who in this context is predisposed rather than predestined.

Because there is a recurring pattern in the relationships among the stars, horoscopy permits individuals to prepare for good or bad periods, and horoscopes can be provided for the collectivity. For example, in addition to the individual horoscopes prepared by soothsayers, the lunar calendar (see Appendix C) advises everyone of auspicious and inauspicious days. There is prescribed behavior for maximizing the good influences of the favorable periods, and avoidance of specific behavior is recommended to evade the

2. The attempt to place social behavior and institutions in proper functional context necessitates discussing numerous cults, practices, and beliefs in other chapters; for example, family cults, such as the Cult of the Ancestors, are described in Chapter 4 on the family, and the Cult of the Guardian Spirit of the Village is discussed in Chapter 8 on the Cult Committee.

bad effects of the unfavorable periods. Rituals also give the individual some control. For example, from the Cung Sao ritual which is performed on the day his star reaches its zenith, the individual can derive the maximal good influences.

Another related concept is harmony. When there is harmony with the existing universal order the individual experiences a sense of well-being; he is healthy, happy, and prosperous. When there is disharmony the opposite occurs. Harmony with the five elements that constitute the physical surroundings is the basis of geomancy. There also is harmony in attaining the favor of good spirits and avoiding evil spirits. To violate a taboo is to invite disharmony and trouble. Existing good fortune for the nation is a manifestation of harmony and the approval of *thien*, the celestial forces, for those in power—that is, the rulers have the mandate of heaven. Floods, droughts, and other catastrophes are indicative of disharmony and the disapproval of heaven. This is the time for "change of mandate," the literal Vietnamese expression for revolution.

The concept of harmony also is intrinsic to Vietnamese folk medicine. If any of the three souls or nine vital spirits that sustain the human body should depart, the imbalance results in sickness, insanity, or death, and the healer's first invocation is for the souls and spirits to return to the victim. In the principles of Nham Than which guide the practitioners of Sino–Vietnamese medicine there are about a thousand vital points in the human body and each corresponds with a specific hour, date, and odd or even number in the lunar calendar. For treating ailments there must be harmony between the point in the body and the auspicious time in the calendar.

Whether Khanh Hau villagers become Christians, receive higher education in Saigon, or for whatever reason become removed from the traditional ways, they continue to retain something of this cosmological view. The notions of destiny and harmony with universal order are deeply ingrained, and it would be an unusual villager (including a Christian villager) who did not consider his horoscope or adhere to at least part of the folk medical beliefs. While this generates a certain conservatism in villagers, it does not commit them to fatalism. Innovation may be viewed with some skepticism although, as will be pointed out in succeeding chapters, villagers do accept technological change when there are patent economic advantages. Also there will be examples to show that villagers, rather than fatalistically accept manifest bad fortune, do everything possible to deter further deleterious consequences. In a drought they do all they can to save the wilting crops, and in illness all available means for a possible cure are employed.

CATHOLICISM

Catholicism has been long established in Vietnam, particularly in the north where the densest concentrations of Catholics are found. According to villagers, Catholicism was introduced in Khanh Hau some time in the early part of the twentieth century, and currently there are twelve Catholic families with a total of about eighty members. Most Catholics reside in the north end of Ap Dinh-B. The first converts were from this part of the village, and some kinfolk living nearby also became Catholics. In addition, marriages between Catholic and non-Catholic villagers usually result in the conversion of the non-Catholic, and the Catholics prefer to live in proximity. Another variable for this pattern may be the fact that the part of the village where they live is closest to the Tan An Catholic church.

The priest periodically visits his parishioners in the village, usually to administer the sacraments to those unable to walk to Tan An. The only Catholic rituals held in the village are daily prayers before the shrine (usually dedicated to the Sacred Heart) in every Catholic house, portions of the marriage rites, or the last rites of the Church administered to a dying villager. In every village where there are Catholic families there is a Church association. Ong Giap, the head of the association in Khanh Hau, owns the Ap Dinh-B rice mill. He was appointed by the parish priest and serves as liaison between the priest and his flock. His responsibilities include visiting Catholic households, disseminating any news received from the priest, and summoning the priest when his services are needed. For example, if a Catholic villager should be gravely ill, Ong Giap keeps a watch so he can hurry to Tan An and bring the priest if necessary. Ong Giap or another household head also represents the Catholic villagers at rituals held in the dinh. Since he cannot participate in the rituals, he serves as recorder of various cash and food contributions made by household heads.

BUDDHISM

Most villagers who are not Catholic or Cao Daist consider themselves Buddhists, and in most village houses there is, in addition to the ubiquitous altar of the ancestors, a shrine honoring a Buddhist deity. Villagers also often make references to Buddha or Buddhist ideals. For example, when one villager gave some of his lottery winnings to the village for the construction of additional classrooms, villagers declared him "a good Buddhist." When conflicts are brought to the Village Council, the arbitrator often attempts to resolve the difficulty through an appeal to "Buddhist mercy."

Khanh Hau has two pagodas: the official one is in Ap Moi close to the Council House and is the responsibility of the village; a more recently established pagoda supported by private means is in Ap Cau, and its affiliation with the Buddhist Association of South Vietnam marks for the first time any real bond between village Buddhism and a hierarchy.

Historically, Buddhism in Vietnam, as in China, was without hierarchical organization. Support of pagodas and the lay monks has been the responsibility of individuals, groups, villages, or towns. In 1951 a group of Buddhist priests and laymen founded the Buddhist Studies Association of South Vietnam in an attempt to form a hierarchy which would, among other things, set standards for monks and nuns as well as preserve the corpus of Buddhist doctrines. Headquarters were established in the Khanh Hung pagoda, located in the modest Hoa Hung quarter of Saigon. With the end of the Indochina War and the influx of Buddhist refugees from North Vietnam in 1955, the activities of the association began to expand.[3] The new headquarters pagoda of Xa Loi was constructed in a fashionable part of Saigon, and by 1959 the organization of the association had enlarged. The Central Committee, composed of monks, *cu si* (lay monks), and laymen, is vested with the highest authority on doctrinal matters as well as responsibility for the administration of the association.

Since its inception the Buddhist Studies Association of South Vietnam has made considerable progress in gaining membership and establishing schools. A school for monks and one for nuns have been organized in Saigon, and several existing schools for religious training have become affiliated with the association. By 1960 membership had risen to over 500, many of whom were monks residing in rural pagodas. Association efforts to gain new adherents also have been manifest. Since 1955 on several occasions monks from the Linh Son pagoda of Saigon have visited Khanh Hau to preach Buddhism and encourage the faithful to spend a short period studying at the association's school in the capital.

About thirty years ago, a cu si from Ap Cau, a brother of Ong Ke Hien, the highest venerable in Khanh Hau, established a private shrine to the Buddha, and he constructed a building to house the shrine with contributions from his affluent kin, one of the wealthiest families in the village. Eventually the building was enlarged and dedicated as a pagoda. At the invitation of the cu si, a Buddhist monk came to reside there and perform

3. Some Buddhists pointed out that organization became necessary because of the growing Cao Daist movement in the south and also because of the hundreds of thousands of Catholic refugees.

the prescribed rituals (see Table 5). A young man from the hamlet fre-
quented the pagoda where the monk gave him instructions in Buddhist
doctrine; after the death of the cu si and the monk, he assumed the role of
resident monk.

TABLE 5. Calendar of Buddhist Rituals

Tam Nguon: The Three Great Annual Rituals

1. 15th day of 1st month*   Thuong Nguon, beginning of the new year
2. 15th day of 7th month   Trung Nguon, midyear festival
3. 15th day of 10th month   Ha Nguon, end of year

Nhung Ngay Via: Lesser Annual Buddhist Rituals

1. 1st day of 1st month   Thich Ca Xuat Gia, Buddha's departure from his family
2. 8th day of 2d month   Thich Ca Nhap Diet, Buddha's first mystical experience
3. 15th day of 2d month   Quang Am Giang Sanh birthday of Quang Am
4. 19th day of 2d month   Pho Hien, birthday of Pho Hien
5. 21st day of 2d month   Chuan De Phat Mau, birthday of Chuan De Phat Mau
6. 6th day of 3d month   Thich Ca Giang Sanh, birthday of Thich Ca
7. 8th day of 4th month   Nhu Lai, birthday of Nhu Lai
8. 12th day of 4th month   Ho Phap Di Da, birthday of Ho Phap Di Da
9. 1st day of 6th month   Quang Am Xuat Gia, Quang Am's departure from her family
                              to become a religious
10. 19th day of 6th month   Dai The Chi, birthday of Dai The Chi
11. 13th day of 7th month   Dai Tang, birthday of Dai Tang
12. 30th day of 7th month   Nhien Dang, birthday of Nhien Dang
13. 22d day of 8th month   Quang Am Thanh Dao, sanctification of Quang Am
14. 19th day of 9th month   Thich Ca Co Phat Nhap Diet, Thich Ca's achievement of
                              nirvana
15. 8th day of 10th month   Di Da Giang Sanh, birthday of Di Da
16. 8th day of 12th month   Thich Ca Dac Dao, Thich Ca became a Buddha

Monthly Rituals

Sam Hoi ritual on 14th and 30th days of each month

Daily Rituals

 5:00 A.M., Cong Phu
 6:00 A.M., (Ap Moi Pagoda) Cong Com
12:00 noon, (Ap Cau Pagoda) Cong Com
 5:00 P.M., (Ap Moi Pagoda) Cong Phu
 8:00 P.M., (Ap Cau Pagoda) Cong Phu

  * Lunar month in all cases.

This pagoda stood near the highway and during one of the wartime
clashes between French troops and Viet Minh it was set afire. Rallying
quickly, the monk and some Ap Cau residents managed to save the sanctuary from complete destruction, and with funds contributed by Ong Ke

Hien a new sanctuary was constructed. The old sanctuary was refurbished and became the monk's quarters. To guarantee continuance of the cult, Ong Ke Hien also donated a hectare of paddy land to the pagoda, and he agreed to give the monk 100 kilos of rice each year.

The sanctuary is dominated by a pyramidal altar on which a large gilded figure of Buddha occupies the highest level. Below it are figures of A-Ana, one of Buddha's assistants, Thich Ca, a reincarnation of Buddha, Ca Dip, who replaced Thich Ca after his death, Dat Ma, the twenty-eighth reincarnation of Buddha, Quang Am, the Goddess of Mercy, and Di Lac, the fat, laughing Buddha on whom frolic six small figures representing Van Thu, the six temporal senses. On the lowest level of the pyramid there is a fearsome polychrome figure representing Quan Cong, the great Chinese warrior. There also are statues of Ong Tieu, who frightens away evil spirits, and Ho Phap, the protector of honest men.

Abutted to the rear is the old sanctuary, and when the monk resided there it was simply furnished with a hardwood bed and a few chairs. It also contained a large gilded figure of Ong Dam, a husky man sitting on a tree stump, leaning on the handle of a large ax. According to legend, Ong Dam was an illiterate woodcutter who had no religious instruction. Nonetheless during the day he often would chant "I venerate the Buddha A Di Da," and for his sanctity he was proclaimed a Bo Tat, the lowest order of sainthood and example of faith for simple, unlettered folk. The monk paid Ong Dam special veneration and considered him the caretaker of the pagoda.

The monk himself came from a large family of tenant farmers, and he was quite young when he began his studies with the first resident monk. He was an ascetic man, a celibate, and he scrupulously observed the prescribed Buddhist diet. His day was spent in prayer, taking care of the pagoda, and tending his kitchen garden. When he performed public rituals, some fifteen to twenty followers usually attended. Hired workers cultivated the pagoda land, and the income was used for repairs to the building and defraying the cost of ritual feasts.

After deciding to continue Buddhist studies, the monk quit Khanh Hau late in 1958 and went to the An Quang pagoda in Saigon. Before his departure, however, he requested that a group of Buddhist nuns be sent from the nunnery in My Tho to replace him. The Buddhist nunnery is a sizable institution and was founded by the niece of Ong Ke Hien. She is a tall, thin woman, hardly distinguishable from a monk with her shaved head and rust-colored robe, and she invariably wears a pair of large sunglasses as a gesture of modesty. Since the nunnery is affiliated with the Buddhist Studies

Association of South Vietnam, the directress had to have the approval of
the central committee to send the nuns to Khanh Hau. When it was received, she dispatched four—a Superior (an elderly woman who had been a
nun for many years and had received formal training in doctrine) and three
ordinary nuns. The latter were of various ages and backgrounds—one an
elderly widow, another a middle-aged woman from a village in My Tho
province, and the third a young girl from a farm family.

In the pagoda the nuns brought about a number of changes in the furnishings and some innovations in the rituals. The figure of Ong Dam was
moved to the main altar, and in the living quarters brightly colored scrolls
appeared on the walls. Flowered pillows were placed on the severe wooden
beds, a fancy green tea cozy replaced the coconut shell used by the monk,
and a library of Buddhist literature was arranged in a corner of the room.
In the semimonthly Sam Hoi ritual to ask forgiveness of Buddha for wrongs
committed, the nuns instituted the practice of public confessions, which
according to the Su Co is an old Buddhist practice.

In this small religious community each nun has delegated responsibilities.
The Superior is the administrator, and she aids in tasks whenever necessary.
One nun is in charge of their newly established school for preschool children
who receive instruction in Buddhist prayers as well as in reading and writing. The other nuns divide the labor of cooking, cultivating the kitchen
garden, and maintaining the pagoda. They hire laborers to plant and transplant their paddy, but they do the harvesting themselves. Also, the nuns ask
for money when they need it rather than receiving a fixed amount of paddy
from Ong Ke Hien.

The nuns observe a strict daily schedule beginning at 5:00 A.M. when they
rise and perform the Cong Phu ritual, kowtowing with burning joss and
reciting prayers before the main altar. Unlike many Buddhist religious,
however, they do not beg food from the faithful. The morning is spent in
delegated tasks, and at noon they gather at the main altar for a ritual offering of food to Buddha. Afterward they take their one daily meal. Work
occupies the afternoon, and at 8:00 P.M. there is another Cong Phu ritual,
accompanied by a ritual offering of soup to the errant spirits. At ten o'clock
they retire. In addition to their regular duties, the nuns often are summoned to pray at the bedside of an ailing villager or before the bier prior
to a funeral ritual, for which services they receive a fee. On such occasions
they may encounter the monk from the village pagoda, but that is the only
contact between them.

The nuns also have been active in organizing meetings at the Ap Cau pagoda. In 1959, under the sponsorship of Ong Ke Hien, they organized a conference to which learned monks from large pagodas in Saigon were invited. A special building was constructed for the honored guests, and women of the hamlet provided food. The monks lectured on the life of Buddha and on Buddhist doctrine. An American travel film was shown by the Ministry of Information, and Ong Ke Hien contributed 100 kilos of rice for distribution among the needy who attended.

The official village pagoda in Ap Moi was constructed over sixty years ago with funds collected from the residents of Tuong Khanh village (Ap Dinh A–B, Ap Moi, and Ap Thu Tuu) and the site, considered particularly auspicious because it is near an ancient gnarled tree venerated by nearby residents, was donated by a well-to-do villager.[4] Other villagers donated plots of paddy land (totaling about 2.5 hectares), collectively classified as pagoda land, a category of village-owned land.

The pagoda is an unadorned wooden structure with a masonry facade and tile roof. The main part is the sanctuary; the rear section serves as a reception room for visitors and a meeting room for the faithful, and when the nearby primary school periodically becomes overcrowded, it is used as a classroom. There are six altars in the sanctuary. In the rear room are several altars, only one of which is dedicated to a Buddhist deity, the goddess Chu An De Phat Mau, a spectacular figure with eighteen arms. An altar in the center of the room contains several tablets honoring villagers who donated land to the pagoda, and a similar altar to one side is dedicated to those who have given donations for maintenance of the pagoda. A small altar on the other side of the room honors the memory of the first resident monk, the present monk's father.

The current monk is a small, thin man of 50 years; after his father's death, several monks appointed by the Village Council had proved unsatisfactory so the present monk was hired. He had learned the prayers, rituals, and Buddhist doctrine from his father, and for several years he studied the traditional calligraphy in a Tan An school. Although he has no contact with any of the large pagodas in Saigon, he possesses several old certificates attesting to the fact that he is a bona fide monk. During the twenty years he has served, he has carried out his functions with only occasional direction from the Village Council.

---

4. Unusual, very old trees traditionally are objects of veneration among the Vietnamese, and villagers explain that the inviting shade attracts the spirits when they promenade. For this reason children are cautioned to avoid these trees, particularly around noon.

This monk contrasts strongly with the monk of the Ap Cau pagoda. The latter is married and has three children; he shaves his head but wears his robes only when necessary, and he does not observe the prescribed dietary restrictions. Daily rituals are performed without the assistance of his parishioners. The monthly Sam Hoi ritual at which Buddha's mercy is implored attracts from twenty to thirty villagers, including a representative of the Village Council. The major act of this ritual consists in writing requests on special papers which are burned by the monk on the main altar. The Village Council is invited to participate in the great annual feasts, and the congregation swells to seventy or eighty. The monk's younger brother usually assists him at the annual rituals, although he does not have an official role in the pagoda.

The pagoda paddy land (2.5 hectares) is rented to the monk for twenty gia of paddy per year (the land normally produces about 200 gia). The income is used to help support the pagoda, and funds are solicited from the congregation. Those attending rituals are requested to bring food for the meals which normally follow. The monk subleases part of the pagoda land to his younger brother, and he hires laborers to work the remainder; in addition he cultivates a sizable kitchen garden and fruit grove, selling part of the produce. To supplement his income he receives fees for praying at the bedside of an ailing villager or at a funeral bier.

Cu si are Buddhist laymen who observe five of the ten monastic interdictions (against killing, drinking alcohol, smoking, sexual pleasures, and stealing). In Khanh Hau there are two male cu si, both of whom have studied Buddhist doctrine with learned monks. The elder is 70 years old and is known as Ong Dao Ba Rau, or Ong Rau, so-called because he has a thick black beard (rau), unusual for a Vietnamese. When he was about 25 years old and already married, Ong Rau journeyed to the mountain of Ta Lon in southern Cambodia to study with Buddhist monks. He also learned Chinese calligraphy and became proficient in preparing folk medicines and amulets and healing through exorcism.

He remained in this retreat for two years, interrupting his studies only rarely to visit his family. When he returned to Khanh Hau he began working as a laborer. He resumed his conjugal life and eventually his wife had three daughters and a son. Ong Rau points out that he does not consider this a violation of the interdiction against sexual pleasures because intercourse with one's wife is a natural thing. Initially he refrained from eating meat, but poor health required that he have a "normal diet." The main room of his house is arranged like the sanctuary of a pagoda with a main altar dedicated to Buddha, represented by a Cambodian Theravada figure. Another altar contains a figure of Quan Cong, and two small altars honor Ho Phap, the protector of honest men, and Cuu Thien, the Ninth Heaven. Ong Rau also has an altar of the ancestors.[5]

At 6:00 A.M., noon, and 6:00 P.M. Ong Rau dons his monk's robe to perform the Cong Phu ritual before the main altar while his wife prays before one of the other altars. Although he does not have rituals marking annual feast days, he does perform Xin Xam, a ritual not observed in either pagoda, to seek a deity's response to a request. Kneeling before the altar, the officiant makes the request and then shakes a container of sticks on which responses are inscribed. The first stick that pops out bears the response of the deity, and it must be interpreted by Ong Rau. In this instance Xim Xam is performed before the altar of Quan Cong.

Ong Rau enjoys a favorable reputation as a healer. He receives patients in his house and visits the sick in the vicinity. He employs amulets and medicines for physical ailments and exorcism for "insanity." In addition to healing, Ong Rau practices a particular kind of geomancy concerned with floor plans of buildings. According to him it is derived from the Taoist principles of *duong* or light, the male principle associated with living things as opposed to *am* or darkness, the female principle associated with death. Feeling that engaging in both duong and am geomancy is dangerous, Ong Rau restricts himself to duong which enables him to find the most harmonious floor plans relative to the cardinal points. He visits the site of the proposed building, examines the surroundings, and then consults his book of duong principles to select the most propitious floor plan. Ong Ke Hien's niece (who founded the Buddhist nunnery in My Tho) consulted Ong Rau when the new buildings were being planned, and he was invited to the dedication.

The other cu si is a man of 57 years and is also a resident of Ap Cau, is married, and has several children. He began to learn Buddhist doctrine at age 14, and studied in a pagoda on the sacred mountain of Ba Den near the Cambodian border and later in the large Vinh Trang pagoda on the edge of My Tho. When the Indochina War disrupted his studies he returned to Khanh Hau and married. Clearing a small plot in a swampy section of the hamlet, the cu si built a thatched hut and became a tenant farmer. Like the

5. Claiming that he turned the house into a pagoda, Ong Rau's landlady demanded higher rent.

house of Ong Rau, this cu si's house resembles a pagoda with altars dedicated to Thich Ca and Quan Cong. In addition to daily Cong Phu rituals, clients come to perform Xin Xam as in Ong Rau's house. This cu si also is a healer, specializing in ailments associated with childbirth.

CAO DAISM

Of the eight Cao Daist sects in Vietnam, four have adherents in Khanh Hau (see Fig. 16).[6] The original sect, the Tam Ky Pho Do, whose head-

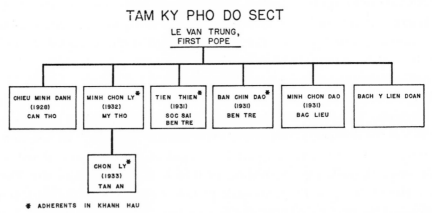

16. Cao Daist Sects: Branches of the Tam Ky Pho Do Sect of Tay Ninh (1926).

quarters or Holy See is in Tay Ninh, claimed the first converts in the village. Subsequently, the Ban Chin Dao and Tien Thien sects, with Holy Sees in Ben Tre and Soc Sai respectively, were established, and eventually both sects constructed temples in Khanh Hau. More recently the Minh Chon Ly sect of My Tho has gained some twenty followers among the villagers.

The first convert to Cao Daism in Khanh Hau was a well-to-do farmer named Vo Van Chieu, currently the chief of congregation in the Tien Thien temple, and in many respects the story of this villager in Cao Daism reflects the history of the movement in the village. In 1926, after hearing of the new religion, Vo Van Chieu attended a seance during which he received a spirit message directing him to embrace Cao Daism. Shortly after, he left his farm in the care of his sons and went to Tay Ninh where he remained two years. During his stay he became a disciple of Nguyen Ngoc Tuong, and when this leader quit Tay Ninh to found the Ban Chin Dao sect, Vo Van

6. For a brief history of the Cao Daist movement, see Appendix B.

Chieu joined him. When a congregation was formed in Tan Huong, the village immediately to the south of Khanh Hau, Vo Van Chieu elected to lend his support to it. He resided in Khanh Hau proselytizing among his fellow villagers, and when the congregation was large enough a temple was constructed in Tan Huong; in 1948 it was burned by French troops.

Shortly afterward, for unspecified reasons, Vo Van Chieu left the Ban Chin Dao to join the Tien Thien sect, and he actively engaged in organizing a congregation in Khanh Hau. His assistant in this task was Ong Khai, current patrilineage chief of descendants of Marshal Nguyen Huynh Duc. During a seance in Can Tho, a group of Cao Daists had received a spirit message from the Marshal advising his descendant to embrace Cao Daism, and Ong Khai complied by joining the Tam Ky. He subsequently shifted to the Tien Thien sect, and in 1949 Vo Van Chieu, Ong Khai, and a farmer from a neighboring village established the Tien Thien temple in Ap Dinh-B.

By 1960 there were an estimated 350 Cao Daists in Khanh Hau, but it would be very difficult to determine the approximate number affiliated with each sect. The pattern has been for adherents to convert kin and close neighbors, resulting in clusters of Cao Daists of a particular sect, particularly around the two temples.[7] Preference for one sect over another for most converts is a secondary consideration, although there is some indication that the Tam Ky sect has been less popular since 1955. In addition to the difficulty between this sect and the government, resulting in diminished activities, the Tam Ky has little formal organization in Khanh Hau. One member is the designated representative of the sect in the village, and his primary function is to disseminate news received from the committee at the temple in Tan An.

Because they have temples in the village, the Ban Chin Dao and the Tien Thien sects have attracted many followers. While each has a core of members who consider themselves exclusively of that sect, many Cao Daists think of themselves simply as Cao Daists in general, and they are apt to attend rituals at different temples in or near the village. There is some shifting from one sect to another for, with the exception of the Minh Chon Ly which differs in doctrine, this involves no conflict. It is difficult to determine whether some villagers who have embraced Cao Daism can be counted as practicing members. For example, the village chief was converted after a

7. The residence patterns around the temples is discussed in detail in the following chapter.

spirit message directed him to do so, but subsequently he left the religion because the dietary restrictions proved deleterious to his health. On occasion, however, he describes himself as a Cao Daist.

In 1955, with funds solicited from the faithful, the leaders of the Ban Chin Dao congregation purchased a wood-tile building in Tan An for 30,-000$ VN. A wealthy member donated a plot of ground in Ap Dinh-A, and the structure was reassembled on it. The interior of the temple is spacious and unusually airy. Brightly colored silk hangings, mandarin parasols, and a set of decorative symbolic weapons to ward off evil spirits adorn the main altar which contains an elaborate throne. A portrait of the founder of the sect rests on the throne, and above there is a painting of the Cao Dai eye. Immediately before the throne are carved polychrome figures representing Ban Chin Dao deities—Lao T'se, Thich Ca, Quang The Am, Confucius, Christ, Ly Thai Bach, Quan Cong, and Khuong Thai Cong. The altar also contains the traditional Vietnamese altar accouterments—gongs, candles, an incense burner, vases of flowers, and offering plates. The sanctuary contains two other altars, one dedicated to Quan Cong, the sainted Chinese warrior, and the other to Duc Ho-Phat (Christ).

The chief of the congregation is elected by the Administrative Committee for a two-year period; this committee in turn is elected by the congregation for an indefinite period. The chief of the congregation sets the elections, and he is responsible for the spiritual and material affairs of the group. He also officiates at specific rituals, acts as chairman at meetings held in the temple, and has the final voice in any decisions affecting the congregation. Three times each year he journeys to the Holy See at Ben Tre to assist at the Tam Nguon rituals and report on the congregation to the Central Committee.

The chief of the village committee is appointed by the chief of the congregation, and his assistant, the "learned man," usually is an elderly member of the congregation. This committee is represented in each hamlet by an assistant, to enable easy contact with the parishioners. The Cult Committee is responsible for organizing annual rituals and feasts. All of those holding high office live in farmsteads close to the temple, and a few of the elderly committee members as well as the guardian live in the subsidiary buildings behind the temple.

Most Ban Chin Dao rituals closely resemble traditional Vietnamese rituals observed in the village (see Table 6). The ritual honoring the dead of the Indochina War illustrates well the traditional form with Cao Daist innovations. It was held outdoors at three altars placed before a large painting depicting a Cao Daist Valhalla. Between the main and middle altars there was a long table covered with plates of cooked rice, meat dishes, cookies, and other delicacies. Men gathered on the right side and women on the left. Four young men in robes of the same style as those worn in dinh rituals stood by the rear altar, and two boys stood by the middle altar. As a choir

TABLE 6. Ban Chin Dao Rituals

*Annual Rituals**

8th and 9th days of 1st month	Feast of Cao Dai, the Supreme Being
14th and 15th days of 1st month	Thuong Nguon, beginning of year
14th and 15th days of 2d month	Anniversary of Thai Thuong Lao Quan, a celestial deity
12th and 13th days of 3d month	Feast of the papal election
8th day of 4th month	Birth of Thich Ca, second reincarnation of Buddha
24th and 25th days of 5th month	Birth of the Pope
14th and 15th days of 7th month	Trung Nguon, midyear feast
14th and 15th days of 8th month	Birth of Goddess Dieu Tri Kim Mau
24th and 25th days of December	Christmas

Monthly Rituals

Eve of 1st and 15th days of each lunar month

Daily Rituals

5:00 A.M.
12:00 noon
5:00 P.M.   } Cong Phu
12:00 midnight

* There are additional rituals held during the year which are fixed by seances; all lunar months except December.

of women chanted, the boys announced groups of male worshippers who kowtowed before the main and middle altars. After the leaders of the congregation kowtowed, they remained kneeling while the four young men made three stylized offerings of burning sandalwood, fruit, and tea, placing them on the main altar. One of the leaders then read an invocation to those killed in the war, afterward burning it on the main altar. The women kowtowed in the final act of the ritual. The participants gathered later in the meeting rooms behind the temple for a feast.

A more typical Cao Daist ritual is the celebration of the birth of the Ban Chin Dao Pope, held at noon on the twenty-fifth day of the fifth lunar month. The 1959 celebration was attended by sixteen of the congregation, nine of whom were elderly women; with the exception of one leader who wore mandarin-like robes, the participants were garbed in white. Two women wore headpieces that resembled those prescribed for mourning, and one of the male leaders wore a black fez. They gathered before the temple for a brief ritual during which a large flag with the Cao Dai eye emblazoned on it was raised. Proceeding inside, the men knelt on the right and the women took places on the left. The ritual, accompanied by beating of gongs, consisted of prayers chanted by the leader, and periodically all would bow low. There was no individual or group kowtowing or any offering.

In establishing the Tien Thien temple in Ap Dinh-B, funds were solicited from members in the vicinity, and a relative of Ong Khai rented them a plot of land. The first temple was a thatched structure that cost 1,000$ VN, but when the congregation raised 39,000$ they purchased a traditional wood-tile house in a neighboring village, dismantled it and reassembled it next to the thatched structure which became a kitchen and residence for the guardian. Continuing to collect money, the congregation eventually was able to construct a sizable two-story building (the only one in Khanh Hau) in front of the existing temple, which since has been used as a reception room and place where some of the sect leaders residing at the temple eat and sleep.

In the sanctuary the main altar is dominated by a large painting of the great Cao Dai eye amid incense burners, candles, offering plates, gongs, and vases of flowers. To the left there is a small altar dedicated to Quang Am, the Buddhist Goddess of Mercy, and to the right there is a small altar over which hangs a print depicting the meeting of all religions, an expression of Cao Daist spirit. Surrounded by celestial clouds is the Cao Dai eye, and below it are Buddha, Lao T'se, Moses, Christ, Mohammed, and Confucius. Other altars honor Lao T'se, Confucius, and Dai Tang, the Buddhist monk who was sent from China to India to seek the true prayers of Buddha.

In the small sanctuary on the second floor is a small altar containing a large print of the Bac Quay, an octagonal symbol designed to protect the temple from evil spirits. There also are altars in the former sanctuary to the rear of the new one. The main altar honors Marshal Nguyen Huynh Duc, and his portrait stands in the middle of it. In spite of the fact that this hero is not officially recognized as a saint by the Tien Thien Holy See at Soc Sai, the Khanh Hau congregation chooses to venerate him with no apparent objection from the hierarchy. To the right stands an altar dedicated to the deceased males of the congregation, and a similar altar to the left is for deceased females.

The Administrative Committee associated with the Tan An Tien Thien temple is responsible for the region, and it has close contact with the Holy See at Soc Sai. The president of this committee visits Soc Sai on the tenth day of every month (Gregorian calendar) when he reports on his region and receives information which he disseminates to the village congregations. The chief of the Khanh Hau congregation also has direct contact with the Holy See, visiting Soc Sai periodically to attend major rituals. While there he reports on the activities of his congregation and receives instructions from the hierarchy. The Administrative Committee in Khanh Hau elects the chief of congregation for a two-year term of office, and members of the congregation elect the committee members for terms of several years (sect leaders were vague on the number of years). The Administrative Committee is responsible for the activities of the congregation, upkeep of the temple and other property, and financial affairs. It also appoints the members of the Committee for New Members which also functions as the Cult Committee. None of the sect officials receives any salary. All describe themselves as farmers, and their official duties require only a portion of their time.

The congregation includes residents of neighboring Loi Binh Nhon and An Vinh Ngai as well as people from all hamlets of Khanh Hau, and by 1960 the rolls listed 150 members. Of these, about thirty attend most rituals in the temple (see Table 7). This "core" includes sect leaders, some elderly

TABLE 7. Tien Thien Rituals

*Annual Rituals**

14th day of 1st month	To honor war dead
15th day of 1st month	Thuong Nguon, beginning of new year
15th day of 2d month	Feast of Thai Thuong, the Supreme Being
14th day of 7th month	To honor war dead
15th day of 7th month	Trung Nguon, midyear festival
9th day of 9th month	Death anniversary of Marshal Duc
14th day of 10th month	Ha Nguon, end of year
15th day of 10th month	To honor war dead
25th of December	Christmas

Monthly Rituals

Eve of 1st and 15th days of each lunar month

Daily Rituals

5:00 A.M., noon, 5:00 P.M.	Cong Phu
11:00 A.M.	Ritual at main altar
7:00 A.M.	Public confessions

* All lunar months except December.

villagers, and a few younger farmers and their wives who live nearby. They often meet for the daily 11 o'clock ritual after which they share a vegetarian meal. They also spend a good deal of their leisure time in the older section of the temple to the rear of the sanctuary. The atmosphere is familial and, typical of the Cao Daists, they invariably extend warm hospitality to any visitors. Annual rituals attract most members of the congregation, but attendance tapers considerably at monthly rituals which are compulsory only for the chief of congregation and members of the Administrative Committee. The daily Cong Phu ritual consists in burning joss and kowtowing, and chanting of prayers.

All members are expected to make at least one retreat of 100 days and, should a member receive a spirit message directing him to make the retreat at a specific time, he must comply regardless of responsibilities or other obstacles. Those on retreat reside in the wood-tile building; male quarters are on one side, the female quarters near the kitchen where the women assist with preparation of meals. At 4:00 A.M., 4:00 P.M., 6:00 P.M., and midnight there are ninety-minute meditation periods for those on retreat. Ideally the participant should achieve a state of complete trance during the meditation. There are also daily yoga exercises at unspecified times, and at seven o'clock each morning public confessions are held. Seances occur frequently, although the only scheduled seance is on the fifteenth day of the second lunar month. A stylized version of the beaked basket is used in seances as prescribed (see Appendix B).

About 1935, during the period when the Minh Chon Ly sect was expanding, several Khanh Hau residents became converts, and by 1960 the sect claimed twenty adherents in the village. The younger brother of the village chief is a member, and one of his neighbors, an elderly lady, was the first convert to this sect in Khanh Hau. The closest Minh Chon Ly temple is in Binh Tam, some 3 kilometers from Tan An; however on the twenty-ninth day of each lunar month, members gather in a private residence near the secondary school in Tan An for a group profession of faith and for traditional rituals, at which one of the school teachers officiates, which involve burning joss, kowtowing, and beating gongs. Occasionally a representative of the Holy See in My Tho visits the gatherings to instruct the congregation in sect doctrine. Members of the sect also perform four daily rituals, similar to Buddhist Cong Phy rituals, in their homes at 5:30 and 11:30 A.M., 5:30 P.M., and midnight. Also prescribed are three daily prayer periods at 9:00 A.M. and 3:00 and 7:00 P.M.

Members of the Minh Chon Ly in Khanh Hau have the usual altars, although theirs have the "heart in the eye" as the central symbol. Also, whereas other Cao Daists are supposed to make daily ritual offerings of food on their altars, the Minh Chon Ly have dispensed with this in the belief that the Supreme Being does not require it. As indicated earlier, members of this sect do not adhere to most traditional cults, nor do they assist at rituals held at the dinh, but they do maintain the Cult of the Ancestors and they burn joss on the altar.

One of the primary school teachers is a member of the Chon Ly Tam Nguyen sect, an offshoot of the Minh Chon Ly; he spends a great deal of time in Khanh Hau and is active in village affairs but is a resident of Tan An. Nguyen Van Kien, the 83-year-old founder of this sect, resides near their only temple on the edge of Tan An. There are few members and they consider their sect the most profoundly religious and theologically the purest. They have no symbol in the temple, believing that it is unnecessary, since each individual has the Supreme Spirit within him. They have no food taboos, and they reject all the traditional Vietnamese cults.

Relations among members of the various Cao Daist sects in Khanh Hau are relatively easy, and most identify themselves as Cao Daists rather than members of a particular sect. Among the leaders, however, the situation differs. The Ban Chin Dao and Tien Thien sect leaders have cordial relations, often visiting each other, and since their doctrines are almost identical they openly permit their adherents to attend rituals at both temples. There have been, however, several incidents between leaders of the Minh Chon Ly and those of other sects, particularly the Tien Thien. On one occasion Ong Khai, head of the Duc family, and one of the Tien Thien leaders invited some members of the Minh Chon Ly hierarchy to attend a Tien Thien conference in My Tho. The Minh Chon Ly delegation disagreed with the Tien Thien hierarchy on doctrinal points, and they left the meeting in anger. A second incident occurred when Ong Khai's father died, and he invited some Buddhist monks and Minh Chon Ly leaders to the funeral. The monks prayed before the bier, and the Minh Chon Ly representatives placed a print of their symbol—"the eye in the heart"—on the coffin. The host left it, but a Tien Thien leader removed it and indignantly returned it to the Minh Chon Ly leaders who were chagrined and immediately departed. Several days later several of the Tien Thien leaders called on Ong Khai to remonstrate with him for allowing the "outsiders" to practice their rituals at a Tien Thien funeral.

OTHER CULTS

The Chinese warrior Quan Cong is widely venerated in Khanh Hau. He is enshrined in the two Buddhist pagodas and in many households, and has become a popular Cao Daist deity. In addition, there is a pagoda in Ap Nhon Hau dedicated exclusively to Quan Cong and supported by a number

of individuals in Ap Nhon Hau and other hamlets in the area. At the end
of the nineteenth century, a group of Ap Nhon Hau residents, all members
of the Cult Committee, sponsored the construction of the original pagoda.
It was a small, simply constructed building, and early in the twentieth century the maternal grandfather of the present Ong Ke Hien collected funds
for a new pagoda. By 1921 this structure had to be replaced because of
termites. The wooden figures representing the deities were burned, and a
new pagoda with new figures was constructed. Although it was untouched
during the Indochina War, it had fallen into disrepair, and when the war
ended a group of prosperous residents of Ap Nhon Hau, Ap Cau, and Ap
Thu Tuu formed a committee to collect donations for a new structure.

Around 45,000$ VN was collected, and the new pagoda was completed in
1958. It was substantially constructed of wood with a tile roof, and resembles
the Buddhist pagoda in Ap Cau, although it is somewhat smaller and less
adorned. There is one main altar containing large polychrome wood figures
of Quan Cong and his assistants Chau Xuong and Quan Binh. To one side
there is a small altar to honor the memory of those who established the original pagoda, and a similar altar on the other side is for those who have given
subsequent contributions.

The Quan Cong Pagoda Committee, charged with maintenance of the
building and rituals, is composed of Ap Nhon Hau Cult Committee members. They also select a resident of Ap Nhon Hau to be guardian and he is
given use of the one hectare surrounding the pagoda. Daily rituals of burning joss and kowtowing are performed by the guardian at 5:00 A.M. and
6:00 P.M. There also are three annual rituals which attract villagers from
the surrounding hamlets. Participants bring offerings of food and cash, and
the rituals resemble those held in the dinh—pigs are sacrificed, and members of the Pagoda Committee kowtow according to ranked order.

On the northern edge of Ap Dinh-B there is a masonry house set among
vegetables, flowers, and fruit trees, which houses a private cult. An elderly
descendant of Marshal Nguyen Huynh Duc lives there with his fourth wife
and several of his daughters and their children. A large, rambling, thatched
addition to the rear serves as living quarters for the family. The main part
of the house had been their residence, but as the man grew older (and
according to his neighbors, senile), he began to venerate an ever-increasing
pantheon of Buddhist deities, Vietnamese culture heroes, and spirits. With
more altars and statues, the family was forced to move into the addition.
The main altar is dedicated to Buddha and the goddess Quang Am, and

there are other altars honoring Quan Cong and the Vietnamese emperors Gia Long, Minh Mang, and Tu Duc. There also are numerous prints of Buddhist deities and Taoist symbols, as well as tablets, candles, gongs, silk hangings, and decorations in the national colors. In the midst of it all there is a canvas camp bed on which the old man sleeps. Before the entrance to the house is a kneeling polychrome figure which the old man identifies as a Khmer goddess. He has reached the stage where he claims belief in all religions and worships all gods. His day is spent in burning joss and praying before the altars, and he also prepares special heavily alcoholic elixirs which he gives to those who visit the shrine.

POPULAR BELIEFS AND PRACTICES

The villagers believe that certain periods in everyone's life are auspicious or inauspicious, and there are prescribed ways of finding out when they occur. There also are practices and rituals designed to maximize the favorable effects and minimize the unfavorable. The first twelve years of an individual's life constitute one cycle, and it is considered a precarious one during which many die. One ritual which will help the child survive and develop is aimed at "cleansing the memory." [8] For everyone, the ages 21 to 23, 31 to 33, 41 to 43, and 51 to 53 are unfavorable periods during which he should exercise great caution in all behavior. In addition there are "bad years" for the individual depending on the relationship of his zodiacal sign with that of the current year. The signs are in three groups: (1) tiger, monkey, snake, pig; (2) dragon, dog, buffalo, goat; (3) mouse, horse, cat, rooster. Those in each category are compatible with one another but not with those of the other two groups. Therefore in the Year of the Tiger those born in the second and third categories must be on guard against the *tam tai* (three misfortunes)—fatal accidents, sickness, and loss of good fortune.

In order to avoid tam tai, the individual consults with one proficient at analyzing the lunar calendar (this would include some elderly villagers, the cu si, and some of the healers) to find a propitious time during the first months of the year for the tam tai ritual. The individual purchases paper figures and talismans, and arranges on a small altar the three symbolic food offerings such as a crayfish to represent sea creatures, some pork for land animals, and an egg for creatures of the air. Reciting prayers, the individual offers the food to the evil spirits, after which he burns the paper figures and talismans.

8. See Chapter 5 for details of this ritual.

During the bad years, it is believed that the star which shone brightly at the time of the individual's birth is hiding its light, depriving the individual of its beneficial influences. Cung Sao Hang is the ritual designed to attract the light of the star.[9] At a date selected according to the individual's horoscope, he writes the name of his star on a tablet which is placed on a small altar arranged before the house, facing the direction of the star. Offerings of fruit, flowers, and burning joss are placed on it, and numerous candles are lighted and set on and around the altar to attract the light of the star.

There are three souls and nine vital spirits which collectively sustain the living body. The primary soul maintains life itself, the second is the seat of intelligence, and the third is related to the senses. The nine vital spirits have no particular properties or designations. When all souls and vital spirits are present, the individual experiences a sense of well-being, but if one or all should depart, sickness, insanity, or death could result. The souls and the vital spirits are targets of evil demons, and when the healer first approaches his patient he usually intones, "Three souls and nine spirits return as quickly as possible." After death, if there is no cult honoring the deceased, he becomes an errant spirit, wandering endlessly and doing great harm to the living.[10]

The pantheon of other spirits is complex.[11] It includes the *ma, yeu, quy, tinh, con hoa, tien,* and several deities such as Thien Loi (the Thunder Spirit), Ba Thuy (the Water Goddess), and Ba Giang Ha (the Falling Goddesses). These are differentiated in a variety of ways—some are inherently wicked, some occasionally wicked, and others capricious or benevolent.

The supernatural beings most commonly discussed among the villagers are the *ma,* phantoms or ghosts, and they command fear, although their degree of wickedness varies. Among the least malevolent are those which once were living animals—*ma heo* (pig ghost), *ma cho* (dog ghost), and *ma meo* (cat ghost). Villagers believe they swarm over the fields after sunset, often getting tangled in the legs of those who tarry too long on the paths. *Ma dung* is the collective term for ghosts associated with horses, oxen, and buffalo, but unlike the other animal ma, they are harmful, and strange oc-

9. In addition to the individual's star, separate stars preside over the fate of males and females.

10. Errant spirits and the Cult of the Ancestors are discussed in Chapters 4 and 5.

11. In his excellent study of Vietnamese religious beliefs and practices Cadière includes a classification of supernatural beings found in central Vietnam. He describes the *quy* as *démons,* the *ma* as *esprits,* and *tien* as *génies,* and he also presents an analysis of the classifier *con* which is used when referring to supernatural beings. (*Croyances et Pratiques Religieuses,* 1957, pp. 80–88.)

currences in the village often are attributed to the ma dung. Ma Than Vong is a specific ghost, the "tightening-knot ghost" which goads people into suicide by muttering *co co* ("neck, neck") into their ears. Ma A Phien is the opium ghost, related to addiction and eventual "death in the pleasures."

Yeu and *quy* are capricious, often wicked supernatural beings, capable of doing unguarded humans great harm. Of all these beings, however, none is so malevolent as the *tinh* who villagers claim use a variety of tricks to induce their intended victims to open their mouths, whereupon the tinh draw out their souls, leaving them insane. Villagers believe that the yeu and tinh inhabit great trees, often appearing as human shadows.

While the supernatural beings of fearful genre are divided into somewhat finely distinguished categories, good supernatural beings are of one kind— the *tien,* who are considered happy and delightful beings. For example, a common proverb in the village is "To eat well and sleep well is to be like a tien." The tien also are thought capable of passing on special gifts such as literary genius, and some impart medicinal secrets. In Khanh Hau the tien are held in reverence but there are no elaborate rituals honoring them as there are in places like Chau Doc and Ha Tien, near the Cambodian border, where the *thinh tien* rituals are scrupulously performed.

With the many watercourses around the village and the large number of ponds, drownings are not uncommon, and to the villagers it is a particularly horrible death, for drowning may indicate *noi,* a curse on other members of the victim's family. Noi implies an irresistible urge to plunge one's face into water, and it falls on the immediate kin of a drowning victim. According to villagers whole families have been drowned as the result of the curse. Some drowned in earthen water jars, one man cursed with noi is supposed to have drowned in a cup of water, and one villager cited the case of a man who stumbled on the road and, because he was cursed with noi, his face was fatally drawn into water that had seeped into a buffalo footprint.

Noi is attributed to a number of water spirits, among them Ba Thuy, the Water Goddess, who can dispel as well as cause noi. While all villagers know of Ba Thuy or Long Than, the Dragon King usually associated with her, few offer periodic rituals, and none maintains a cult to either deity. Boat dwellers on the larger streams such as the Mekong or the Vaico are conscientious in their rituals to Ba Thuy, and most have gilded altars honoring her. Throughout the year ritual offerings are made at prescribed times, and fierce weather always provokes rituals to Ba Thuy. Some villagers contend that Ba Thuy protects drinking water from contamination, although this belief is not manifest in any ritual act.

Ma troi is the ghost of a drowned person who, not having been restored to the family tomb or to the altar of the ancestors, has become an errant spirit. Ma troi manifests itself by a phosphorescent glimmer over a body of water or near a fire where villagers say it is attempting to warm itself. Normally the ma troi is the ghost of a victim whose body has not been recovered, and its manifestation is a sign that the victim's kin should continue the search. If the search is futile, a ritual is performed by Ong Thay Phap, the sorcerer, to bring peace to the tormented ghost. It consists in summoning the ghost from the depths and capturing it in a jar which is placed on the altar of the ancestors.

The most fearful of the water spirits—those associated with noi—are the *ma da*. These are ghosts of the drowned who cannot find peace until they have secured another victim to replace them in their misery. The ma da lurk in the water, awaiting a victim, usually a kinsman, and their favorite prey are children. In Khanh Hau, children are cautioned about the ma da, and many wear metal bracelets which repel the ma da who may attempt to pull a child into water. From time to time one hears the expression "drowned by the ma da" in reference to a drowned child. Often ma da manifest themselves as large, ominously black amorphous masses which hover over the water wailing "It is cold—so cold."

Ba Hoa, the Fire Goddess, and *con hoa,* ghosts of those who died by fire, are greatly feared by villagers because of their destructiveness. Thatched houses are a favorite target of the fire spirits, who are supposed to cause the fire themselves or induce someone else to start it. New houses never are constructed on the site of a house that burned. There are no prescribed cult practices to propitiate Ba Hoa or con hoa, but rhinoceros horns or horns from a mountain goat, both extremely rare in the delta, are known to be very effective talismans against the fire spirits.

Villagers refer to thunder as a "blow from heaven," believed to be directed by the Spirit of Heaven against evil spirits on earth. Associated with this is the Thunder Spirit, sent to earth to mete out punishment to evil spirits and criminals. He carries an ax known as *luoi cam set;* he uses a bronze one against humans and a stone ax against animals and evil spirits. According to popular belief, if one digs deeply in a place where lightning has struck, it is possible to find the luoi cam set, which may be used as a powerful talisman. Many sorcerers carry small axes which they call luoi cam set.

Meteors are believed to be manifestations of goddesses descending to earth. Villagers refer to them as the Goddesses of the Nine Heavens, the Mistresses of the Spirits, or simply the Buddhist Goddesses. When a falling meteor disappears behind trees, it is thought that the goddesses are descending via the tree, so in their honor a small shrine should be constructed at the base of the tree. There are many such shrines in the village. Some are simply constructed and maintained for a limited time whereas others, usually constructed by well-to-do villagers, are of masonry with a tile roof and are scrupulously looked after for a long period.[12]

HEALERS

Ong Thay Phap (Master of Sorcery) is a particular type of practitioner who receives from his patron deity special powers, especially the power to meet evil spirits and exorcise them. Since evil spirits are believed to cause a wide variety of maladies, the sorcerer's power to exorcise makes him a sought-after healer. There is no resident Ong Thay Phap in Khanh Hau. Some villagers claim that a man in Ap Dinh-B is one, but he denies this, saying that although his father practiced sorcery, he never learned the secrets (those who claim he is point out that his five wives have died, the result of his dealing with evil spirits).

There are several Ong Thay Phap in neighboring villages, and one is hired each year to perform special rituals for the Cau An celebration held at the Ap Dinh-A dinh.[13] Between 1958 and 1961 the same Ong Thay Phap was selected for the village celebration. He is 55 years old and has two wives and four children, all of whom share his wood-tile house in a village near Tan Hiep, south of Khanh Hau. He farms seven cong of paddy land, his primary means of support, and practices sorcery to supplement his income. Both his father and his father's father were Ong Thay Phap, and he learned the ritual forms, magic formulae, and art of making amulets by assisting his father. In his family the rule is that the eldest son learns the secrets, and currently his 18-year-old son serves as his apprentice, assisting in simpler rituals. As his proficiency increases, he will participate in more complicated rituals, such as the Cau An. Women never are admitted to this circle, since they marry out of the family and might divulge the secrets.

The main altar in the Ong Thay Phap's house is dedicated to Ong Thay Thuong, the patron deity from whom he derives his mystic powers. Tablets on the altar also honor the deity's five assistants, all warriors of ancient Chi-

12. There are numerous other spirits and deities known by the villagers, although they receive no special form of veneration. Among them are the Wave Spirits which lie on the bottom of large rivers and periodically ascend, causing great waves and agitation, and Lord Whale, Lord Crocodile, and Lord Tiger.

13. This is discussed in Chapter 8.

nese legends. Food offerings are placed each day on the altar, and Ong Thay Phap performs a simple ritual, kowtowing and burning joss. Being a Buddhist, he also has Buddhist altars and scrupulously performs the prescribed daily Buddhist rituals. In addition, the Ong Thay Phap has responsibility for cult rituals venerating several patrilineal ancestors.

Specialization is common among the sorcerers, and this one is particularly adept at curing mental illnesses. Exorcism of the evil spirit is part of the cure and is combined with use of amulets. The usual procedure is to cut the victim's upper arm or tongue to obtain blood with which to write a special formula designed to frighten the evil spirits away. Ong Thay Phap admits that he fails in some illnesses, the real cause of which he feels must be organic. Fees for services depend on the patient's means and the gravity of the ailment. Poor patients usually are charged only the cost of transportation, should that be necessary. Well-to-do patients either pay cash or present the sorcerer with gifts. He supplements his income by selling amulets and talismans.

In addition to the Ong Thay Phap there are several Khanh Hau residents who heal certain types of ailments but without exorcism. They have patron deities, but they have no contact with the evil spirits.[14] One impoverished woman in Ap Dinh-A (who was abandoned by her husband) is known as Ba Cot (Madame Healer), and over twenty years ago she discovered she had the power to cure children's illnesses and certain female ailments, particularly those affecting the breasts and eyes. This power is derived from the goddess Ba Linh Son Thanh Mau for whom Ba Cot maintains a shrine in her thatched house. Ba Cot also has an extensive knowledge of traditional Vietnamese medicine which she prepares for her patients; she also prays over them, invoking the power from the goddess. In addition to giving children herb medicine, she employs a talisman of colored strings woven into a necklace. Ba Cot often is called upon to perform the services of midwife. At the risk of losing her power, she is forbidden to charge fees, although she is free to accept tokens of gratitude.

Another resident of Ap Dinh-A, a tenant farmer, is a healer. Known as Ong Thay Sau Thoi, this 58-year-old man felt the power to heal come over him some ten years ago and, being a fervent Cao Daist, he assumed it was a gift from the Supreme Being. It was not until 1956, however, that he actually learned healing techniques and preparation of traditional Vietnamese medicine. His friend, the cu si known as Ong Dao Ba Rau, had been study-

14. One healer who relies exclusively on folk medicine without intervention of a supernatural being is discussed in Chapter 6.

ing these methods with the hermits in the Seven Mountains. When he returned to Khanh Hau in 1956 he agreed to impart some of his knowledge
to Ong Thay Sau Thoi, who did not learn the secret of exorcism but did
learn how to prepare medicines and employ traditional techniques. Eventually, Ong Thay Sau Thoi also learned the principles of Nham Than,
wherein over a thousand vital points in the human body are related to cor-
responding hours, days, and months in the lunar calendar. This guides treatment to a more effective cure; violation could aggravate the ailment or
bring death. For example, there are certain hours of certain days when
specific parts of the head can be treated by letting blood, the most common
technique employed. In addition, Ong Thay Sau Thoi uses magic cloths.

CHAPTER 4

The Kinship System

THE VIETNAMESE have a patrilineal kinship system. The *toc* or patrilineage found in northern and central Vietnam is reckoned through the
male line to a male ancestor in the fifth ascending generation (some families
trace ancestry farther). In Khanh Hau, however, with the exception of
several families, the common ancestor is in the third ascending generation.
Reference terminology clearly distinguishes patrilineal from nonpatrilineal
kin, and males in Ego's and ascending generations in the patrilineage are
age graded, a feature related to the traditional means of selecting the
truong toc or head of the patrilineage according to age priority. Again
Khanh Hau deviates from tradition; in most village families the truong
toc is selected by a council of adult male and female members of the
family. According to custom, jural authority in the patrilineage rests with
the truong toc, and he is responsible for rituals venerating the common
ancestor. He also holds title to the patrimonial land, the income of which
must be used to defray the cost of rituals and feasting integral to the Cult
of the Ancestors. He maintains family tombs, and should the family keep
a genealogy book, the truong toc is charged with making the proper entries. Well-to-do families attempt to conform to these prescriptions, but for
most village families they represent only the ideal.

KIN TERMINOLOGY

The concept of nuclear terms described by Feng in his analysis of Chinese
terminological composition is applicable to Vietnamese kin terminology.[1]

1. Nuclear terms express the nuclear group of relationships and, linguistically, are
independent of modifiers. Each nuclear term possesses a primary meaning and one or
more secondary meanings. The primary meaning is assumed when the term is used
independently, and when it is used in combination with other elements the secondary
meaning or meanings become paramount. Basic modifiers for the most part express col-

There are nuclear terms for parents, parents' siblings, siblings, and Ego's children. In their primary meaning they express generation, lineage, and in some cases relative age to Ego and Ego's father. Modifiers may be added to some terms to indicate sex and age priority, but they are not intrinsic. Some of the nuclear terms are used to refer to other kin, assuming a secondary meaning. Lexically, the syntactical principles of the isolating, monosyllabic Vietnamese language permit an exactness in designating relationship to Ego by the use of various modifiers (see Tables 8 and 9 and Fig. 17). Nuclear terms, qualified by modifiers, are used for affinal kin, and they constitute the basic vocatives (as well as basic pronouns in Vietnamese grammar).

The family of Marshal Nguyen Huynh Duc is one of the few in the village that trace ancestry beyond the third ascending generation with names, birth dates, and death dates carefully recorded in one of the rare genealogy books in Khanh Hau.[2] *To* is the term indicating ancestors in general. The patrilineal ancestor of the fifth ascending generation is Ong Ky Noi, and should his wife also be honored, she is referred to as Ba Ky Noi. Ong and Ba are respect pronouns used in address or reference, and they also serve as sex modifiers in referring to many kin of ascending generations. *Ky* indicates the fifth ascending generation, and *noi* is a modifier designating patrilineal kin. Patrilineal ancestors of the fourth ascending generation are Ong So Noi and Ba So Noi. *So* is the modifier for the fourth ascending generation, and *co* indicates the third ascending generation.

Nonpatrilineal as well as patrilineal kin are recognized in the second ascending generation. There is no term to indicate the generation itself. Ong Noi and Ba Noi are the paternal grandparents; the maternal grandparents are Ong Ngoai and Ba Ngoai. The modifier *ngoai* literally means "outside" and is often used when referring to nonpatrilineal kin. For example, when villagers discuss their kin they usually specify *ben noi* (on the patrilineal side) of *ben ngoai* (on the nonpatrilineal side). *Cha* is the term for father, although when referring to one's own father it is more polite

---

lateral relationship and generation status and cannot be used independently as kinship terms. The nuclear terms form the basis for kinship extensions, and the basic modifiers locate the exact place of the relative in the total scheme. The combinations and recombinations of these two classes of elements constitute the modern standard system which is the norm of all other terminologies. The referentials modify the standard system into proper forms for referential use in specific applications. Vocatives, aside from their primary usages, transform them into direct forms of address between relatives. (Feng, *Chinese Kinship,* p. 9.)

2. The Duc family, as it often is called, is discussed in Chapter 10.

TABLE 8. Syntax of Kin Terminology

	Sex	Generation	Lineage
Fifth Ascending		Ky	
Fourth Ascending	Ong (male)	So	Noi (patrilineal)
Third Ascending	Ba (female)	Co	Ngoai (nonpatrilineal)
Second Ascending	Ong (grandfather)		
	Ba (grandmother)		

		Generation	Lineage
First Ascending		Cha (F)	
		Me (M)	
		Bac (FoB)	Patrilineal
		Chu (FyB)	
		Co (FSi)	
		Cau (MB)	Nonpatrilineal
		Di (MSi)	

	Siblings		Collateral	
Ego's				
	Anh (oB)	Hai (eldest)	Anh Ba Con (PoSbS)	
	Chi (oSi)		Chi Ba Con (PoSbD)	
				Ben Noi (patrilineal)
	Em (ySb)	Trai (male)	Em Ba Con (PySbCh)	Ben Ngoai (nonpatrilineal)
		Gai (female)		

	Lineal		Collateral
First Descending		Hai (first born)	
	Con (Ch)	Ba (second born)	Chau (Cousins' Ch)
		Tu (third born)	
	Chau (SbCh)	Ben Noi (patrilineal)	
		Ben Ngoai (nonpatrilineal)	

	Generation	Lineage
Second Descending	Chau	
Third Descending	Chat	Noi (patrilineal)
Fourth Descending	Chut	Ngoai (nonpatrilineal)
Fifth Descending	Chit	

to use the honorific term Ong Than. *Me* is the popular word for mother, and Ba Than is the polite form of reference. Age grading of patrilineal male kin begins in the second generation. The father's older brothers are *bac;* the younger brothers are *chu. Co* is the term for father's sisters. The mother's brothers are *cau,* and her sisters are *di.*

TABLE 9. Affinal Kin

A. Affinal Kin: Male Ego
B. Affinal Kin: Female Ego

A.

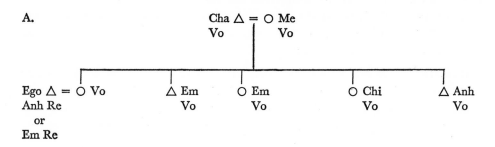

B.

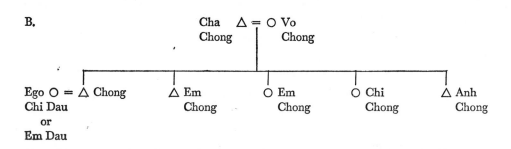

All of Ego's siblings are age graded: *anh* for older brothers and *chi* for older sisters; younger siblings are *em,* with *trai* for males and *gai* for females. Kin numeratives usually are added to sibling terms. The first born is *anh hai* or *chi hai. Hai* literally is "two," and villagers explain that num-

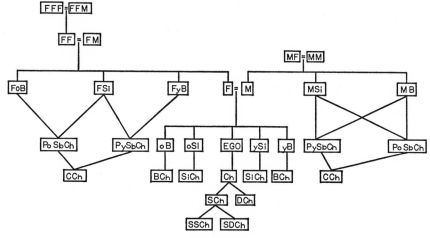

17. Structure of Kinship Normally Recognized in Khanh Hau.

ber one is a superlative reserved for persons of great honor such as the emperor. The second born is *ba* (three) while the third is *tu*, a term to indicate fourth persons or days (*bon* is the more general term for fourth). The usual numeratives are employed for the remaining siblings, and the youngest generally is referred to as *em ut*. The modifier *ruot* may be added to any sibling term to specify those born of the same parents, a necessary distinction in polygynous families.

With modifiers added, sibling terms are used for cousins who are age graded according to the relative age of the parents. The older sibling terms anh and chi also designate parents' older siblings' children, and em is applied to parents' younger siblings' children.[3] The addition of the compound modifier *ba con*, which translates as "kin," may be used to indicate close collateral kin, i.e. those related through the parents' siblings. As already indicated, this type of relationship often is described further by adding the modifiers ben noi for patrilineal kin and ben ngoai for non-patrilineal kin. One can also explicitly indicate through which parent collateral kin are related to Ego; *ba con chu-bac* means that he is related through the father's brother without specifying which parent is older; *ba con ban di* indicates that they are parallel cousins, related through the mother's sister. One expression, *ba con co-cau* (literally "father's sister–mother's brother"), summarizes cross-cousin relationships. Collateral kin further removed may be age graded according to the relative-age-of-parents principle, and the modifier *ho* would indicate that they are more than one degree removed. In general, ho has come to mean "family" and in the broadest usage it indicates family name.[4]

In the first descending generation, Ego's children are *con*. Kin numeratives invariably are added, and often the child is referred to by his numerative. The sex modifiers trai for males and gai for females also may be added. *Chau* is a general term for siblings' and cousins' children as well as other collateral kin of the first descending generation. The modifiers ben noi and ben ngoai to distinguish patrilineal and nonpatrilineal kin may be added. The term chau also is used to designate lineal kin of the second descending

3. In "An Analysis of Annamese Kinship Terms," Benedict considers the principle of age grading according to relative age of parents incongruous with the terminology, and he refers to it as "retrograde differentiation implied but not actually present in a term or set of terms."

4. In some works on Vietnamese history and culture, the term ho often is defined as the Vietnamese term for clan. While more historical research might reveal that present-day Vietnamese family names once were clan names, at the present time there is no evidence to support this.

generation, and the modifiers noi and ngoai distinguish patrilineal and non-patrilineal kin. *Chat, chut,* and *chit* are terms for third, fourth, and fifth generations respectively, and again the modifiers noi and ngoai separate patrilineal from nonpatrilineal.

Nuclear terms with qualifying modifiers are used for affines. Parental terms are extended to the husband's or wife's parents, and sibling terms are used to refer to a spouse's siblings, who are age graded according to the relative age of the spouse. For the male speaker, affinal relationships are indicated by the modifier *vo* (wife) to indicate they are his wife's kin, while the female speaker uses the modifier *chong* (husband). Sibling terms also are extended to spouses of siblings, and they are age graded according to the relative age of the siblings. *Re* refers to a sister's husband, and *dau* to a brother's wife; for example, a younger brother's wife would be *em dau,* an older sister's husband *anh re.*

Vocative terms are somewhat more complicated. When a couple is newly married, the husband addresses his wife as *minh* or *em hai,* both intimate expressions. He also may call her *nha toi,* which translates literally as "my house" (equivalent to the English "my own"). The young wife addresses her husband as *cung* or *anh,* both of which might be translated as "my darling." [5] After their first child is born they shift to a teknonymous usage, addressing each other as "father of so-and-so" or "mother of so-and-so." For example, if the child is a male named Teo, the husband addresses his wife as *ma thang* Teo, and she addresses him as *cha thang* Teo. If the child is a female named Chao, the husband becomes *cha con* Chao and the wife is called *ma con* Chao.

Children call their father *ba* or *tia* and their mother *ma* or *me,* and parents usually address their children by numeratives. Siblings customarily address one another by the referential age-grade terms—older brothers are anh, older sisters chi and younger siblings em. Kin numeratives may be added. After siblings marry, the form of address may change. A male who has children addresses his younger brother as chu, father's younger brother. Younger brothers, however, continue to address their elder brothers by the term anh. Males with children address their sisters as co, or father's sister, while females with children address their sisters as di, or mother's sister, and their brothers as cau, or mother's brother. Villagers explain that these are

5. The kin terms anh and em when used as pronouns in the second person singular imply a relatively close relationship and, in certain contexts, intimacy. In the intimate usage, a male speaker addressing a female as em will use anh for the first person singular; the female addressing a male as anh will refer to herself as em. The use of the numerative hai lends both intimacy and respect.

the terms their children will use, and this is a means of demonstrating proper form. The one exception is the older brother whom the children will address as *bac,* or father's older brother. Kin of the third and fourth ascending generation are addressed by their referential terms.

THE PATRILINEAGE

In Khanh Hau the patrilineage (toc) normally is reckoned from a male ancestor in the third ascending generation, and its most important function is veneration of the ancestors. For the villager, immortality lies in his undying lineage, but bliss in the afterlife can be attained only by proper cult veneration, without which the deceased becomes a malevolent errant spirit. Within the patrilineage the division of cult responsibility is such that all deceased members will be venerated. With three ascending generations there will be a minimum of six ancestors—the parents, the father's parents, and the father's father's parents. Prescriptively, but not obligatorily, the patrilineage head (truong toc) venerates the father's father's parents while rituals honoring the father's parents are the responsibility of one or more other male members, and the eldest son in the family maintains the cult for his parents. The truong toc also sees to it that other ancestors, such as unmarried female members of the toc, are properly venerated.

The patrilineage assumes the character of a corporate kin group when it has huong hoa (patrimony), the income from which, according to Vietnamese custom and law, must be used to defray the cost of rituals and feasting associated with the Cult of the Ancestors. Collectively owned by adult members of the toc, guardianship of the patrimony is vested in the head of the patrilineage who is charged with properly allotting the income. In southern Vietnam there are two kinds of huong hoa—*vinh vien* is inalienable but *co phan* is alienable with the consent of all adult members of the toc. Although there is one case of huong hoa vinh vien being divided between disputing descendants,[6] there are no instances of patrimony being sold.

Also desirable for the Cult of the Ancestors is a substantially constructed house that will endure for generations to become an ancestral house. To the villager *nha* (house) is not simply a physical structure; it is a symbol of family and hearth. The ancestral house is the central sanctuary for altars honoring the ancestors of the toc, and it is the place where cult rituals and feasting take place. Similar sentiment is attached to the stone tombs that

6. This case involves the village chief and Ong Xa Khanh, one of the wealthiest residents in the village, and is discussed in Chapter 10.

will stand through the years as mute reminders of past generations. Villagers express their feelings about house and tomb in the oft-quoted proverb, "When alive, one must have a house, when dead, one must have a tomb."

Lineage cohesiveness is highly valued by the villagers. The patrimony, the ancestral house, and the stone tombs are symbols of lineage longevity, and lineage solidarity is perpetuated by prescribed reunions to venerate the ancestors. Members of the patrilineage gather at the lunar New Year and during Thanh Minh, an annual period specified for visiting and refurbishing family tombs. On these occasions they reconfirm their kin bonds and introduce new members to the group. Among the well-to-do these gatherings bring kin from distant places.

In Khanh Hau the patrilineage in which Marshal Nguyen Huynh Duc is an ancestor is unique in having retained most features of the traditional Vietnamese toc (still found in northern and central Vietnam more than in the south). Ancestors to the seventh ascending generation are venerated (see Appendix A), and toc members' names, birth dates, and death dates are carefully recorded in the genealogy book. In addition to huong hoa and stone tombs, there is a splendid ancestral house that also serves as a museum and shrine honoring the Marshal. Family celebrations attract kin from Saigon and My Tho as well as from surrounding villages, and in recent years the celebration of the Marshal's death anniversary has become a village event.[7]

Typical of southern families with huong hoa, the Duc family selects the patrilineage head on the basis of good character rather than seniority. The current truong toc, the second son of his father, holds title to the huong hoa, keeps the genealogy book, and maintains the ancestral house and the tombs. He venerates all of the male ancestors; other male members are responsible for the females.

In the Duc family as in other village families with huong hoa, any serious breach in his responsibility may result in calling a council of adult members to select a new truong toc. Villagers contend this control is necessary to avoid having an irresponsible head squander the income of the patrimony, and they cite examples from Khanh Hau and other villages where this has happened (the errant truong toc usually was prone to gambling and/or opium). There also are other reasons for wanting to change the patrilineage head; for example, when Ong Xa Khanh's elder brother, the truong toc, was

7. The Cult of Marshal Nguyen Huynh Duc has become a responsibility the family shares with the Village Council. In addition to organizing the drive for funds to construct the new shrine, the Village Council assists in organizing the death anniversary which is attended by district and provincial officials. The Village Council's role in this cult is discussed in Chapter 7.

converted to Catholicism, the family held council and gave the title to Ong Xa Khanh. Should the head refuse to relinquish his role, the family may resort to legal action and, although airing family difficulties is frowned upon, such action is not rare. The most recent case in Khanh Hau occurred in another family when the truong toc became a Catholic; his siblings sought to have him removed on the grounds that as a Catholic he no longer could perform the prescribed rituals. The truong toc took the case to the district tribunal which ruled that although as a Catholic he could not kowtow before the altar of the ancestors, he could have masses said for the ancestors with income from the huong hoa, and he also could continue to have the feasts. His being a Catholic was therefore no bar to continuing in the role of truong toc.

Variable wealth within the patrilineage sometimes results in shifts in the functions of truong toc and in the use of huong hoa. It is not unusual that a well-to-do member, although not the head, may be permitted to assume cult responsibilities for ancestors of the third and second ascending generations, leaving the truong toc to expend patrimonial income on his parents' cult. Such is the case of the hamlet chief of Ap Moi, a landowner, whose elder brother, the lineage head, is a poor tenant farmer. In some instances income from huong hoa is not expended on the cult. For example, the village chief is head of his patrilineage and guardian of the patrimony. Since he is wealthier than his two brothers, however, he pays for cult rituals and feasting out of his own income, letting his brothers farm the huong hoa.

Most families in Khanh Hau have no land, and consequently numerous village toc are without income for the Ancestor Cult. The members' houses are of perishable thatch, and their graves are mounds of earth that will be unidentifiable after a decade in the floods of the rainy seasons and the pulverizing sun of the hot seasons. The one institution they carefully preserve, however, is the Cult of the Ancestors. Without means to provide for many guests, their gatherings for rituals are small, and most of those who attend come from within walking distance. At most death anniversaries, for example, from five to ten guests may attend whereas in a family as prosperous as that of Ong Ke Hien there might be 100 guests.

Cohesiveness or corporateness, such as may be found among the wealthy, are not characteristic of most patrilineages in the village. Many, if not most, of them are fissioned, particularly as members move from the locale, and only segments of the patrilineage gather for the cult celebrations. The term truong toc tends to be loosely used—most often referring to the eldest of the patrilineal group living in the same part of the hamlet—and without any property functions there is no need for serious council to decide on the new truong toc. Because of the fissioning, several members are likely to be designated truong toc for different segments which are not in contact. Consequently there is apt to be duplication of rituals venerating the common ancestor (duplication of rituals causes villagers no concern, but omission does).

In spite of the fact that most patrilineages in the villages are segmented, and roles and functions have deviated from traditional prescription, villagers realize that every man potentially is a common ancestor, and every nuclear family a nascent patrilineage. They therefore strive to attain the adjuncts of the patrilineage, the things that hold the family together—sons to perpetuate the line, land that can be declared huong hoa, a house that will become an ancestral house, and stone tombs.

HOUSEHOLD COMPOSITION AND RESIDENCE PATTERN

Prescribed residence is patrilocal. The youngest son is expected to remain in the paternal house to care for the aging parents while other brothers also reside there for a temporary period before establishing their own households, preferably in the vicinity. Females reside with their husbands who usually are from outside the hamlet, often from another village. There are, of course, exceptions to the residence rule. A son may not be able to remain near the paternal house if there is no available land or an alternative means of supporting his family. On the other hand a girl may inherit land, so it may happen that her husband will come to live in her part of the village. If the girl is the only child (although adoption of sons is common) she is expected to care for her aging parents; her husband may then reside with her parents. It is common also for a widow to return to her natal village, and some second wives remain in their paternal households.

Adherence to the patrilocal residence rule and exceptions to it are reflected in both household composition (see Table 10) and residence pattern. Including couples without children, all of whom are relatively young (and presumably will have children or adopt a son in conformity with custom), complete nuclear families without dependents comprise slightly over half (51.6 per cent) of the households in the village (the residence pattern which will be discussed presently indicates that there is a predominance of patrilineal kin clustered together, and most are brothers and their families). Also reflecting patrilocality are the 11.3 per cent of the total village households composed of a nuclear family with either the husband's mother or father living with them. Most of the joint households (11.0 of the 11.7 per cent of

TABLE 10. Percentage Household Composition in Khanh Hau, 1958

I. Nuclear Family Households				87.91
A. Nuclear Complete			69.30	
Husband and wife		3.39		
Husband, wife, and children		48.20		
Nuclear plus dependents		17.71		
a. Patrilineal Kin		16.02		
Husband's father	3.04			
Husband's mother	8.28			
Other	4.70			
b. Nonpatrilineal Kin		1.18		
c. Both		0.51		
B. Nuclear Disintegrated			18.61	
Single males		2.88		
Single females		1.52		
Woman and children*		7.10		
Other		7.11		
II. Joint Households				11.66
A. Polygynous			0.17	
B. Patrilineal			10.99	
C. Nonpatrilineal			0.51	
TOTAL				99.57

* Not specified as widows. Some are second wives, others are separated from their husbands. Widows are included in "nuclear plus dependents," "single females," "nuclear disintegrated," and "other" categories.

the total village households) consist of a son or sons and their families living with the paternal nuclear household. Only three households (0.5 per cent of the total) are comprised of a nuclear family with a daughter and her nuclear family.

In the category of disintegrated nuclear families single residents constitute 4.4 per cent of the total village households. Widows returning to their natal place often prefer to reside alone, and many elderly men also prefer living by themselves. Several elderly villagers pointed out that their children's households invariably included many children, they found it difficult to get enough rest with the noise, and it was easy to construct a small thatched hut near their kinfolk where they could prepare their own simple meals and receive their friends. The 7.1 per cent of women listed as head of household with children (mostly minors), includes women separated from husbands temporarily (the husband is working in another place, doing military service, or active in the Viet Cong) and women separated from their husbands permanently.

An examination of the residence pattern of Ap Moi reflects the broader village pattern. For this analysis the hamlet can be divided into sections A, B, C, and D. Section A is the southern end of the hamlet; Section D is the northern end where the hamlet converges with Ap Dinh-A. The houses are numbered more or less according to the system devised for the five-family groups[8] (see Fig. 18, and see Appendix F for kin groupings).

Reviewing the overall pattern of the hamlet, 57 households—over three quarters of the total 73—have kin ties in the hamlet (see Table 11). Exactly

TABLE 11. Ap Moi Residence Pattern

Section	Number of Households	Households without Kin Ties in the Hamlet	Households with Kin Ties	Number of Kin Groupings	Patrilineal Groupings	Patrilineal and Nonpatrilineal
A	24	2	22	6	3	3
B	10	5	5	2	2	0
C	20	1	19	2	0	2
D	19	8	11	4	2	2
TOTAL	73	16	57	14	7	7

half the 14 kin groupings are exclusively patrilineal and consanguineal, while the remaining have patrilineal and nonpatrilineal kin. The latter groupings are larger, and they include affinal as well as consanguineal kin. Generally, however, patrilineal ties predominate, and by and large it can be stated that the patrilocal residence rule is adhered to in most instances. Many of the patrilineal groupings and segments of the mixed groupings are composed of brothers and their families or families related through brothers.

Some exceptions can be noted. Widows returning to live near their siblings are found in Chart 1 (d and e) and Chart 3 (a) of Appendix F. In two other groups, for different reasons the husbands preferred to live near their wives' kin. In relation to unaffiliated households, it is interesting that the largest number is found in Section D. More than likely this is so because this part of the hamlet is closest to the administrative center of the village. It is a convenient place for the shopkeepers and the nurse, and furthermore, during

8. In 1956 the five-family groups were established in Khanh Hau, and by 1959 there were some 120 in all hamlets. Each group has five households located in the same part of the hamlet. Houses are numbered, and the group selects a leader who is responsible to the hamlet chief. Periodically, the leaders meet with the hamlet chief to report on their groups and receive instructions or information to be passed on to the member families. Also, from time to time there are meetings of all five-family group leaders at the Ap Dinh-A dinh.

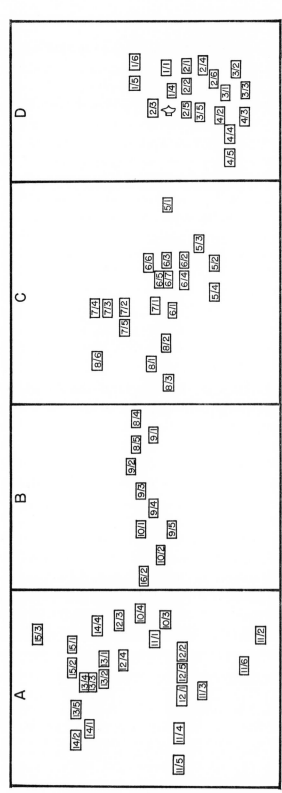

18. Ap Moi Residence Map.

94

the troubled periods, the presence of the stockade attracted settlement by villagers, particularly the well-to-do.

Most of the larger kin groupings in Ap Moi are part of a broader kin network that includes 33 of the 73 households in the hamlet. Linking households through patrilineal and nonpatrilineal as well as affinal ties, this network also extends into Ap Dinh A–B. The entire network can be traced to a couple who settled in Khanh Hau during the nineteenth century.

One of the daughters of the settlers was the maternal grandmother of Ong Ca Duoc (profile in Chapter 10), matrilineally linking numerous households. The youngest son of the settlers was a maternal grandfather of the former village chief who maintains one of his households in Section D of Ap Moi, and through his siblings he has extensive kin ties in Ap Dinh A–B. One kin grouping in Ap Dinh-A is comprised of his three brothers, one of the brother's sons, and another brother's daughter. A deceased sister's husband continues to reside in the group as does a son of another deceased sister. The grouping also includes one of the former village chief's younger sister's sons and a daughter's family. The sons include Ong Lam, a prominent resident of the hamlet and his brothers, the younger of whom became police agent in 1961. As already indicated, two brothers of this sister's husband reside in Section D of Ap Moi, and there are additional households linked through the husband's sister and another brother in Ap Dinh-B.

The network could be extended through affinal ties to other groupings in other hamlets in and around the village. For example, Ong Lam's daughter married the son of Ong Xa Khanh, one of the wealthiest residents in Khanh Hau, who has numerous kin (including the village chief) throughout the village, and Ong Lam's brother Ong Chi is married to a daughter of Ong Ke Hien, the highest venerable in the village; he also has extensive kin ties throughout Khanh Hau and the neighboring village of Tan Huong.[9]

Despite the fact that none of the families in this network keeps genealogy books, most can trace their relationships. This awareness of broad kin ties within the local area appears to be related to the strong taboo against marrying consanguineal kin (most of the kin ties in the network are consanguineal). It also is significant that this particular network includes many of the prosperous landed families of these hamlets, bearing out villagers' observation that the gentry usually intermarry. This network is essentially a residential group that in its entirety has no functions. It has no cohesive-

9. Ong Lam and his brothers as well as Ong Xa Khanh and Ong Ke Hien are mentioned in several other chapters, and profiles of all of them are included in Chapter 10.

ness or corporateness. These qualities are found in some of the groupings within the network patrilineages or segments thereof and residence groupings.

As already indicated, patrilineages with huong hoa, an ancestral house, and stone tombs are more likely to have the corporate group characteristics so highly valued among the villagers. Proximity of residence therefore is secondary to property relations in the collective ownership of huong hoa and common participation in cult rituals. For example, within the network, the toc of which Ong Tien Bai has patrimony, an ancestral house and stone tombs, and at his cult celebrations all patrilineal kin in the network are present as are patrilineal kin from the surrounding area, Saigon, Can Tho, and My Tho (in addition there are numerous nonpatrilineal kin in the network and some unrelated neighbors).

Residence, however, is very important in permitting segments of fissioned patrilineages without material possessions to generate closer relationships and reconfirm kin bonds at their gatherings. In the village, primary group relationships are found for the most part in the residential clusters. Living close together, the residents have daily contact, and among the households in the clusters there is a great deal of mutual aid. For the relatively well-to-do, mutual aid usually consists in lending money when necessary and giving assistance with large family gatherings. For other families, mutual aid also involves assistance in thatching roofs or making house repairs, and in aiding with farm work, particularly the harvest.

Prevalent in the residence pattern of Khanh Hau are clusters of brothers and their families and similar groupings—segments of patrilineages which in most instances have fissioned. They manifest considerable cohesiveness and for them kinship is a reality in the veneration of common ancestors. The importance of proximity, however, is illustrated by the fact that in many residence clusters there are non-kin, and usually they participate in these primary group activities—mutual aid, ancestor worship, and other family celebrations. The sentiment underlying this is expressed well in the villagers' oft quoted proverb, "Sell distant kin, buy close neighbors." Close neighbors are treated as kin, and in this respect proximity of residence might be considered a more universal determinant of strong social bonds in the village than kinship.

Since the construction of the Cao Daist temples there has been a tendency for some adherents to locate their farmsteads nearby. The collection of farmsteads around the Ban Chin Dao temple in Ap Dinh-A is somewhat apart from the rest of the agglomeration, and it came into being after the temple was built. There are 19 households, 15 of which are divided among three kin groupings (see Fig. 19).

The land of the Tien Thien temple, its subsidiary buildings, and the farmsteads of the adherents belong to the patrilineal descendants of Marshal

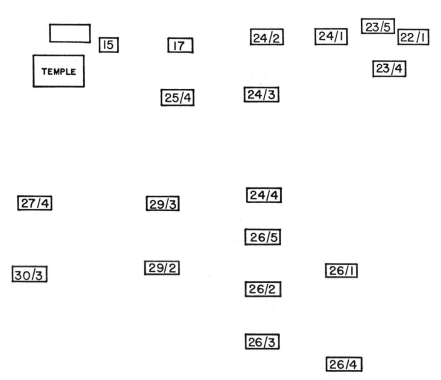

19. Residence Pattern of the Ban Chin Dao Temple Section of Ap Dinh-A.

Duc. Of the nine households in this section (Fig. 20), six are included in a kin grouping and, since they trace ancestry to the hero, they are not expected to pay rent.

Residence patterns around both temples do not differ from the Ap Moi pattern. Most of the households belong to kin groupings, and there is a predominance of patrilineal kin with an increase in nonpatrilineal kin in the larger groupings. There are some exceptions to the patrilocal residence rule. According to villagers, many nonpatrilineal descendants of Marshal Duc have settled on rent-free family land in Ap Dinh-B, and this probably accounts for some of the women who have remained near their paternal homes. These groupings also indicate that the Cao Daists tend to proselytize among their kinfolk and, according to the leader of the Ban Chin Dao sect, after groups of Cao Daist kin settled near the temple, several marriages took place among them. (See Appendix F for kin groupings.)

Solidarity of the Cao Daist residence groupings appears to be stronger

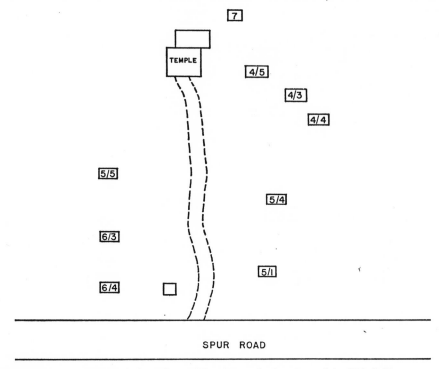

20. Residence Pattern of the Tien Thien Temple Section of Ap Dinh-B.

than among other residential groupings. In addition to kin ties, they have religious ties which frequently are reconfirmed by participation in Cao Daist rituals. As indicated above, the Cao Daists also intermarry. Mutual aid extends to residents of the section rather than to the clusters of households. It is common for prosperous Cao Daists to lend plows and water wheels to other adherents without charge, and most families are members of a Cao Daist cooperative which provides coffins for members.

CHAPTER 5

The Family as a Social Group

DURING most of their lives villagers are surrounded by kin. Few people in Khanh Hau live alone, and among those who do, there are no real isolates— all have relatives somewhere in the village. Kinfolk share their daily tasks and pleasures. In the fields they labor together, and when work is done they gather to pass leisure time in the house or a nearby shop. Adult members of the household group invariably take meals together, and at night, young and old share the hardwood beds. The yearly cycle is marked by a series of family celebrations in which all members of the kin group participate and, as the villager's life spins on, family rites of passage mark the movement from infancy into childhood, on to adolescence, and finally into adulthood and old age. Death is no real departure from the family—one joins the ancestors to exist as an unseen but nonetheless present member.

MARRIAGE

The goal of all villagers is to have a mate, children, and a house of one's own. *Nha* does not simply mean "house" in the sense of a physical structure; it implies the household group, the hearth, or the center of the individual's world—concepts reflected in the endearing *nha toi* used by a young husband to address his wife or when a villager refers to things (such as land) *cua nha,* "belonging to the household."

Marriage is one of the most important events in the life of a villager. He now will found a family and become perpetuator of a line, and in the continuance of the line he will realize his own immortality. The most favorable marriage age for a male is 21 and for a female 17; ages 20 for males and 18 for females are inauspicious. Children of the prosperous tend to marry early —as early as 16—but children of poor parents must wait until they can support themselves and have accumulated sufficient money for a proper feast. Often they are past the ideal age when they marry.

Most marriages in Khanh Hau are arranged by the parents. Two friends often agree that their children will marry when they reach the proper age; the children are brought up with this idea, and they accept it without complaint. It also is common for the young man's parents to arrange with her parents marriage to a girl recommended by kin or friends. Girls no longer remain in the semiseclusion of their own homes as they did in the past. With the expansion of educational facilities there has been an increase in social contact between boys and girls, and if a boy selects his own mate, she is likely to be a girl of his acquaintance. If he has no particular girl in mind, the usual procedure is to seek information about available girls in Khanh Hau or neighboring villages. This is easily done through the matchmaking older women.

There are definite qualifications for the ideal wife: she must be of a respectable family without a history of bad health or oddities of any sort, and preferably of the same social level as the young man. It is imperative that she be a capable housekeeper, and robust good health is more important than a fair face. Although it is desirable that the girl be a virgin, it is not a prerequisite so long as she is not known as a woman of easy virtue.

The Vietnamese used to consider it incestuous for consanguineal kin, regardless of how distant the relationship, to marry. Violation was thought to bring great misfortune. Older villagers recall that when they were young it was absolutely forbidden to marry anyone with the same surname, and although it continues to be something to avoid, it no longer is considered incestuous per se.[1] Hamlet exogamy, observed before World War II, no longer is imperative, although many villagers still feel it is preferable to marry outside the hamlet.

Once the selection has been made, either the young man or his parents ask an older male or female acquaintance to act for them. The intermediary should be a person of good character, the parent of many children, and it is generally considered desirable that the male matchmaker have a beard, the sign of age and wisdom. After consulting with the young man's parents the intermediary informally visits the girl's parents, and whether or not they are aware of the purpose of his coming, they are expected to register great astonishment. They consult the horoscopes of the boy and girl to determine whether the two are compatible and their future together holds the promise of many children, happiness, and prosperity. In most instances this is simply a formality, since both families are aware that formal overtures are about to be made, and they have done the necessary research on the other family,

1. There are 37 surnames in the village, which are listed later in this chapter.

including the essential inquiries into predestined compatibility. When the girl is formally told of the overtures she is expected to feign reluctance, although if she really does disapprove (and in most cases it would be a surprise to her parents, since she certainly is aware of the situation and could have expressed disapproval sooner), the negotiations are broken off abruptly with the excuse that she is too young or that their horoscopes do not indicate future bliss.

If all parties are agreeable to the match, they consult the lunar calendar to determine an auspicious day for the *coi mat* (literally "show the face"), the first meeting of the parents so that the young man's parents can view the girl (regardless of how well acquainted the families may be). On the appointed day the young man, his parents, and the intermediary proceed to the girl's house bearing gifts of rice alcohol, fruit, and flowers. Her parents await them at the entrance, and after greetings are exchanged the visitors are invited to enter the house where they are seated before the altar of the ancestors. After they have chatted several minutes, the girl appears with a tray containing tea, cookies, perhaps some candied fruit, and with her eyes cast down she serves them without speaking. In addition to the formal purpose implied by the name, coi mat also provides an opportunity for the young man's parents to see the girl's house.

If they are pleased with the visit, they extend an invitation to the girl's parents to visit them. At this stage both parties are anxious to become better acquainted, and the young man's parents are expected to appear eager that the girl's parents see what a fine family their daughter is entering. With continued accord, the parents again consult the lunar calendar to determine a favorable day on which they can hold *le hoi,* the engagement celebration. On such days it is common to see young men, their intermediaries, and a group of male kin dressed in traditional clothes hurrying single file on their way to the girl's house. The groom, usually looking very intense, leads the group. He carries a tray containing the traditional engagement gift of gold earrings and, if he is of a wealthy family, other jewelry. His companions carry bottles of rice alcohol and fruit.

The girl's house has been decorated with green boughs, palm fronds, and flowers, and candles burn brightly on the altar of the ancestors. Her close kin are gathered, and they sit drinking tea in the main room. Greeted at the entrance by the hosts, the young man enters and proceeds directly to the altar of the ancestors where he kowtows—the act of presenting himself to the girl's forebears. He then kowtows before the girl's parents and offers them the gifts. These ritual acts constitute the le hoi, and with them the engagement is complete. The affianced and their parents are then led to places of honor at the table, and when the guests all have been seated, a large meal is served. The couple's parents already have consulted horoscopes to select the most auspicious day for the wedding, and in the course of the meal they announce the date. Normally the wedding is held several months after the engagement, but since it is forbidden to wed during a mourning period, the wedding will be held as soon as possible if a relative should be gravely ill. This is known as *cuoi chay tang* (marriage running ahead of mourning).

After the engagement the parents meet to agree upon the bride price, the amount of which depends on the means of the fiancé's family. Wealthy families are expected to present a sizable bride price of such things as bolts of cloth, jewelry, food, jars of rice alcohol, and a large sum of money. Poor families simply give the prescribed minimum bride price, the symbolic *mam trau cau,* a tray of betel leaves and areca nuts which traditionally represent unity and faithfulness. If other gifts are made, all but the mam trau cau are sent to the bride's house before the wedding. Vietnamese law continues to observe the French-instituted regulation of announcing the banns by registering the marriage eight days before the marriage ritual.

A traditional Vietnamese practice which continues to be observed in Khanh Hau is *lam re* (literally "to be the son-in-law"), a service period the fiancé is expected to perform at the fiancée's house prior to the marriage as a demonstration of good character and his ability as a farmer and bread-winner. Older villagers recall that when they were young, lam re was required of all fiancés, and they worked in the fields or cut wood and carried water. While this continues to be the case in families of small tenant farmers and laborers, among other village families lam re consists of token performances such as a daily appearance by the fiancé during which he stands about never speaking unless addressed, to display his good deportment.

As the day of the wedding approaches, both families begin feverish preparations. Since weddings are anticipated long in advance, money is saved for the great event regardless of financial position. In order to accommodate the many guests, the fiancé's house is enlarged by removing the front wall and constructing a thatch and bamboo shelter. In both houses the main room is decorated with gaily colored festoons, and palm fronds are fixed to pillars and beams. Tables, chairs, glasses, chinaware, and chopsticks are borrowed from kin and neighbors. The altars of the ancestors also must be made ready—brass altar accouterment is polished, fresh candles are put in place, and prosperous families purchase new silk or satin hangings to drape around the altars. Furniture is cleaned and polished, and new mats are placed on the hardwood beds in the main room. If it is to be a particularly large gathering, a thatched addition may be constructed to the rear of the house to serve as a kitchen. Several days before the event, female kin of the bride and groom gather at the groom's house to begin preparation of the staggering variety of dishes that will be served at the feast. Braziers, fueled by coconut shells, burn constantly and the women sit chatting while they chop vegetables, meat, and fish. Most families fatten several pigs to provide exquisite pork dishes for the feast, and wealthy families also slaughter several oxen or cattle. Some even hire cooks from Tan An to direct the activities in the kitchen.

The festivities usually begin at the groom's house on the eve of the wedding when friends of his family gather to eat and drink in an atmosphere of informal gaiety. Candles are lit in the main room, and music fills the air as guests arrive to present the groom's father with cash gifts to help defray the cost of the wedding. Often the celebrating lasts well into the night, and it is not unusual for some guests to remain until dawn. On the morning of the wedding, guests gather early at the groom's house to sip tea until the procession is formed. Offerings of fruit, rice alcohol, and tea have been placed on the altar of the ancestors, and a small altar dedicated to the Spirit of the Soil has been arranged in front of the house. When the final preparations have been completed the groom dons the traditional blue silk robe, and his father gives the signal for the procession to the bride's house.

Places in the wedding procession are clearly prescribed: it is led by a close friend of the groom who acts as his assistant, carrying gifts of gold earrings and rice alcohol, as well as a red silk wedding robe and a large circular hat, both rented from the Village Council. These will be worn by the bride on the return procession and subsequent marriage ritual. The groom follows, carrying a large, round red and gold box containing mam trau cau, the traditional wedding gifts of betel leaves and areca nuts which symbolize unity and faithfulness. The best man and groom are flanked by assistants holding long-handled mandarin parasols. After them come the intermediary and usually the groom's male kin, many of whom carry large black umbrellas. Younger married and unmarried women dressed in pastel colors, their gold necklaces glistening in the sun, come behind the men, and the older women, invariably garbed in black, bring up the rear. Should the bride live in a neighboring village and one of the families be well-to-do, vehicles more than likely will be provided to transport the guests. In this case care must be taken that the betel leaves and areca nuts are well covered, for belief has it that if they are exposed disaster will come to the carrier.

At the bride's house, kin and friends have gathered in the main room to await the groom's procession. As it approaches, the bride's parents go to meet the groom; the intermediary presents them with small glasses of rice alcohol and explains that they have come for the bride. Begging their permission to enter the house, the intermediary gives the bride's parents the tray of areca nuts and betel leaves, which is placed on the altar of the ancestors when the whole group moves inside. An elderly male friend of the bride or groom's family or both fathers perform a ritual in which red candles, held aloft, are lit before the altar of the ancestors while prayers are recited. It is believed that should the candles go out during the ritual, the couple will not have a happy married life (some villagers slyly suggest that flammable fluid usually is poured on the candle wicks). As a gesture of respect, the groom then comes forth to kowtow before the altar of the ancestors, after which he kowtows before the bride's kin—males first and then females. He then carries the wedding garb to one of the rear rooms where the bride has been waiting. By this time the guests have been served tea and iced drinks and are chatting. Attracting little attention, the bride and groom emerge and pass from table to table displaying the tray of gifts brought in the procession.

Shortly thereafter the procession to the groom's house forms. The groom leads, followed by the bride, the best man, and the intermediary. The bride's kin and guests join the rest of the procession.

The returning procession wends its way across the paddy fields. When the guests arrive at the groom's house they quickly disperse, most of them seeking the cool shade of the house. The bride and groom pause by the altar honoring the Spirit of the Soil, and with burning joss clasped in their hands, they kowtow, asking permission to enter the house. Meanwhile the guests have been shown to their tables where refreshments are served. Elderly men are seated at a table in front of the altar of the ancestors while other men occupy tables around the main room. Women are placed on the periphery, usually under the temporary shelter. Older women invariably converge on the hardwood beds in the main room where trays of betel leaves, areca nuts, and pots of lime have been placed for their convenience. Honored guests are seated with the old men.

When beer and soft drinks have been served, the din of conversation and laughter fills the room as the bride and groom enter, accompanied by their fathers, and proceed to the main altar of the ancestors. After the intermediary lights two candles which he holds high as he informs the ancestors of the marriage, the couple step forward and kowtow three times. Then taking a mat, they move about the room kowtowing before their kin—first the elderly males, then the younger males, and the females last. At most weddings it is necessary for an elderly man such as the intermediary or one of the fathers to guide the couple through the prescribed sequence of ritual acts.

With the wedding rituals performed, collection of cash gifts for the bridal couple follows. Taking the tray containing gifts brought by the groom, the couple pass it among their male kin, each of whom is expected to give at least 100$ VN. The elderly ladies, who until this moment have been chewing betel and areca while they gossiped, turn their attention and their privileged frankness on the men. "Anh Tam there," a gray-haired lady is apt to shout, "you had a good harvest, and we know you have money hidden in your house, so give these children some of it!" Amidst the laughter another lady might add, "You, Muoi Hai, you miser, give them two hundred more—such a small sum for a rich man." More than one man sheepishly plunges into his pockets to add to his gift, but they never retort. These gibes are made in a joking spirit, and they reflect the license accorded elderly ladies in village society.

The wedding feast follows the gift giving. When the hot dishes have been placed on the tables, the guests wait for the older men to begin and then consume their food with polite restraint, stopping frequently to put down their chopsticks and chat. The atmosphere of the gathering, however, is not restrained. The sounds of many conversations fill the air. Men are served beer and rice alcohol (the women are given soft drinks), and some men become boisterous, much to the amusement of everyone. The bride and groom move among the tables seeing that the guests are well supplied with food and drink—the bride is responsible for the female guests and the groom the males. The bridal couple never join the feast nor are they permitted to speak to each other, and they are expected to appear grave.

The bride's parents and other kin must leave at a preselected auspicious hour. After bidding farewell to their hosts, they walk to the entrance of the farmstead accompanied by the bride. As they move across the paddy fields, the bride returns to the house, hiding her face as she quietly weeps. Feasting is likely to continue until early evening, and finally toward the end, the bride and groom remove their wedding robes and go to the kitchen to eat. After the guests have departed, the house is cleaned and put back in order, and the bridal couple retire to a room or partitioned area set aside for them. Passing into the bridal chamber, they observe a simple ritual act wherein the bride steps in first while her husband stands back to avoid her stepping on his shadow, in the belief that if this happens he will be a henpecked husband.

Traditionally the newly married couple was expected to refrain from sexual intercourse until after the ritual visit to the bride's parents three days after the wedding. In Khanh Hau at the present time, however, this visit may take place within a reasonable time after the wedding, so there is no longer a restriction on the consummation of the marriage. When the couple do make their ritual visit, they are met by the bride's parents who accompany them to the altar of the ancestors. There an elderly male kin or friend of the bride's family performs the ritual which consists of opening the box of areca nuts and betel leaves placed on the altar the day of the wedding. The nuts are sliced and wrapped in the leaves and are later distributed to kin and friends as a symbolic announcement that the marriage is final.

Cao Daists observe the traditional rites described above. Catholic marriages, however, mix traditional Vietnamese and Catholic practices. Although many Catholic marriages are arranged, since the young man and woman probably attend mass at the same church in Tan An, they more than likely know each other. The common pattern is for Catholics to marry only Catholics. Premarriage observances are similar to those already described. After the first meeting of the parents the couple usually visits the priest in Tan An to discuss the marriage and receive counsel. The engagement celebration is observed with the traditional presentation of gifts, and the young man prays before the Catholic shrine in the main room of the girl's house. Three weeks before the wedding, the banns are announced in the Tan An church. On the day of the wedding, the bride price is carried to the bride's house, but the couple meet at the church for the ceremony (which may or may not include a mass, depending on the relative means of the groom's family). Everyone then proceeds to the groom's house where the couple pray before the family shrine and kowtow before their kin. After the gift giving, a feast is served.

Permanent patrilocal residence is prescribed only for the youngest son who will inherit the paternal house. For other sons, temporary patrilocal residence is customary and is designed to integrate the new bride into her husband's family; this usually is a trying period for her. Since most marriages are arranged, it is still not uncommon that the bride and groom are strangers. In most village houses there is little opportunity for them to be alone, and in many houses they are fortunate to have their own bed.

A bride is expected to treat her husband's parents with marked deference. While she has little to do with her father-in-law, she must be particularly submissive to her mother-in-law. The girl's housekeeping ability is at first harshly criticized by her mother-in-law, and she is also given the most servile tasks, which she must perform without complaint. Her mother-in-law's comfort and satisfaction must be her primary consideration. Unless her brothers-in-law are children she must avoid them, but she is free to establish an easy, informal relationship with her sisters-in-law. Adjustment for some young wives is difficult; the new household is strange and ways of doing things are different. Villagers point out, however, that most girls are prepared for these difficulties, and after all the daughter-in-law of today is the mother-in-law of tomorrow.

In many respects the young people are ready for the new roles which marriage brings. The husband usually continues working with his father, although now he is breadwinner rather than a contributing son, and the girl now does housework as a wife rather than a dutiful daughter. They have learned through the example and counsel of their parents to manage their own affairs. The husband is expected to turn over to his wife whatever cash he receives. She makes the necessary purchases, saving some cash for future contingencies, and the husband receives some for tobacco, for food when he is away from the farmstead, and for recreation such as drinking with friends in a hamlet shop.

Pregnancy and Birth

When a Khanh Hau woman first becomes pregnant she begins to observe a set of taboos and certain prescribed behavior designed to ease the strains of pregnancy and guarantee the birth of a well-formed child. She should avoid foods considered "unclean"—such as beef, dog, mouse, rat, and snake —lest the child be an imbecile. Alcohol is considered deleterious, although it is permissible to chew betel and areca, or smoke tobacco. The woman is cautioned against having sexual intercourse during the entire period of gestation. The pregnant woman also should avoid such work as carrying heavy loads, and she is advised to walk with great caution to avoid stumbling.

Certain behavior is considered taboo. She should remain at home as much as possible and avoid weddings and funerals at any cost. Her attendance at a wedding may cause bad luck for the newlyweds, and the atmosphere of a funeral may affect her badly so that her child may cry incessantly. It also would be wise for her to shun places of worship and shrines in the village for fear of incurring the wrath of the spirits residing in these places. For the same reason she should avoid the roads and footpaths of the village at noon and five o'clock in the evening, the hours when the spirits leave their sanctuaries to promenade. In the house she must be careful not to step over one of the hammocks out of fear that the child will be inflicted with a lethargy causing it to keep its eyes closed for seven days after birth. The pregnant woman also can be a source of misfortune to others; for example, if she should step over a hammock where her husband lies sleeping, he may be afflicted with a sleeping sickness. This also could occur if he should finish a glass of beverage left by his wife.

As the time for birth approaches, a special bed of bamboo without a mat is arranged behind the altar of the ancestors or some other relatively private part of the house. When labor pains begin, the woman takes to this special bed, and an experienced older woman or a woman who has received some training in midwifery is summoned. (In Khanh Hau the preference is for older women because they are considered more experienced, and modern methods of delivery continue to be regarded with some suspicion.) Several female neighbors and kin are called in to assist, and the husband is expected to remain out of the house during labor and birth.

No matter how difficult the delivery, the woman must not cry out, for it would draw the attention of the neighbors, and the family would suffer great embarrassment. Traditionally, the umbilical cord was cut with the sharp edge of a china cup or rice bowl, but knives or scissors are now used in most cases. Another traditional practice which is diminishing in the village is to swaddle the newborn child in the castoff clothes of the other children. The infant is bathed in tepid water, swaddled, and given to the mother as soon as possible, after which the husband is permitted to enter the house and see his child. After the birth, a brazier of burning wood is placed under the bed in the belief that the mother has dissipated the heat of her body, and it must be replenished. For several weeks she is served highly seasoned food to increase this heating process. After two or three days, a small pot filled with hot coals is passed over her body periodically to tighten the skin and prevent sagging of the abdomen. After this "ironing" of the body, the woman is bathed in water in which cinnamon and other fragrant herbs have been boiled, to "cleanse and sweeten her." There is also a ritual "to cleanse the child."

The child is kept with its mother almost constantly and after seven days they are moved to one of the ordinary beds in the main room of the house. The bamboo bed is either discarded or burned, and the brazier is placed under the new bed where it will remain as long as the woman is bedridden. The prescribed period is one month, but in Khanh Hau most women quit their beds after ten days to resume household activities. After the birth of the first child the parents are expected to refrain from sexual intercourse for at least 100 days, but for subsequent births there is no restriction.

NAMES

The Vietnamese, like the Chinese, place the family name first, then a middle name (usually a sex designation, *van* for males and *thi* for females), then the given name. In Khanh Hau there are 37 family names, Nguyen being the most common in the village as it is throughout Vietnam.[2] In naming a child it is important first of all to find a name that has never been held by any living or deceased member of the family. Second, in normal circumstances the name should import something propitious such as Tot (good), Phuoc (luck), Tho (longevity), or Loc (abundance). Poetic names, such as Minh Chau (beautiful pearl), Dao (peach blossom), or Xuan (spring), also are popular and some may be given to males and females alike. If the firstborn should die, however, the family may try to ward off the evil spirits who snatched away the infant, and who may covet the second child, by giving him an unfavorable name such as Meo (cat), Cho (dog), or the more extreme Cat (penis) for males or Lon (vagina) for females.

Avoidance of given names is general in Khanh Hau. The only time a villager ever uses his real name is on official records. Villagers refer to and address one another by kin numeratives or nicknames, and those with titles are usually called by them. It is not uncommon for an individual to have several nicknames, and it is a popular practice in Khanh Hau to bestow nicknames on the basis of some outstanding physical characteristic. The real name is akin to the soul, and to use it is to invoke the spirits by calling attention to the soul, whereas nicknames confuse them.

ADOPTION

If, after several years of marriage, a couple does not have a child or if they have had numerous daughters, they will adopt a son to maintain the lineage

2. These are Vo, Ho, Nguyen, Mai, Le, Pham, Luong, Phan, Quach, Truong, Tran, Han, Ly, Dao, Ngo, Doan, Ha, Duong, Dang, Phung, Hong, Tan, Ta, Huynh, Lam, Loi, Chau, Bui, Diep, Do, Trinh, Cao, Van, Dan, Kieu, La, and Vuong.

and the Cult of the Ancestors. The procedure is informal, and there is no recourse to legal authority. It is preferable that the child be very young and a member of the husband's lineage, but if this cannot be arranged the couple looks for a male infant in the village. Some compensation may be offered if the family is not related to the couple, although there is no evidence of systematic selling of male infants. Should a family be very impoverished, however, and have numerous sons, they may let it be known that one or several are available for adoption. In addition to receiving something for a child, the parents have the comfort of knowing that their son will have more opportunities. Adoption of girls also occurs in the village, although much less frequently.

SOME ASPECTS OF CHILD REARING

Parents in Khanh Hau are reluctant to have infants sleep alone, so the mother of one of the parents often comes to sleep with the child. If this is not possible the child sleeps with the parents. Small siblings all share the same bed, usually in the same room with their parents, regardless of the size of the house. An infant spends a great deal of time with its mother, who carries it around, holding it with one arm while its legs straddle her hip. The child is kept nearby while she performs her household tasks, and should it cry, she immediately picks it up. She may even hold the child while it naps; one very common sight in the village is that of a woman reclining in a hammock with her child comfortably sleeping in her lap. When the child is more than a year old, it is cared for a great deal of the time by one of its older siblings or by a cousin who lives nearby.

Some time during the first twelve years of the child's life—within the first cycle of the lunar calendar[3]—the parents must perform the ritual called *cung do dot*. It is the popular belief that since the child has come from an "unhealthy" part of the mother's body, it is essential to "cleanse the memory" in order to spur the child on to bright intelligence and a healthy adulthood. On this occasion a small altar dedicated to the Twelve Goddesses of Birth is arranged in the house. The parents place twelve bowls of an extremely sweet soup made of soybeans and sugar on the altar, after which they burn twelve strips of paper. Each strip contains a sketch representing one of the twelve animals of the calendrical cycle.

This is a time when the child also must be protected from evil spirits, who are particularly covetous of small children—little boys especially. The name-ploy already mentioned is one means, and there are many talismans

3. For details on the lunar calendar twelve-year cycles see Appendix C.

which also can be employed; for example, a brass bracelet worn by the child wards off evil spirits who cannot tolerate the bracelet's cold touch. The spirits also can be hoodwinked into thinking a little boy is a girl by having him wear an earring. Children are cautioned to avoid the shrines, the road, and such outstanding natural features as the large gnarled tree by the pagoda in Ap Moi at noon when the spirits promenade. Children also can be placed under the protection of a household spirit or a Buddhist deity; the Spirit of the Hearth is a known protector of children, as is the Buddhist Goddess of Mercy.

By and large, there is a good deal of permissiveness with children in the village. They continue to suckle until the age of three or four; when a child is hungry, it simply asks for food and in most instances receives it. Children are not expected to take their meals with the adults, and it is a common sight to see them standing about in front of the house or on the road at odd hours of the day, scooping rice and perhaps some fish from a bowl with chopsticks. Small children are rarely swaddled; they usually are garbed in a light garment that covers only the upper part of the body. Fondling the genitals is one means of calming the crying infant, and sex play appears to be common among the small children. Toilet training is casual; small children are permitted to relieve themselves anywhere but in the house.

Children have the run of the section of the hamlet where they live; they may wander into the neighbors' houses without fear of being punished. Indeed, in most cases, neighbors are likely to be kinfolk, so they are welcomed as members of the family.

Fathers usually assist in caring for the small children, and public displays of paternal affection are considered normal in the village. Villagers in general are very conscious of fondness toward children, and parents are judged by the way they treat them. As the figure of authority in the family, the father is expected to administer any severe punishments, although either parent may spontaneously chastise the child who misbehaves in his presence. Most chastisements are swift and brief, and the child is left to its own misery afterward. Every child is expected to learn certain forms of politeness, the foremost of which is respect for the aged, a reflection of the strong value placed on filial piety. It also is important for a child to know how to greet adults. When a guest is having tea with a villager, it is a source of great pride to the host when his children enter with arms folded, bow low and say "Chao ong." They also are expected to *chao* (act of greeting with respect) in the same manner when they meet the schoolmaster or some equally respected member of the community on the road. Great deference must be paid the grandparents, although relations between grandparents and grand-children often are very easy. Grandparents never punish the children, and they invariably bring gifts to the children when they visit.

Most children attend school for several years at least. Girls assist their mothers, and they tend to remain close to the farmstead as they grow older. Boys, however, are free spirits in the village. They have many companions with whom they play marbles or have cricket fights, and they are free to wander about the hamlet or explore the waterways in a pirogue. Swimming in the fish ponds is a favorite pastime, and in the dry season they trap fish in the canals or cast a line from the bank of the stream. The paddy fields in the rainy season provide them with vast seas in which they may fish with poles, nets, or a variety of traps.

The Mid-Autumn Festival is essentially a children's celebration. They troop through the village carrying lighted, colored-paper representations of the moon or a carp, and they gorge themselves on moon-cakes, made especially for this day. Children swarm into the dinh for village celebrations, and when troupes of traveling actors perform, the children form a large portion of the audience, some of them even squatting on the stage—the best place to watch the performance.

POLYGYNY AND CONCUBINAGE

Although polygyny and concubinage are distinguished conceptually by villagers, it often is difficult to tell one from the other by outward manifestations. While the first marriage is considered a contractual arrangement between families, there is likely to be some element of romance in subsequent relationships. Affairs with other women of the village or relations with prostitutes in Tan An or My Tho may take place at any time, but generally a man takes a second wife or concubine only after ten or fifteen years of marriage. There are no known cases in the village of polygyny among men under 30 years of age.

Well-to-do villagers usually adhere to the prescribed means of taking a second wife—a practice which normally only this segment of village society can afford. There is no ceremony; an arrangement is made between the parties, and consequent behavior makes it apparent to villagers that the man has taken a second wife. If the "little wife" (meaning the second wife) lives with her family, her husband is expected to provide a house for her. In some cases, however, the second wife already has her own house (as does the village chief's second wife), or she may be living with an aged parent, so she may remain there. In those instances where the little wife is going to

share the same house with the "big wife," permission of the latter is required. It would be unusual if she did not assent, for the little wife is
younger in most instances and, being subordinate, she is expected to be
responsible for most of the housework, the children, and other duties which
a wife finds more demanding as she becomes older. Although this arrangement is thought to have great economic advantage, maintaining separate
households for the wives is favored by most villagers who practice plural
marriage. They prefer keeping the wives separated, and it provides two
households between which the husband can divide his time as he pleases.[4]
Such cases clearly constitute polygyny; the women are recognized as second
wives, and their children are considered the legal offspring of the father
with rights of inheritance equal to those of the first wife's children.

Polygyny serves a variety of functions. Having a second or third wife is a
manifestation of affluence, a mark of prestige. If the first wife has failed to
produce male offspring after ten or twelve years, taking a second wife
increases the possibility of having male heirs. The wealthy, aging villager
also may be attracted to a younger woman, a situation often linked with the
failing attractiveness or failing health of the first wife. Finally, there are
economic motives for some cases of polygyny—an unmarried girl with an
inheritance or a widow with a house and land makes a desirable second wife.

In Khanh Hau there is no concubine installed in a house as is a second
wife. Concubinage usually takes the form of a liaison which is considered
temporary from the outset. In most instances the girl continues to reside
with her family, and her lover may have visiting privileges. With poorer
villagers it is difficult to determine whether, in such arrangements, the
woman is considered a concubine or a second wife whom a man cannot
afford to support. Children born of such a relationship may dispel some of
the uncertainty. If the woman is considered a concubine, the father has the
right to decide whether or not to recognize them as heirs and, by the same
token, the mother can affirm or deny any claim he may make. If she is a
second wife there is no question that the children are the legal heirs of the
father.

In one case, a young woman who had been abandoned by her husband
gave birth to a son. The father was a relatively prosperous villager already
married, and he refused to claim the child as his legal son, indicating to all
that the woman was his concubine. His wife, however, desired to have the

4. The Family Bill, passed by the National Assembly of Vietnam in 1959, made both
polygyny and concubinage illegal, although the effect of this legislation is not yet manifest at the village level.

child because it was a male. She approached the young woman and pleaded with her to sell her the child; she offered a sum of money which the young woman refused.

Temporary affairs are not uncommon in the village. When men gather to drink rice alcohol and gossip, boasters often hold the attention of the group with tales of their sex conquests and the number of *meo* (literally "kittens"), the popular term for girl friends, they have in the area. Several of the wealthy villagers are reputed to have several wives and many meo in neighboring towns and villages. Stories such as these are intended to enhance one's reputation as a great lover, and give high status in the drinking groups. While many of these stories represent the Khanh Hau version of barracks braggadocio, they do reflect the villager's concern with public appearances and reputation. Since it is almost impossible to have a clandestine affair in the village, it is advisable to have it elsewhere.

SEPARATION

There are no recorded divorces in Khanh Hau. If a couple has no children, and they decide they can no longer live as man and wife, they usually agree to separate without recourse to legal authority. If a couple has children, however, they are subject to strong social pressures, particularly on the part of kinfolk, to remain together in spite of their incompatibility. In such instances the wife tends to bear the brunt of the difficult situation; she is expected to accept her unhappy role stoically, showing no outward sign of discontent. She must carry out her responsibilities as wife and mother with all the scrupulousness of a happily married woman. The husband, on the other hand, has several outlets for his discontent. If he is well-to-do, he can take a second wife and establish another household where he may spend most of his time or, regardless of wealth, he may console himself with a concubine.

When a couple can no longer tolerate living together, they separate by mutual agreement or one party leaves without warning. There appear to be more instances of husbands than wives leaving, and generally the children remain with their mother. If the woman's parents are alive she may go to live with them, otherwise she will have to support herself and her children, usually receiving some assistance from kin and friends.

DIVISION OF LABOR IN THE FAMILY

Division of labor in the family depends on economic level, season, and household composition. Taking the nuclear family as the model, families of laborers, landowners with very small holdings, and tenant farmers tend to divide labor in much the same way. They are closer to the subsistence level than other families, so all able-bodied members are expected to contribute to the sustenance of the group. Critical years (such as 1958 when drought reduced the rice crop) affect these groups, forcing some of the males to leave the village to improve their fortunes elsewhere, with only a slim chance that they will return.

The principal breadwinner of the family is the father. Laborers usually work for the same farmers, and they can expect steady, if seasonal, employment. The small landowners and tenant farmers also are most active during the growing season, and they have the added chores of repairing implements and caring for draft animals, if they are fortunate enough to have any. Like the laborer, however, they must seek dry-season employment to supplement their incomes. Within the village some farmers hire laborers to aid in repairing the bunds and irrigation channels, and currently the School of Fundamental Education hires labor for their projects. But many continue to seek work in Tan An. Those who do find employment usually also seek a place for kin and friends with the same employer.

In families of laborers, small tenant farmers, and small landowners, grown sons usually work with their fathers and continue to do so after marriage. Grown daughters also are expected to contribute to the family income, and should the son remain in the paternal house after marriage, his wife may have the same responsibility as the daughters. Most of the women who work for hire in transplanting and harvesting teams are from this economic group. Also, in families of small tenant farmers and small landowners, girls assist with the field work, doing such things as weeding, harvesting paddy, winnowing, weighing paddy, and storing it in the bins. Wives usually sun the grain, raking it in front of the house. Women also help the men carry straw collected in the fields back to the farmstead. A few girls may work periodically as domestics for wealthy families, and some may be fortunate enough to be apprenticed to seamstresses in the village.

Older women often weave mats and baskets on demand, and most of them tend small kitchen gardens, selling part of the produce. Some women engage in small commerce, vending sugar cane or coconuts purchased in the markets at Tan An or Tan Huong, and a few make rice cakes to sell along the road. The only women engaged full time in commerce are those whose husbands are deceased or disabled or have abandoned them.

The primary role of the women remains that of housewife and mother. Responsibilities are fairly routine, with the meal schedule altering somewhat with the agricultural cycle. Normally during the dry season when there is little activity only two meals are prepared—one between ten and eleven in the morning and another at four in the afternoon. When the men are working in the fields, however, they eat a breakfast at 5:00 A.M., another meal around 10:00 A.M., and a large meal when they return from the fields at five in the evening. Wives remain in the farmstead most of the day. A few may be called upon to assist in the field work, and some labor on the transplanting and harvesting teams. Marketing trips to Tan An are infrequent, since they have neither the need nor the means to purchase most of the goods sold there. Local shops satisfy demands for most items that must be purchased from day to day, and foods are readily accessible in the village. Small tenants and small landowners have their own paddy, and laborers often receive part of their pay in kind; if necessary they can purchase paddy from kin or neighbors. The wife or the daughters periodically carry baskets of it to the local rice mill to be husked and polished. They also make daily trips to the local shops to buy dried fish, vegetables, perhaps fruit, and condiments.

Household tasks include preparing meals for the family and for the transplanting team, during the season. The house must be swept every day and clothes must be laundered frequently. Carrying water is a daily task, and several times each week the women seek firewood. Much of the wife's time is spent in caring for the inevitable infant—nursing it, rocking it to sleep in the hammock, and bathing it. A periodic responsibility of the women is to prepare the meals that are served at family celebrations. Among these villagers the meals are never very elaborate, although they do require time and effort.

Younger children usually have some responsibilities. They are expected to care for younger siblings, and they search for firewood around the village. If the family raises ducks, the small sons are responsible for guarding them, and they also herd the family buffalo. Some small boys contribute directly to the family larder by fishing in the flooded paddy fields, canals, and streams, and some are hired to guard buffalo belonging to wealthy villagers. Another amusing and productive pastime is searching for wild fruit. Village boys are very dexterous at disengaging the fruit from the highest parts of the trees with loops attached to bamboo poles. At harvest, children of very poor families invade recently harvested fields to glean sprigs of paddy. In many of the very poor families the aid of children often is essential, and it is common to hear the expression "the need to aid the parents" when referring to children who do not attend school.

Division of labor alters somewhat as the family's economic lot improves.

The relatively well-to-do farmers usually hire laborers for necessary work in the fields, although they still must supervise planting, transplanting, and harvesting. While sons are relieved from having to work in the fields, they, as well as grown daughters, usually assist in the harvest because of the need to complete the task as quickly as possible. Among the wealthy there is little mutual aid; they are able to hire laborers, and usually they live in houses that require specialists to build and repair.

Wives in prosperous families have essentially the same responsibilities as other village wives, and in many respects more demands are made on them. Their houses are larger and better furnished and consequently require more care. Wealthy villagers have larger wardrobes, they eat more elaborate meals, and they entertain more guests. Family celebrations among them normally are large, and their social position demands that they have impressive meals, all of which involve planning and supervision by the wife as well as trips to the Tan An market. Only one family in the village has a full-time domestic, and few have part-time help. On the other hand, the wealthy can afford certain amenities which relieve wives of some household labor. Polygyny is found more often among them, and the second wife assumes responsibility for much of the work. Wealthy villagers recently have been adding concrete cisterns to their houses, eliminating the need to carry water. In addition, most have the costly new brick ovens which can be fueled with rice husks as well as kindling, and they facilitate cooking.

HEALTH

Health is primarily the affair of the family. Parents are responsible for the well-being of their children, and should an adult member fall ill, his kin are expected to take some form of action.[5] Since the villagers believe that the individual is predisposed rather than predestined (in addition to realizing that such things as disharmony with universal order are ultimate causes of ill fortune), they recognize immediate causes of sickness and have culturally prescribed ways of coping with them.

There are several means of preventing sickness. Villagers generally are aware of the need for a proper diet, and certain foods are served from time to time because they contribute to good health. For example a bitter-tasting melon known as *kho qua* is considered good for "refreshing the stomach and

5. A great many villagers complain of ailments, most of them seemingly minor—slight fevers, headaches, insomnia, mild digestive disorders, and periodic diarrhea. There also are serious illnesses; several women appear to be in the advanced stages of tuberculosis (one died in 1960). Skin eruptions indicating some kind of pox are fairly common among children.

the intestines," and red chili peppers which are consumed frequently are thought to prevent worms. Chewing areca and betel "refreshes the heart." There also are numerous alcoholic preparations which are drunk from time to time to promote robust health—porcupine belly or snakes in rice alcohol are two popular preparations—and at times certain foods must be avoided.

Attempts to introduce modern hygiene have met with mild success. When he was director of the School of Fundamental Education, Nguyen Van Mung had a group of villagers look through a microscope at water from an earthen jug before and after it had been boiled. Shocked at the "animals" in the unboiled water, they agreed to boil their drinking water. After Nguyen Van Mung left the village, however, they discontinued this practice, pointing out that rainwater really is pure and boiling it destroyed its "fresh flavor." The smallpox inoculation organized by Nguyen Van Mung was well received by many villagers. The Village Council informed residents when the inoculation team would visit their hamlet. Many brought their children, although only few of the adults would submit to inoculation. Finally, the School of Fundamental Education aided some residents of Ap Dinh-A and Ap Dinh-B in constructing latrines over their fish ponds as examples to other villagers, but few followed suit.

Probably the most widespread preventive techniques are rituals which are aimed at preventing ill health either by requesting protection of a deity or by propitiating an evil or errant spirit. Within the framework of formal religions, many women maintain special shrines to the Buddhist goddess Quang Am for protection of their children and for easy childbirth. Cao Daists observe the same practice, and some of the Catholic families give special veneration to the Blessed Virgin for the same reason.

Among the numerous family rituals already noted are those concerned with prenatal and natal practices. Ritual offerings on the thien shrines before every house, the Cult of the Spirit of the Hearth, and the Cult of the Ancestors all involve protection of family health among other things. Also an annual ritual called Trung Nguyen, observed by the family, is designed to placate errant spirits capable of causing illness, and there are numerous amulets available to protect one from evil spirits that cause ailments.

When ailments do occur, the family tries every means at its disposal rather than resort to outside agency. Some home remedies are made from kitchen-garden plants; one locally grown plant is used in preparing a gargle for throat irritations; another provides the basic ingredient in a medicine for curing conjunctivitis.[6] Many families keep bunches of unhusked paddy

6. Cultivation of medicinal plants is discussed further in Chapter 6.

which when cooked is considered nutritious for those with digestive disorders. Glutinous rice also is given to anyone suffering a gastrointestinal ailment. For a number of minor sicknesses such as colds, headaches, or upset stomach there are patent medicines available at both Chinese pharmacies.

Some afflictions are considered temporary and not serious, and go untended. Open wounds rarely are treated and, in the belief that skin pustules are caused by an ill wind, children suffering from pox are covered with a scarf and allowed to mix freely with their playmates.

When an outside agency is required, villagers almost invariably look to practitioners of traditional Sino–Vietnamese medicine. In addition to selling patent preparations, the Chinese pharmacists prepare "northern medicine," the Vietnamese designation for Chinese drugs, as well as "southern medicine," which broadly indicates traditional Vietnamese drugs, which in southern Vietnam include an accumulation of northern and central Vietnamese healing substances together with those adopted from the Chams and Khmers.[7] Both pharmacists also visit the sick to diagnose ailments, administering medicine or employing traditional healing techniques such as pinching, bloodletting, or suction with tubes. Traditional therapy also is performed by an Ap Dinh-A farmer known as Ong Thay Muoi Le who specializes in bone fractures and sprains. As already indicated, some practitioners such as the two Buddhist lay monks, Ong Thay Sau Thoi and Ba Cot (healers in Ap Dinh-A), and Ong Thay Phap (the sorcerer) combine Sino–Vietnamese medical techniques with mystical practices, and many families seek their cures when illness strikes.

Should traditional therapy be of no avail, some families try Western medicine. Many villagers continue to be somewhat skeptical of it, however, and its high cost is another factor in its restricted use. Some Western patent medicines such as aspirin are sold in the pharmacies.

Khanh Hau has two male nurses. One specializes in inoculations; the other, the official village nurse who worked six years in the Tan An hospital, employs a wider range of techniques. The village medical supply, however, is very limited, and although the village nurse has a private practice, few can afford his services.

Among villagers who accept Western medicine, inoculations are very popular, and at times the number and variety of shots given a patient seem

7. Cham medicines are thought to be particularly powerful. The Cham of south central Vietnam continue to prepare a potent medicine for back ailments. Groups of Cham medicine vendors often are seen in My Tho, Ben Tre, and Can Tho along the Mekong River, where they have regular clients among the Chinese and Vietnamese pharmacists.

excessive.[8] Hospitalization is anathema to most villagers. They point out that not only is the patient in the hands of strangers, but he will not be properly fed. If a villager does agree to be hospitalized (and there is space for him in the overcrowded Tan An hospital), it is on condition that a member of the family can remain close and cook for him. News of someone dying in a hospital spreads rapidly, reinforcing villagers' prejudices. After one resident of Ap Dinh-B died in the hospital, and his sister manifested the same symptoms, she adamantly refused to undergo the same treatment, and her kin and neighbors supported her refusal. When all possible means have been tried and the ailment worsens, villagers become fatalistic. If a man's legs swell or a woman's face puffs up, there is nothing to do but wait for death.

FAMILY RELIGIOUS PRACTICES

Signs of religion are omnipresent in villagers' houses. Practicing Buddhists always have an altar dedicated to one or more Buddhist deities, usually sharing a prominent place in the main room with the altar of the ancestors. Additional altars, often almost hidden in dark recesses, also are common, and in smaller houses the Buddhist altar may be attached high on a wall or on a cross beam. Thich Ca, a reincarnation of Buddha, is one of the more popular deities as is Quang Am, the Goddess of Mercy, or Cuu Thien, both considered protectors of households and children. In addition to attending periodic rituals at the pagoda, very orthodox Buddhists observe the daily Cong Phu, consisting of burning joss, kowtowing, and reciting prayers at 6:00 A.M., noon, and 6:00 P.M. Each day food offerings and tea are placed on the main altar.

Cao Daists invariably have altars dedicated to the Supreme Being, usually represented by an eye emanating rays of light. The one exception is found in the only family of the Minh Chon Ly sect which symbolizes the Supreme Being with the eye-in-the-heart. Buddhist deities often are enshrined on these or additional altars, and Cao Daists retain their ancestral altars. On entering a Catholic home in Khanh Hau, one may at first easily mistake the Catholic shrine for a Buddhist or Cao Daist altar. It is in the same place and contains the same incense burner, candles, and flowers. Upon closer scrutiny,

8. One elderly man in Ap Moi was suffering from fever, severe coughing, and body pains, and in the course of several weeks the nurse inoculated him with penicillin, Histamycine, Thioderazine, Solucamphor, Septicemine, Teoneptale, and vitamin B_1. The man recovered.

however, it becomes clear that the stylized figures are Christian deities. Most Catholic families venerate the Sacred Heart, and there also may be altars honoring the Blessed Virgin and the Infant Jesus of Prague. In the evening, Catholic families always recite the rosary before the shrine.

On the fifteenth day of the seventh lunar month, every family should observe the rituals that mark the beginning of Trung Nguyen, the midpoint of the lunar new year. The popular beliefs surrounding this feast are based on an old Chinese legend which is well known to villagers.[9] The primary aim of the ritual is to placate the errant spirits. To avoid their wrath, each family heaps offerings on the altar dedicated to the Spirit of the Soil, which stands before the house. The head of the household begs permission of the spirit to make ritual offerings to the errant spirits. A mat is then placed on the ground and offerings of rice, fruit, and rice alcohol are put on it. Before the 1955 law forbidding opium in Vietnam, a pipe was prepared as part of the offerings. The errant spirits are summoned to partake of the offerings by striking a gong or two pieces of wood. Members of the family hold burn-

9. In ancient China there lived an elderly lady named Thanh De, and being a fervent Buddhist, she often took baskets of rice to the monks at the pagoda on the edge of her village. On one such visit, the monk who received her at the gate refused her offering, saying that it was insufficient for the number of monks residing at the pagoda. Taking back her rice, Thanh De started for home, and as she mulled over the rudeness of this refusal, her anger arose, and impetuously she flung the rice into the river, a shameful waste.

When she arrived home, she immediately began to plot some revenge against the monks. After much thought, she settled upon a diabolical scheme that would surely shame them and satisfy her need for retribution. She organized a feast which she called Lam Chay, and dedicated it to the errant spirits, those unhappy and malevolent spirits of the dead who have no cult. It was an elaborate feast, and Thanh De herself prepared the *pièce de resistance,* a rice cake called *banh bao,* and in each cake she inserted some dog flesh. In consuming the cakes, the monks would violate the taboo against eating flesh, and this would be compounded by another breach against the taboo forbidding the consumption of dog flesh, because the dog is the guardian of the house. The feast was held, the monks came and partook of it, and Thanh De savored her sweet revenge.

Not long after, Thanh De died, and as a result of her wicked behavior, she was plunged into hell. Her son Muc Lien became a Buddhist monk, and upon his death he was admitted to the ranks of the sanctified Buddhas. He visited hell and finding the soul of his mother, he interceded in her behalf, and she was granted the state of nirvana. This occurred in the seventh lunar month, and it set a precedent for possible salvation of errant spirits. On Trung Nguyen the gates of hell are opened and the errant spirits return to earth where they wander aimlessly in the hope of finding a cult being offered for them. They cause misfortune if they remain unsatisfied, so the object of the Trung Nguyen is to provide ritual offerings for the errant spirits to propitiate them and grant them rest in death.

ing joss as they kowtow, after which they burn votive papers on the altar. This ritual is performed outside the house because of fear that, given the opportunity to enter, the errant spirits might install themselves on the altar of the ancestors.

There are many occasions when the family pays homage to the Spirit of the Soil. This deity is honored prior to construction of framework for a new house and before a bride and groom enter the groom's house for the wedding ritual. Also, before planting rice seedbeds, most farmers continue to make five small ritual offerings to this spirit.

Altars of the Spirit of Heaven are found before most village houses, and they range from simple planks set on a post or tree trunk to rather elaborate concrete shrines, models of pagodas. On the first and fifteenth day of each lunar month, offerings of three cups of tea or rice alcohol, a small dish of rice, a small package of salt, and some burning joss should be placed on the altar to entice the spirit to remain there and protect the house and its occupants. The spirit in the altar also observes the behavior of those in the house and reports it to the king of Hell, the deity who judges the dead. The rigidity with which villagers make the prescribed offerings varies considerably. Some altars are noticeably devoid of offerings throughout most of the year, while others are heaped with food at the prescribed times. One villager with a particularly large, almost spectacular altar remarked that he is happy to have the spirit observe the excellent conduct of his family so he provides well for him.

There are many household talismans found in Khanh Hau, their use depending on a number of circumstances. Some are employed because of illness or persistent misfortune while others are geomantic or are designed to provide general protection against evil spirits. The most common is the "crossbeam talisman," so named because of its place in the house. Within the octagonal frame, the central circle is divided into the white Ye (light and the male principle) and the black Yang (darkness and the female principle) (the Yin and Yang of the Chinese cosmology). The remaining part of the talisman contains the eight elements—thunder, wind, mountain, water, fire, earth, torrents, and storms—spelled out in black Sino–Vietnamese characters on a red background. Geomantic talismans are similar, but instead of the divided circle they have a mirror in the center. Another very common household talisman is a print of the powerful legendary sorcerer Ong Tu Vi perched atop a tiger, holding the crossbeam talisman in his right hand. His left hand clutches a box containing his credentials and seals issued by the Celestial Court.

DEATH

In Khanh Hau as a man grows old he prepares to join his ancestors. In many respects his whole life has been a preparation for this. A man labors to accumulate land for succeeding generations, particularly land to be designated huong hoa. He also strives to construct a substantial house to contain the altars of the ancestors. As old age comes upon him, the man who can afford it purchases a coffin of carved wood which is set in the main room of the house,[10] and the provident man sets aside money for his tomb. It is consoling for the elderly villager to see the coffin and tomb in which his mortal remains will rest. Some cautious villagers obtain coffins when they are 40 or 50 years old, and often these reminders of death stand in the house for 20 or 30 years.

The ideal tomb, the type constructed by the wealthy, is of stone or concrete, on a site selected by a geomancer. Ong Ke Hien, the highest venerable in Khanh Hau, and his wife have large concrete tombs, each of which cost 50,000$ VN. Both are near the pagoda which Ong Ke Hien sponsored in Ap Cau. Often they visit their tombs to supervise the work being done on them.[11] Villagers of lesser means usually have stone markers on their graves, and the poor merely have graves marked with mounds of earth.

When a man dies, kin living in the village immediately gather at the house to assist with the numerous preparations for the funeral and burial. One member of the family is dispatched to the Council House to report the death to the civil status secretary and request permission to keep the body for a specified number of days. In most instances, an experienced elderly villager is summoned to advise the family on the prescribed behavior for mourning and the ritual for the funeral. He also consults the deceased's horoscope to determine the auspicious days and hours for rituals. The family then divides the various tasks which are part of the preparations for the funeral. The house must be cleaned and perhaps expanded by removing the front partitions and attaching a temporary thatched shelter. Tables and

10. The Vietnamese have specific designations for coffins of various types. *Hom* is the popular term for coffins in general, and *sang* is the more elegant designation. *Tho* is the coffin purchased in advance of death. *Linh cuu* refers to the coffin of a high personage such as a mandarin, and *quach* is the popular word for a child's coffin.

11. Some of the most elaborate stone and concrete tombs in Khanh Hau were constructed by men who were born in the village and left it to make their fortunes in the cities. Several of these were district chiefs in the French Administration. Although they no longer had kin there they continued to be strongly attached to Khanh Hau as their natal village and desired to be buried there. In Vietnam, one always returns to his natal village, perhaps in old age, perhaps in death.

chairs must be borrowed from neighbors, and the coffin must be purchased if this has not already been done. The monk is notified, and someone is sent to inform kin in other villages.[12] The women gather in the kitchen to prepare the many dishes that will be served during the funeral period.

The first ritual act is to wash the corpse and dress it in the traditional tunic and turban. Many families in Khanh Hau retain the traditional practice of placing a few grains of rice in the mouth of the corpse. A variation of this is to place a bunch of bananas on the chest of the body in the belief that this tantalizing food will divert the appetite of the Celestial Dog, who descends to eat the entrails of the deceased. Male members of the family lift the corpse into the coffin while the women stand by weeping, and then the clothes of the deceased are tucked around the sides of the coffin. Some families continue the old practice of placing a bowl of rice by the head of the coffin, for the corpse may rise up, and the rice is thrown at it to force it back in place.

If the deceased is the truong toc, his bier is arranged before the central altar of the house, otherwise it is placed in front of one of the side altars or to the side of the main altar. Candles are lit on the altars, and several lighted candles are placed on top of the coffin. Some families place an oil lamp under the coffin. The immediate reason for this is to dispel any odor from the coffin. There is, however, an old legend which relates this practice to a hope for resurrection.[13] A small altar is placed at the foot of the bier, and

12. Traditionally, the announcement of death to those of the ascending generations in the patrilineage or to village authorities was done formally, first presenting a tray containing some betel leaves and rice alcohol, the symbols of respect for authority.

13. According to the legend, in ancient China there lived a noted philosopher named Khuong Thuong. Being dissatisfied with the state of things in the kingdom, he disassociated himself from it by spending his time fishing. He did so, however, without using a hook on his line. One day while sitting on the river bank in the languid afternoon, Khuong Thuong met an old woodcutter named Vo De. They became friendly, but when Vo De noted that Khuong Thuong neglected to put a hook on his line, he ridiculed him. Chagrined at this rudeness, Khuong Thuong predicted that on his next trip to the wood market, Vo De would die. This dire prediction came to pass; laboring under an enormous load of wood, Vo De stumbled, and the wood crushed him. Vo De's tortured soul sought out Khuong Thuong to beg forgiveness. Khuong Thuong forgave him, and granted him life anew.

At this time there was a great and fearsome mandarin named Bao Cong, at the Imperial Court, and he had the power of judging the souls of the dead. He heard of Vo De's death and grew impatient when his soul did not appear to be judged. Aware of the possible consequences, Khuong Thuong advised Vo De to place a lighted lamp under his empty coffin. Vo De did this, and it prevented Bao Cong from examining the coffin. The ruse was successful, and Vo De lived to a ripe age.

when the preliminary arrangements are complete the family gathers before this altar for the ritual offering of food to the soul of the deceased—three bowls of rice, three small cups of tea, and several other dishes. The family kowtows three times in priority of relationship to the deceased; that is, the wife or husband and children first, then siblings, and so forth. For the duration of the funeral period, three such ritual offerings will be made each day. Mourning clothes are distributed, sometimes by the Buddhist monk. Those in high mourning (widow, widower, children, and patrilineal grand-children) wear roughly made robes of gauzy cotton with patches sewn on them to lend abjectness. The males wear a headpiece of roughly twined straw and the females wear a veil. The remaining kin in low mourning wear white bands neatly wound around the head. The widow is expected to ob-serve a mourning period of two years during which she withdraws from society. The mourning period for a widower is one year, and the children observe semimourning for one year.

With mourning clothes distributed, the *nhan dieu* begins, a vigil period that corresponds to the Western practice of holding a wake. Kin, neighbors, and friends, dressed in traditional clothes, come to pay their respects. The sons stand before the bier to receive the visitors who express their sorrow and kowtow. Visitors bring offerings of cash, food, or alcohol.[14] For wealthy villagers, particularly men who were high in the Cult Committee, the nhan dieu may last from five to seven days in order to permit kin and friends to come from distant places. They usually bring large, colored satin or silk banderoles on which the good qualities of the deceased are extolled in Sino–Vietnamese characters. Most villagers purchase less elegant banderoles pre-pared by specialists who crudely draw the characters on cheap white cloth with the charred end of a burned bamboo stalk.

Prosperous families usually hire musicians to provide music during the daytime. Food and drink are served to the guests, and in many instances the nhan dieu becomes merry in contrast to the earlier period of sadness and weeping. As at the wedding feasts, some of the men become boisterous as they consume increasing quantities of alcohol. For these large gatherings, the seating arrangement is similar to that of the wedding feasts—men occupy tables at the center of the room with elderly men and honored guests nearest the bier, while the women are seated around the periphery. Elderly women

14. At the funeral of one wealthy villager who enjoyed the reputation of being a hearty drinker there were innumerable bottles of rice wine and Bordeaux red wine piled high on the altars and around the bier, giving a wine-cellar aspect to the room.

usually gravitate to one of the beds where they sit chewing betel and areca while they gossip. For most village families, however, nhan dieu is observed more modestly, and it normally lasts only one day.

At the end of this period the family gathers at the bier to kowtow prior to burial, which in some instances is very elaborate. *Giang do* is the generic designation for all things needed in the funeral cortege—musicians, draperies, a catafalque, and pallbearers. All of these are provided by a service in Tan An that few villagers can afford, and in 1959 a group of Ap Nhon Hau residents formed an association to make giang do available to members at a low rate. There is also a group of organized pallbearers for hire in Khanh Hau without the other trappings.

One of the most elaborate funerals in recent years was for Ong Tien Bai, the second highest venerable in the Cult Committee and one of the most prominent villagers. In addition to having hired pallbearers and trappings, the family retained the services of the four young attendants who assist in the rituals at the Ap Nhon Hau dinh. Dressed in the same robes worn at village rituals, and performing with the same stylized movements, they made offerings of tea, sandalwood, and rice alcohol at the altar of the ancestors before the coffin was removed. Movements involved in lifting the coffin and transporting it to the grave were very mannered, and the pallbearers performed under the direction of a leader called the Bai Quan. For the act of carrying the coffin out of the house, Bai Quan signaled by taps with two sticks of special wood. The twelve pallbearers approached the coffin and kowtowed four times. Two strokes directed them to place their hands under the coffin, and three strokes was the signal to lift it and carry it out. It is imperative that the coffin be carried as level as possible so the Bai Quan sat on the shoulders of two assistants to survey and signal whether it was tilting. As most village funerals these ritual acts are performed less elegantly and without professional assistance. Usually young kin and friends of the family carry the coffin, and although they take care, they cannot match the measured movements of the hired pallbearers.

The funeral cortege is formed according to a prescribed order. In Ong Tien Bai's lavish funeral, large, brilliantly colored banderoles were carried at the head of the procession. These were followed by the satin banderoles sent by kin and friends, and two assistants carried a small portable altar containing photographs of the deceased surrounded by burning joss, flowers, and altar tablets. The coffin rested in a gilt and red catafalque of carved wood borne by the pallbearers who chanted the traditional dirges to the accompaniment of horns, drums, and stringed instruments. The deceased's sons,

bent low and leaning on roughly cut sticks, followed close behind the
catafalque, and then came the widow, daughters, and other kin. The remaining mourners trailed in no particular order. Paper money was strewn
along the route to placate any errant spirits that might attempt to bar the
way, and the route was planned to avoid any places of worship. At the tomb
the Buddhist monk recited prayers, and the family kowtowed. Funeral cor-
teges of the well-to-do approximate Ong Tien Bai's, but while most villagers'
processions follow this order and have the portable altar, they do not have
the splendid banderoles, the musicians, or the catafalque, and few have the
monk recite prayers at the grave. None of the rites described is observed in
a child's death. After a brief ritual at the altar of the ancestors, the child is
buried immediately, and it is honored with a special altar arranged in the
main room of the house.

After the ritual at the grave, the family returns to the house for recitation
of the five prayers entreating the soul of the deceased to leave the grave and
reside in the altar of the ancestors. The objects and offerings which were
carried on the portable altar are placed on the altar of the ancestors, before
which members of the family kowtow in the last ritual act of the funeral.
Three days after the burial, members of the family again don their mourning
clothes and return to the grave for the rite designed to permit the soul of
the deceased to depart from it and go to the ancestral altar. Joss is burned,
and a chicken is tied to a stick of sugar cane to be led around the grave three
times.

Funerals in Khanh Hau can be a curious mixture of somber mourning
and festive gaiety, and there are occasional incidents which at first appear
to be irreverent, but in context reflect only a persistent type of humor found
among the villagers. At one funeral, for example, the pallbearers, who were
young neighbors of the deceased, remained to bury the coffin after the
mourners departed. An elderly friend, a small man with eyeglasses askew
and somewhat inebriated from the feasting at the house, stayed to supervise
the burial. Although he clearly expected recognition of his authority, he
received only the amused tolerance of the young men who were engaged in
piling large chunks of dried earth over the coffin in the shallow grave. They
had providently supplied some rice alcohol and a pot of tea with which to
refresh themselves in the heat of the afternoon and, when they paused to
drink, several began to chide the self-appointed supervisor. "Is it true that
you'll be the next hamlet chief, sir?" one inquired, much to the amusement
of the group. As one young man sipped alcohol, he addressed the grave:
"You're dead. Why did you leave your friend the boss here? He's sad now

that he's alone." These remarks reduced the young men and those watching to fits of laughter. The old man, however, dramatically expressed outrage at these remarks and asked the strangers present for some paper and a pencil so he could record what had been said. He declared that the young men had no respect, and he would complain to the Village Council. As he wrote, the young men threw small bits of earth to harass him mildly. Then they all departed together to return to the festivities at the house.

Cao Daists in the village observe the traditional funeral rituals with few innovations. They place the bier in front of the shrine honoring Cao Dai and, instead of having the Buddhist monk participate, they invite a group of the faithful Cao Daists to pray before the bier. Other members of the congregation to which the deceased belonged often bring traditional banderoles, bearing Cao Daist symbols and prayers. Many purchase their coffins from a Cao Daist coffin cooperative in Tan Huong. Members of the Tien Thien sect in surrounding villages donate time and labor in the production of coffins at the cooperative, and the coffins are then sold to members of the sect at reduced prices. The profits are divided between the workers and the Tien Thien temple in Tan Huong. When one poor member of the sect died in Khanh Hau, his coffin cost 1,300$ VN, a relatively low price, and it was paid for by the donations of the mourners.

Catholic villagers observe funeral rituals which vary considerably from the traditional practices. Ong Giap, the leader of the small Catholic group in the village, is expected to keep a death watch if a Catholic villager is dying. When it appears that death is near, he summons the priest from Tan An to administer the last rites. If the family of the deceased is wealthy, they may transport the corpse to the church in Tan An for funeral services which in such instances include a requiem mass to which the friends and kin are invited. In most cases, however, the funeral is held at home. The coffin is arranged before the Catholic shrine in the main room of the house, and the priest comes from Tan An to lead the rosary before the bier. Catholic families follow the traditional form of receiving guests and serving food, although they never have giang do. In the paddy fields on the northern edge of Ap Dinh-B there is a small plot of ground consecrated by the priest from Tan An, which is the cemetery for Khanh Hau Catholics. After the services in the house, the cortege is formed, and the body is transported to the cemetery for the burial.

After death and the traditional funeral, villagers observe a series of prescribed rituals which elevate the deceased to his place among the ancestors. Ritual prayers in the house after the funeral, and at the grave three days after the burial, properly belong to the complex of rituals associated with the Cult of the Ancestors. Subsequent to them, there is a series of prescribed, but not obligatory rituals during the first year, but they are not observed by most villagers because of the expense involved. After the graveside rite, something symbolizing the deceased (a photo and/or tablets on which his name is inscribed in characters) is placed on the altar of the ancestors. The name of the deceased must never be spoken, so the family refers to him by a pseudonym. The first 49 days for deceased males and the first 63 days for deceased females are marked by rituals every seven days. These are referred to numerically, e.g. Bay Ngay is the ritual of the seventh day, Muoi Bon Ngay is the ritual of the fourteenth day, and so on. On these occasions the family gathers at the house of the deceased where they place offerings on the altar of the ancestors and kowtow. Wealthy families usually retain the services of a Buddhist monk to lead prayers at these rituals. Services on the twenty-first and forty-ninth days are considered particularly important, so they tend to be more elaborate. With candles aglow on the flower-bedecked altar, the sons, in their gauzy mourning costumes, stand on either side of the altar to greet kin and friends who attended the funeral. Offerings are placed on the altar by members of the family, after which they kowtow. On the forty-ninth-day ritual, a paper containing the deceased's name, birth date, and death date is burned on the altar, a gesture to show that the proper funeral rituals have been observed. Both celebrations are followed by copious feasting.

The one hundreth day is marked by a ritual similar to those performed on each seventh day; there is also a first anniversary observance, celebrated by rich and poor alike. On the eve of the anniversary, the family gathers before the altar of the ancestors to recite vigil prayers (among the well-to-do these prayers are led by the Buddhist monk). On the following day the eldest male performs the first offering of food, tea, and clothes to the deceased. Dressed in mourning clothes, members of the family take burning joss and kowtow before the altar. Guests usually arrive after the ritual, and everyone sits down to a meal. A celebration marks the second anniversary, and it also signals the end of the mourning period. After the usual offerings of food and alcohol the officiant leads prayers and, after the family kowtows, their mourning clothes are burned on the altar. Subsequent death anniversary celebrations are similar in form. Among the wealthy they may last several days with 50 to 100 guests participating in the rituals and lavish feasting. Most villagers, however, have modest celebrations, inviting from 5 to 25 guests, and serving them simple fare. Catholic families usually have a mass said for the deceased, after which they return home to pray before the family shrine and receive guests for a meal.

As the lunar new year comes to a close and the harvest is gathered, the people of Khanh Hau give themselves over to a holiday mood, indulging in numerous village and family celebrations. Thuong Dien, the village feast marking the end of the harvest, is followed closely by Tet, as the lunar New Year celebration is commonly called. It is the time for everyone, even the urban dweller, to return to his natal village or to the village where his family tombs are located. There he re-establishes bonds with kinfolk, and for one week he becomes a villager again, participating in the simple pleasures of peasant life.

The first Tet ritual, held during the twelfth lunar month, is the fixing of family tombs, and it may be observed in one of two ways. First the family gathers at the house of the truong toc, and they may carry the necessary joss, votive papers, and the prescribed offerings of cake, chicken, tea, rice alcohol, and paper money to the graves. After requesting the Spirit of the Soil for permission to disturb the earth, the truong toc offers the food to the ancestors, and adult members kowtow before the graves and place burning joss on them. They then weed the plot, pile earth on the graves, and whitewash the stone tombs—tasks which they perform scrupulously, for the state of the graves reflects on the family. When their labor is finished they settle down to a picnic of the food offerings.

It also is permissible to return to the house of the truong toc after refurbishing the tombs and make the food offerings at the main altar there. This is followed by a feast to which guests usually are invited. Most villagers prefer having the food offering and meal at the tombs, and only a few prosperous families consistently have feasts at their homes. Several villagers go about fixing the graves of those who no longer have kin in the village. Most of these burial places have been reduced to barely visible weathered mounds, and a few chunks of dried soil may mark them for the coming year. Joss also is placed on them to prevent the deceased from becoming errant spirits.

On the twenty-third day of the twelfth lunar month the family celebrates the departure of Ong Tao, the Spirit of the Hearth, who is represented in the kitchen by three stones on which cooking is done, and honored with a small altar in an auspicious corner. Ong Tao observes the daily activities of the family, and on this day he returns to the celestial realm where he reports to the Emperor of Jade all he has observed during the year. He consequently can influence the family's destiny, and it is not uncommon for parents to place their children under his protection. Daily offerings are placed on his altar, and for the Tet ritual, red paper containing a sketch, which depicts the departure of Ong Tao on a large carp, a celestial horse, or a phoenix, is burned on the altar. The family then partakes of a feast which should include two traditional Tet dishes—glutinous rice cakes and the excessively sweet soybean soup. A bowl of the rice usually is placed on Ong Tao's altar, but during his absence no joss is burned on it.

On the thirtieth day of the twelfth lunar month, each family gathers at its house to prepare for the arrival of the souls of the ancestors and the return of Ong Tao. A few families retain the traditional practice of placing before the house a symbolic tree made from bamboo branches on which votive paper, a rectangular talisman of straw, a small sack of rice, and a container of water are tied. Joss burns continuously on the altar of the ancestors. Around nine o'clock in the evening the usual calm of the village is shattered by bursts of exploding firecrackers intended to chase evil spirits, and anyone entering the house must wash his feet.

While awaiting midnight, the hour for receiving the ancestors and Ong Tao, women prepare the soybean soup while the men continue to set off firecrackers, careful to guard a good supply for midnight so the entrance of ancestors and Ong Tao will not be marred by the presence of evil spirits. At midnight all adult members of the family, dressed in traditional clothes, gather before the ancestral altar where the eldest male makes an offering of food and burns red votive paper. Each member then takes a stick of burning joss and kowtows before the altar. This ritual is followed by a meal in which special Tet dishes are served. Prayers are recited at the altar through the night as a vigil for the first day of the new lunar year.

Mon Mot is the first day of Tet, and with it comes a certain anxiety that bad luck will enter the house and plague the family during the entire year. The primary function of the symbolic tree is to bar the entrance of the Celestial Dog, a bearer of ill fortune. Since firecrackers have the same effect, the tree is not absolutely necessary (which probably explains why many villagers do not bother to prepare one). Many villagers purchase leafless branches of an apricot or pear tree that they hope will burst with exquisite blossoms on the first day of Tet, portending good fortune for the family. On this day there is a great deal of visiting, so some members of the family remain at home to receive guests and serve them tea, rice alcohol, and candied fruits and vegetables. Guests with favorable names such as Tho (longevity), Loc (abundance), and Kim (gold) are particularly welcome in the belief that they bring the good fortune their names import. On the other hand, those with unfavorable names such as Meo (cat), Cho (dog), or

Lon (vagina) are not encouraged to visit. Around six o'clock in the evening, offerings are made at the altar of the ancestors, and the family sits down to another meal of Tet dishes.

On the third day of Tet some villagers observe a ritual honoring two military heroes of antiquity—Hanh Binh and Hanh Truong. Chicken boiled in a special way is served at a large feast during which the host invites the two heroes to participate, requesting that they in return protect the house during the coming year. After the meal the feet of the chicken are attached to one of the rafters. If the claws draw inward after a while, it is considered a good sign, but if they open out they release bad luck. The important ritual of the fourth day of Tet is the departure of the ancestors. This resembles the other rituals honoring the ancestors, and it also is an appropriate time for exploding firecrackers. The fifth day is inauspicious for traveling, having feasts, and engaging in a number of other activities, so it tends to be un-eventful as is the sixth day. On the seventh and last day of Tet, the symbolic tree is removed, and the various talismans are kept in the house during the year. The family has a final meal to mark the end of the new year celebration.

INHERITANCE

According to Vietnamese tradition, ancestral cult land always is the trust of the truong toc, who represents adult members of the patrilineage or a segment of it as collective owners. In Khanh Hau, on the death of the truong toc, a family council of both male and female adult members selects his replacement. Inheritance of the paternal house also is relatively well defined. Whereas primogeniture traditionally determines inheritance of the paternal house in Vietnam, ultimogeniture is the rule in Khanh Hau. With other real and mobile property, the usual practice is for parents to agree on the division among their children, after which the children are informed, and they are expected to accept it without complaint. In wealthy families this decision generally is expressed in written form.

Should the father die first, his widow assumes control of all family property and, if no arrangement has been made for its distribution, she may do so. If both parents die without arranging for the inheritance, the children are expected to divide it among themselves. Females inherit land, although males have prior claim should the amount of land be too small for equal distribution. In the case of a minor child, the eldest brother usually assumes trust of the inheritance until the child reaches maturity.

Inheritance presents no problem for most families in Khanh Hau for they have little to leave to their children, but the wealthy villagers are scrupulous about arranging inheritance. They invariably declare some land to be huong hoa and, in some instances where landholdings are large, titles are distributed prior to death.[15] Land inheritance is the cause of some squabbling among kin, and as landholdings diminish because of fragmentation with each generation, equitable division becomes a problem.[16] One solution is to pass title to the sons in common with the agreement that each will have use of the land for a fixed period. Villagers point out that this rotating usufruct has the advantage of giving each son a greater, if intermittent, income than if the land were divided. They also emphasize that with this arrangement the family landholding remains intact (at least for one generation).

15. In one such case described in Chapter 10, Ong Ke Hien, the highest venerable, has declared five *mau* of his large landholding to be huong hoa, and he already has granted land titles to some of his heirs.

16. Some inheritance difficulties brought to the attention of the Village Council are discussed in Chapter 7, and one case of downward social mobility related to fragmentation of family landholding is described in Chapter 10.

CHAPTER 6

Livelihood Patterns and the Economic System

CULTIVATION of rice is the most important activity in Khanh Hau, and practically everyone is engaged in it. In many respects it might be considered a highly structured social institution. Rooted in a tradition of several thousand years, the cycle of preparing, planting, tending, irrigating, and harvesting is reassuringly repetitious. Rice cultivation in the Mekong delta not only reflects this tradition, but also reflects the alterations that have taken place in it as the Vietnamese peasants in their southward migration adjusted to new physical environments, sometimes devising new techniques and sometimes borrowing from the indigenous Cham and Khmer farmers. Drawing on this experience, the settlers in Khanh Hau learned to maintain the necessary balance among soil, seeds, water, sun, and available fertilizer. In time they also selected artifacts they considered functional—a harrow, waterwheels, a Khmer plow, water scoops, knives, sickles, threshing sledges, baskets, winnowing machines, granaries, and rice mills. The result is a well-defined pattern of planting.

In rice cultivation as in any social institution, there are clearly drawn roles—landowners, tenants, laborers, rice millers, rice merchants, and gleaners. There also are things sacred. Specific deities associated with successful rice cultivation are venerated in individual and collective rituals, and should there be a catastrophe such as a drought, tradition provides the proper ritual to cope with it.

Secondary crop cultivation is less structured. Fruit cultivation for a cash crop on what might be considered a commercial scale is relatively new, and most secondary crops are found in kitchen gardens. There is a wide range of fruits and vegetables from which the villager may choose, and households vary in their gardening techniques. Animal husbandry is widespread, and more families raise chickens and pigs than buffalo, cattle, or ducks. One family has a pair of oxen, one man breeds doves, and one woman keeps two goats. Several villagers raise fish on a commercial scale, and many villagers engage in fishing. With the exception of an occasional snake chase, there is no hunting. Food gathering is not uncommon, although only a few villagers do it from necessity.

Most other occupations and specializations are ancillary to agricultural activities. All artisans farm as do the medical practitioners (two male nurses who deal in Western medicine and the variety of traditional healers). Entrepreneurs, including rice millers and rice merchants, are landowners who rent part of their land and hire laborers to cultivate the remainder. Rice agriculture supports all the religious specialists: the Buddhist monks and nuns hire laborers to work the pagoda land, and the leaders of the Cao Daist congregations and of the Catholics are farmers. Only some shopkeepers (vendors of general goods, pharmacists, tailors, and barbers) and women engaged in petty commerce neither own nor rent land.

RICE CULTIVATION

When the last of the paddy has been harvested in March, the air becomes still and the soil parched and dusty in the yellow heat of the dry season. Fortunate laborers with dry-season work assist their employers in repairing bundings, clearing irrigation channels, and other tasks best done at this time of year. The less fortunate usually seek work in Tan An. Most villagers also occupy themselves with house repairs—replacing thatching with the aid of kin and neighbors or fixing roof tiles. This also is an opportune time to repair or replace tools.

For those engaged in rice cultivation, the dry season means planning for the next crop. According to Delvert and Coquerel [1] the *Oryza sativa* species of rice predominates in both Cambodia and the Mekong River delta in Vietnam, although *O. glutinosa* also is cultivated. In Khanh Hau, both species are cultivated. Villagers distinguish between early or "hasty" *O. sativa,* harvested about 90 days after transplanting, and "rice of the season" or late *O. sativa,*[2] harvested close to 120 days after transplanting. They also have local designations for the array of subspecies they grow (see Appendix E). Some names are Vietnamese, and they often are descriptive; for example Rang Chon means "fox's fang," so called for its long thin grain, and Trang

1. Delvert, *Le Paysan Cambodgien,* pp. 332–42. Coquerel, *Paddys et Riz de Cochinchine,* p. 1.
2. In some parts of the delta, rice of the season and late rice are distinguished as two types of rice.

Nho is "little white." According to villagers, some designations such as Soc Nau and many beginning with *nang* are deformations of Khmer terms.

Several factors affect the farmers' decisions concerning which type of rice to cultivate. It is advisable for farmers with relatively high fields such as those found in Ap Moi to cultivate early rice because water drains easily from them, and it is less risky to have the crop mature sooner. Some varieties of rice are popular because they are considered hardy and are able to resist light floods or droughts. One of these is *ve vang*, which according to villagers was introduced into the village by the Service Agricole some 25 years ago. The amount of working capital a farmer has at the beginning of the planting season and the cost of fertilizer also are essential considerations in selecting types of rice. Fine varieties of rice, such as *nanh chon* known throughout the delta for its delicious flavor and exquisite fragrance while cooking, bring high prices on the market, but farmers are convinced they require more fertilizer than do other types.

Anticipated market price of rice probably is the factor most often discussed among the farmers during the dry season. Prices of the previous year are talked about in informal conversations, and the opinions of such successful farmers as Ong Ke Hien and the village chief are heavily weighed. In 1958, for example, most farmers decided not to cultivate any glutinous rice because the price had fallen drastically the previous year. A few of those who did plant it pointed out that there always is some demand for it—it is the prescribed type of rice for offerings in rituals, it is considered particularly nourishing for children and the aged, and is a convenient rice to feed labor gangs because it can be eaten by the handful with some salt. These farmers were willing to gamble on a price rise, given the demand and a reduced supply.

Late in April or early in May, the southwest winds bring rain to the delta, signaling the beginning of the planting season in Khanh Hau. When the first rains have sufficiently softened the soil the seedbeds are plowed, preferably to a depth of only 5 centimeters, so the soil will be finely tilled. The seedbeds then are harrowed. The seedbed is then left for a two-day "airing," after which it is plowed and harrowed again (some farmers repeat the process five or six times). Some farmers also favor rolling the surface to permit better drainage.

The plow currently used in Khanh Hau is a Khmer type adopted by villagers some thirty years ago in preference to a heavier Vietnamese plow, more difficult to maneuver. It is of wood with a metal plowshare fixed to an iron moldboard (see Fig. 21), which is drawn by a team of water buffalo

Plates

"Ap Dinh-A contains the primary school [far left], the Council House [structure at right with thatched roof], . . . and the century-old dinh" (p. 20).

"Most Ban Chin Dao rituals closely resemble traditional Vietnamese rituals observed in the village" (p. 68).

"Shortly after the feasting ended . . . the Village Council and members of the Cult Committee gathered outside the dinh to bring the imperial decree . . . from the shrine of Marshal Duc to the dinh" (p. 225). At left, the police agent who was slain by the Viet Cong.

"Food offerings were placed on the concrete slab before the tablet and also on the two shrines" (p. 231).

"The police agent, finance secretary, and civil status secretary kowtowed once and remained kneel-ing before the altar" (p. 224).

"The two boys in mandarin hats and robes took their positions beside the altar and announced the worshippers" (p. 231).

"The returning procession wends its way across the paddy fields" (p. 104).

"Older women invariably converge on the hardwood beds in the main room where trays of betel leaves . . . have been placed for their convenience" (p. 104).

"As they move across the paddy fields, the bride returns to the house, hiding her face as she quietly weeps" (p. 105).

"With their heads shaded by conical hats and cloths, the transplanters move across the fields in a row" (p. 138).

"Standing on the edge of the water source, the operators drop the basket into the water, and . . . lift the brimming basket, . . . swinging it so that it empties into the higher field" (p. 142).

"The thresher . . . grasps a bunch of plants by the stalks and beats it" (p. 146).

"Women usually carry the paddy, and they also spread it out before the house to sun it" (pp. 146–47).

"Most of them are poor elderly villagers or children of poor families, and they carefully search . . .
for sprigs containing grains" (pp. 147–48).

"Weaving for home consumption is done when the need arises, and for profit when an order is received" (p. 167).

"Known to all by his title, Ong Ke Hien [the highest venerable], he has the highest position on the Cult Committee and is the wealthiest resident of Khanh Hau" (p. 258).

"His only son is married, and Ong Ca Duoc is making plans to . . . acquire additional land to be declared huong hoa patrimony" (p. 263).

and guided by the farmer. The harrow, which looks like a large rake with rather widely separated teeth, also is pulled by buffalo and while one man guides the animals, another stands on the harrow to weigh it sufficiently. In order to protect the health of the animals and conserve their energy, the

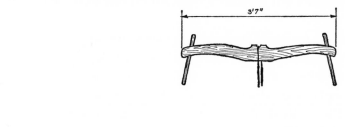

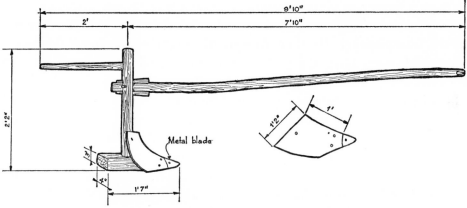

21. Plow.

usual working day is five hours (from 6:00 to 11:00 A.M.). For those who must hire the team, plow, and plowman, the rate is 60$ VN per workday. Farmers who own the plow and team, but must hire the plowman, pay him 30$ and one meal, although the price may be somewhat higher for those plowmen considered singularly adept.

Before sowing, most farmers perform a simple ritual to the Spirit of Agriculture, asking him for an abundant crop. This consists of offering some tea and cooked rice, but the usual joss sticks are absent because, as the farmers pointed out, burning joss closely resembles wilting rice plants —a bad omen. Rice seeds are soaked in water for two or three days after which they are kept in a dampened basket until they germinate. The sprouting seeds are scattered on the muddy surface of the seedbed, and for several days no water is allowed to collect until the seeds have settled.

If the rains continue, the farmers begin to prepare their fields for the transplanting which must be done before the seedlings are too high. Fields are plowed once, usually 8 to 10 centimeters deep, and harrowed twice in two directions at right angles. The man who can plow a straight and deep furrow enjoys a good reputation in the village, and he commands a higher than usual price if he should rent his services. Plowing normally takes five or six days for one hectare, but harrowing varies from one to three days per hectare.

When the fields are prepared and the seedlings are high, the farmer usually consults the lunar calendar for an auspicious day to transplant. Inauspicious days actually are few, and avoiding them would not entail a serious delay in transplanting. Many farmers in Khanh Hau hire transplanting teams organized by individuals in each hamlet. The organizer arranges with each farmer to do the transplanting on a specific day, and they agree on the number of workers, according to the size of the fields and the exigency of the transplanting. He then recruits his laborers from poor families— young girls, some boys, and perhaps several needy widows. The usual wage for each transplanter is 15 to 20$ VN per day plus two meals—a breakfast of glutinous rice and salt, and a lunch of soup, a vegetable, fish, and steamed rice. The team begins work at six in the morning, stops for lunch and a rest at eleven, then continues on until five in the evening. From time to time, usually owing to the necessity of getting a large area planted, teams work longer hours, but farmers estimate that one eight-hour day is sufficient for a team of twelve to transplant one hectare, and they figure the cost between 220 and 280$ VN, including the cost of the two meals.

The heavy work associated with transplanting requires male laborers, who are hired by the farmer. One laborer uproots the seedlings, collecting a bunch of thirty or so which he frees of mud by slapping them vigorously against his leg. He then ties them into bundles with palm-frond cord; another laborer collects the bundles, puts them into baskets suspended from a shoulder board, and carries them out to the flooded fields. With their heads shaded by conical hats and cloths, the transplanters move across the fields in a row. Clutching a bundle, a worker plants four seedlings at a time, each group 18 to 25 centimeters apart, and particular care is taken that the roots are sufficiently covered by the mud. The team organizer supervises the work, and generally the farmer will be present. Older villagers recall that the transplanting teams once sang to maintain the work rhythm and to relieve the monotony of the labor.

Insufficient rains can disrupt the planting pattern with catastrophic results. In 1958, when the rains were very light until the end of June, the seedlings began to wither. Although the fields were cracked and hard, some farmers began to plow in the hope that the rains would increase. Others attempted to sell their seedlings, but few were successful because either the roots were damaged when the plants were pulled up, or the plants had rotted from being left too long in the close-packed seedbed. The few farmers who did find buyers (most of whom were from villages closer to the Mekong where fresh water sources are more abundant) worked rapidly using hired laborers, loading the seedlings on trucks and boats. A few farmers with fields near the still-brackish watercourses reluctantly irrigated their seedbeds and fields with the saline water which they realized would have a deleterious effect on the soil. Finally despairing, many farmers let their livestock graze among the flaccid seedlings.

All rice farmers in Khanh Hau use chemical fertilizer. Before its introduction most farmers employed a mixture of buffalo manure, ashes, and a compost of straw and dead leaves—a fertilizer now restricted to gardens. Exactly when and how chemical fertilizer was introduced into the village are points of disagreement. The consensus is that it occurred over 20 years ago when a French entrepreneur proposed to Ong Ke Hien that he experiment with a sample on several hectares. The results were favorable; the plants visibly were hardier and had heavier heads than plants in other fields. Ong Ke Hien agreed to purchase a large amount of the fertilizer, and within 15 years all farmers were using it.

Prior to 1958 the most popular brand of fertilizer was Than Nong,[3] a phosphate tricalcic, containing 30 per cent P_2O_5. Importation of this product was discontinued in 1957; it was replaced by Than Tai which had the same ingredients and Tam Tai which varied somewhat, containing 25 per cent P_2O_2. Two brands of ammonium sulfate, Chim and Tien, both referred to as *diem* (sulfate) by the villagers, are available locally, and both contain 20 per cent nitrogen. Purchasing either type is an annual financial problem for most villagers; fertilizer is used relatively late in the growing season when most farmers are short of cash, and fertilizer prices have fluctuated in recent years, usually rising, sometimes as much as 400 per cent, when the need is greatest. Several aid programs designed to fix prices and make fertilizer available by extending government credit have been organized. In 1958 the Agricultural Credit Program of the government extended its benefits to the village, and with low-interest loans, many farmers were able to purchase fertilizer during the planting season. The National Revolutionary Movement, the predominant political party of the village, also organized a cooperative to purchase chemical fertilizer at lower prices for its

3. Farmers refer to the various chemical fertilizers by their brand names.

members, and this was the primary function of the Village Agricultural Cooperative which was dissolved in 1959, and the more recently organized Farmers' Association launched by the government.[4]

The use of fertilizer is based on one's past experience, and consequently it varies considerably. Most farmers mix the phosphate tricalcic with rice husks or ashes, but they prefer the ammonium sulfate in its pure form. The common preference seems to be to use phosphate tricalcic shortly after transplanting and one application of the ammonium sulfate about a month before the harvest. Some farmers time the second application of fertilizer by the appearance of the buds; others feel that the best time is when the plants are about 1 meter high. Farmers cultivating rice of lower quality sometimes mix the phosphate tricalcic and ammonium sulfate (1:2) for the second application.

There is a common belief that the more fertilizer employed, the more abundant the harvest. A well-to-do farmer is therefore apt to use a good deal more than the poor farmer (and with the agricultural credit loans, the amount of fertilizer employed in the village has undoubtedly increased greatly). Some farmers reported that they normally use 100 kilos of phosphate tricalcic and 25 kilos of ammonium sulfate to the hectare, while others claimed they used 250 and 150 kilos respectively. Another common belief among the farmers is that after years of applying chemical fertilizer, abandoning the practice would result in soil infertility.

After transplanting, the farmers usually check whether all plants are firmly rooted; wilting plants must be replaced. When the plants have begun to thrive, the major responsibilities are maintaining the bundings, weeding, and preventing crop damage by insects and disease. Weeds present no great problem, and a number of the farmers contend their fields do not require weeding. Where it is necessary, it is done by the women before the plants are 2 feet high, and the collected weeds are taken back to the farmstead for fodder. Farmers feel that after the plant has reached the height of 2 feet, weeds cannot inhibit the continued growth.

Most crop damage is caused by insects and disease. Green-winged insects, about the size of a rice kernel, attack the leaves and stem of the plant. Another pest is a worm that bores into the stem, gradually rotting the plant. Some older farmers contend that there has been a marked increase in these pests in the past twenty or thirty years, noting also that this correlates with the introduction of chemical fertilizer. Farmers previously relied on sudden heavy rains to rid the plants of pests, but pesticides are now available in Tan

4. These programs are discussed in detail below.

An. These are costly, however, and are used only by the well-to-do and farmers who cultivate large areas. Pesticides are generally considered more effective against surface insects than against borers.

Flying over the floating world of the Mekong River delta, it is difficult to conceive that water is a problem. In most of this area, however, tidal action carries brackish water a considerable distance inland. The rains usually begin in late April or early May and when the watersheds of the Annamite Cordillera have swelled, they flush the brackish water from the streams and rivers throughout the delta. The rains also flood the paddy fields, but irrigation still is essential to a successful crop. For the villagers the anxious period is from early May until August, when ample water is necessary to sustain the plants to almost mature height.[5]

In the 1958 drought the Village Council considered requesting the provincial authorities for permission to perform the traditional ritual asking heaven for rain.[6] This consists of gathering a large group of men, all with sticks, on the main road. Shouting invocations to heaven, they move the sticks as though they were paddling pirogues. The ritual was not necessary, however, as the rains came in great force within a week. In 1959 rainfall was normal and, because of its proximity to the Plaine des Joncs, Khanh Hau was not affected by the 1960 Mekong River floods which devasted large areas of the delta farther south; 1961 was described as an "ideal year."

The consensus among Khanh Hau farmers is that about 10 centimeters of water is the desired depth; more than that will drown the plants and with less they have a tendency to dry up. Given steady rains, maintaining the proper level is simply a matter of letting the water drain off by breaching the bunds. In unusual years, however, when the rains are too plentiful, there is great danger that the water level of the streams and canals will rise to that of the fields. When the plants reach maturity and the buds begin to sprout, the farmers drain their fields slowly so that by harvest time the soil is still soft and moist but not muddy. In addition to making harvesting easier, it is said to prevent rot in the base of the plant.

Three methods of irrigating the fields are used in Khanh Hau. The scoop

5. Villagers also fear disease when the supplies of potable water are low and, significantly, part of the Cau An celebration held in June is an exorcism of the cholera spirit from the village. During the 1958 drought, a 12-year-old girl died suddenly, and a rumor that she had died of cholera caused by drinking canal water spread through the village. The Village Council quickly refuted it.

6. Villagers were unable to explain why provincial permission was necessary. It is conceivable that provincial authorities under French rule were reluctant to permit the large gatherings that this ritual entails.

or basket lift, the foot-powered waterwheel, and the recently introduced gasoline-powered pump. According to older villagers, waterwheels were introduced into the village some 25 years ago; prior to that, irrigation was done exclusively by scoops and baskets. Two types of foot-powered waterwheels were brought to the village, but only one of them continues to be used. This is an arrangement of wooden paddles set at about 45° on a hub that moves clockwise, pushing the water forward. Circular wooden pedals are attached to either side of the hub, and the operators, leaning on an attached bar, tread on the pedals which move the paddles forward, pushing the water up to a height of half a meter. The other waterwheel, still used in central Vietnam, is larger and has a longer paddle mechanism, but the villagers found it cumbersome and heavy and prefer the smaller, simpler wheel.

There are several variants of the scooping method. For a one-man operation, a long triangular scoop is suspended from a tripod placed over a narrow water channel. The operator straddles the channel, and holding the small end of the scoop he shovels the water into an irrigation ditch. An alternative way requires two men, and the device is a conical basket with double ropes attached to each side. Standing on the edge of the water source, the operators drop the basket into the water, and then in unison they lift the brimming basket by stepping back and tightening the guide ropes, swinging it so that it empties into the higher field or channel. This is done rhythmically and quickly, and although it appears to be done with ease, it is the most difficult of the irrigation techniques.

The gasoline-powered pump is the most flexible technique in terms of lifting water to various heights, and it also can throw water some distance from the source. On the other hand, the pump is heavy, making it more difficult to transport to the fields. It also requires technical skill in its maintenance, and it is the most expensive method of irrigation. The deputy chief owns the only gasoline pump in the village, and when he is not using it he rents it to other villagers at the rate of 60$ VN per hour. At one point the village chief and deputy chief conceived of several schemes for purchasing or borrowing additional pumps for the village. They considered requesting funds from the provincial authorities, and they also discussed the possibility of forming two groups of a dozen or so prosperous farmers to buy pumps. It might have been possible, through the Fundamental Education School, to borrow a pump from the Department of Agriculture, but when the rains came suddenly this and the other schemes were no longer necessary.

Irrigating fields adjacent to water sources is no problem, but complexities arise when the fields are at some distance. One technique is to flood the fields closest to the source, then breach the bunds and allow the water to flow into the other fields. A more arduous but quicker method is to construct a temporary channel by building a low dike parallel to the bunding. (One group of farmers even received permission to cut a temporary channel through the spur road.) Distribution of water involves cooperation that is not always obtained, and the village authorities report that each year they must arbitrate conflicts over water. When there is cooperation, mutual-aid groups are formed to divide the task of irrigating. One group, for example, consisted of kin and friends, all of them Cao Daists of the Ban Chin Dao sect, and they farmed adjacent fields in Ap Moi. Being poor, they were unable to rent waterwheels, but they managed to borrow one from a fellow Cao Daist, and the guardian of the dinh lent them another one. Dividing into pairs, they took turns pedaling the wheels, and time was measured by burning joss sticks. In order to take advantage of the late morning high tide, they varied the usual meal schedule, taking breakfast at 7:00 A.M. and the main meal at 2:30 P.M. rather than at 11:00 A.M.

Another outstanding example of cooperation was the construction of the canal in Ap Thu Tuu. Early in 1958 a group of Ap Thu Tuu residents approached the Village Council with the proposal that a narrow canal be dug from the small branch of the Rach Don that courses through the hamlet to the main highway, where a small channel could continue under the highway through a conduit and connect with other channels fed by the Can Dop in Ap Dinh-A. While this would not increase the amount of navigable waterways in the village, it would permit better water distribution in the hamlet. The council, some of the venerables, and the residents of the hamlet met to decide the issue. The highest venerable gave his approval, and most residents were in favor (one woman protested that it would cut away too much of her paddy land). It was decided that each household benefiting from the canal would be responsible for digging a section 1 meter 60 centimeters long, 3 meters wide, and 1 meter 20 centimeters deep.

Kinsmen and friends cooperated to do the digging for households without many adult males, and only one work group, consisting of two boys 13 and 14 years old, appeared undermanned. In spite of the hard ground and a sun blazing with the intense heat of the mid-dry season, the work groups manifested glints of typical village humor. One worker loudly remarked that perhaps it would be more agreeable if the women came out and prepared tea for them, and then he added that they would have to work harder (indicating that they would be bound to show off). To this another worker responded, "Yes, but then the young men would be too busy looking at the women to work." When one work group diligently dug deeper than those on either side, one villager noted for his wit stopped them and admonished, "You work too hard. Don't you realize that if you keep it up, we'll have to shovel dirt into your hole to keep it at our level." Shortly afterward when a bus passed slowly by, someone shouted from it, "Are you building a new road?" to which the group wit replied, "Yes, a new road so we can drive our American automobiles over it."

As the plants thrive, the anxieties that mark the early part of the cycle begin to subside, and when the first fields of hasty rice turn a dull gold and the fragrance of ripened paddy is carried on the wind, the villagers feel reassured. There is exhilaration in the air as the harvest begins. In Khanh Hau it has three phases—the early harvest, usually beginning in mid-September; the middle harvest in December; and the peak harvest of the season in January and February, which tapers off with the last paddy gathered in March. It is a time of great activity. Piles of paddy appear before the houses, and vehicles of all descriptions as well as boats converge on the village to transport the gunny sacks of paddy to the farmsteads, rice mills, and markets.

All village families, even the wealthy, rally every able-bodied member to assist in the fields. It is imperative to complete the harvest as soon as possible; ripened grains easily fall to the ground, and rain beats down the already top-heavy plants, rendering them difficult to reap. The size of the field determines the number of workers in a harvesting team, and in some of the particularly large fields, several teams are necessary. Both men and women reap the plants. If threshing is to be done by hand, it is essential to cut the stalk at the base; a plant may be cut nearer the grains if it is threshed by treading or rolling. *Luoi hai* is the crudely fashioned sickle long used in the village (see Fig. 22); a more recently introduced sickle better suited to cutting a stalk midway is the *vong hai* which has a long blade and long handle with a **V** where the blade is connected. The **V** enables the worker to separate a group of plants, the stems of which are then wrapped around the blade and cut. Since this sickle also can be used to cut at the base of the plant and it requires less bending, its use is increasing.

Until thirty or forty years ago, threshing was done by treading or rolling, but only a few farmers continue to employ these techniques. After being cut, the plants were brought to the farmstead and spread on the ground. In the treading method, a draft animal (buffalo or ox), tied to a stake, moves in a circle treading on the plants. The same result is obtained by having an animal pull a heavy stone roller over the plants. The disadvantage of either

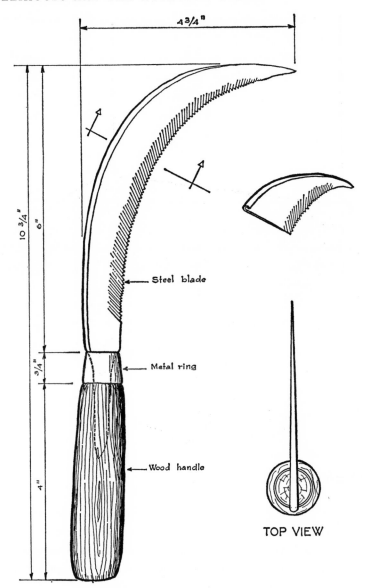

22. Sickle.

technique is that empty husks are not separated. On the other hand, tread-ing or rolling softens the stalks, making better fodder.

Co dap lua, the threshing sledge now used in Khanh Hau (see Fig. 23), consists of a wood and bamboo frame set on wooden runners, permitting the farmer to pull it through the mud, and since the sledge is light in weight, one able-bodied man can carry it on his back to and from the place of work.

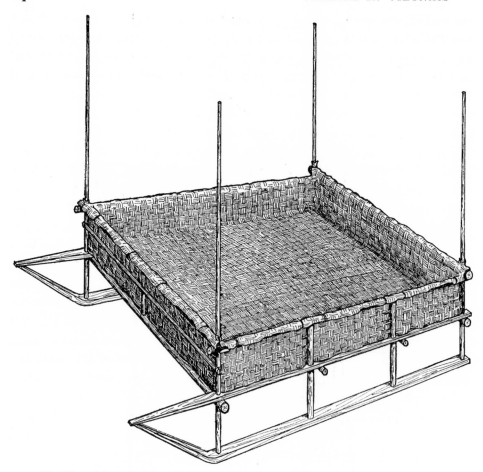

23. Threshing Sledge.

Reed matting is placed on the bottom and around the side, and for thresh-ing, larger mats 7 or 8 feet high are fixed as a wind screen around three sides. A wooden grill is fixed 4 or 5 inches from the bottom. The thresher, most often a man, grasps a bunch of plants by the stalks and beats it three or four times against the grill and side of the sledge, which usually cleans the plant of grains, although some empty husks remain attached. Villagers claim that paddy threshed in this manner commands a higher price on the market.

From time to time the paddy accumulated in the sledge is emptied onto mats and although some farmers prefer to measure it in the fields, using 1-gia (40-liter) containers, others simply pour it into sacks which are carried on shoulder boards to the farmstead to be measured. Women usually carry the paddy, and they also spread it out before the house to sun it.[7] A few families have their own wooden, locally-made winnowing machines which are hand operated. Families without these machines rely on the traditional method of slowly spilling a basketful of paddy while standing on a chair so that the wind separates grain from chaff. Many villagers have abandoned winnowing, merely raking the paddy as a means of cleaning it.

When the paddy is threshed, winnowed, and dried, most farmers separate the amount to be consumed by the family during the coming year from paddy to be used for rent, sold, or paid to hired workers. Farmers estimate that an efficient team of three, working from six to eleven in the morning and from two to five in the afternoon can produce from 18 to 20 gia of paddy per day, and currently they are paid 10 per cent of the total. Many of the poorer farmers simply pile their paddy in the corner of a room, but most villagers have cylindrical woven-reed bins, kept in one of the rear rooms of the house. These are available in varying sizes at the Tan An market, and usually are placed on straw, wood, or woven mats for protection against the damp ground. Rodents are a constant problem, and most villagers let their chickens feed freely on the stored paddy. Prosperous farmers with very large amounts of paddy commonly rent storage space in one of the local rice mills, and most of this is sold later in the year when the prices tend to rise. In August 1958, for example, the deputy chief was reported still to have 500 gia of the exquisite Rang Chon rice, 200 gia of Ve Vang, and 300 gia of Soc Nau; Ong Xa Khanh, a wealthy farmer, had 1,000 gia of Soc Nau and some 400 gia of an unspecified variety of glutinous rice.

In areas of the village where water is plentiful, farmers usually cultivate a second rice crop. Generally, however, it is considered a risky venture. They feel that the soil has been sapped to some extent by the first crop, which demands more fertilizer, and the yields invariably are smaller than the first crop. Also there is the danger that the rains may diminish sooner than expected, and the second crop may suffer from lack of water. On the other hand, it is not necessary to plow or harrow the fields before transplanting the second crop. Most farmers simply roll the fields, crushing the stubble left from the first harvest.

When the harvest workers have left the fields for the tasks of drying, winnowing, and storing the paddy, the gleaners appear. Most of them are poor elderly villagers or children of poor families, and they carefully

7. Some rice merchants in the village complain that a number of farmers do not properly dry their paddy, resulting in many broken grains when it is milled.

search among the plant stubs for sprigs containing grains. Some even scrupulously collect grains that have fallen from the plants or grains left in the threshing area. For some farmers, the final act of the cycle is to burn the brittle stubble to provide ash fertilizer.

CULTIVATION OF FRUITS AND VEGETABLES

In his stratified-sample survey of households in Ap Moi, Ap Dinh-A, and Ap Dinh-B, Hendry[8] found that approximately half raised both fruits and vegetables, but 22 per cent did not raise either. Vegetable and fruit cultivation appeared to be more common among upper economic level villagers, and only a few households in the sample sold any portion of their produce. In 1959 the pattern of fruit cultivation began to change. There was considerable talk about the high profits of fruit producing, and several well-to-do villagers planted fruit groves in former paddy fields. In addition to the experimental fruit and vegetable garden established in Ap Dinh-B (which will be discussed presently), several farmers in Ap Moi and Ap Dinh-A planted groves with banana, orange, grapefruit, and lime trees, and by 1962 there were several sizable fruit groves along the national highway. One farmer in Ap Dinh-B planted a crop of sugar cane, but the 1958 drought destroyed the plants and the venture ended. In 1959 several families also began cultivating vegetables as a cash crop. One family living near the Ban Chin Dao Cao Dais temple in Ap Dinh-A planted a large vegetable garden in a section of their paddy land, and with the aid of kin and friends dug a deep reservoir for irrigating the garden and their rice seedbeds as well. The produce of the garden was destined for the Tan An market.

A wide variety of vegetables is cultivated in Khanh Hau kitchen gardens (see Appendix E). Potatoes are supposed to have been introduced into Vietnam by the French, as were some varieties of beans (French haricot is used redundantly with Vietnamese *dau* to designate bean), and deformation of French terms is seen in *cai sa-lat* (*salade*) for a variety of lettuce, and *ca to-mat* (*tomate*). Green beans and potatoes usually are only served on festive occasions, and the latter are prepared in a French-style ragout with saffron or curry powder added. A few of the local vegetables have no known Latin and/or English designations. One of these is *cai cu*, a tuber, cultivated in most gardens. The root is boiled and served in soup; the leaves are preserved in brine, and they too may be added to soup.

Among the most popular vegetables are a white-stemmed Chinese cabbage

8. *Economic Activities,* p. 144.

also preserved in brine and usually consumed in soup. The plant produces a small yellow flower which, when powdered, is the basis for a mustard-like substance used in cooking. Many garden arbors contain the prickly balsam pear, and it can either be served in soup or stuffed with ground meat and steamed; although extremely bitter, it is very popular and is thought to have the medicinal effect of "refreshing" the stomach and intestines. Red chili peppers crushed or sliced are eaten with most meals, and mint is served with meat dishes. Carrots are pickled in brine and customarily added to fish sauce as a condiment.

Several varieties of onion are widely cultivated, and green leafy vegetables are consumed almost daily by villagers. Boiled corn provides a convenient snack, and yams, a low-prestige food, are eaten only during lean times as a substitute for rice. In 1957, through the agency of the Village Council, some so-called American varieties of tomatoes and corn were introduced, but they were not accepted. Villagers felt that foreign varieties (in spite of their having French varieties) were not suited to their conditions, and they thought the new strain of corn had an inferior flavor.

Garden techniques vary with the different types of plants, and households sometimes differ in their methods. Hendry summarizes the general pattern in the following description:

> Most households prepare the ground by turning it with shovel or pickaxe, then mounding it in rows so that water will collect between the rows and the moisture will be retained. Practically no households use draft animals on garden plots. Chemical fertilizers are used if farmers can afford it, but otherwise they use buffalo manure, ashes, and on rare occasions, night soil. It is difficult, however, to get firm information on the use of night soil. Most people deny they use it, but if questioned, they will also say that some other households use it occasionally.
>
> One common practice is to spread ashes on the ground after it has been turned, and then wait 20 days before planting. Just prior to planting, a second treatment of ash is added, sometimes together with chemical fertilizer or buffalo manure. Both phosphate tricalcique and ammonium sulphate are used, but there seems to be a preference for the former. Buffalo manure is collected by individual households if they are poor, or purchased if the family can afford to do so. The manure is sometimes mixed with ashes and straw, but it is often applied

directly to the garden plot. The timing of fertilizer applications also varies, with most farmers adding fertilizer throughout the growing season as they feel there is need for it.[9]

Another common garden fertilizer is prepared by mixing animal dung and rice husks.

It was pointed out previously that because of a vein of sandy soil, the central portions of Ap Moi and Ap Dinh A–B are considered the best places in the village for garden cultivation. Water in these sections, however, is scarce, and while rainfall is sufficient for ordinary kitchen gardens, irrigation is necessary for larger, cash-crop gardens. The aforementioned reservoir is one solution, and although villagers consider wells costly, a few farmers recently have investigated the possibility of wells for garden water. One group of Ap Dinh-B farmers pooled money to retain the services of a Tan An man noted for his ability to locate well sites. When he had found a likely place, the farmers insisted on performing a ritual, making offerings of joss, tea, chicken rice soup, boiled chicken, and rice alcohol to the Spirit of the Soil, asking permission to disturb his domain.

While parts of other hamlets are near good sources of water, the heavy clay soil renders them unsuitable for garden cultivation. Residents of Ap Cau and Ap Nhon Hau have water and good soil, but the lush vegetation around their farmsteads provides too much shade for good kitchen gardens. A few villagers have taken advantage of rent-free land and availability of water to arrange small, elongated gardens on the dikes along the canals. A curious kitchen garden also is kept by the Self-Defense Guards along the road between the dinh and the military stockade. Watered by the drainage ditch, rows of vegetables grow amid the barbed-wire entanglements.

Many varieties of fruit are cultivated in Khanh Hau (see Appendix E). Some of these require considerable care and others grow almost wild in the village. Coconut palms abound, and all three varieties common to the delta are found in Khanh Hau. *Dua xiem* is a relatively short tree that is supposed to be native to Thailand (Xiem is the Vietnamese name for Siam), and *dua ta* is the most common type of coconut palm found in Vietnam. The *dua gan quan* palm produces a yellow-colored nut that is considered the best fruit of the three varieties. Some four or five years after a nut is planted, the tree begins to bear fruit. It is preferable that the tree be close to a good source of water, and each year fresh mud is banked around the base of the tree. When it begins to bear fruit, latania fronds often are tied around the

9. Pp. 149–50.

trunk to prevent rats from reaching the fruit, and care must be taken to remove worms that bore into the trunk (these worms are eaten as a delicacy).

Coconut trees produce throughout the year, and the number of nuts produced increases annually, reaching a maximal production of five to ten coconuts per month after twenty years. This number diminishes somewhat after thirty years, but a tree will continue to bear fruit until it dies (some trees in Khanh Hau are over eighty years old). Coconut trees grow thickly in Ap Nhon Hau and Ap Cau, and close to the water sources in the other hamlets. Some farmers plant a grove with channels for water between the rows of trees, but most coconut palms are simply planted here and there around the farmstead. A few farmers with groves dry the meat and sell it to merchants in Tan An for copra oil, but most prefer to sell the whole nut. Within the village the market for coconuts is good. The meat is shredded into the milk and is served to guests, and this combination also is used in preparing a sweet soup served on festive occasions. Coconut milk also is used extensively in cooking. The shells, when dried, make excellent fuel.

Tall, graceful areca palms thrive particularly well in Ap Cau and Ap Nhon Hau, and they are planted and cared for in much the same way as the coconut palm. After four or five years they begin to produce clusters of rust-colored nuts. Betel vines usually are planted to twist around the trunk of the areca palm. The sliced nut is wrapped in betel leaf and garnished with lime; it provides a mild stimulant when chewed. It is particularly popular among elderly women and some elderly men and is thought to "refresh the heart." Betel leaves and areca nuts are sold in the village, but since the local supply is insufficient to meet the demand, they are also brought in from the Tan An and Tan Huong markets.

Lime, grapefruit, tangerine, orange, and mango shoots must be purchased in the vicinity of My Tho town, and since they are relatively costly, cultivation is limited to the prosperous. These fruit trees require considerable care, and the produce, particularly the mangos, commands high prices in the local markets. Several households in Ap Dinh-B, near the Cao Daist temple, grow a type of tea plant with rather large leaves. They are difficult to cultivate, but in addition to being practical, their box-hedge appearance makes them very decorative.

Banana trees are ubiquitous in the village, and in most farmsteads they grow in disorganized profusion. *Chuoi gia,* long, green bananas, are the most commonly cultivated variety. *Chuoi com,* also known as *chuoi cao,* is an exquisite small yellow banana that is very sweet to the taste and, because of its delicate appearance, is considered singularly appropriate as an offering in rituals. *Chuoi su,* a short, fat, yellow banana, is best for deep frying. Some of the better varieties are sold, but most bananas are consumed by the family. Usually they are eaten raw as dessert, and some shopkeepers prepare a confection of the chuoi gia by drying them in the sun and sprinkling them with sesame seeds. In spite of the seeming abundance of bananas, villagers continue to purchase them, particularly the chuoi su and chuoi com in the Tan An market. Papaya trees, like banana trees, are everywhere. They grow rapidly, require no real care, and produce amply. A few papayas are sold in the local shops, but they are too easily cultivated to be a valuable cash crop. Papaya cut into slices often is served to guests. Peach trees and other fruit trees listed in Appendix E are much less widely grown.

Some of the numerous trees that grow wild in the village (see Appendix E) produce seasonal fruit which is gathered either by those on whose property the trees are located or by small boys (using a loop attached to a bamboo pole for fruit growing high). Tamarind trees grow here and there, and the thin crescent-shaped fruit is used in a fish soup, although many do not care for its acrid flavor. *Trai keo* or *keo tay* is a small round sweet fruit that appears around the lunar new year, heralded by mauve-colored blossoms. *O-moi* (wild black fruit) is plentiful during the second lunar month; it is a long, sausage-like fruit with a hard skin, and it has a sweet, but indistinctive flavor. Some villagers slice it into an earthen jar of rice alcohol which is then buried for at least 100 days, producing a pleasant liqueur considered good for the digestion. *Binh linh* is a type of wild tree usually found in the tangled hedge growths around farmsteads, and it produces a small seed that poor villagers grind and brew as a substitute for tea.

Three not very common wild trees in the village produce fruit that villagers of all ages enjoy gathering. *Trung ca* (literally "fish eggs") are so called because they are bunches of berries that resemble large fish-egg clusters. *Le ki ma* is the mamey sapodilla or mamey sapote, a round, orange-colored rather sweet fruit, and *mang cau,* known in English as anona or custard apple, is a small, green fruit. Wild vegetables are gathered by needy families for the most part. *Rau dang ruong* is a bitter vegetable that grows in the paddy fields. *Den den gai,* a wild spiney type of green leafy vegetable, resembles spinach, and *rau muong* is a floating vine. Other vegetables of this genre are *rau cang cua, rau mo,* and *rau ma,* all of which may be eaten raw or cooked, and they often are used with shrimp in a soup.

INDUSTRIAL CROPS

Latania water palm provides the most commonly used construction material in the village. A mature plant produces a large segmented nut with an edible center, but most villagers prefer to plant the nut in the soft mud on the edge of a water course to grow a new tree. This palm has no trunk; the fronds sprout directly from the soil, and in order for them to be thick and sturdy, fresh, soft mud and fresh water are necessary. After approximately one year, the fronds reach a height anywhere from 10 to 25 feet; they are then cut and dried and used as thatch.

Bamboo, another widely used construction material, is planted by villagers in their farmsteads, and stands also grow wild amid the tombs, in the hedge growths, and along paths. It takes about three years for a stand to mature. Because of their particular fondness for bamboo, villagers prefer to preserve whatever is growing around the house and purchase what they need in the nearby markets. Kapok trees are planted by some villagers, and they also grow wild in drier parts of Ap Dinh A–B and Ap Moi. Kapok cotton is used primarily for stuffing pillows.

Medicinal Plants

Some medicinal plants are cultivated in kitchen gardens; others are gathered in and around the village. As indicated earlier, chili pepper is considered a preventive against worms (in addition to being a popular condiment), and is grown in every garden. One farmer in Ap Moi, with a long history of respiratory ailments, has fashioned a gnarled cigarette holder from the root of this plant in the belief that the heat contained in the root (and manifest in the pepper) is disseminated to his lungs when he inhales, alleviating his difficulties. Other local medicinal plants are *cay muon,* which is applied to herpes and other skin disorders and *co muc,* which provides a gargle. *Voi voi* is good for backaches, and *day mong toi* applied to the eyes is supposed to cure conjunctivitis.

The Experimental Garden

In 1958 an experimental garden was established in Ap Dinh-B with funds donated by the Asia Foundation of San Francisco. Mr. Nguyen Van Mung, then the UNESCO representative in Khanh Hau, was instrumental in obtaining the money and supervising its use. The Village Council organized the project, announcing it to the villagers and accepting bids for the labor. The group that won the bidding was led by Ong Quan, a tenant farmer who at one time was information officer in the village, and who occasionally supervises the cooking at large weddings and village feasts, Ong Thu, a farmer from Ap Dinh-B, and Ong Trung, a farmer also skilled in carpentry.

The site of the garden was a plot next to the spur road, rented from the village chief. Long islands were made by digging deep ditches, connected with a channel fed by the Can Dop, on which the plants were cultivated. Shoots and small trees were purchased from the government nursery in My Tho, and there the group also received some instruction in improved techniques for garden cultivation. For example, mango trees are difficult to grow, and the government agents advocated placing small bits of buffalo hide in the hole with the newly planted shoots. They also gave instructions in using bone and composting for preparing fertilizer. Chemical fertilizer was recommended for the guava, mango, lime, and grapefruit trees, and a mixture of phosphate tricalcic and water for the vegetables.

Banana trees, 128 of them, dominated the garden and provided shade for small plants that might wilt with too much sun. The 12 mango shoots also were carefully shaded by pieces of palm frond stuck in the ground. There were 20 lime trees, 20 guava trees, and 19 grapefruit trees. Rows of corn were planted on the outer edge of each island, and kitchen-garden vegetables were cultivated between the rows of trees. The plots were fenced against animals by barbed wire strung through concrete posts, which were cast in wooden forms by the contractors.

Late in 1959 the garden appeared to be doing well. Some bananas had been picked and sold in the Tan An market, and the trees were producing amply. With the exception of the corn, the vegetables were thriving as were the fruit trees. By 1962, however, the garden was considered something of a failure. The corn and vegetables were gone. Banana and coconut trees were withering, and only the mango trees continued to grow amid the weeds that had invaded the islands. From the start, many villagers had been pessimistic about the garden, regarding it as an interesting but costly venture. Some living nearby attributed its failure to relatively poor soil and intense heat.[10]

ANIMAL HUSBANDRY

Villagers attribute success in pig raising to *tay* (literally "hand") which appears to be akin to the notion of a "green thumb," and often they speak of tay in association with *phan* or destiny, indicating a divinely ordained talent. The concept also extends to raising other animals, and it tends to generate a certain amount of apathy among those who manifestly do not possess this gift. They feel that without it, raising animals beyond a very small scale is a fruitless endeavor. Those who engage in small-scale pig

10. Signs of neglect were striking, and it is possible that since the garden was supported by American funds, the political difficulties of the 1960–62 period had something to do with the failure. Often the Viet Cong threaten villagers cooperating with government or American Aid projects.

raising usually purchase one or two piglets each year, keeping them for six or seven months, after which they are sold in the Tan An or Tan Huong markets.[11] Pigs usually are fed rice bran mixed with banana tree pulp, and table scraps are collected for them. They also forage for food in the house and yard, and only in a few farmsteads are they confined to sties.

A few farmers with tay raise pigs on a grander scale, and they exercise greater care with them. Sows are not bred until they are at least five months old then not more than twice a year. The birth of a litter is carefully supervised to prevent damage to the piglets, and for the first 15 days they are kept apart from the sow to prevent their being smothered. Feeding also is supervised, and the piglets are carefully rotated so each will receive ample milk. When a sow has produced a litter, she is fed a mixture of rice and rice bran. Over a period of one month, the amount of rice is reduced and the bran correspondingly increased in the belief that with this diet the sow will have piglets with better skin and hair as well as longer ears—all characteristics of robust health.

Disease is a prevalent problem in pig raising, and the only recourse when illness is manifest is to purchase a Veterinary Service inoculation from the village nurse.[12] Some villagers admitted trying to sell a sick pig to an individual buyer or a slaughterhouse, often with success. Although it is required by law that the death of an animal be reported, few villagers bother to do so, usually consuming the meat at home or trying to sell it in the local markets.

In 1956 the Ministry of Agriculture introduced pigs of new strains into Khanh Hau. These pigs were distributed with the requirement that those who received them would repay the government with one or two piglets from the first litter, to be given to other villagers under the same arrangement. Disease struck, however, and despite widespread inoculation, most of the new stock died. As one of the program participants, the guardian of the Ap Dinh-A dinh received a Yorkshire sow which produced one litter of six piglets, all of which died in the epidemic. On a daily diet of 40 liters of rice bran and chopped stalks of banana trees, however, the sow has grown to be the largest in the village, and the guardian shares the opinion of other villagers that the new strains really were no more susceptible to disease than

11. Hendry, p. 169. In Hendry's stratified sample, two fifths of the households raised pigs, and of these there was a large proportion of middle economic level villagers (identified as those who own between 2 and 4 hectares or rent between 2.5 and 5 hectares of paddy land). Hendry also found that two thirds of the households raised one pig annually, and only 10% raised as many as three or more pigs. Finally, around 92.5% of the pigs raised were sold in nearby markets.

12. *Toi* is the generic term employed by the villagers for any disease striking livestock.

the local strains. Also, they feel that the hogs produced through interbreed-ing of the new stock and the local are more robust, and the meat has a better flavor.

Most families in the village raise some chickens and many also keep a few ducks.[13] Because of the relatively small ponds and lack of space, however, duck raising on any commercial scale is difficult; most families keep only a small number to provide a delicacy for special occasions such as weddings or anniversaries of ancestors' deaths. One family in Ap Dinh-A who had a large flock of ducks herded them into the muddy paddy fields that already had been harvested to forage for grains, but moving them from one field to another caused some complaints from owners of unharvested fields, who contended the ducks did damage to their crops. At a sacrifice to their schooling, the children tended them, and of the 1,000 ducks in the flock at its maximum, 900 survived for market.

Chickens abound in the village, and limitations on chicken raising lie for the most part in diseases. Normally the chickens are allowed to roam freely in the farmstead, feeding on whatever is available. They have access to the bins where the paddy is stored and scurry through the house, some-times competing with the dogs for scraps from table and brazier. They rum-mage through the gardens, pick along the roads, and even invade shops and pagodas. At times they seem to be omnipresent. Some families feed their chickens regularly—rice scraps from the bowls and pots, and often children have pet chickens for which they gather paddy. Generally, however, the chickens fend for themselves, and in their quest for food, small young chickens sometimes are prey for snakes.

The only recorded innovations in poultry raising were attempted by Mr. Nguyen Van Mung when he was director of the UNESCO School of Funda-mental Education. New poultry stock was provided by the Ministry of Agriculture center in Tan An, and Mr. Mung arranged for their reception by 15 families in Ap Dinh A–B. These families already had received instruc-tion in building chicken coops and new feeding methods, including a mix-ture of broken rice, paddy, leaves of vegetables, grass, rice bran, egg shells, ground shrimp, and various types of fish. Unfortunately, the chickens pro-vided for this experiment died within a short period of time. The reaction of the villagers was mixed—some attributed the deaths to diseases that

13. Nearly four fifths of the households in Hendry's sample raised chickens, ducks or both. Of all, about two thirds did so for home consumption, and a larger number of lower economic level households sold part of their poultry. Not one family in the sample sold either duck or chicken eggs. (P. 168.)

affect the local strains, others were skeptical of the adaptability of new strains, and a few felt it was celestial retribution for misdeeds. Many of the villagers who participated in the experiment, however, were not discouraged by the negative beginning, and they have continued to use the same techniques, but with indigenous stock, happily reporting an increase in egg laying as well as in the size of the chickens. Another innovation was the introduction of small kerosene-burning incubators with eggs supplied by the Ministry of Agriculture center in Tan An. Villagers by and large were not enthusiastic about this device. They felt it was not a marked improvement over the natural method of hatching eggs. For the villagers it remained more economical to pay four or five piasters for day-old chicks in Tan An than to risk hatching the two-piaster eggs in the incubators.

One woman in Ap Dinh-B tends two goats for her sister, a resident of Tan An. These are the only goats in the village, and their milk is highly prized as a food beneficial to the ailing. The man in Ap Dinh-A who operates a motorcycle transport between the village and Tan An supplements his income by breeding doves valued for their beautiful singing, which he sells to wealthy families in the vicinity. Pets are common in the village. Children often keep chickens and ducks as pets, and captured birds are found in some houses. One family has a monkey, fat with age and lack of exercise. Cats are rarely seen (perhaps because cat flesh is a great delicacy), but dogs are everywhere. Villagers point out that unlike the northern Vietnamese, they do not eat dog because they are the "guardians of the house."

The initial cost of large animals and their limited usefulness are major deterrents to widespread ownership in Khanh Hau.[14] Grown cattle and buffalo sell for at least 4,000$ VN and calves for around 2,000$. In 1956 the Agricultural Service initiated a program under which a farmer could borrow up to 3,500$ to purchase buffalo imported from Thailand. Although some farmers felt the Thai buffalo were smaller and did not work so well as the local buffalo, they welcomed the opportunity to obtain livestock under these conditions. After one year, however, for reasons unknown, the program ceased.

Cattle and buffalo are little used as beasts of burden. Of the two, buffalo are considered better for farm work, but aside from the plowing, harrowing,

14. In Hendry's sample survey, three fifths of the households reported that they owned neither cattle nor buffalo, and only 5% of the sample owned both. There also were fewer (18%) of the households with buffalo than cattle (27%). Most families with buffalo owned two; only one family had one and several had four or more. With cattle, however, the pattern is different; one third of the sample had one cow, and nearly three quarters owned two or more cows. (P. 170.)

and occasional threshing, they are unproductive. Cattle are raised primarily for sale or slaughter. Some village families consume beef frequently, and at all family celebrations there are some beef dishes. Cattle also are taken to the Tan Huong or Tan An markets where buyers bid for them.

Cattle and buffalo are kept in a stable on the farmstead, and normally they are fed straw and water. During the day they often are allowed to wander the hamlet in search of grasses and herbs along the edges of the roads, paths, and bundings as well as among the clusters of tombs (some villagers grow prickly plants on their graves to keep off the grazing animals). After the harvest, buffalo and cattle are turned loose in the fields, watched by small boys who often sit on their backs. Delicate white herons, seeking small fish in the pools, also perch on the backs of these massive animals, feasting on the leeches that plague them.

Villagers contend that because of government-supplied inoculations, cattle and buffalo are not so susceptible to disease as are other farm animals. Because of the poor pasturage, the cows generally give no milk—a relatively small loss since, with the exception of children and some sick people, Vietnamese villagers do not consume milk or other dairy products. The only milch cow in the village is being kept by a farmer with the support and supervision of the Provincial Veterinary Service. It is larger than the ordinary village cows, and because it is being raised as a milch cow it is fed a special diet of straw, grass, rice bran, bananas, sugar cane, and water.

Animal dung, sometimes mixed with straw or paddy husks, often is used as fertilizer on kitchen gardens. Some farmers also sell their animal dung, collecting a sizable pile which the buyer is expected to remove. One group of dung buyers comes from neighboring Tan Huong, and each year they visit Ap Dinh A–B with their rented truck, purchasing from the same farmers. They estimate the amount of dung, bargain with the farmer, and haul it away. In 1959 they made two trips to the village, and by their calculations they purchased some 1,500 gia of dung.

FISHING

Many varieties of fish, shellfish, and frogs are found in the streams and canals in the village, and during the rainy season they invade the inundated paddy fields. Fishing is a secondary subsistence activity, and while many villagers engage in it at the height of the planting season, throughout the year fishing is primarily an activity of children and young adult males. Fresh fish in large quantities are available in the Tan An market, and all local shops sell several kinds of dried fish.

Various fishing techniques are employed. The most common is trapping, and several kinds of traps are used (see Fig. 24). Most villagers prefer the *ong mieng thoi* (A) which usually is combined with the *cai thoi* (B). Fish swim into the large open end of the ong mieng thoi, passing into the receptacle of the cai thoi where they are trapped. These traps may be placed in a narrow channel or at the breach in a bund when the fields are being drained, and often one or several men standing in a line push the traps into the current of a stream. The cai thoi also may be used separately, either setting it in a breach or simply placing it in the shallow water on the edge of a stream or canal where the current is not strong enough to topple it. In this position it is considered a particularly effective trap for prawns and small crabs.

Another popular device is the *cai nom* hand trap (Fig. 24, C). Holding it at the small opening, the trapper walks through the flooded paddy fields, plunging the trap rapidly and rhythmically into the water. If a fish or frog is caught, the vibrations caused by efforts to escape warn the trapper who reaches into the opening to grab the catch. The cai nom also is commonly used by boys in the canals. They wait until low tide when the receding water creates a swift current, forcing fish and frogs to the edge where they

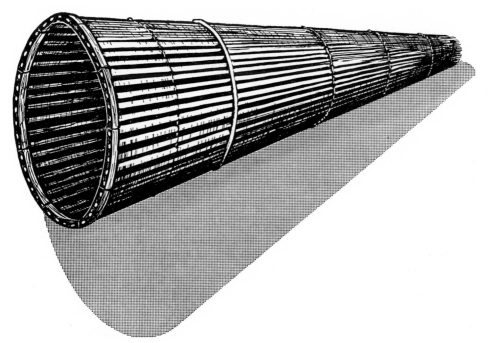

24A. *Ong mieng thoi,* a trap for prawns and small crabs.

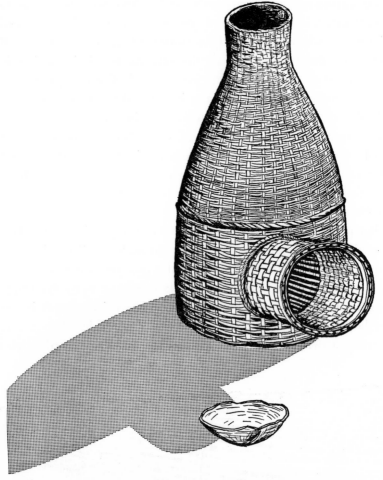

24B. *Cai thoi,* a trap for small fish, lid is made from half a coconut.

nibble on the grasses and herbs. Moving in small groups, the boys swiftly plunge their traps against the bank just below the water line. Frogs' legs are broken to prevent their escaping. Two types of basket, the *cai duc* and the *cai gio* (Fig. 24, D and E), tied around the waist, are used for carrying the catch. The cai gio is good for lively, relatively large fish; the cai duc is better suited for frogs and crustaceans.

Probably because they are more difficult to make and have more restricted use, the *cai bung* and *cai rong* (Fig. 24, F and G) are less popular than traps already described. The cai bung is set in shallow water, preferably where there is current to sweep fish into the trap, and it is considered effective for catching small fish which abound in the paddy fields. The cai rong is a floating trap, usually anchored in a canal or stream to snare fish swimming close to the surface.

Net fishing is fairly common in the village, particularly in Ap Cau and Ap Nhon Hau where the watercourses are relatively large. A few Nhon Hau residents have large standing nets that are raised and lowered by lever action, and one tenant farmer of Ap Dinh-A maintains a net of this type where the Can Dop empties into the West Vaico a few kilometers from his farmstead. He purchased the net for 800$ VN and realizes sizable catches when floods from the paddy fields are drained and swell the Can Dop with fish making their way to the main stream. The fish are marketed in Tan An. Village children employ the same technique on a smaller scale, using a handkerchief-sized net with the four corners attached to the end of a bamboo pole. They also use small delicate nets resembling butterfly nets, with which they scoop the edge of a watercourse, ensnaring fish or frogs.

24C. *Cai nom,* a hand trap.

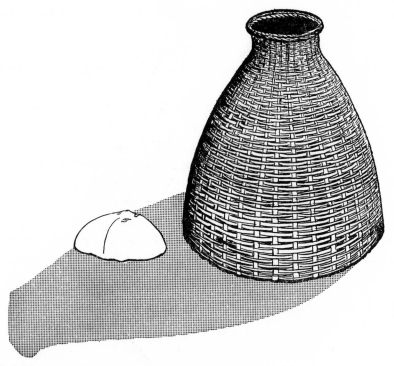

24D. *Cai duc,* a carrying basket for crustaceans.

Young men and boys commonly fish with hook and line in the paddy fields or from the banks of canals or streams. Bait may or may not be used, and some of the boys claimed that with this technique they caught larger fish than with the traps. At the end of the harvest small fish often are left in small pools as the fields are drained, and villagers collect those thrashing in the mud. A kind of mollusk also is found in the paddy fields and along the edges of the streams; poor families usually gather them for soup.

Fish are raised throughout the village, and in well-watered Ap Cau, Ap Nhon Hau, and Ap Thu Tuu fish ponds tend to be larger and more abundant than in the other hamlets. In Hendry's survey,[15] he found that one fifth of the sample raised fish regularly, and only one household did so on a scale large enough to be considered commercial. The well-to-do are more likely to be engaged in fish raising. Commercial feed is too costly for most villagers, and only a few ponds have latrines over them.

Ponds vary considerably in size. When the hole has been dug, a channel

15. Pp. 157–67.

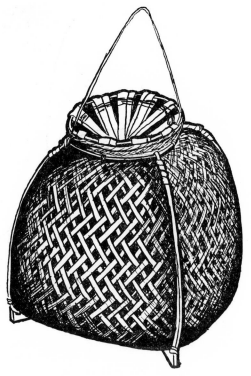

24E. *Cai gio,* a carrying basket for large fish.

is cut to the nearest water source, and when the level reaches about 1.5 meters, the channel is blocked before stocking the pond with fish. Usually an enclosure of cactus and other growth or wire is arranged around the pond to prevent animals from using it. If the fish are to be sold, they may be fed rice bran for about a month to fatten them before they are removed. If there is a latrine over the pond, it is removed during the bran-feeding period. Villagers are reluctant to consume fish raised in a pond with a latrine, and the month-long diet is supposed to erase the taint of the latrine.[16]

The types of fish commonly raised for sale are *ca tra,* a type of catfish, *ca do,* a long fish with a flat head, and *ca ro,* a variety of trench. Ca tra are bred in the vicinity of Chau Doc, near the Cambodian border above the Gulf of Siam, and fish dealers sell them in Khanh Hau in lots ranging from

16. Latrine construction is a recent innovation, organized by the UNESCO School of Fundamental Education. The program, however, has been implemented only in Ap Dinh A and B. There also have been some difficulties because of it; for example, the Village Council ordered one villager to remove a latrine he had constructed close to a canal which was the major source of potable water in the vicinity.

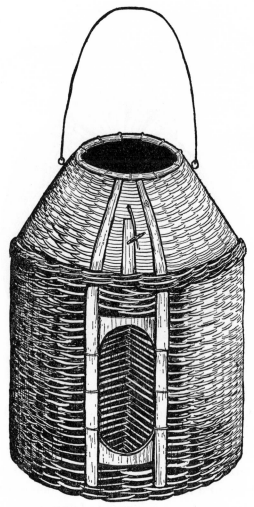

24F. *Cai bung,* a trap for small fish.

100 to 1,000 fingerlings. Villagers estimate that they grow at the rate of 1 kilo per year, and although they mature in two years, it is best to sell them after one year. Ca do are widely raised in the village, but ca ro are less popular; they are smaller and, since they should be fed rice bran during the growing period, they are somewhat costlier to raise. Most fish raised in Khanh Hau are sold in the Tan An market, and from time to time Chinese merchants visit the village to purchase fish which they transport to Cholon.

In 1956 the government launched a program to introduce *tilapia,* a fast-breeding fish imported from the Philippines, into the rural areas of Vietnam. Some villagers in Khanh Hau accepted small batches of tilapia fingerlings,

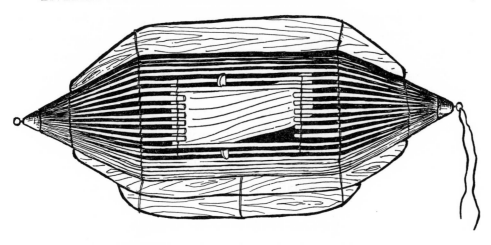

24G. *Cai rong,* a floating trap.

but by 1958 they had completely abandoned raising them, giving various reasons. Some felt the tilapia could not thrive in the hot sun, and others pointed out that they were ill suited to the brackish water of the dry season. Several women said they thought the tilapia had a peculiar flavor, and in addition they were very susceptible to diseases. Another factor undoubtedly was Viet Cong propaganda, which insisted that the tilapia were carriers of leprosy, tuberculosis, and other dread diseases.

CARPENTRY AND IMPLEMENT MAKING

In Khanh Hau there are three or four implement makers and between 25 and 30 carpenters. Most of them also are engaged in agricultural activities. The demand for their services is greatest during the dry season when farmers purchase or repair implements and construct or repair houses; thus these specialists are free to farm during the season. If a craftsman has a workshop, it is located on his farmstead, usually indistinguishable from other subsidiary buildings. Several of the carpenters perform tasks for residents of surrounding villages, and the services of outside craftsmen, particularly those skilled in decorative woodwork, are sometimes demanded by people of Khanh Hau.

The usual pattern is for carpenters and implement makers to pass on to their sons the skills of the trade as well as the tools—saws of various sizes, chisels, planes, bow-powered drills, hatchets, squares, metal rulers, plumb lines, pliers, and hammers. One exception was a carpenter in Ap Dinh-B who, because his son lacked propensity for the trade, took one of his brother's sons as an apprentice, later accepting him as a full partner. Some young men complained that there is a tendency to accept only kin as apprentices, and they cited the example of a young laborer who was unable to become an apprentice in the village, so he learned carpentry working in a Tan An lumberyard.

The most successful carpenter in the village originally had been trained in boat construction, shifting to house construction when he moved to Khanh Hau. Specializing in houses for prosperous villagers, he employs some of his boat-construction techniques. Another carpenter previously had specialized in making hand-operated rice mills, but with the advent of the machine-operated mills he was forced to turn to general carpentry. Some craftsmen refuse to do jobs outside of their specialization; for example, one resident of Ap Moi turns wood for elegant tables, and although the demand for his services is not great, he declines offers to do other types of carpentry.

Both carpenters and implement makers work on the basis of special orders, and in many instances the buyer furnishes the material. Rooted as they are in tradition, most of the designs and forms are very patterned, and only a few well-to-do villagers are likely to request innovations reflecting current Saigon modes.[17] Some artisans have introduced new tools into the village, however. It is believed that the first threshing sledges and Cambodian plows were brought to Khanh Hau by craftsmen, and an Ap Dinh-A artisan proudly displays his new, recently devised waterwheel in which the axle is set on imported ball bearings, greatly reducing the physical work of pedaling.

Artisans generally try to attract clients through reputation for good workmanship rather than the lure of low price. Cost of a job is based on a consistent estimate of labor time with material costs added. Wood for any kind of work requiring specialists must be brought in—Bien Hoa and Thu Dau Mot are the best sources for good hardwood—and it is not uncommon to request wood one year in advance to guarantee proper seasoning. If the amount of required wood is relatively small, it may be purchased on the Tan An market, and some carpenters bring in logs of inexpensive wood, cutting it by hand into planks and pieces as needed.

WEAVING

Weaving is a marginal economic activity in Khanh Hau. While it is done by some women of all economic levels (many villagers feel that weaving is a skill every girl should acquire) it would be safe to say that only among the

17. Some of these were indicated in Chapter 2, and they also are discussed in Chapter 10.

poor is it done for profit. Since weaving materials are not indigenous to the village, production costs are relatively high. Reeds gathered in the Plaine des Joncs area are sold in Tan An, and the length of the reeds determines the cost of a bundle. After being soaked in water for about thirty minutes, the reeds are pounded to flatten them, and after this process has been repeated the three or four times necessary to make them pliable, they are put in the sun to dry.

Weaving for home consumption is done when the need arises, and for profit when an order is received. The range of things woven is not broad— bed mats, rice baskets, and small, compact bolsters are the commonly demanded items. The forms never vary, and village weavers do not use colors. Only when weaving a baby's mat is there a design, and this is to indicate where the head should go. Villagers believe that if the head is placed where the feet have been, the intelligence of the child will be dimmed.

Medical Practitioners

The specific roles of medical practitioners in Khanh Hau vary considerably. Some already discussed are the Buddhist lay monks and others who rely on mystical powers to achieve cures. The only one who dealt in medicine to the exclusion of other economic activities was the Chinese pharmacist in Ap Dinh-B who left the village in 1959. The other Chinese also is a shopkeeper, and the remaining practitioners are engaged in agricultural activities; their medical activities supplement their incomes. Ong Thay Phap, the sorcerer, has set fees for most of his services. Although they do not have fixed fees, the two Buddhist lay healers accept tokens of gratitude.

Ong Thay Muoi Le specializes in healing bone injuries, a profession which brings him an income equal to that derived from his tenant farming. His paternal grandfather and his father also were healers, and he enlarged on the range of techniques learned from them. For fractures, Ong Thay Muoi Le bandages the swollen area, changing the dressing every three days. He also gives the patient an alcoholic medicine to ease the pain and stimulate blood circulation. For a break he mixes a medicated paste which, when applied, hardens into a cast. Bamboo splints, held in place by bandages, are arranged over the cast. The patient is instructed to remain in bed for several weeks, after which the bandage and cast are removed, and the limb is massaged. Ong Thay Muoi Le adjusts his fees to the means of the patient, and he often is summoned to treat patients in surrounding villages. During the Indochina War his services were much in demand after clashes between the French troops and Viet Minh.

Prior to its closure, the Chinese pharmacy was a fragrant place with its extensive collection of herbs (some of which would be sun dried before the shop), powders, and liquids for preparing medicines. There also were medicines prepared by large Chinese pharmacies in Cholon and patent medicines from Saigon firms. The pharmacist had learned his profession by working several years in a large Cholon pharmacy, and in addition to preparing *thuoc bac* (Chinese medicine) and *thuoc nam* (Vietnamese medicine), he was adept at bloodletting, pinching, suction cups, and other traditional healing techniques. He treated patients in the shop and made house calls when necessary, charging fixed fees for medicines and services.

The nurse in private practice is a young tenant farmer who has received instruction in giving inoculations. With some syringes and medicines as well as written authorization from the provincial authorities, he practices a very limited type of medicine. Although inoculations are the most popular form of Western medicine, demand for his services is not great. Recently, however, he has been called upon to inoculate ailing animals. The village nurse, who also has a private practice, is a tenant farmer with eight cong of paddy land in the neighboring village of Tan Huong. Having worked as an assistant in the Tan An hospital for six years, he is authorized to practice general nursing. After he married a Khanh Hau girl who is a seamstress, the nurse constructed a small shop and house on the spur road near the military stockade. His role as village nurse requires his presence at the Council House each morning to tend the ailing. The village budget pays his salary and a small allotment of funds is earmarked for medicines. In his private practice, he employs only Western medical techniques.

SHOPKEEPING

There are shops of varying types and sizes scattered throughout the village. Some shops deal only in foodstuffs but a few also stock a relatively wide range of manufactured items. Most shops have several tables where tea, soft drinks, beer, or rice alcohol are served, and some also serve food—sandwiches of French bread and bits of pork fat or sausage, along with bowls of noodles, rice, and simple meat and vegetable dishes. They are gathering places for those who live in the vicinity. Women may take tea after making purchases, men returning from the fields may stop for some food and something to drink, and in the evening men gather to sit in the orange-amber glow of the oil lamps to drink beer and discuss their crops or news.

There are six shops on or very near the spur road in Ap Dinh A–B, and among them are the largest shops in the village. There are no shops in the scattered clusters of Ap Moi, and those in the other hamlets are very small, usually set back from the footpaths that serve as the main line of land communication. All village shopkeepers launched their businesses themselves, and most of them have had to borrow to maintain stocks. Usually this is done through open-book credit from supplying merchants to participating in a village *hui,* a mutual credit society or tontine.[18]

All the village shops contain the living quarters of the owners and their families, and shop construction ranges from simple thatched buildings to relatively large masonry structures with tile roofs. Operation of the shop is a family affair. With the exception of the two Chinese shops, women tend to the customers and maintain the accounts. Grown children also assist, and in none of the shops is there need for hired help. Most of the shopkeepers have had previous experience; both Chinese, for example, served as apprentices in Chinese pharmacies, and one shopkeeper learned the trade from his father while four of the female shopkeepers had prior experience either as shop assistants or as petty merchants.

The Chinese who operates a small general goods shop and pharmacy near the primary school in Ap Dinh-A came to Khanh Hau from Cholon in 1953 (and since then other shops in the vicinity have noted a drop in their sales). In addition to being a pharmacist and practitioner employing traditional Chinese and Vietnamese medical techniques, he has an extensive stock of merchandise—the most complete in the village. Standing in his crowded shop, one is surrounded by metal pots and pans, chinaware, water jars, writing materials, chopsticks, canned milk, tea, canned foods (some of which are imported from France), wines, brandy, beer, soft drinks, joss, votive paper, candles, lamps, kerosene, textiles, ready-made clothing, mosquito netting, hats, haberdashery, flashlights, wooden clogs, rubber sandals, fish traps, woven-reed mats, baskets, shoulder boards, sickles, knives, rope, glassware, tobacco, cigarettes, betel leaves, areca nuts, lime, spices of various kinds, fish sauce, fermented pounded pork, fermented shrimp, cookies, hard candies, coconuts, dried fish, fresh fruits, and fresh vegetables.

Petty Commerce

Most petty merchants in Khanh Hau are on the spur road; some have temporary stands and others are ambulatory. Fresh fruits and vegetables, fish sauce, and fish—dried, salted, or live (usually in kerosene cans filled with water)—are items most commonly vended. Weighed down by their shoulder boards, the ambulatory merchants pass from house to house, displaying their

18. The hui is explained later in this chapter and in Appendix D.

wares and bargaining with those interested in purchasing. One widow in
Ap Dinh-B buys fruits from villagers, reselling them in front of her house.
She also prepares sweet glutinous rice cakes wrapped in banana leaf, which
her daughter sells along the road (some days she sells about 50, charging
1$ VN apiece).

Two elderly women, one with an infirm husband and the other a widow,
maintain a small temporary food stand in front of the primary school. Their
menu consists of dried fish, manioc grilled over a charcoal brazier, glutinous
rice cakes, and sandwiches of pork fat or sausage, garnished with hot sauces.
Most of the customers are school children and men returning from the
fields. The only male participant in petty commerce pedals a canopied stand
down the road, selling ice, beer, soda pop, and cups of shaved ice flavored
with syrup which he prepares with sugar, water, and fruit extract.

RICE MILLING AND RICE MERCHANDISING

The development of local rice mills since 1950 has increased rice merchandising and rice market competition in the Tan An area, dispersing the
previous concentration in Cholon. Prior to 1950 most of the rice mills in
southern Vietnam were in Cholon. Paddy, transported by boat and truck,
was processed, and the polished rice was carried to the local markets. In
Khanh Hau a number of villagers used hand-operated, locally made wooden
rice mills or grindstones, and those without either had to take their paddy
to Tan An where the only local mills operated. Machine-powered rice mills
are one of the most advanced technological innovations in the village to
date, and by 1959 there were two in Khanh Hau, three in the neighboring
village of Tan Huong, and six in Tan An. All are owned by Vietnamese,
and they have proven a success to the point where home rice milling has all
but disappeared. Idle hand-operated mills can be seen stored in corners of
rooms throughout the village, and the village rice-mill producer has turned
to general carpentry.

Villagers expressed a number of reasons why local milling has expanded
since 1950. Several mill operators stated that during the war years they and
their families had accumulated funds for investment, and for the first time
they found themselves able to go into business. Further, several had gained
some knowledge of the needed machines and their maintenance as well as
the rice-marketing procedure by working for Chinese or French firms.
Equally important was a relaxation of French and Chinese control over the
importation and sale of milling machinery. Also, Presidential Ordinance
No. 53 issued on September 6, 1956, closed eleven occupations to foreigners,

lessening Chinese control and opening new entrepreneurial doors to the Vietnamese.

One rice miller pointed out that while means of transporting paddy to Cholon had improved, the increased number of check points inhibited movement. Before the Indochina War there had been two control points between the delta cities of Can Tho and Cholon, but by 1959 this number had grown to 56, 10 of which were between My Tho and Cholon. At these control points taxes are levied and the truck is inspected. Villagers indicate that, since the inspecting official can easily find some violation, and paying a fine is no guarantee of exemption at the next control point, bribery is common and shippers must allow for it in their estimated costs. Control points also are an additional means for local administrations to gain revenue, and they are designed to restrict the flow of rice into certain areas such as those near the Plaine des Joncs and the Cambodian border where it might fall into the hands of the Viet Cong.

One of the rice mills in Tan Huong is partially owned by a resident of Khanh Hau.[19] The two mills in Khanh Hau are east of the national highway, one near the bridge in Ap Cau and the other on the eastern edge of Ap Dinh-A on the banks of the Can Dop. The rice mill owners are from old, relatively wealthy village families, and they have been engaged in agriculture as well as in some other entrepreneurial activities. Both mills are small, and their clients are local residents who usually carry in small amounts of paddy on shoulder boards, to be milled for home use. Those desiring to sell rice in large quantities transport their paddy to the larger mills in Tan An or Tan Hiep.

The Ap Dinh-A mill was constructed in 1952, and it is owned by a family with two other rice mills in distant villages. The mill is a wooden structure with a metal roof, pleasantly shaded by palm trees, and since it is on the Can Dop, some villagers can transport their paddy by pirogue. The machinery, which the mill operator complains breaks down frequently, was manufactured in Cholon and assembled by specialists from there. The mechanism is run by a gasoline-powered motor outside the building. Paddy brought to the mill is weighed and measured in lots by the miller's assistant who keeps records of each batch. The paddy passes first through a hopper to remove foreign matter, and a conveyor then carries it to the top of the mill where it descends through sifters and polishers which separate rice bran and husks and broken grains. If the client pays the highest milling rate, he

19. Ong Nam, the youngest brother of Ong Lam, whose profile is included in Chapter 10.

retains the bran, otherwise it is stored and later sold by the miller. The miller always keeps the husks which he sells for fertilizer and fuel.

With the beginning of the harvest in September, the flow of rice to the market increases steadily, reaching a peak in December and January. Economic level, of course, determines willingness or need to sell rice. Farmers of the lower economic level do not cultivate rice for the market; those of higher economic levels sell much of their crop immediately after the harvest, and while some continue to sell throughout the year, only those with large landholdings, and rentals paid for the most part in kind, retain supplies of rice for later sale. Although the usual pattern is for farmers to supply their home needs from the crop, there are some who sell their entire crop, purchasing rice of lower quality for home consumption.

The recency of local rice merchandising is reflected in the fact that very few of the villagers engaged in it learned from their fathers. Since this business requires capital and is considered somewhat risky, it is restricted to the wealthy villagers, all of whom have considerable land. Some also view it as a temporary venture, illustrated by the fact that there may be twenty or thirty villagers in rice merchandising one year and only ten the following year. In order to be successful, the rice merchant must be keenly aware of current prices and cost and have a good deal of experience with rice; for example, he must be adept at estimating the amount of whole milled rice that will result from a given batch of paddy. Overestimations have ruined many village merchants.[20]

There are no official rice-price reports from Saigon, and although price ranges are fixed by the government for average-quality rice, there are no prices set for rice of superior or inferior quality. Usually farmers discuss prices with friends and relatives, and estimates are based on prices paid the previous year. Condition of paddy is an important consideration in estimating price—that which is properly dried and winnowed commands a higher price. Merchants, however, are better informed on current prices which gives them an advantage over the village seller. Gathering in the rice mills and in market towns, they have contact with other merchants with whom they can compare prices. Some also visit Cholon, the market center of southern Vietnam, and price fluctuations they find out about there will not reach the Khanh Hau area for days.

20. Some villagers also contend that the 1957 government ban on rice exports put many merchants out of business because of an ensuing price decline. Many merchants had stored large quantities of rice in anticipation of a greater demand with accompanying higher prices as exports increased. Saigon sources, however, say that exports were limited, not banned.

Rice merchants in Khanh Hau usually are small operators with an annual turnover of several thousand gia. They have no place of business, storing paddy in local rice mills until it is sold. Unfamiliar as they are with Cholon market practices, most merchants prefer to remain in the Tan An area. The few with relatively extensive experience have their paddy milled and transport it by boat or truck to Cholon where samples are given to the wholesalers, letting them compete for the lot.

In spite of the fact that commercial people have traditionally been ranked low in Vietnamese society, these entrepreneurs are not regarded with disdain, and among them are members of the Village Council and high-ranking members of the Cult Committee. For example, the village chief was a rice merchant (and in 1959 he invested in a new gasoline station in Tan An), and Ong Ke Hien owns several rice mills and has a thriving rice merchandising business (in a Tan An shop completed in 1961). There is, however, a tendency for villagers to deprecate Vietnamese commercial ability. Some feel that Vietnamese do not trust one another sufficiently to form workable partnerships and business arrangements. They also point out that because of inexperience (previously most business was in the hands of Chinese), Vietnamese businessmen are disorganized; they fail to keep proper records and are slow to seize opportunities. One devout Buddhist villager gave up rice merchandising because one had to be "a teller of lies." By and large, however, the entrepreneurs themselves are proud of their roles, and Ong Lam, one of the most venturesome businessmen, summarized this spirit in his motto, "The home of the truly big man, the clever man, is everywhere." [21]

CREDIT AND SAVINGS

According to villagers, most borrowing is for food and other essentials for the maintenance of the household.[22] Purchase of fertilizer, medical expenses, ritual expenses, and farming costs also account for debts. Some engaged in

21. Hendry, pp. 198–230.
22. Ibid., pp. 282–95. Two thirds of the households in Hendry's sample had debts of some kind. Only about one quarter of the families in the upper economic level had debts, while close to two thirds of families in the middle and lower economic level owed money. Some 18.5% of the middle level and 28.1% of the lower level reported that they borrowed to buy food and other necessities, but a much larger percentage of middle-level households borrowed to purchase fertilizer and meet other farm expenses. Lower-level households reported a greater need to borrow for medical and ritual expenses than the other two levels. Over one third of the total owed less than 2,000$ VN, and a slight majority owed less than 3,000$. More than one quarter, however, had debts of 5,000$, and about 10% had debts greater than 10,000$.

pig raising borrow money as do a few of the entrepreneurial villagers. Sources of credit vary. Shopkeepers in the village and surrounding markets extend credit to their regular clients, and some village storekeepers report that as many as one third of their customers have open-book credit with them. Most shopkeepers also complain that too often they are not paid. Before his departure the Chinese pharmacist noted that one of his clients had died without paying his bill, and he lamented, "One generation in medicine, three generations indigent." It was pointed out earlier that the shopkeepers themselves usually receive open-book credit from their suppliers.

Kinfolk, friends, and neighbors also are sources of credit. Some well-to-do villagers lend money, but they usually are reluctant to do so without considerable security, and most prefer lending in the market towns where borrowers are merchants, rice mill operators, and other relatively good risks.[23] In order to borrow money, some villagers participate in hui, a type of mutual aid society found throughout Vietnam and probably derived from a similar Chinese institution. In addition to being a source of credit, the hui is a form of gambling, and there is a convivial social air to hui meetings. Participation is limited to those with some available resources and, since monthly payments are part of the hui, a steady source of funds also is essential. The number of members and the amount of money the organizer gets depends to some extent on the need and resources of those who participate, but the hui lasts only long enough for each member to receive funds once.

Two relatively unsuccessful agricultural cooperatives have been tried in Khanh Hau. In 1956 a group of farmers from different hamlets banded together to form a Village Agricultural Cooperative. The primary aim was to establish a credit system so the members might avoid having to sell unharvested paddy to money lenders or rice merchants. The cooperative also planned to purchase fertilizer at wholesale prices. Shares were sold for 100$ VN each, and members could purchase up to five. At the outset the cooperative claimed 95 members from all hamlets, but initial optimism was dampened by financial problems—of the 31,200$ VN pledged, only 18,000$ was collected.

Membership began to diminish, and by 1958 the cooperative was practically nonexistent. In June of that year when the planting was beginning, a

23. In his survey, Hendry found that one third of the loans were made without interest. In slightly less than one third of the loans, the rate of interest was 5%, and another one third had a rate of interest between 1 and 4%. A little more than 10% of the loans were at rates in excess of 5% per month. Some 53.6% of the loans made by kinfolk were reported to be without interest. (Pp. 289–94.)

meeting of the members was called at the headquarters of the National Revolutionary Party to decide the fate of the cooperative. The group leaders reported that attempts to get government aid were unsuccessful. One faction proposed that they affiliate with the thriving cooperative in neighboring My An Phu, and another faction favored dissolution. There was a decided lack of solidarity, and in spite of its being comprised exclusively of Khanh Hau farmers, many expressed a reluctance to entrust their money to the group. Discussion continued, but no final decisions were made. When the government-sponsored Farmers' Cooperative was proposed in 1959, the Village Agricultural Cooperative disbanded, and members were given refunds.

The Farmers' Association grew out of a presidential decree issued in December 1958. In April 1959 agents of various bureaus of the Thu Thua district visited the village to explain the aims and organization of the program. Held in the Council House, the meeting began by paying homage to the national flag. The district information service agent presided, and after stating the aims of the meeting, he spoke about the need for cooperation among the villagers especially after their having lived "under the yoke of feudal landlords, French imperialists, and Communists." He then set forth the organizational features (including membership dues of 10$ VN monthly) and the advantages of cheaper fertilizer and group marketing. The only response from the audience was a complaint from an elderly farmer that the dues would be a burden to him and others like him.

The following speaker changed the tone of the meeting. Emphasizing the need for political security, he pointed out that one important function of the association would be to organize political instruction classes in the village. He then upbraided the villagers for their lack of cooperation in the anti-Viet Cong campaign:

> A revolution cannot be carried out by an army or by a security organization or a police force but only by all the citizens, all the inhabitants of the countryside. Why are we still far from being efficient in our fight against the Communists? Because we have not succeeded in putting all the villagers in the same political organization [that is, the National Revolutionary Movement] and because the villagers still have an indifferent attitude toward the anti-Communist policy of the government.
>
> By the latest pennant hanging in Ap Dinh A and B by the Communists, we know that some opposition elements still remain here.[24] The

24. This refers to the incident late in 1958 when banners bearing antigovernment slogans were found early in the morning in Ap Dinh A–B.

division into five households is not efficient enough to control opinion. I think there are still some agitators hidden in the Ap Dinh A–B households.

During this year I hope that none of you will pay the agriculture tax to the Viet Cong and that all patriotic villagers will fight enthusiastically against the Communists. The inner man in some of you has two antagonistic tendencies: one for the National Government in the daytime, and the other for the Communists in the night.

This was followed by another speech about the villagers' responsibility to cooperate with the authorities and government programs, which also chided the villagers for their "indifference."

In June 1959 elections were held to select the hamlet committees, each of which consisted of two members. An election board was appointed, which selected candidates from each hamlet. At the election of the association officers, a meeting at the primary school, the province chief addressed the estimated 200 villagers gathered, emphasizing the concern of the central government for the well-being of the rural population as well as the advantages of the Farmers' Association. Some villagers who did not vote later voiced the opinion that the election was a formality—the winning candidates had been preselected. When the results were made known, the two winning candidates in each hamlet had received 100 per cent of the votes. By December 1959 the promised program still had not been implemented, and with the increased insecurity in 1960, all rural programs began to stall. In 1962, the Farmers' Association still existed, but villagers pointed out that it had not achieved a great deal—the Agricultural Credit Program was responsible for most credit extended to villagers, and no agricultural innovations had been introduced.

Since 1955 three government-sponsored agricultural credit programs have reached the village. It has been pointed out that in 1956 loans for purchasing buffalo were issued in the village. Four-year loans were granted early in that year, and 21 farmers were able to borrow 3,500$ VN each. In midyear, 1956, one-year loans were given to 36 farmers out of a total of 100 who applied, and they received amounts ranging from 500$ to 2,000$ with over four fifths receiving the latter figure. When 100 villagers again requested similar loans in 1957, none received them, because of unexplained complications on administrative levels higher than the village.

In July 1958 the National Agricultural Credit Office (NACO) program reached the village with 153 application forms, which were given to hamlet chiefs who distributed them among the heads of the five-family groups. As organized, the recipient of a loan had to be (1) a resident of the village, (2) an active farmer, (3) a small landowner or tenant, (4) in need of credit. The applications were processed by the Village Council and sent to the district headquarters at Thu Thua where the NACO office decided on the amount to be lent. The Village Council made no effort to select the neediest cases, and a number of villagers complained of favoritism. About one quarter of the village households benefited, and despite complaints many of the needy villagers received loans.

The maximal loan in 1958 was 3,000$ VN for farmers with relatively large holdings, and the minimum was 800$ for those with one hectare or less. The rate of interest was set at 1 per cent per month, and 142 applicants received loans. In the eleven rejections, five were too young or too old, two had made out their forms incorrectly, one had not paid his 1956 loan, one had too much land, and two did not have rent contracts. By the 1960–61 planting season, the amount loaned in the village reached a peak of 559,000$ VN, and decreased to 340,000$ during the 1961–62 season, primarily because of late payments on loans of the previous year. This reflected a general pattern throughout the delta. In many areas the lateness or lack of repayment was attributed to the Viet Cong; many of the authorities contend Viet Cong cadremen approached recipients of the program, threatening violence if they repaid the loan. Since by April 1962 some 540,000$ of the 559,000$ lent in Khanh Hau had been repaid, the tardiness would seem to be due to other factors.

NACO loans, by and large, were well received in the village. One suggestion many villagers had was that it might be better to distribute the fertilizer rather than extend cash credit. Many villagers felt that particularly among the very needy this would remove the temptation to use the credit for other purposes, and it also reflected the distrust of fertilizer merchants. Something along this line was done by the National Revolutionary Movement in 1958. The central party organization distributed fertilizer to district party headquarters for delivery to the villages. Prices were set below the market price, and both party and nonparty members were eligible to buy, although the former could purchase on partial credit. During the distribution period, membership in the National Revolutionary Party increased by fifty households.[25]

25. Hendry, p. 312.

CHAPTER 7

Village Administration and Law

ADMINISTRATION of the village is in the hands of the Village Council and its representatives in each hamlet, the hamlet chiefs. The vested authority and responsibilities of the Village Council are derived from two sources—administrative legislation and tradition. Delegated administrative functions depend on the place of the village in the larger polity—the state or nation—and owing to historical events these functions have undergone a series of changes. Traditional council functions, however, are rooted in the role of the councillors as leaders in village society and consequently are more conservative. Although some of these traditional functions, such as the place of the councillors in the Cult Committee (which will be discussed in Chapter 8) are not "official," they continue to have the silent sanction of higher authorities.

In administrative matters, the Village Council is directly responsible to the district chief of Thu Thua, one of the seven districts that constitute Long An province. The council also has frequent contacts with provincial authorities, particularly the province chief (more so, probably, than other councils have because Khanh Hau is the scene of some community development projects and the site of Marshal Duc's shrine and tomb). Since 1904, attempts by the central administration to integrate villages into the larger political superstructure have increased contacts with higher authorities and given them a greater voice in village affairs. The result is that the prerogatives of the Village Council have been steadily diminishing.

CHANGES IN THE VILLAGE COUNCIL: 1904–1962

The administrative legislation of 1904 marked the first attempt by the French colonial government to standardize the structure of Vietnamese village political institutions. During the preceding forty years, the colonial government had relatively little concern with village political affairs, and by 1903 some administrators were becoming alarmed at what they considered to be manifestations of village council disintegration. A study committee was formed, and in 1904 its recommendation provided the basis for legislation to create closer ties between the villages and the central administration. The result was that the village councils became smaller, and positions not viewed as administrative (those concerned with the Cult of the Guardian Spirit of the Village and village celebrations) were eliminated. Some of these sacred functions were absorbed by the cult committees, which emerged unofficially in every village subsequent to the legislation.

Under the 1904 legislation, the Village Council was composed of eleven positions, some of which were retained from the traditional village council, and additional functions were outlined for them. In the traditional council the Huong Ca was dean of the notables by virtue of age; he now became head of the council (viewed as an administrative body), and to him was delegated the responsibility of keeping the village archives. The Huong Chu, Xa Truong, Huong Quan, and Huong Than remained, but their functions were altered. Other titles were kept, but the character of the positions was changed completely (see Table 12).

The right of the Village Council to impose punishments was altered. Traditionally, ordinary villagers guilty of a legal violation were beaten with a rattan cane; notables were fined. When the colony of Cochinchina was established, the French administration forbade these punishments as too harsh. Vietnamese officials, however, registered formal complaints, contending that this repression of power greatly diminished the prestige of the village leaders. As a compromise, the 1904 legislation granted the village councils the right to demand additional days of guard duty as punishment for males and the right to impose certain penalties for damage to public property or fraud relative to alcohol and opium regulations.

Legislation in 1927 brought about further changes in the Village Council. The administrative reforms broadened the base of personnel eligible for membership in the council, and the promotion process was made more flexible. A twelfth position, that of civil status secretary was created to deal with vital statistics and health. The functions of the Huong Ca were expanded to include supervision of all village services, thus giving him more administrative authority. There also were some shifts in existing functions —responsibility for keeping the archives went from the Huong Ca to the Huong Bo who already was keeping records, and the Huong Bo also assumed control of the village budget.

TABLE 12. The Traditional and the 1904 Village Councils

Traditional	*1904*
Huong Ca: First notable, by virtue of age	Huong Ca: First notable; presiding officer and keeper of archives
Thu Chi: Keeper of archives	
Huong Chu: Official advisor	Huong Chu: Deputy chief and inspector of village services, reporting to first notable
Huong Su: Intermediary between village and mandarins	Huong Su: Advisor on laws and regulations
Huong Lac: Advisor of the council	
Huong Truong: Advisor on execution of orders from higher authority	Huong Truong: Advisor on village budget and assistant to teachers
Huong Chanh: Official advisor	Huong Chanh: Arbitrator of minor conflicts among villagers
Cau Duong: Village magistrate	
	Huong Giao: Instructor of young notables and secretary of council
Huong Quan: Police chief	Huong Quan: Police chief; supervisor of transportation and communication
Thu Bo: Treasurer	Thu Bo: Guardian of rolls and accounts, village buildings and materials
Huong Than: General administration	Huong Than: Intermediary between judicial authorities and council
Xa Truong: Intermediary between administration and Village Council	Xa Truong: Executive notable; intermediary between administration and Village Council; conservator to village seal; tax collector
Thu Bo: Tax officer	
Huong Hao: General administration	Huong Hao: Executive notable
Huong Nhut: First notable	
Huong Nhi: Second notable	
Huong Le: President of ceremonies and rituals	
Huong Nhac: Chief of musicians	
Huong Am: Organizer of public fetes and banquets	
Huong Van: Composer of verses in the mood of the Guardian Spirit of the Village	
Thu Khoan: Guardian of the communal paddy land	
Cai Dinh: Guardian of the dinh	

Payment for services was based on the amount of time spent on council duties and, with a twelve-man council, time demands on any one member were not great. Also, the council members were primarily concerned with council affairs or "housekeeping operations" rather than village affairs. At this time, the legislators also created two subgroups within the Village Council—the executive council and executive notables.

The Village Council of the 1920s and 1930s had the right to select replacements for vacancies, subject to the approval of the provincial authorities, and legislation of this period specified that new council members be chosen from a select group of villagers—such people as landowners, retired military officers, and retired district or provincial officials. Salaries were modest but, as some of the elderly Khanh Hau residents continue to point out, the high prestige of being a member of the Village Council was sufficient compensation, and these positions were sought after by the village gentry. Ex-members of the Khanh Hau council also report that during this period, new appointees held lower positions for a two-year period, moving upward subsequently.[1]

In August 1945 a brief but drastic change took place in the village councils. With the end of Japanese occupation in August of that year, the Viet Minh seized control of the rural areas, organizing administrative committees in every village. The Administrative Committee in Khanh Hau consisted of six members—the chairman, two police agents, a public works secretary, a finance secretary, and a civil status secretary. All were selected from the Viet Minh cadre in the village, and although most were tenant farmers, the chairman and one of the police agents were brothers from a relatively well-to-do landowning family. Viet Minh control was short-lived, however; when the French re-established the colonial administration in January 1946, the former council was reinstated.

With the onset of the Indochina War, the village councillors were particularly susceptible to accusations of being pro-French or pro-Viet Minh, and from time to time some of them were forced to flee the village. On the other hand, several villagers contend that the confusing war years provided an opportunity for unscrupulous members of the council to exploit their authority, and it was widely known that one village official was guilty of having extorted money from villagers by threatening to denounce them as Viet Minh.

Legislation following the end of the Indochina War brought about many changes, particularly in the way council members were selected. From 1946 until 1949 the council was composed of eight members, divided into two administrative committees, and there was provision for popular elections. In 1949, legislation called for a council of from six to eight members appointed by a provincial committee. Universal suffrage to elect village councils was the first provision of the 1953 legislation during the period of Emperor Bao Dai's government, and this legislation also brought about changes almost matching those of the Viet Minh. Council organization was

1. Woodruff, *The Study of a Vietnamese Rural Community*, Vol. 1, pp. 33–35.

made flexible—a minimum of three and a maximum of nine positions were allowed. Specific duties were outlined for the three members of the council, and the distribution of responsibilities for additional members was left to the council itself. Also, the position of the head of the council was greatly strengthened. All titles were changed; Huong Ca became Chu Tich or chairman, the same designation introduced by the Viet Minh, and with other positions the term *huong* (meaning communal with honorific associations) was replaced by *uy vien* (literally, commissioner).

In June 1956 the Secretary of State at the Presidency in Saigon authorized the province chiefs to replace the elected village councils with appointive councils, ranging in size from three to five members, depending on the size of the village. The council first was called the Administrative Committee, the same term used by the Viet Minh, but it soon was changed to Village Council. Khanh Hau had a council of five members (see Table 13), all

TABLE 13. Changes in Structure of the Village Council

I Prewar Council

1. Village chief
2. Deputy chief
3. Advisor on laws and regulations
4. Advisor on village budget; assistant to teachers
5. Arbitrator of minor conflicts among villagers
6. Secretary to council; trains young notables
7. Police chief
8. Advisor on village rolls and accounts
9. Intermediary between judicial authorities and Village Council
10. Intermediary between village and administration; keeper of village seal; tax collector

11. Executive notable
12. Civil status officer

II Viet Minh Council

1. Chief
2. Police chief
3. Finance officer
4. Public works officer
5. Civil status officer

III 1958 Council

1. Chief
2. Deputy chief
3. Finance officer
4. Police chief
5. Civil status officer

appointed by the provincial authorities for an indefinite period, and this council persisted through most of the period under consideration here. An attempt was made to draw the membership from the different hamlets. The chairman referred to throughout this study as the village chief was a man from Ap Dinh-B.[2] He served as general coordinator and executive of the Village Council, with an assistant chairman called the deputy chief, a landowner from Ap Moi. The police agent, a landowner from Ap Nhon Hau,

2. There is a profile of the village chief in Chapter 10.

was responsible for maintaining law and order in addition to serving as chief of the Self-Defense Guards and the Hamlet Guard, and he described himself as one of the district intelligence officers. Collection of taxes and upkeep of village financial records were the major responsibilities of the finance officer, a member of the Duc family and a resident of Ap Dinh-B; the civil status officer, one of Ong Ke Hien's twin sons, who lives in Ap Moi, recorded vital statistics and also served as village information officer.

During the 1956–62 period, other innovations were introduced. All members of the Village Council for the first time were required to undergo some training at Tan An, which lasted about a month, and participants followed a set schedule with classes in administrative matters, propaganda (anti-Communist for the most part), and self-criticism in which fellow students were supposed to point out each other's faults. The village chief contended that councillors continued to employ this technique in the village. Salaries were raised in 1958. The village chief's salary increased 66 per cent, the deputy chief received 11 per cent more, the police agent 62 per cent, the finance councillor 17 per cent, and the civil status officer 22 per cent. Hamlet chiefs and other civil servants' salaries remained the same.[3]

Late in 1959 the finance councillor resigned, and the village chief assumed his responsibilities. The deputy chief subsequently was appointed to the newly revived position of canton chief, and his functions temporarily were taken over by the village chief until a new member was appointed. Finally, the civil status position was abolished, and the duties associated with it were absorbed by the village chief. By 1961, the Village Council had dwindled to three members, the smallest in village history (see Table 14).

The role of the hamlet chief in the village has remained relatively unchanged. He is selected by the Village Council, usually from a family of good reputation. The Ap Cau hamlet chief (who in 1962 was arrested as a Viet Cong committee leader, but subsequently was released) is a well-to-do landowner; the remaining five hamlet chiefs are tenant farmers. The major function of the hamlet chief is to act as liaison between the Village Council and residents of his hamlet, and since 1958 they have become responsible to the police agent in matters of security. When new programs are being implemented, the hamlet chief, either directly or through the heads of the five-family groups, explains the aim of the program and the role of the villagers in it. Also, from time to time the hamlet chief organizes meetings of the five-family heads to disseminate any news or propaganda received from the village information agent.

3. Woodruff, pp. 47–49.

TABLE 14. Administrative Organization of Khanh Hau, 1961

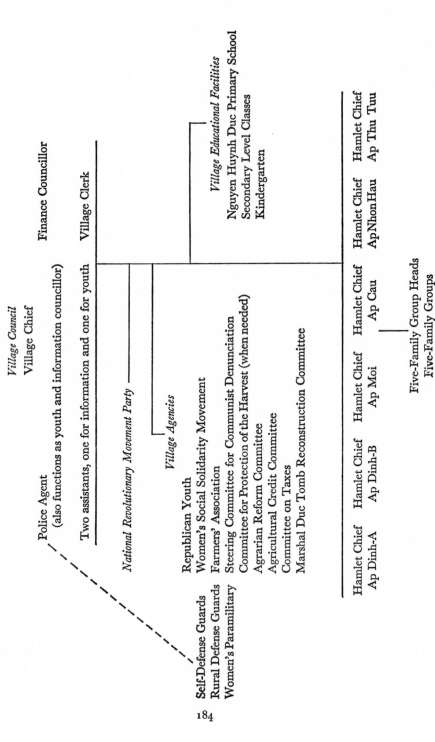

Village Council
Village Chief

Finance Councillor

Police Agent
(also functions as youth and information councillor)

Two assistants, one for information and one for youth

Village Clerk

National Revolutionary Movement Party

Village Agencies

Republican Youth
Women's Social Solidarity Movement
Farmers' Association
Steering Committee for Communist Denunciation
Committee for Protection of the Harvest (when needed)
Agrarian Reform Committee
Agricultural Credit Committee
Committee on Taxes
Marshal Duc Tomb Reconstruction Committee

Self-Defense Guards
Rural Defense Guards
Women's Paramilitary

Village Educational Facilities
Nguyen Huynh Duc Primary School
Secondary Level Classes
Kindergarten

Hamlet Chief
Ap Dinh-A

Hamlet Chief
Ap Dinh-B

Hamlet Chief
Ap Moi

Hamlet Chief
Ap Cau

Hamlet Chief
ApNhonHau

Hamlet Chief
Ap Thu Tuu

Five-Family Group Heads
Five-Family Groups

184

When a village project is being carried out in his hamlet, the chief usually acts as overseer. During the construction of the canal in Ap Thu Tuu, the hamlet chief was kept busy trying to find drinking water for the workers and listening to the complaints of landowners who opposed the canal. Hamlet chiefs also pass on requests received from residents to the Village Council. When families of Ap Cau and Ap Nhon Hau decided they would like a branch of the primary school in Ap Nhon Hau, they met with Ong Ke Hien and their hamlet chiefs who approved it and submitted it to the Village Council.

Traditionally, welfare for individuals or individual families has been more the affair of the hamlet chief than the Village Council.[4] In 1958 the Village Council once ordered a hamlet chief to organize a fund collection for a pregnant woman with an infirm husband and a child hospitalized with hepatitis. Without prodding from the council, however, the Ap Dinh-A hamlet chief collected cash and rice for a kin group in which a brother and sister died of the same illness.[5] Shortly after, the hamlet chief of neighboring Ap Dinh-B organized relief for the destitute family of the barber (mentioned earlier) who was jailed after a fatal fight with a neighbor.

In addition to administrative duties, hamlet chiefs have roles in the Cult of the Guardian Spirit. They assist in organizing the rituals at the dinh and, like the councillors, they have a fixed place in the kowtowing. At the Ap Nhon Hau dinh the hamlet chiefs of Ap Cau and Ap Nhon Hau have a particularly important role. Three of the four annual rituals held at both dinh are on the same day, making it impossible for members of the Village Council to be present at the Ap Nhon Hau rituals, so they are represented by the hamlet chiefs.

The changes in the Village Council since 1953 have not met with the complete approval of many villagers, particularly former members of the council. Several of the ex-village chiefs complained that the councillors had simply become civil servants with stipendiary roles that lack prestige, and the titles were arid—that is, without the title huong there was no aura of honor and dignity. A group of older men, many of whom had served on the council, laughed heartily when one noted that "the people used to be the servants of the Village Council, now the Village Council is the servant of the people."

There also were indications that because of the insecurity, village gentry

4. The creation of the Spring Tree celebration, explained later in this chapter, has altered this somewhat.

5. A profile of this family is included in Chapter 10.

were less desirous of holding council positions. Several times during the research, the village chief frankly expressed his distaste for the job, and after many requests that he be allowed to resign, he was permitted to do so in 1962. His successor accepted the position under protest, unhappy that he was unable to remain with his family in the village after dark. The slaying of the police agent and the arrest of the Ap Cau hamlet chief also increased the apprehension of those holding public office.

THE COUNCIL HOUSE

The Council House in Ap Dinh-A is in what is considered the "center" of the village—the vicinity of the dinh, primary school, and military stockade (see Fig. 1). It is of moderate size and has a wood frame and plank walls; in 1959 the exterior was faced with concrete to prevent dust and rain from entering the innumerable chinks. The roof is thatched, and the front of the building has louvered doors, opened about eight o'clock by the clerk and locked at six in the evening by the last one to leave. As part of the 1959 refurbishing the interior walls were whitewashed, and the pounded-earth floor was covered with bricks.

The interior of the Council House is a curious combination of the sacred and the secular. In the rear there is a large altar dedicated to the "venerable ancestors"—deceased members of the Cult Committee. It contains the usual altar accouterment: incense burner, candles, vases, and offering plates, as well as sizable tablets on which the names of the honored dead are written in Sino–Vietnamese calligraphy. On either side of the altar are racks, each containing twelve symbolic weapons intended to ward off evil spirits. In the rear corners of the room are large hardwood beds on which councillors from other hamlets may take midday naps, and during village celebrations the beds serve as platforms on which food offerings are placed or where the musicians sit. The beds are somewhat hidden by two light wood cabinets which resemble French armoires and are used for village records and storing stationery. In front of the altar a low octagonal table with glass top, surrounded by carved chairs, occupies the place of honor where guests or high venerables are served tea. At the entrance there is a long table flanked by equally long benches, used for the most part by members of the Village Council when they are present. Four desks complete the furnishings—one for the clerk who usually is busy with his archaic, clattering typewriter, the others for councillors or villagers who require a place to fill in applications, registrations, and other forms.

The Council House also is a village gathering place. In addition to villagers who go there for administrative reasons, there often is a group of men from nearby hamlets, particularly during the dry season, gossiping and discussing news, crops, and weather. They sometimes are joined by hamlet chiefs who are expected to report to the council periodically, and high venerables who drop in to chat with the councillors or assist in planning village celebrations. These gatherings lend an informal atmosphere to the Council House. Although the village chief and his deputy spend more time there than do other members of the council, they have no set schedule, often absenting themselves because of farm or family responsibilities.

AGRICULTURAL AFFAIRS

The Village Council has a variety of responsibilities related to agriculture; it passes agricultural information on to higher authorities and disseminates information received from them. It also handles rent adjustments and in 1958 tried to cope with the water crisis. Such government enterprises as the Agrarian Reform and Agricultural Credit Programs require cooperation from the Village Council for successful implementation. It also had a role in organizing the unsuccessful Village Agricultural Cooperative as well as its successor, the Farmers' Association, and the council functions as liaison between the village and the Fundamental Education school.

During the first three months of 1958 the Village Council received from fifty to seventy requests from higher authorities for information on agricultural activities in Khanh Hau. In January the district chief requested an estimate of the total number of agricultural credit loans and total amount that would be needed during the coming year. At the same time, the interprovincial tax inspector sought information on businesses in the village, and a district office asked for data on communal land, waste land, idle land, and the number of uninhabited houses. The Agrarian Reform Agency wanted to know how many landlords had title to more than 100 hectares, and one provincial agency had to know the number of horses between the ages of 5 and 6. Estimates on the volume of the last paddy harvest and the amount of paddy earmarked for sale outside the village was desired by the Provincial Agricultural Service, and this was followed by a provincial agency's request for information on the number of rice mills and sawmills and the number of building permits issued during the past year. A district agency wanted to know the number of 1958 licenses of all types thus far issued in the village, and Civil Action asked for a general census concerning family income, standard of living, educational facilities, and the number of illiterates. With the last request, the village chief complained that while much information was easily supplied, it would take the council considerable time to determine such things as standard of living. His chagrin was heightened with receipt of a special letter sent to all villages by the district chief admonishing the councils for inaccurate reports. Too often, the district chief wrote, councils indulge in imaginary reporting—"pulling figures from the sky."

According to Woodruff,[6] the Vietnamese government relies heavily on administrative channels to disseminate information, and the Village Council passes along considerable information concerning agricultural matters. Early in 1958, most of this information came from the Department of Land and Agrarian Reform. A notice of intent to survey all lands was sent to the village, and the council was directed to post it in a public place. This was followed by other brief communications about aspects of the program and a note emphasizing the need for "counter-propaganda," advising the Village Council to forward questions raised by the farmers to the district headquarters. The district chief also forwarded an announcement from the secretary of Land and Agricultural Reform explaining procedures for obtaining public lands from the government. Additional instructions relating to application for public lands followed, and with one set of instructions was included a notice to avoid cutting timber as part of a national effort to conserve existing woodlands. Other information received concerned rental rates for multicrop fields and a tract recommending a specific brand of chemical fertilizer approved by the Institut Pasteur in Saigon. The general commissariat for Agricultural Extension also sent a warning that any villagers who attempt to resell animals purchased from the government would be punished.

In years of lean harvests, village tradition calls for a rent reduction which normally is a matter for landlord and tenant to resolve. With the severe drought of 1958, however, the district chief authorized the Village Council to form an agricultural committee for the purpose of making "on-the-spot" adjustments. The committee included the village chief, several other members of the Village Council, two landlords, and two tenants. They toured the village, examining the state of the crop just before harvest, and of the 100 claims submitted, 70 adjustments were made with no appeals to higher arbitration.

The 1958 drought also stimulated Village Council action to meet the need for potable water as well as water for crops. Since some villagers had begun to use canal water for cooking and tea—increasing the danger of cholera—the village chief requested aid from the district chief in bringing

6. Pp. 225–33.

water to the village. Army trucks already were transporting potable water from the deep wells in Tan An to villages in the surrounding area, and on orders from the district chief, they brought several truck loads to Khanh Hau.

Most village projects classified as "public works" have to do with agriculture, and since 1957 many have been carried out in conjunction with the School of Fundamental Education. The most successful of these were completed when Nguyen Van Mung was director of the school. Living in the village and working closely with the Village Council and the venerables, he initiated the successful Tuong Khanh canal project which served as a model for the Ap Thu Tuu canal. Relations between the council and school were very close, and a spirit of optimism pervaded the annual meeting of the school staff and villagers in November 1958.

In the months that followed, however, relations between the village and the school became strained. Nguyen Van Mung had been replaced by a director who lived in Cholon, and the staff of the school had removed themselves to the gleaming new buildings on the national highway. Although the school staff had restricted themselves very much to the administrative center of the village in Ap Dinh-A, they now made only occasional visits to the primary school. The Village Council was annoyed by Mung's dismissal, and felt slighted when the school staff members visiting the primary school failed to make a protocol visit to the Council House.

In the early months of 1959 several incidents aggravated the situation. On one occasion the school director hired some twenty village laborers to dig a reservoir. When payment for the work was not forthcoming, the laborers sought the aid of the village chief who appealed to the province chief, who in turn ordered the school to compensate the workers immediately. Several additional occurrences resulted in loss of face for the school. Unable to repair their broken gasoline-powered pump, some of the school staff asked the assistance of village farmers, promising to let them use it. When several villagers did repair the pump, news of it spread, and it was considered something of a joke. Also, villagers and members of the council visited one of the school's rice cultivation projects and found the results disappointing. The deputy chief told Woodruff: "They showed us how to plow, spread seeds, and what level of water to use, but their output was not as high as that of the villagers." [7] The deputy chief also expressed the council's intention to request no further assistance from the Provincial Agricultural Service or the School of Fundamental Education. By 1962 relations between

7. Pp. 233–34.

the school and the Village Council had improved, although lack of security prevented them from initiating any new projects in most parts of the village.

FINANCIAL AFFAIRS

Khanh Hau, as all other Vietnamese villages, is responsible for its own budget. It is prepared by the finance councillor and submitted to the Village Council for approval, after which it is presented to the province chief prior to the new fiscal year, which is the calendar year plus twenty days. Woodruff [8] describes the processing of the budget in the following passage:

> Budget processing for Khanh Hau required at least two months. After the entire Council had signed the draft, it was forwarded through channels to the provincial budget officer in the provincial headquarters. As explained by this officer, his major task concerned checking the arithmetic. Upon completing his review he would return it through channels to the village for final drafting which consisted of preparing four copies "in ink" to be resubmitted for final approval by the Province Chief. Although this procedure should be completed prior to the beginning of the calendar year, for 1958 the budget officer had not received the final copies by the 28th of March. Delays as such seemed to be accepted as part of the village–provincial budget system, and insofar as this observer could determine it seemed to have no adverse effect on administration in Khanh Hau.

Once in effect, the village officials were responsible for balancing the budget, and this was done in a relatively easy fashion. When a deficit occurred, the budget was put back in balance merely by adding the amount to the revenue column of the budget form as "subventions" from the province. The district chief pointed out that only three of the nine villages in the district did not need subventions because they had extensive communal paddy land.

Sources of village revenues include those from village property (communal lands, garden plots, pagoda land and dinh land); tax surcharges on paddy land, garden plots, farmstead sites, and houses; licenses, animal tax, vehicle tax, fines, and fees of various types; contributions for village celebrations; loans; and subventions. Between 1956 and 1958 the major local source of revenue was from cong dien, village communal paddy land, but this income was diminishing. In 1958 the provincial authorities issued a decree that cong dien rentals would be reduced because of the drought. In

8. Pp. 73–75.

addition, the province chief decided to adjust cong dien rents to the rates set in the Agrarian Reform Program rather than by competitive bidding which might raise the rentals. The end result was a 30 per cent reduction in these revenues—from 27,158$ VN in 1957 to 20,000$ in 1958. When open bidding was reinstated in 1959, however, the revenue increased to 35,000$ (22 farmers attended the bidding for the 19 lots, the largest of which was 1.2 hectares, and the rent was fixed at 40$ per gia of paddy harvested).

Village officials lament that the village is "poor" because its relatively small amount of communal land provides small revenues.[9] Before World War II the village ceded 2 hectares to a neighboring village in an agreement with the provincial authorities and in 1958, as the result of a decision made at the provincial level, 5 hectares were leased to the School of Fundamental Education on a long-term basis. This diminished the cong dien by 30 per cent, and some of the poor tenant farmers complained. Although communal land in principle is for the needy (and is intended for welfare rather than for revenues), in recent years the police agent and village clerk, both of whom are landowners, were among the renters.

During the 1956–58 period, assistance from the provincial budget increased steadily, amounting to 56 per cent by 1958. Interesting too is the fact that taxes on animals produced increasing revenues, and by the end of the period they surpassed the tax on private paddy fields as a source of village income. The taxes imposed by the village actually are surcharges of existing taxes set by the provincial and central governments. The taxable possessions and rates are fixed by the higher authorities each year, and the village simply adds to them to gain its own revenues.

Tax payments on paddy land are made in three ways for most villagers. The villager can pay his taxes at the Council House either voluntarily or after being warned by village or district authorities. A village representative —the finance councillor or perhaps the village clerk—might go directly to the taxpayer's house (as the security situation worsened, this involved having an armed guard). The taxpayer may pay directly into the provincial treasury, a practice common for most nonresident landlords. The exception is Ong Hue, the largest landowner and resident of Saigon, who authorized the village chief to collect the tax due from the cash payments of rent made by each tenant.

As already indicated, the tax assessment depends on the quality of paddy

9. In the section on land use in Chapter 2 it was pointed out that communal land in Khanh Hau is 1.83% of the total area cultivated, somewhat less than the pre-World War II estimated average of 3% for southern Vietnam.

land in terms of its productivity,[10] the basic tax rate, and the village and provincial surcharge rates. Woodruff[11] notes that between 1956 and 1958 none of these varied, and (according to the village clerk) a former finance councillor had put all paddy land in the village into the higher-quality levels, and although these were known to be inaccurate they remained unchanged, apparently to obtain the maximal revenue. In 1959, however, tax rates on paddy land did diminish somewhat as a result of the 1958 drought, and the Village Council was authorized to make reductions of rent, which had been done after a tour of the village to inspect the state of the crops.

All house sites are taxed, but only houses with tile roofs are taxed, and in 1957 there were 34 such houses on the village rolls. Each was levied 29.70$ VN, and of this, 5.40$ was for the central government, 10.80$ for the provincial government, and 13.50$ for the village (a surcharge rate of 250 per cent of the national tax). Licenses were required of some general goods shops, and both Chinese pharmacists had to have special licenses. Surcharge taxes on buffalo and oxen are 15$, on horses 40$.

In examining the question of timing and delinquency in tax payments, Woodruff draws the following conclusions:

> This examination of the rice field tax collections was designed to provide some additional insights into the financial affairs in Khan Hau Village. Emphasis was placed on analyzing the pattern of payments made by the resident landowners. The examination showed the timing of tax payments. It was found that the tax year itself did not provide a significant proportion either of the total assessment or of the amount collected during the first 20 months of tax payments. The major peak in tax payments occurred from 12 to 14 months after the initial collections. Contrary to what might have been anticipated, smaller landowners seemed to have been more responsive during the first year than the larger landowners. However, by the end of the total period exam-

10. Since 1956, a committee, appointed by the province chiefs in the various regions (south, central, and highlands) have determined this classification, and in 1958 there were the following gradations:

Class	Kilos of Paddy Produced
Superior	2,000 +
First	2,000–1,200
Second	1,200–700
Third	700–500
Fourth	500–300
Fifth	300–

11. Pp. 75–82.

ined, smaller taxpayers were as a group more delinquent. This held true also in the identification of the "chronic delinquents," those land-owners who had failed to pay taxes for two consecutive years. Although the range itself for the delinquent group extended far into the larger landowner portion, the majority of the resident delinquents were the smaller taxpayers.

Concern about the lack of satisfactory tax collections obviously had been expressed many times and in many ways by the higher officials. Various devices ranging from praise to threats against the public officials, and from court suits to crop seizures against the villagers had been proposed, if not employed. These variations or these experiments indicated some bewilderment among the officials. In sharp contrast with the higher authorities, Khanh Hau village officials displayed little concern either about rice field tax collections or improvements in the overall tax system. Various factors might have brought about this lack of interest, such as: (1) awareness of the availability of financial assistance from the higher authorities; (2) unsympathetic identification of tax collection with central governmental rather than with village welfare; and (3) preference for a system of contributions rather than an expansion of the tax program even for village activities.[12]

Village expenditures are carefully recorded, and any expenditure exceeding 200$ VN must have the advance approval of either the district or province chief. (Table 15, derived from tables of monthly expenditures prepared by Woodruff,[13] indicates how available funds are allocated.) Salaries of the councillors, which according to the village records began on a regular basis in August 1957, were paid only sporadically, owing to lack of funds. According to members of the council, late salary payments are chronic, and they are forced to pay the clerk and laborers, as well as many other pressing expenses, out of their own pockets. When the President of the Republic visited the village in a tour of the area, the village chief paid the cost of arches and a tribune, for which he would presumably be reimbursed by the provincial budget when funds became available.

Early in 1957 the salaries of the canton secretary and the messenger were eliminated. In 1958 hamlet chiefs began receiving regular monthly payments, and in 1959 the Self-Defense Guards' salaries were increased and were paid monthly. Between 1956 and 1958, minor payments for such things

12. Pp. 118–22.
13. P. 100.

TABLE 15. Annual Village Expenditures, 1956–1958

Item	1956	1957	1958
		(Vietnamese dollars)	
Council		28,626	43,269
Clerk	9,030	10,920	10,920
Hamlet chiefs			16,200
Laborers	18,545	15,840	7,200
Stationery	2.580	1,374	1,378
Office equipment	1,216		
Lighting	1,320	1,425	1,320
Ceremonies*	3,371	2,160	500
Council travel	2,400	2,400	2,730
Canton secretary	4,551	1,755	
Canton messenger	4,230	1,278	
Self-Defense Guard	2,595	516	1,451
Information agent	9,600	5,400	
Youth programs	1,200		
Education	600		
Election lists	315		
Communist Denunciation Committee	223		
First aid agent		3,000	
Travel, cult committee†		450	
Military‡		1,370	300
Public opinion			
Box			130
Meat inspection			
Stamp			100
Information material			170
Extra expenditures	2,000		

* Expenditure for other than annual ceremonies such as those held in the dinh.
† For a delegation of venerables to attend a graduation ceremony of a training program of leadership for rural youth at the district headquarters in Thu Thua.
‡ Travel for draftees.

as travel, stationery, and illuminating gas for the Council House had been regularized. There also were intermittent "ad hoc" expenses for a ceremony honoring Marshal Duc, uniforms for the Self-Defense Guards, materials for the Communist Denunciation Committee, and travel expenses for the Self-Defense Guards to attend a rally in a neighboring province and for the soccer team captain to attend a youth meeting. Between 1960 and 1962, expenditures associated with increased security measures rose considerably. The membership of the Self-Defense Guard rose from about 15 to over 100.

Ad hoc expenditures during this period were for more uniforms for the Self-Defense Guards and additional materials for the Communist Denunciation Committee. Although implementation of the Strategic Hamlet Program was being largely financed by provincial funds and villagers' contributions, it nonetheless meant additional expenditure by the village.

Woodruff[14] points out that "in view of the limited role of self-government in Khanh Hau it was not surprising to see the systematic and frequent check made on village financial activities." These checks are in the form of monthly, quarterly, and annual reviews. At the end of every month the receipt books, which are the financial records of the village, are carried to the district chief's office for his review, after which the village is notified that the records will be returned. The quarterly review is similar in procedure, but the records are submitted to the provincial administration, and a standard form is provided to systematize the information. The annual report, submitted to the district and forwarded from there to the province, is a single-page statement entitled "Condition of Taxes and Revenues."

LAW AND ORDER

One of the most important functions of the Village Council is to maintain order in the village, and while this has been expanded to include matters of political security, traditionally it simply meant punishing the guilty and arbitrating disputes. Crimes are rare in Khanh Hau. Most disorders are torts, and there are numerous conflicts between individuals and families. In the traditional Village Council, justice was a matter for the Huong Chanh, and the usual procedure was for the accused and accuser to swear to the truth of their statements before the altar of the Guardian Spirit of the Village. Each would have a live chicken, and as they made their oaths, they would cut or tear off the chickens' heads, begging the Guardian Spirit to strike them dead if they lied. Traditional punishments were cane thrashings for ordinary villagers and fines for notables.

In general, villagers attempt to resolve their difficulties themselves. When a difference remains unresolved, it usually comes to the attention of the five-family group head or the hamlet chief. Either can arbitrate, and should the decision prove unsatisfactory, it is taken to the Village Council. Rarely is a case appealed beyond this level. Villagers fear having their problems presented to harsh or cold strangers at the district tribunal. The council also prefers to keep village problems from district authorities whose legal deci-

14. Pp. 122–28.

sions are too rigid, and having Khanh Hau disputes recorded there would cause the village to lose face.

Between August 1956 and May 1958, an estimated sixty to ninety cases —three or four each month—were brought to the Village Council for arbitration. For the most part they concerned marital relationships, family lands, irrigation problems, physical assaults, rent issues, and land use. At first glance it is surprising that family problems should be included, since there are strong sanctions against airing them in public. Villagers feel strongly that difficulties between members of the family should be resolved within the family, and usually this is the responsibility of the truong toc in collaboration with older male and female members. In examining the recorded cases, however, with the exception of some disputes over land, family problems are marital—between affinal rather than consanguineous kin.

While most disputes come to the attention of the Village Council through a hamlet chief, some are brought to the council directly, either in writing or, more commonly, orally. One example of a written complaint is the following letter:

> To lodge a complaint:
> My name is Vo Thi Chinh, I submit this application to the Village Council to solve a problem of *hui*[15] in which Madame Huong Bo Dien has been involved with me.
>
> The *hui* will last for 500 days. So far there are in all six openings but she has contributed only once and missed the five others. I have asked her many times for money, but she has always promised to pay me later. I have no money to pay other participants: they are very dissatisfied. Madame Huong Bo Dien still refuses to pay me in order that I may pay others.
>
> Now I submit this application to request a solution from the Village Council. Thank you very much.

In principle, any member of the Village Council may hear a case. The police chief, however, in declaring to a villager, "Don't bring it to me unless it's 'bloody,'" made it clear that he prefers to deal only with criminal offenses. The Self-Defense Guard which is under his control, however, serves as an arm of the law in the village and may be called upon when needed regardless of the gravity of the difficulty. When disputes are brought to the Council House, whichever councillor is present may arbitrate. Procedures

15. See Chapter 6 and Appendix D.

are informal. The disputing parties usually stand on opposite sides of the room, and each presents his version of the case. Witnesses for either or both then are heard.

Part of the pattern is for the arbitrator to appear somewhat disinterested, often continuing to read a document or carry on some business with another villager or the village clerk. The Village Chief employs two techniques. One is to invoke a moral message, the other is to treat the situation lightly; sometimes he combines them. For example when Ong Ke Hien brought action against a tenant farmer for cutting down a banana tree on his property, the village chief advised him to be lenient, noting that he already had abundant worldly goods, and mercy would befit the highest venerable. Ong Ke Hien was moved by this argument and dropped the case.

The seeming facetiousness of the second technique appears to be a mechanism for preventing discussion from becoming too heated. In one case concerning nonpayment of rent, the plaintiff, a woman known to be well-to-do and somewhat miserly, was becoming increasingly excited as she explained her side of the case. The defendant, in contrast, sat huddled, looking at the floor. Suddenly the village chief, who had been giving orders to the clerk, motioned for the woman to stop. "Madam," he said calmly, "why don't you forget the rent? This man is poor, and if you are kind, perhaps he will pray to Buddha for you in gratitude." After a pause he added, "You are getting old, you know, and you will need prayers more than money." Everyone in the Council House laughed, the plaintiff became calm, and the case was settled.

On another occasion, a woman from Ap Cau and her sister appeared at the Council House with a complaint against their neighbor who, in the course of an argument, struck her on the face. She pointed out to the village chief that this man was known for his aggressiveness, and she emphasized this by citing an incident during which he hit his own father. Since she would require medical treatment, she wanted her assailant to pay the bills. The village chief agreed to give her a medical certificate to visit the clinic in Tan An but was reluctant to pass judgment on the man's conduct. Another member of the Village Council advised her to forget it, saying that he would receive his punishment "according to the principles of justice." He also pointed out that perhaps the man already regretted his violence but was too shy to ask forgiveness.

The woman, however, was not placated. She retorted that if she did not bring charges against her neighbor he might well interpret this as a sign of weakness and strike her even harder should they argue again. She also added that having one side of her face swollen as it was made her ugly, whereupon the village chief suggested that she let her neighbor strike her on the other side of the face so as to restore the balance. This brought laughter, even from the woman, and she agreed to drop her charges and accept the certificate for medical treatment.

Personal relationships are occasionally invoked as a means of influencing the judge. In one such instance a young man was accused of behaving in a very forward manner with a young woman of a neighboring family. The defendant's mother pleaded on his behalf, and after presenting several arguments for dropping the case, she pointed out that the presiding councillor was a kinsman of hers, and he therefore should be lenient with her son. The councillor refused to be swayed, and the boy was fined 40$ VN. A councillor may refuse to hear a case because one party is a kinsman or close friend. On one occasion a councillor was approached by his younger brother to hear a case, and the councillor refused, advising his brother to forget about it because it was nonsensical.

In Chapter 6 it was pointed out that villagers consider duck raising on any large scale impractical because of lack of ponds and sufficient space for sizable flocks. It is interesting that two of the three 1957 property damage cases in the village records concerned ducks. In one case the ducks swarmed into a villager's field and ate some of the paddy; the owner of the flock, a wealthy woman, offered to pay for the damage but the property owner refused, saying that the ducks had purposely been let into the field. Being wealthy, he argued, she could well afford to pay. In the discussion that ensued, one of his kin struck the woman. The case reached the Village Council but both sides refused to settle, and it was continued indefinitely. Another case involved the head of a five-family group. A landowner had killed some ducks in a flock that passed over his fields, and the five-family head declared that he had witnessed no damage by the ducks. The property owner retorted that when he had asked the five-family head and the owner of the ducks to keep them off his field, neither took action. The Village Council ordered the landowner to apologize, and when he refused he was fined 40$ VN. Also the penalty was posted in the Council House for all to see as a mark of his disrespect for council orders.

During this period, nine cases of physical violence were recorded with the Village Council. One record simply consisted of a statement signed by a man and his sister's son that they would refrain from quarreling. Another case, brought to the council by a Self-Defense Guard, was against a girl who struck her mother-in-law. She apologized and was fined 8$. Another concerned a charge by a young farmer that the hamlet chief had assaulted his father during an argument while the two were returning from a funeral. Several days later, changed testimony of the young man made it clear that his father had been intoxicated and fought with the hamlet chief when the latter tried to assist him home. An example of appeal was a case in which a woman found her child fighting with another child, and she slapped the other child's face, causing his nose to bleed. The Village Council ruled that an apology would be sufficient, but the injured child's mother refused to accept the verdict on the ground that there had been medical expenses. The council changed its decision, imposing a fine of 100$ for medical expenses.

Another reported incident of physical violence involved a hamlet chief who, during a struggle with a man and his wife, struck the woman, injuring her badly. At the hearing in the Council House, the hamlet chief agreed to pay the 2,500$ medical expenses (the highest expenses involved in any recorded case). Another costly case concerned a dispute between two families over a debt of 28$ which led to a fight, during which one of the wives was injured. She asked for 1,000$, refusing a 700$ compromise settlement suggested by the Village Council. When this happened, the council referred the case to the district chief.

Village records included three cases of land disputes, two of which, although lacking details, involved kin. One was a complaint written by a young man who contended that while he was in the army, his father's younger brother had unfairly assumed control of family land. Another was a dispute between a man and his younger brother's son (who was described in the file as "tough") over some family land. No action had been taken in either case. The remaining case involved a landlord who asked the council to notify his tenants that their rent contracts were terminated; this came to the council when the tenants refused to agree and requested a two-year extension.

There also are several recorded disputes over property. One concerned ownership of a dog, and another was between a man and his brother-in-law over two houses. Disputes over water usage are many, although most are resolved without recourse to the council. In one such case, Farmer A contended that Farmer B tricked him into pumping water into his field. It seems A's fields were removed from the stream, and B gave permission to flow water through his fields. After one day of pumping, when B's field was flooded and the water was only beginning to run in A's field, B refused to allow A to continue pumping. The case went to the Village Council, then to the district chief who ordered Farmer B to pay Farmer A 1,000$.[16]

Marital difficulties brought to the attention of the Village Council included allegations of adultery, desertion, and incompatibility. In one case a villager accused his wife of adultery, specifying that she had had relations with another man on three occasions. When the Village Council summoned her to present her defense, she failed to appear, and no action was taken. Three desertion cases were recorded. A young bride had deserted her husband, going to Saigon with another man. The Village Council communicated with her, advising her to return, but she refused. Another woman left her husband and took her children with her. In a meeting of the husband, wife, and her parents at the Council House, the parents agreed to settle the dispute within ten days. In the third case of desertion, the wife took 6,000$ when she departed, and her whereabouts were unknown.

Village records contain several formal requests for separation. In one case the separating couple met at the Council House with the hamlet chief, the head of their five-family group, various kinfolk, and some neighbors. The husband presented a written statement authorizing his wife to remarry. Shortly thereafter, however, the couple decided to renew cohabitation (and the Village Chief pointed out that had they really wanted a separation, legal action would have been necessary). Another case was somewhat more complicated. The wife made the request for separation on the ground that her husband refused to work, but when the hamlet chief examined further, he found that they had not actually been married, and also that on one occasion she had threatened to kill him. The Village Council decided to fine the woman 40$, whereupon she fled the village. When she returned, the Self-Defense Guard took her into custody, but she was released when she and her alleged husband agreed to a separation and property division.

Woodruff [17] attended the hearing of one marital difficulty centered on a girl of 18 who had just been married and refused to remain with her husband. The boy, his parents, and the girl accompanied by her mother presented the case to the deputy chief. The girl's mother declared the boy at fault (noting that her own husband was opposed to discussing the problem before the Village Council; she, however, felt it had to be settled even if it meant going to court). The boy's father responded that the girl had left her husband because he was ill. After a discussion concerning who was re-

16. Woodruff, pp. 175–91.
17. P. 186.

sponsible for dealing with the girl—getting her to return to her husband—the girl firmly declared that she would not rejoin him. If her parents would not take her back, she would leave the village. She and her mother then departed. The boy's father concluded that separation was inevitable, but he wanted an agreement that his son could marry again. The boy's father reminded the deputy chief that, although tradition prescribed that the girl return the bride price, he would not demand it, in order to facilitate the settlement.

Many villagers lament that the long years of war have disrupted the normally tranquil life of the village and that, in addition to breeding a great deal of conflict, there also has been a lessening in the deeply rooted respect villagers have always had for one another. Worst of all, there has been violence, and even before the violence of the 1960–62 period, there were several incidents that jarred village society. One occurred late in 1959 when a fight between two villagers resulted in the death of one. A group of men, including the jovial barber from Ap Dinh-B and a prosperous farmer from the same hamlet, were drinking rice alcohol one warm afternoon, and the two became engaged in an argument. This ended in a fight during which the barber pushed the farmer, who fell backwards, hitting his head on the exposed root of an old tree. Before medical assistance could be summoned, the farmer died.

The police agent and other members of the council took the matter in hand before the provincial police came to take the barber to jail. Villagers were shocked, and a group gathered in one of the shops agreed that the barber was not to blame. When the village chief organized welfare for the barber's almost destitute family, most residents in the hamlet contributed either cash or food, and Ong Ke Hien donated twenty liters of rice. The barber remained in custody for more than a month, after which the death was ruled accidental, and he was released. In the meanwhile, however, his shop had been dismantled by the landlord because rent had not been paid. Again the Village Council rallied and collected money for a new shop.

Another disturbing incident took place in May 1958 when a villager attempted suicide, the first anyone could recall. "The Suicide," as everyone referred to him for a period, was a man of thirty, unmarried and living with his mother in a small thatched house. He had been employed as a driver by one of the companies that operate jitneys from Tan An to My Tho, and his neighbors described him as a poor man. They also pointed out that although he had reached the age of thirty, he had not yet married, implying that this somewhat abnormal state might shed some light on his state of mind. He had taken an overdose of sleeping pills which he had purchased in Tan An, but before they could have their effect, his mother summoned help.

Prior to taking the pills, he wrote a note addressed to the Village Council, which read:

> I accuse nobody
> To accuse somebody would cause much trouble
> I have had enough of life, and I want to die
> I have taken sleeping pills.

He also wrote another note expressing the following anomic sentiment:

> I am discouraged with life on earth
> I want to see the nether world
> Nobody needs me
> I shall kill myself.

The village chief talked with the man several times, but no other action was taken.

Since 1955, maintaining security (which means keeping the Viet Cong in abeyance) has become a responsibility of the Village Council. Numerous organizations have been launched with the aim of generating loyalty to the central government, and anti-Communist propaganda has made its way into many village celebrations. Anti-Communist slogans on banners, signs, and pamphlets and shouted from sound trucks have become part of the village scene. Support of the central government is the major theme of the National Revolutionary Movement, which is the only official political party in the village.[18] Its membership includes most of the village leaders—members of the Village Council and the high venerables of the Cult Committee—and it has its headquarters in Ong Van's[19] house near the primary school.

Recruiting members for the party is one responsibility of the Village Council. During 1958 and 1959, at some of the large village-sponsored gatherings, speakers emphasized the necessity for villagers to join the party to demonstrate their loyalty to the government and their will to fight the Viet

18. With the coup d'etat of November 1, 1963, and the end of the regime of President Ngo Dinh Diem, the National Revolutionary Movement was disbanded.

19. Ong Van is the villager who won 1,000,000$ in the national lottery; his profile is included in Chapter 10.

Cong.[20] On these occasions the villagers appeared impassive. As far as could be determined, membership in the party was relatively small, and in spite of attractive programs such as the party cooperative to sell cheaper fertilizer to members, villagers still appeared reluctant to affiliate themselves openly with any political party.

The most military of the new organizations is the Self-Defense Guard, all of whose members are from Khanh Hau. Centered in the Ap Dinh-A stockade, the Self-Defense Guard is under the direction of the police agent. Until 1959 there were about 15 guards, all volunteers from poor families in the village, but with the increase in Viet Cong activities in 1960–62, young men from all ranges of village society were pressed into service, swelling the ranks to over 100. They receive a monthly salary of 900$ VN and are given black uniforms. When on duty they carry bolt-action rifles and eat and sleep in the stockade.

The Self-Defense Guards maintain observation posts around the village, go on night patrols, and provide escorts when needed (e.g. councillors collecting taxes in Ap Nhon Hau). During the 1960–62 period they had several nocturnal encounters with Viet Cong patrols. In one such clash the police agent was slain, and in another a guardsman was killed. As indicated earlier, the guardsmen sometimes bring quarreling villagers to the Council House, and they also carry messages for the Village Council. They often participate in such village projects as construction of the new pagoda honoring Marshal Duc.

The Hamlet Guard, which was replaced by the Rural Defense Guard in 1962, also was under the police agent. It was not voluntary nor were the members paid. With few exceptions, membership was required of all village "youths" between the ages of 18 and 45. Their primary duty was to stand night guard duty at various points throughout the village. Armed only with

20. Woodruff, p. 146, quotes two speakers at such gatherings in the following passages:

A revolution cannot be carried out by an army or by a security organization or a police force but only by all citizens, all the inhabitants of the countryside. Why are we still far from being efficient in our fight against the Communists? Because we have not succeeded in putting all the villagers in the same political organization, the National Revolutionary Movement, and because the villagers still have an indifferent attitude toward the anti-Communist policy of the government.

Myself, when I popularize the governmental policies, I directly participate in the political life of our country. Why not you? Why are you somewhat afraid of politics? Comfort yourselves, I would say. Since the top leader of the organization—the National Revolutionary Movement—is our President himself, any of you who fails to join shows evidence of his indifference and could be regarded as guilty.

poles 2 meters long and a short piece of rope, they were not intended to engage in combat with Viet Cong patrols, but rather to signal the Self-Defense Guard on bamboo or wooden drums placed around the hamlet.

The five-family groups, in addition to providing a mechanism for disseminating news and instructions, are designed to generate a spirit of communal solidarity through mutual aid. Group leaders also may be called upon to arbitrate difficulties among members. It is through these groups that attendance for meetings is rallied, and they are supposed to form a surveillance network in which the movements of strangers in the hamlet or suspicious activities of any member of the group are reported to the leader who in turn informs the hamlet chief. By and large, the operation of the system is very uneven. Some groups are active while others are not. There also is a pattern of frequent change of group composition, with the result that some families have no idea to which group they belong.

In 1956 the central government launched a program to establish village associations throughout the rural areas. Four associations were formed in Khanh Hau—one each for men and women between the ages of 18 and 45, another for those from 45 to 60. Membership in principle was voluntary, but all were expected to join. There was a province committee as well as a district committee, and at the village level there was a central committee for each association. The village police agent served as the head of each committee, and in each hamlet there was a committee under the hamlet chief. The aims of the associations were similar to those of the five-family groups. Officially they were designed to stimulate mutual aid, create more community solidarity, and induce more active participation in village affairs. Since the village associations cut across five-family group lines, they were supposed to be a supplementary means of maintaining security.

By 1959, the only active village association was that of the younger men. In addition to supplying recruits for the Self-Defense Guard, it also maintained a soccer team. From time to time the police agent arranged to have military physical culture instructors visit the village to lead the young men in calisthenics, and on several occasions the young men organized well-attended concerts of classical Vietnamese music at the dinh. The young women's association functioned more or less as an auxiliary to the young men's association, and it had no program of its own. Villagers pointed out that this was due to "the natural shyness of young women in the village." The police agent attributed the inactivity of the older groups to the fact that they were too busy with households and farms to support the associations.

Early in 1962, with the launching of the Strategic Hamlet Program in the village, some organizations were changed, and plans were made for establishing new ones. The village associations were replaced by the Republican Youth group which includes all villagers between the ages of 18 and 35. By April 1962 some 40 residents of Ap Dinh A–B formed the initial group, and plans were made to extend the organization into other hamlets (Ap Nhon Hau, Ap Cau, and Ap Thu Tuu still were very insecure—to all intents and purposes under Viet Cong control). The Hamlet Guard was replaced by the Rural Defense Guard which has the same form and functions. Also plans were drawn up for the Women's Social Solidarity Movement and a women's paramilitary organization intended to supplement the Self-Defense Guard.[21] The Village Council already had received notice that registration of women between the ages of 16 and 30 had begun at the provincial headquarters. One of the primary propaganda vehicles in the village is the Communist Denunciation Committee, which consists of 24 members who, according to the village chief, are drawn from the "elite" of the village (including all members of the council and some high venerables). Every Saturday evening there is a hamlet Communist denunciation meeting, and the hamlet chief and five-family leaders are responsible for seeing that all male residents over 18 years are in attendance. On the fifteenth day of each lunar month there is a general Communist denunciation meeting held at the dinh in Ap Dinh-A. The committee in collaboration with the information agent organizes this meeting, and usually they provide a speaker from Civic Action, the Civil Guard, or the Provincial Information Service. Villagers dutifully assist at these meetings, but most do not appear particularly attentive. Some squat outside the dinh chatting in low tones while a few read newspapers. After one denunciation meeting, a young farmer regaled his friends in one of the nearby shops by imitating the speaker of the evening. In addition, the committee distributes posters and banners, some of which exhort villagers to "love the fatherland" and "improve agricultural production," while others decry the "Communist crooks" and "Viet Cong, engaging in pillage, assassination, and arson against their compatriots."

EDUCATION

According to villagers, in 1925 the French administration constructed a primary school in Ap Dinh-A and named it after Marshal Nguyen Huynh

21. After the coup d'etat on November 1, 1963, the Republican Youth, the Women's Social Solidarity Movement, and the planned women's paramilitary organization were abolished by the new government.

Duc. It consisted of three classrooms and offered instruction in the first three grades of the five-grade Vietnamese primary education. Late in 1945, when the Japanese had withdrawn from Vietnam and the Viet Minh assumed temporary control of the village administration, the school was burned. Several months later, the villagers rallied and constructed a new wooden school with a thatched roof. In 1949 two classrooms were added, and several teachers were hired to expand the course of instruction to five grades, permitting village children to receive the primary education certificate.

That same year the new director of the primary school launched a campaign to raise funds for the construction of a more substantial school building. The villagers responded enthusiastically with practically every family in the village donating some money. The central government allotted 50,-000$ VN, enabling construction of a five-classroom masonry building with a corrugated iron roof. In 1952 Ong Van, the tenant farmer who had won in the national lottery, generously contributed 130,000$ for the construction of an additional five-classroom building with a large concrete water tank abutted. Late in 1958 the school acquired another frame building when the UNESCO School of Fundamental Education abandoned its original quarters and moved to the new buildings constructed beside the national highway.

At present the Nguyen Huynh Duc school consists of three long buildings, each containing five classrooms, arranged in a compound. The central area is shaded by trees and serves as a playground.[22] In 1945 the enrollment was 120, rising to 636 by 1950, and in 1959 it increased to 778, approximately half of whom were girls. Pupils come from all of the hamlets as well as from the neighboring villages of Tan Hoi and Loi Binh Nhon. In spite of the constant physical expansion of the school, there continues to be a shortage of classrooms, necessitating use of the dinh and the rear section of the Ap Moi pagoda.

Primary education is free, and although the Ministry of Education supplies a limited number of textbooks, most pupils must provide their own. There is no library, nor is there a refectory. Pupils living in Ap Dinh-A, Ap Dinh-B, and nearby sections of Ap Moi go home for their midday meal, but those from distant parts of the village and neighboring villages carry their own food. At noon the children gather in the shade around the schoolyard and the dinh to eat from metal containers or banana-leaf wrappings. Most have rice garnished with a bit of fish, perhaps a cooked vegetable, and usually a condiment such as crushed fermented pork or fish sauce. Only a

22. Boys seem to prefer tag, kicking soccer balls, cricket fights, and races, while the girls usually play jacks or jump rope.

few have meat. Some children purchase food from the vendors who set up small stands near the school, and others purchase sandwiches in nearby shops.

The curriculum is the standard primary school program prepared by the Ministry of Education in Saigon. Prior to 1958 the Provincial Education Service was directly responsible for administration of the school, and the provincial budget paid teachers' salaries. When the School of Fundamental Education was established, it assumed technical responsibility for courses at the primary school. This proved fortunate for Khanh Hau; the security situation was making it increasingly difficult to get teachers in the villages, and 9 of the 15 teachers at the Nguyen Huynh Duc school were provided by the School of Fundamental Education (and it paid their salaries).

Also in 1958 the Village Council began to take a more active interest in the primary school, chiefly, according to Woodruff,[23] because of community dissatisfaction with the administration of the school. The village chief outlined the history of conflicts between the parents and the school directors: the first director was too old and had little contact with the parents; the second director was too young, and he aroused the ire of the parents by allegedly keeping the tank water for his own uses, giving the pupils canal water. At the request of the parents he was transferred. The current director is more popular because he organized a prize-giving ceremony, but he failed to invite the high venerables to the 1958 presentation.

Interest in school affairs has resulted in considerable cooperation between the Village Council and the school director. The council sought to aid the school in obtaining some equipment promised by the province chief, and the finance councillor served as special chairman on a committee to raise funds for the school. The council also allowed the school to use space in the dinh and the pagoda for classrooms. The school has reciprocated by assigning three teachers to assist in the village census, and the school's Boy Scout troop participates in major village celebrations. Members of the Village Council also are invited to the annual prize awards at the end of the school year.

The prize-giving ceremony held in 1959 was a mixture of religious ritual, anti-Communist propaganda, awards for scholastic merit, and entertainment by the pupils. The province chief was represented by his deputy, a young army captain. The district chief, members of the Village Council, and several high venerables had places of honor in the front of the room, near a temporary altar with the usual large brass incense burner, candles, vases filled with flowers, and several offering plates piled with fruit. The first act of the

23. Pp. 258–64.

ceremony was to honor the deceased school teachers. The school director, the deputy province chief, and the district chief, holding burning joss, kowtowed before the altar. After this brief ritual, the school director addressed the assembly, giving thanks to the honored guests for their assistance. The district chief then read a message from the President of the Republic, and the deputy province chief followed with a speech decrying the disastrous effects of Communism in the schools—"the pupils become treacherous toward friends and disrespectful toward parents." Before the awards a voice from a hidden microphone sounded: "At the present time, Communist North Vietnam is burdened with hardships. Our south is peaceful." The guests presented the awards to deserving pupils, and the celebration ended with songs and dances by the pupils.

In 1957, Nguyen Van Mung, the first director of the School of Fundamental Education, organized a class of primary school graduates for instruction at the sixth-grade level—secondary education in the Vietnamese system. At that time, only a very small number of Khanh Hau children continued on to the secondary level. In addition to being costly, many families felt that secondary education was not essential. Also, conditions in most village houses are not conducive to serious study; lighting is very poor and there is a lack of privacy (in only a few houses are there any books).

Six of the sixty primary school graduates registered in Mung's first class, and after Mung's departure one of the former primary school directors assumed responsibility for the courses. By September 1958 there were 41 students being instructed by five teachers, all of whom had regular teaching posts in other Long An province secondary schools. By village standards, tuition is rather high—160$ for the sixth grade and 170$ for the seventh. Currently, with the approval of the Village Council, classes are held in a Quonset hut constructed by the French troops near the Council House, and variously used by the staff of the School of Fundamental Education and the Self-Defense Guards.

In addition to establishing a secondary school in Khanh Hau, Nguyen Van Mung also made it possible for the village to have its first kindergarten. Before leaving the village he turned over to the village chief money he had received from the Asia Foundation for the kindergarten project. The village chief proceeded with the project, and late in 1958 a one-room structure with thatched roof, latticed walls, and brick floor was constructed. Equipment was obtained from the canton chief, a friend of the village chief. A lady from the hamlet, who had received seven years' education and was considered of "honorable character" was appointed teacher, with a salary of 1,000$ monthly, paid by the district authorities.

As early as 1952 a program for adult literacy instruction was launched by the central government. Known as Popular Education, the program received a great deal of national support in 1956, and the Bureau of Primary and Popular Education was responsible for extending the program to all sectors. In Khanh Hau the Village Council, working with district authorities, implemented the program, and classes in the national language continue to be held each day for an hour and a half at 7:30 P.M. for illiterate villagers between the ages of 13 and 50. The Village Council sends members of the Self-Defense Guard to the homes of those who do not attend, to "advise them of the Village Council's interest in the program."

HEALTH AND WELFARE

Threats to the general health of the village are met with some form of action by the Village Council. Recent examples of such action were the council's successful petition to have military trucks bring water to the village during the 1958 drought, and their willingness to organize the traditional rain-making ritual during this crisis. Also, the Village Council quickly suppressed a rumor about a cholera death in the village at the height of the drought. Even in years of normal rainfall, the council, in collaboration with the Cult Committee, hires a sorcerer to perform a special ritual exorcising evil spirits from the village, particularly the dread spirit of cholera, as part of the annual Cau An celebration. When a bubonic plague struck parts of southern Vietnam in 1959, the council disseminated precautionary measures outlined in a letter from the district health office.

The Village Council also has been instrumental in bringing Western medicine to the village. As part of his hygiene program, Nguyen Van Mung organized a team of students to visit each hamlet and give smallpox inoculations, and with the cooperation of the Village Council the project was carried out successfully. A medical cabinet containing 25 different kinds of Western medicines was received in the village through the American Aid Program, and until the village hired a nurse in 1959 it was the responsibility of the civil status secretary. Since then the nurse has used it (getting replacements from Tan An) for his daily sick calls (most patients are children with coughs and mild digestive upsets).

The most recent health project in the village is the maternity center, completed in 1962. Financed by the Asia Foundation, it was planned by the

School of Fundamental Education and the Village Council. Prior to its construction, the school launched a campaign to interest villagers in it, but some of their techniques produced negative results. For example, one leaflet titled "Victim of Poor Sanitation" told in poetry how a lady in Ap Nhon Hau began to have labor pains, and her husband went on a fruitless search for a nurse. When she began delivery, everyone panicked, and someone used an unclean betel knife to cut the cord. As a result the child died "of tetanus, not due to fate." This unfortunate tract precipitated a rumor that a child actually had died in Ap Nhon Hau. The hamlet chief registered a verbal protest with the Village Council because he felt the story shed a bad light on his hamlet. Other villagers pointed out that the story was foolish because no one panics over a thing like childbirth, and few village women rely on the services of a nurse (they prefer an elder, experienced kinswoman or neighbor). Also, according to tradition, the cord is cut with a broken rice bowl. When the center did open a few women used it, and the Village Council felt that if all went well—that is, if no one died in it—the maternity center would attract women from the surrounding area.

Although in Khanh Hau communal paddy land has not been used exclusively for the needy, communal garden plots are let only to poor families, and there is a small patch of public burial ground for those who need it. The recently instituted Spring Tree celebration marks an attempt to provide a new source of welfare. Launched by the district chief, the Village Council was made responsible for implementing it. The first step was to organize a committee, which consisted of the village councillors, the director of the primary school, a representative of the National Revolutionary Movement, and the hamlet chiefs. With the aid of schoolteachers they began a fund collection for the village needy.

In 1957, the first year of the drive, only 167$ VN was collected (the deputy chief explained that this was because villagers already had contributed to three different programs). The 1958 collection, however, amounted to 3,000$, and the Village Council prepared a list of 31 adults and 14 children in need of assistance, including elderly villagers without support, young married laborers without work, the infirm, those with very low incomes, and children of the very poor. On the day of the Spring Tree celebration, during the lunar new year period, the gifts were distributed, and the village chief reported to the district chief that the recipients "seemed happy and grateful to the government." [24]

24. Woodruff, p. 156.

THE CULT OF MARSHAL NGUYEN HUYNH DUC

Until 1957 the prescribed cult rituals venerating Marshal Nguyen Huynh Duc were the responsibility of his descendants, particularly Ong Khai, the truong toc of the family. In that year the village chief and deputy chief conceived a scheme for improving the neglected tomb of the southern hero, and after meeting with Ong Ke Hien, some high venerables of both cult committees, and the hamlet chiefs, they called a general meeting which attracted about fifty villagers. The Village Chief reminded the gathering that in 1927 the French administration had authorized the village to refurbish the tomb and had paid the cost, and he informed them that now the village was again prepared to act. After this meeting the village chief explained the plan to the province chief who agreed to contribute 10,000$, also suggesting that the council organize a fund drive.

In response to this advice, the Village Council formed a committee of prominent citizens from the village and Tan An. These included Ong Ke Hien, who served as chairman, the village chief, deputy chief, a representative of the National Revolutionary Movement, director of the primary school, an ex-director of the primary school, and a well-known jeweler from Tan An. A goal of 300,000$ (later raised to 400,000$) was set. Also the plan evolved from simply restoring the existing tomb to construction of a new shrine which also would function as a museum containing Marshal Duc memorabilia. There would be two buildings—Lang Dong or East Shrine and Lang Tay or West Shrine.[25] In discussing the new scheme, the village chief pointed out that new buildings would be better than simply restoring the tomb because they would be gestures of greater honor, thus invoking even stronger protection from the Marshal's spirit; he also noted that new shrines would be more likely to attract tourists who would spend money in the village.

The village chief and deputy chief were the most active members of the committee. They prepared a leather-bound "Golden Book" in which the names of donors and amounts donated were carefully entered. The procedure for soliciting donations changed several times, and on the advice of the district chief they settled on a system whereby district chiefs would inform the wealthy—merchants, rice millers, and landowners—of the fund drive and then arrange a general meeting with the committee members visiting

25. *Lang* literally refers to a mausoleum or structure associated with an elaborate tomb such as an imperial tomb, and usually it is a place where rituals venerating the dead may be performed. Shrine, therefore, would be about the most appropriate English word to use.

the district. Provincial and district agencies also donated funds. By September 1959 the contributions amounted to 600,000$ or 200,000$ in excess of the goal. In addition to the 100,000$ collected by the committee, some 240,000$ was contributed by the National Institute of Archaeology and Preservation of Historical Monuments, and 250,000$ was obtained from the Mutual Assistance Fund of Long An province with the authorization of the province chief.

While the fund drive was being conducted in 1958, the Duc family celebrated the anniversary of the Marshal's death on the eighth day of the ninth lunar month. Whereas this is normally a family affair, because of the revived interest in the memory of Marshal Duc it was attended by the province chief, the Village Council, some high venerables, and several visitors, giving it the air of an official village celebration. The ritual took place at the main altar in the house. Candles burned brightly, the vases were filled with flowers, and food offerings were piled on platters. (According to members of the family, until the advent of Cao Daism, food offerings consisted of chicken, beef dishes, and pork, but a spirit message from the Marshal ordered his descendants to offer him non-meat dishes, so the offerings were soybean cakes, fruit, and vegetables.) Boys in robes such as those worn during rituals at the dinh stood beside the altar while the male members of the family, male guests, and female members of the family kowtowed. After the ritual a vegetarian meal was served to the guests.

The assemblage then moved outdoors where about forty villagers were gathered. The village chief introduced the province chief, who spoke of his disappointment at the neglected state of the Marshal's tomb and shrine. It was wrong "that the Marshal's altar should be under a worn roof." It was, he emphasized, the responsibility of the Duc family, the Village Council, and the people to raise money to restore the tomb and shrine. When the councillors and Ong Khai gathered for tea after the speech, the province chief was more specific in his admonishments—there were no flowers on the tomb, and he complained about the indifference of the villagers. The following year the province chief was represented by his deputy, but the Village Council had assumed some responsibility in the preparations. There were many flowers, including a large wreath provided by the village chief, and there also were more villagers in attendance.

As the fund drive was being carried out, the National Institute of Archaeology and Preservation of Historical Monuments retained an architect to draw plans for the first building, the West Shrine, which was to be traditional in form with "a modern look." Before excavating the foundation, a temporary altar was arranged and a ritual honoring the Spirit of the Soil was performed. Afterward, each member of the Village Council carried a basketful of soil for the site (they explained that this was a symbolic gesture of their participation in the project). Needy laborers hired by the village then began excavating.[26]

By December 1959 the completed shrine stood gleaming in the middle of a newly planted garden of brilliantly colored plants and miniature trees set in ceramic pots. Constructed of masonry with a tile roof, the new shrine combines modern simplicity with lilting touches of traditional elegance. The district chief, members of the Duc family, the Village Council, numerous members of the Cult Committee (including the high venerables), representatives from the neighboring villages of Loi Binh Nhon, An Vinh Ngai, and Tan Hoi, as well as a scattering of visitors, gathered for the inauguration of the shrine on December 24, 1959. Converging on the old shrine, they paid homage to the Marshal by kowtowing at his altar. Male members of the Duc family were first, then the district chief and other male villagers followed the kowtow order prescribed for rituals in the dinh. After the kowtowing, documents containing the Marshal's royal titles were placed on a palanquin which had belonged to him. Borne by older students from the primary school and accompanied by musicians playing drums and gongs, the palanquin led the procession to the new shrine. After the treasured documents were placed on the new altar, the kowtowing was repeated.

The inauguration ended with a brief address by the district chief who first apologized on behalf of the province chief for his absence because of pressing administrative affairs. He emphasized his belief in the need for the government to be aware of the cares and desires of the people, respecting even their veneration of spirits. The village chief thanked the district chief and added that construction of the second building would begin shortly. Owing to the increase in Viet Cong activities, however, plans for the second building were postponed. By spring of 1962 no work had begun on the second building and, according to villagers, cult rituals honoring the Marshal had been very small, and very few tourists had visited the new shrine.

26. They were paid at the rate of 30$ per cubic meter, and each was expected to dig 1.5 cubic meters a day.

CHAPTER 8

The Cult Committee

INFORMATION obtained from elderly Khanh Hau residents indicates that before the administrative reform of 1904 the Village Council shared responsibility for the dinh and the Guardian Spirit cult with a body of notables consisting of ex-councillors who retained their council titles and respected citizens who were given honorary titles. After the 1904 legislation and the emergence of standardized and secularized village councils, the body of notables became known as the Ban Hoi Huong, or Cult Committee, and this pattern was repeated in most southern villages. Since the earlier body of notables had no particular structure and composition, organization of cult committees varies from village to village. Vietnamese tradition, however, defines their primary functions: to organize and perform rituals honoring specific deities revered by the whole village, the foremost of which is the Guardian Spirit of the Village, and to maintain the dinh.

In southern Vietnamese society the Cult Committee encompasses that group of males most active in village affairs, and it invariably includes the village elite. During rituals at the dinh each member of the committee kowtows before the Guardian Spirit's altar according to a priority based on relative rank in the committee (see Table 16). This kowtowing order reflects a great deal about the relative place of the participants in the sociopolitical structure of the village.

COMPOSITION OF THE KHANH HAU CULT COMMITTEES

With two dinh, Khanh Hau has two Cult Committees, and a successful effort has been made to maintain organizational uniformity between them. Primary responsibility for perpetuating the dinh and rituals associated with the Cult of the Guardian Spirit of the Village lies with the ceremonial staff in each committee. Preserved from the traditional body of notables, this

TABLE 16. Cult Committees in Khanh Hau

Ap Dinh-A and Nhon Hau   *Common to the Hamlets*
(one for each hamlet)

HIGH VENERABLES   HIGHEST VENERABLE

Tien Bai   Ke Hien
Chanh Bai
Boi Bai
Pho Bai   VILLAGE COUNCIL
Chanh Te   Chanh Chu Tich (village chief)
Huong Quan   Xa Truong or Tai Chanh (finance)
Huong Ca   Canh Sat (police)
Huong Le (or Thay Le)
Ca Truong

NOTABLES

Chu Truong   Huong Bo
Giao Su   Huong Than
Huong Su   Huong Nghi
Huong Truong   Huong Luan
Huong Chanh   Huong Nhut
Huong Giao   Huong Nhi
Pho Huong Quan   Huong Huan
                                   Huong Hao
                                   Huong Ho

INITIATES
Pho Luc Bo
Thu Bo
Thu Bon

committee consists of five former village chiefs who hold the highest positions. In ranked order, they are the Ke Hien, wisest and most respected in
the village (as Table 16 indicates, there is a common Ke Hien for both
committees), the Tien Bai, Chanh Bai, overseer of celebrations in the dinh,
and their assistants, the Boi Bai and Pho Bai. The remaining titles in the
category of high venerables have no specific function. The incumbents are
expected to lend some assistance in organizing celebrations at the dinh and
contribute more cash than do those in other categories.

In spite of the 1904 legislation, the Village Council continues to have an
unofficial role in the activities of both cult committees, particularly in the
Ap Dinh-A committee because the dinh in that hamlet is the responsibility
of the Village Council. This includes maintaining the structure, appointing
the guardian, and administering dinh land. The village budget has an
allotment of funds for ceremonies at the Ap Dinh-A dinh, and from time
to time the village budget includes expenditures for travel by members of

village cult committees. Normally, members of the Village Council are active in organizing the annual celebrations associated with the dinh and, as village representatives, they play an important part in the rituals—it is they who make the offerings to the Guardian Spirit. Also, the village chief and deputy chief have a voice in naming new cult committee members as well as recommending higher titles for the deserving. Finally, it is necessary to have served as village chief in order to attain all but the Ca Truong title of the high venerable category of both committees. Although the Village Council is not included on their organization charts, in both committees it properly belongs below the high venerables. The next category includes the notables, and most members hold titles at this level; as the designation indicates, the initiates are those newly admitted to the cult committees.

While only one person may hold the title of Ke Hien, Tien Bai, Chanh Bai, Boi Bai, Pho Bai, or Chang Te, or any of the positions in the Village Council, more than one may hold any one of the other titles. For example, in 1958, 23 had the title Huong Chanh in the Ap Dinh-A committee while 20 had the rank of Huong Giao. There were 11 Huong Bo, whereas there was only one Huong Nghi and one Huong Luan. The size of the cult committees consequently varies from year to year. Between 1958 and 1962 the Ap Dinh-A committee membership ranged from 120 to 163, and the Ap Nhon Hau committee numbered about 110.

A villager must be of good character and manifest an interest in village affairs to become a member of the Cult Committee. The Ke Hien, Tien Bai, and Chanh Bai together with the village chief and deputy chief decide who will be offered membership and who will be advanced in rank. Since having a title in the Cult Committee is an honor bestowed by the village, acceptance is compulsory. Villagers agree there is prestige in being on the committee—indeed, it is essential if one is to join the ranks of the sociopolitical elite in village society. For the ordinary villager who cannot hope to move up to the higher ranks, however, membership often is a burden. One young laborer pointed out that he had to accept the Huong Hao title in spite of the fact that the 200$ contribution he was expected to make at the Cau An ritual forced him to borrow from kin. A tenant farmer expressed the opinion that the 200$ donation was too high for a low-ranking title and, while it did carry prestige, he got nothing else for it.

Should the burden of a title become insupportable, the accepted recourse is to present a convincing argument for resigning from the committee. In a group gathered in a shop, a laborer drew nods of assent when he stated that if he were sufficiently articulate, he would go to the council and talk his way out of his title. Hardship is not the only excuse for leaving the committee. Ong Xa Khanh, one of the wealthiest villagers and a former council member, resigned his title on grounds that his increasing landholdings demanded too much of his time.[1]

Upward mobility within the Cult Committee depends on age, moral character, wealth, education, and family background, with one or more factors assuming importance at different levels in the ranked order. Titles of initiate are given to young men of good character, usually sons of committee members. Eighteen is the minimum age, and most of the present initiates are about 21. With the exception of some young men who enter the committee at the Thu Bo or Pho Luc Bo levels, a new member commonly receives the rank of Thu Bon which he must retain for a minimum of two years before moving upward. Although these are low-level titles with no particular associated responsibilities, it is considered essential for a young man who aspires to high status in the Cult Committee to pass the apprentice period as an initiate. All those in the high venerable category as well as members of the Village Council had once been Thu Bon, Thu Bo, or Pho Luc Bo.

Position as a notable differs only in relative rank and in kowtowing order at rituals. Most have held title as an initiate, although a new member considered too old to be an initiate commonly is offered the rank of Huong Hao which he must retain for a minimum of two years before moving to a higher rank. Although it is possible to skip ranks, most notables spend at least two years in each position. Age becomes important at the level of Huong Bo, which requires that the member be at least 50. Chu Truong is the second eldest member in each hamlet, and Ca Truong, the only rank in the high venerables category that does not require a member to have served as village chief, goes to the eldest member in each hamlet, the highest position to which most members of the Cult Committee can aspire.

Membership in the Village Council provides an opportunity for the qualified villager ultimately to enter the ranks of the high venerables. As already noted, having served as village chief is requisite for all but one rank among the high venerables and, in principle, any member of the Village Council eventually may become village chief. Wealth, education, and age are necessary for membership in the Village Council. Tradition demands that councillors have the wisdom born of experience (it has been noted that some older ex-councillors complained of the "youth" of the present village chief and deputy chief), and practical demands in time and money require

1. A profile of Ong Xa Khanh is included in Chapter 10.

that members of the council be relatively prosperous. At the present time a primary school education also is considered essential.

Before the 1956 administrative reform, when the Village Council had from nine to twelve members, it was not uncommon for young men of well-to-do families to move from the initiate category or the lower ranks of the notables to one of the lesser positions in the council. For example, the village chief held the Thu Bo rank and was appointed directly to the public works section of the Village Council; the deputy chief went from the Pho Luc Bo position to assistant civil status secretary. This pattern, however, has been disrupted by the ever-lessening size of the Village Council.

In the pattern of movement from lower to higher position, the councillor who serves well more than likely will eventually become village chief. Councillors who leave office without having served as village chief usually are given titles in the category of notables, and those who serve at least one term as village chief move upward to the rank of Huong Le or Huong Ca. Beginning with the rank of Chanh Te, longevity is the primary determinant in further mobility. Having already established himself as a man of wisdom and high moral character as well as a man of means capable of meeting the "noblesse oblige" of high venerable status, a villager may succeed to the ranks of Pho Bai, Boi Bai, Chanh Bai, and Tien Bai and, should he outlive his confreres, he may attain the rank of Ke Hien, the highest venerable in the village.

THE DINH

Vietnamese tradition prescribes some of the basic architectural features of all dinh. The sanctuary, which is the repository for the imperial document naming the guardian spirit and the place where altars honoring the guardian spirit (also perhaps village ancestors) are housed, normally is closed to the public. Each night the custodian is expected to enter and burn a stick of joss on the altar of the guardian spirit, and from time to time the high venerables enter to inspect the imperial document. Also, the sanctuary is opened for the four annual village celebrations. The open section of the building contains provisory altars only during some village celebrations, and this area serves a wide variety of uses in most villages. Roofs are of the traditional style (such as described for wood-tile houses in Chapter 2), and there inevitably is a dragon-motif decoration on the peak of the roof.

Dinh vary considerably in architectural and decorative elegance. The Ap Dinh-A dinh is over 100 years old, and although it has been refurbished a number of times it is shabby compared to the Ap Nhon Hau dinh which was newly constructed after the old structure was burned during the Indochina War. Indeed, in spite of the fact that the one in Ap Dinh-A is the official village dinh, the Cult Committee feels that in view of its tawdriness it is preferable to keep the imperial document in the shrine of Marshal Nguyen Huynh Duc and bring it to the dinh in a ritual procession during the two celebrations specifically honoring the Guardian Spirit of the Village. Undoubtedly another factor in this arrangement is the great reverence paid this culture hero who many villagers feel is as powerful as the guardian spirit (and with the construction of the new shrine, Marshal Duc has in many respects become a guardian spirit of the village).

In the sanctuary of the Ap Dinh-A dinh, there are five altars, the largest of which (see Fig. 25, notably altar A) is dedicated to the Guardian Spirit

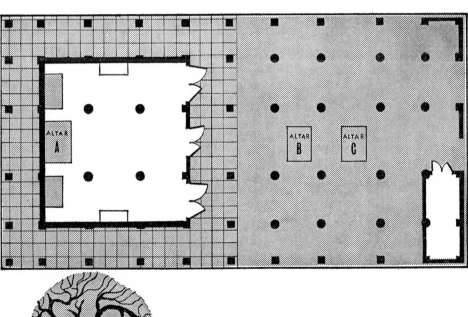

25. Floor Plan of the Ap Dinh-A Dinh (1/1000). Altars B and C are erected only during rituals.

(the singular is used regardless of whether there are multiple guardian spirits). The red and gold carved wooden box containing the imperial document naming the seven military mandarin spirits is in the center of the altar. Periodically, after selecting an auspicious day and fasting for a short period, Ong Ke Hien and several other high venerables open the box to ascertain that the document is intact. Only they know the names of the deities, and custom forbids that they mention them to anyone. Behind the box, gold characters on a red wooden tablet spell out the title of the guardian spirit—Ban Canh Thanh Hoang. There also are the usual brass incense burner, candles, vases, and offering plates. Altar A is flanked by two smaller altars honoring the "assistants" (unspecified deities) of the Guardian Spirit. The remaining small altars, located along the side walls, are for the ancestors of the village—all deceased adult villagers. Before altar A there are the twelve symbolic weapons and two polychrome wooden male phoenixes, 5 feet tall, symbolizing authority.[2] A large drum, used to summon participants to rituals, hangs from the ceiling.

In addition to annual rituals there are numerous meetings in the open part of the dinh—meetings of the Cult Committee and general meetings of villagers to discuss proposed projects or have the Village Council explain a new government program. Attendance is compulsory at Communist Denunciation rallies, which fill the open section, with the overflow standing or squatting outside. Occasionally there are large feasts honoring visitors and, with canvas drawn around the sides (to prevent spectators who have not paid), it is an adequate setting for plays, concerts, and classical opera performed by traveling troupes. And, because of insufficient space in the primary school, classes are held there.

The dinh in Ap Nhon Hau is similar, although it is somewhat smaller and more elegant. Because it is not the official dinh, it does not have altars honoring village ancestors, nor is it the site of village gatherings and feasts. The same type of table representing Ban Canh Thanh Hoang occupies a central position on the main altar as does the red and gold box which is empty, since the imperial document was destroyed and with it, the identification of the guardian spirit. The sanctuary also contains the symbolic weapons and the two carved male phoenixes.

With the approval of the high venerables, the Village Council appoints the custodian of the Ap Dinh-A dinh. The present custodian's father had been appointed to the position in 1941, and when he died in 1947 his son

2. One of the four sacred animals (dragon, unicorn, tortoise, and male phoenix) customarily represented in the dinh.

was given the job. He lives in a rambling wood and thatched house behind the Council House, and his duties include caring for the dinh and the Council House, both of which must be swept out each day. Every night he lights a stick of joss on the altar honoring the guardian spirits. When rituals are held in the dinh, he assists with the preparations—particularly securing additional tables and chairs—and putting the building in order afterward. He also provides tea for members of the Village Council and their guests. When they wish to summon him, the clerk strikes a large orange drum (made from a wine cask) suspended from the ceiling. A certain rhythm is the signal for the custodian to come and another rhythm indicates that tea is desired.

Until mid-1957, he received a monthly salary of 1,550$, but this was reduced to 600$ for some unspecified reason. He does, however, have the right to rent, for 30 gia of paddy annually, the 1.5 hectares of dinh land. This rice is served in feasts at the dinh. (In addition, he rents 3 hectares from a landowner in Ap Moi and, as already indicated, he participates in the government-sponsored hog-raising program and owns the largest sow in Khanh Hau.)

Ritual Responsibilities of the Cult Committee

The Cult Committee is responsible for organizing four annual village celebrations, two of which include several rituals honoring multiple deities. Cau An is the most important of the four, held in the Ap Nhon Hau dinh on the fifteenth and sixteenth days of the second lunar month and in the Ap Dinh-A dinh on these days of the fourth lunar month. The primary purpose of this ritual is to request peace and prosperity from the Guardian Spirit of the Village. Ancestors of the village also are honored, and evil spirits are exorcised from the village. Ha Dien or Descent to the Fields, held early in the planting season on the fifteenth day of the sixth lunar month in both dinh, and Thuong Dien, Ascent from the Fields, on the fifteenth day of the tenth month, both honor the Spirit of Agriculture as well as the Guardian Spirit. Chap Mieu or Le Lap Mieu marks the end of the harvest, and it includes rituals honoring the Spirit of Agriculture, the Guardian Spirit of the Village, and village ancestors. In both dinh it is held on the fifteenth day of the twelfth lunar month.

Preparations for the Cau An celebration at the Ap Dinh-A dinh in 1958 began weeks in advance. Because of the fund drive for the new shrine honoring Marshal Nguyen Huynh Duc, the Village Council and some high venerables of the Cult Committee decided that expenditures for the Cau An be curtailed. At a very informal meeting attended by the police agent and about eight members of the Cult Committee, it was decided that the classical opera of the Chinese tradition be eliminated. (It was included in the 1959 celebration, and there was opera in the Cau An at the Ap Nhon Hau dinh both years.)

Another expenditure that had to be dealt with was the higher fee asked by Ong Thay Phap, the sorcerer.[3] He was from Tan Hiep in My Tho province, and his services were required for certain rituals integral to the Cau An celebration. He came to the Council House to plead for a higher fee. He said he had three assistants, had to travel from Tan Hiep with equipment, and had to purchase materials for such things as the spirit boat—all of which necessitated a fee of 700$ rather than the 400$ of the previous year. While he was explaining this to several members of the Village Council, the Ap Thu Tuu farmer, holding the title of the ritual master, was summoned. With his arrival the bargaining began. The ritual master informed the sorcerer that expenditures for the ritual were being cut so it would not be possible to pay him more. The sorcerer, however, felt that his services were worth more than 400$: "I do everything necessary for preparing and performing the ritual, even writing the *lien* and *van te*."[4] The village chief responded that in Khanh Hau neither was used in the rituals. Without hesitation the sorcerer pointed out that since he furnished his own red turban, this relieved the village from having to purchase one. No one responded.

Turning away, the sorcerer then addressed an appeal to the observers in a voice loud enough for the village officials to hear. "Performing the ritual is difficult and fatiguing," he groaned. "It is like a classical play where everything must be done at the right time in the right manner. Then too it is physically demanding—I must cut my tongue and upper left forearm for blood to prepare amulets, and the ritual involves being up all night drinking rice alcohol." The council members and ritual master conferred among themselves during the sorcerer's plea, and when he had finished, the ritual master repeated his offer of 400$, adding with an air of finality, "That is all we can pay. Besides you don't need three assistants and extra things." Pondering a moment the sorcerer pointed out that if he did not receive more money he would have to make the ritual simpler, whereupon the ritual master laughed and warned, "If you leave something vital out, the Guardian Spirit of the Village will cut your head off!" Nonplussed, the

3. The sorcerer is described in detail in Chapter 3.
4. Both invocations to spirits.

sorcerer departed, and several days later he returned, offering to perform the ritual for 400$.

The sorcerer's fee and other expenses are met with funds contributed by members of the Cult Committee, the Village Council, and heads of households in Ap Moi, Ap Dinh-A, Ap Dinh-B, and Ap Thu Tuu. High venerables are expected to give between 300$ and 400$ as well as a tray of glutinous rice or a large can of cookies; other members contribute 200$. The sum expected of household heads depends on relative wealth—20$ minimum from the poor and 200$ from landowners. In 1958 the collection for the Cau An at the Ap Nhon Hau dinh brought 34,000$, of which 31,000$ was expenses, and for the Cau An at Ap Dinh-A, some 48,000$ of the 57,000$ collected was spent. (The surplus is supposed to be used for dinh maintenance.) Sacrificial animals and food for the feasting account for most of the expenditures. Four sacrificial pigs and two heads of cattle to furnish meat for the meals were purchased in the village. Ordinary rice, vegetables, beer, rice alcohol, and necessary condiments also were purchased. Labor is voluntary, and generally the same group of men and women prepare the food in a shack next to the Council House.

Several days before the celebration, a group of volunteer workers descended on the dinh to remove the wall separating the closed sanctuary from the open section. Some repainted the red and gold on the main altar while others cleaned the altars and polished the wooden pillars. Under the supervision of the ritual master, they arranged two temporary altars in the open section and another altar at the entrance to the Council House. Brass incense burners and candle holders were carefully polished and placed on the temporary altars.

Formally, the Cau An celebration lasts three days—Yet Than is the first day, Dan Ca is the second, and Ton Vuong is the third. Actually in both the Ap Dinh-A and the Ap Nhon Hau dinh, the Cau An rituals take place during a two-day period, and the third day is given over to some amusement such as the classical theater. On the first day, the initial ritual is Tien Hien, honoring the deceased members of the Cult Committee and Village Council, and in Ap Dinh-A it takes place in the Council House where there is a permanent altar dedicated to the village ancestors. On the morning of the fifteenth day of the fourth lunar month, members of the Cult Committee, dressed in traditional clothes, began converging on the Council House. High venerables carried offerings of glutinous rice cooked in saffron and coconut milk, neatly arranged on circular trays, or red tin boxes of cookies. They filed into the Council House to join other members of the committee in the rear where offerings were recorded by the village clerk and a representative of the Catholic families in the village (to symbolize their participation in the celebration).

As the time for the ritual approached, a group of villagers (including the monk from the Ap Moi pagoda), carrying drums, horns, gongs, and stringed instruments gathered on one of the hardwood beds in a corner of the room. Four young men and two boys known as the ritual students, dressed in blue and black robes and hats modeled along the lines of traditional mandarin costume, entered and were directed to the temporary altar by the ritual master. The boys flanked the altar while the young men stood by a table placed behind it.

Three rumbles of the large drum followed by three measured strokes on a small drum signaled the beginning of the ritual. Fast rhythmic music began in the back of the room. Everyone stood as the three highest venerables, Ke Hien, Tien Bai, and Chanh Bai, removed their shoes and moved to positions on a mat before the temporary altar. Prompted by the ritual master, the two boys lowered their heads and clasping their hands while raising them high, they announced the titles of the worshippers. With lighted joss sticks held at the level of their foreheads, the three venerables performed the prescribed ritual kowtowing. They were followed by the Boi Bai, Pho Bai, and Chanh Te titles and, beginning with the Huong Quan, those with the same title kowtowed in groups of three.

After the high venerables had kowtowed, the prescribed offerings were made to the village ancestors. Representing the village and each wearing a satin band in the national colors (saffron yellow and red) across his chest, the police agent, finance secretary, and civil status secretary kowtowed once and remained kneeling before the altar. The four young men, bearing the offerings, moved forward from behind the altar, walking in a slow step, raising their legs high, and dipping deeply in a movement reminiscent of the stylized actions in the classical Chinese opera. The first two held oil lamps before them, the second two carried dishes containing an offering of fragrant burning sandalwood which they proffered to two of the village representatives. Taking them, the councillors held them in a gesture of offering, and then passed them back to the young men who continued in their stylized procession and placed the offerings on the altar of the ancestors. Ritual offerings of rice alcohol and tea were performed in the same manner.

The ritual master then kowtowed before the temporary altar and unfolded the *van te,* an invocation to the ancestors, and a list of the members of the Cult Committee, in black calligraphy on red paper. In a high-pitched chant, the ritual master identified the village, then read the list of members, and concluded with the request of the village ancestors for peace and prosperity. Afterward he placed the van te on the altar and the offerings continued. The fourth offering was of rice alcohol and the fifth of tea. When they were completed, Cult Committee members of the notables and initiates kowtowed in groups of three. In the final act of the Tien Hien, the ritual master burned the van te on the altar.

After the ritual, the participants were invited to sit at the food-laden tables for the first of several feasts that would take place during the next two days. The high venerables were seated at the long table immediately in front of the permanent altar; other members of the Cult Committee moved to other tables at random. Members of the Village Council acted as hosts, seating people, directing the servers, and generally seeing that the guests were well supplied with food and drink.

While the Tien Hien ritual was in progress, the sorcerer and his assistants had been preparing for their ritual. In the open section of the dinh, they had arranged two altars, the larger dedicated to the sorcerer's patron deity; the other had tablets honoring the deity's assistants, all warriors of ancient Chinese legends. They also had constructed a spirit boat 4 feet long, of light wood and colored paper. A flag on the top contained the names of evil spirits written in Sino–Vietnamese calligraphy, and under the roof three paper soldiers were fastened to each side. A paper drum and small wooden oar had been placed inside, and the boat was fixed to thick bamboo logs.

Shortly after the feasting ended (about 3 P.M.), the Village Council and members of the Cult Committee gathered outside the dinh to bring the imperial decree naming the Guardian Spirit of the Village from the shrine of Marshal Duc to the dinh. The Village Self-Defense Guard led the procession, followed by two files of school children dressed in blue and white uniforms. Behind them two men carried a small altar, and several men held a banner bearing the slogan "Than Tam Dan Le" (Attend the ritual with a reverent attitude). Next came the reliquary, a large, elaborately decorated red and gold model of a dinh, flanked by men holding brightly colored mandarin parasols. In no particular order, the participants walked behind the reliquary. As the procession moved along the spur road into Ap Dinh-B, villagers hurried to their doorways to watch.

At the shrine the procession was greeted by Ong Khai, the head of the Duc family and keeper of the Marshal's shrine.[5] The children lined the garden path, and the participants filed into the shrine which contained several

5. The role of Ong Khai is explained in Chapter 10.

altars and a collection of Marshal Duc memorabilia. Ong Ke Hien, Ong
Tien Bai, and Ong Chanh Bai proceeded to the main altar where they
kowtowed while other Cult Committee members kowtowed at the two
smaller altars. When all had paid their respects to the spirit of Marshal Duc,
Ong Khai stepped forward and removed the red and gold box containing
the imperial decree from the main altar. He presented it to the finance
secretary who, with the police agent and civil status secretary, kowtowed.
Leaving the shrine, they placed the box in the reliquary, and the procession
regrouped. Along the route, flowers and offerings had been placed on the
small Thien altars in front of the houses. The villagers stood in reverent
silence, and a soccer game in a dried paddy field next to the road came to an
abrupt halt as the players stood facing the procession. At the dinh, the
finance secretary removed the box and placed it on the main altar. Accompanied by the police agent and the civil status secretary, he then kowtowed.
The Thinh Sac ended with all members of the Cult Committee kowtowing
according to ranked priority as in the Tien Hien ritual.

After the Thinh Sac, Thay Phap Vao Dam, the sorcerer's ritual took place
in the open section of the dinh. The function of this ritual is to exorcise evil
spirits from the village, particularly the Spirit of Cholera which is thought
to appear at this time of the year when the water supplies are low. On the
two altars arranged by the sorcerer, candles flickered, joss burned, and there
were offerings of cookies and three small glasses of rice alcohol. Three false
black beards had been attached to either side of the print depicting the
patron deity. One of the assistants sat on a mat next to the larger altar
holding a banderole on which an invocation to the sorcerer's deity was
written; the other assistant donned a red skirt and red wig. Some of the
musicians from the Tien Hien ritual began to play frenzied music as the
sorcerer entered wearing a short robe and a headpiece fashioned out of red
prayer paper known as a *so*, a special request made of a powerful spirit.
Swaying and spinning to the music, the sorcerer seemed to go into a trance,
and suddenly he stopped to read alertly the invocation from the banderole
held by his assistants. Then both assistants joined him in the dance, and
finally all three prostrated themselves before the altar.

The ritual continued as the assistant in the red wig put on one of the false
beards, and dancing in circles he chanted an invitation to the spirits of the
military mandarins to assist in the celebration. When he finished, the sorcerer sat before the deity's altar and read incantations from a book while
his assistants beat small drums. The three then retired behind a tattered
curtain they had strung across a corner of the room.

After a brief interruption, the second phase began with the re-entry of the sorcerer and his two assistants dressed in multicolored robes of bits and pieces of cotton cloth, their faces made up in the fantastic style of the Chinese theater and wearing the black beards. The sorcerer stood before the main altar and, removing the prayer paper which had been his headpiece, he read an appeal to the spirits of those who had died violently and all other evil spirits, particularly the cholera spirit, asking them to assemble at the dinh to partake of the food offerings which had been placed on the altar of the Patron Spirit. Carrying a small portable altar on which offerings of pork had been placed, the assistants preceded the sorcerer out of the building to join several men carrying a large orange-colored drum which they beat frenziedly. The sorcerer and his assistants called to the spirits in loud voices as the group moved along the road to carry their appeal to all hamlets of the village.

Darkness had descended and oil lamps had been lit in the dinh and Council House. Behind the dinh several sacrificial pigs were being scrubbed, and when one of them was prepared it was tied to a pole and carried into the open part where it was placed before one of the temporary altars. A villager known as Ong Te Gia, the honorable housekeeper, a specialist in sacrificial slaughtering, entered and proceeded to the main altar of the sanctuary. Holding his special knife and a basin, he kowtowed and asked permission of the guardian spirits to sacrifice the pig and make an offering of it. While two men held the pig's head back, Ong Te Gia poured rice alcohol into its mouth (later he explained this was to increase blood circulation so the animal would expire sooner). He then took a drink of the alcohol himself, after which he deftly cut the pig's throat with one sweep of the knife. The gushing blood was collected in the basin, and when the animal ceased its movements, it was carried outside to be eviscerated and dissected.

Two more pigs were slaughtered in the same manner, and after dissection the parts were distributed according to village custom. The heads, considered the most honored parts of the animals, and the prestigeful tenderloins were placed with the glutinous rice and cookies on a table before the altar of the Guardian Spirit in the dinh. After the celebration, the heads were presented to the four highest venerables—Ke Hien, Tien Bai, Chanh Bai, and Boi Bai—while some of the tenderloins were given to Ong Khai, the head of the Duc family. Slices of the bacon were placed on all the altars in the dinh, and small morsels of pork fat were put on all the offerings of glutinous rice and cookies. Each member of the Cult Committee also received a morsel of pork. Some of the elders pointed out that the well-known proverb, "A morsel of flesh from the village is worth more than a basketful of flesh from the market," expresses the symbolic value of this presentation. Finally, entrails and other parts remaining were carried to the kitchen to be cooked for the feasts.

An evening meal was being served to members of the Cult Committee in the Council House while a large crowd of villagers gathered in the dinh for the final phase of the sorcerer's ritual. Entering the dinh from their tour of the village, the sorcerer and his assistants put lighted candles and food offerings, including twelve bits of flesh from twelve parts of the sacrificial pig (to represent the twelve years of lunar cycle), into the spirit boat. Music began as the sorcerer approached his patron deity's altar, again producing the prayer book from which he read a final invitation for the spirits to enter the boat and partake of the feast prepared for them. Four villagers then lifted the spirit boat and, followed by the sorcerer, his assistants, and a group of villagers, they proceeded to the Rach Ong Dia, the stream that forms the southern border of the village. After the sorcerer had recited some prayers, they pushed the boat into the current of the receding tide. Spinning erratically, it drifted seaward. The sorcerer pointed out that villages along the route were expected to see that it continued on its way; should it stop, the spirits might disembark.

At midnight, Chuc Kien, the major ritual of the Cau An celebration, took place in the dinh. In addition to honoring the guardian spirits of the village, Chuc Kien includes a formal request for peace and prosperity. Food offerings and flowers had been placed on the main altar and on provisory altars B and C (see Fig. 25). Candles blazed and colorful satin decorations graced the sanctuary, lending a particularly festive air to the place. In form, the Chuc Kien was very similar to the Tien Hien ritual. Under the direction of the ritual master, the two boys flanked altar B and announced the first group of worshippers—the Ke Hien, Tien Bai, and Chanh Bai. They first kowtowed at altar B and then repeated the act at altar A. The other high venerables, village chief, and deputy chief followed, and rather than making the offerings as in the Tien Hien, the notables and initiates also kowtowed. When all had finished, the finance secretary, police agent, and civil status secretary kowtowed before altar C while the venerable Chanh Te kowtowed before altar B. They remained kneeling, and after gongs and drums sounded three times, the four young men moved forward, carrying lamps and offerings of sandalwood which were given to two of the village representatives. As in the Tien Hien, they offered them and returned them to the young men who proceeded in their stylized step to altar A.

There were two offerings of rice alcohol and one of tea (at the Cau An ritual in Ap Nhon Hau there were three offerings of rice alcohol, and all offerings were carried by male and female members of the classical opera troupes, dressed in their theater costumes and wearing colorful makeup). After the offerings, the ritual master read the invocation to the Guardian Spirit, asking peace and prosperity for Khanh Hau. He also read a list of the Cult Committee members. The final act of the ritual was to burn the invocation on altar A. Most participants then gathered at the Council House where a simple meal of rice soup containing entrails from the sacrificial pigs was served.

At eight o'clock the next morning, members of the Cult Committee began gathering at the Council House for a breakfast of pork dishes and glutinous rice from the trays brought by the high venerables. Customarily the donor retains half the glutinous rice, and the remainder is served at the feasts. In the rear of the room the village clerk and the Catholic representative continued to record contributions. A group of elderly women entered and, after making small contributions of 10 to 15 piasters, they sat together at one of the tables where they were served breakfast. Some of the high venerables explained that all either were widows or abandoned by their husbands and, as their children were married, they lived alone. This gave them special status in the community, and they were the only females invited to partake of the feast. Since they were household heads, however, they were expected to make cash contributions regardless of how small.

At eleven o'clock the beating of a large drum summoned participants to the ritual sacrifice of the one remaining pig. The two boys in mandarin hats and robes stood at altar A and announced the Tien Bai and Chanh Bai, who moved forward and kowtowed. The pig, trussed to a pole carried by two men, was brought to the altar and, after asking the Guardian Spirit to accept the offering, the Tien Bai simulated the sacrificial act by passing a knife close to the animal's throat. The pig was then taken to the rear of the room where Ong Te Gia did the actual killing as he had done before.

After a large meal served in the early afternoon, the Dan Ca, the final ritual venerating the Guardian Spirit, took place in the dinh. There was only one notable difference in the arrangement of offerings for the Dan Ca —whereas in the Chuc Kien the sacrificial pigs had been cut apart, now the whole carcass of the pig was left intact and spread out to dominate the food sacrifices. The ritual itself varied somewhat from the Chuc Kien and Tien Hien. Rather than kowtowing after the high venerables, the village chief and deputy chief followed the initiates. The hamlet chief of Ap Moi replaced the finance secretary as a village representative, and pork replaced the tea offering. Finally, the Chanh Te tasted both the rice alcohol and the pork before the young men placed them on altar A. The ritual ended with the burning of the membership list and invocation to the Guardian Spirit.

Gia Sac, the act of returning the imperial document to the shrine of Marshal Duc, marks the final phase of the Cau An celebration. In form it was like the Thinh Sac in reverse. After the participants had kowtowed at altar A, the police agent removed the box containing the document, and the procession accompanied the reliquary to the Duc shrine. The kowtowing was repeated before the altars at the shrine after the box was replaced. After the ritual, many participants remained and were served tea.

In addition to honoring the guardian spirits of the village, both Descent to the Fields and Ascent from the Fields are primarily intended to pay homage to the Spirit of Agriculture. Behind the dinh, the altar honoring this deity consists of a large stone tablet, set on a massive concrete slab. The name of the Spirit of Agriculture, in Sino–Vietnamese calligraphy, is carved on the tablet. The altar is flanked by two small shrines, one dedicated to the Five Elements (metal, wood, water, fire, and earth); the other honors the Spirit of the Mountain. The Ascent and the Descent rituals are similar in form and, as indicated, they are held in the Ap Dinh-A and Ap Nhon Hau dinh on the same days at the same hours.

In 1958 planting already had begun when the Descent ritual was held at the Ap Dinh-A dinh on the fifteenth day of the fourth lunar month. During the early morning the sanctuary was opened, and the altars were decked with flowers. Under the supervision of the ritual master, an altar containing a large incense burner, candles, a vase of flowers, a cruet of rice alcohol, several small glasses, and offerings of bananas and pineapples was arranged in front of the shrine of the Spirit of Agriculture. Vivid red and gold mandarin parasols and racks holding the twelve symbolic weapons to ward off evil spirits were placed on either side of the altar. Members of the Cult Committee, some bearing offerings of glutinous rice, cookies, or long loaves of French bread, filed into the Council House. Since the cost of this feast (as well as the Thuong Dien and Chap Mieu celebrations) is relatively low —3,500$ in 1958—smaller donations for this and the Ascent ritual were expected—120$ from the high venerables and from 80$ to 100$ from other members. Contributions from household heads were not fixed. According to some of the high venerables, before the Indochina War each food offering was accompanied by a chicken, but because this imposed a hardship it was discontinued. Since the end of the war, however, the village offering has become more elaborate. Whereas it had been a chicken, it now is a pig, a more prestigious sacrificial animal. The Descent to the Fields drew a smaller attendance than the Cau An. While most members of the Cult Committee attended the Cau An (about 150), only 70 members assisted at this celebration.

Food offerings were placed on the concrete slab before the tablet and also on the two shrines. After Ong Te Gia ritually slaughtered the pig in the dinh as he had done during the Cau An celebration, the head was prominently displayed, and bits of flesh were put on each offering. (After the ritual the food was distributed as it had been after the Cau An.) Drumbeats summoned the participants, and when all had gathered behind the dinh, the musicians who had played at the Cau An began their frenetic music. The two boys in mandarin hats and robes took their positions beside the altar and announced the worshippers—first the Ke Hien (since the Ap Dinh-A dinh is considered the official dinh, the Ke Hien attends rituals there in the event of a clash of schedules) and then the other members of the Cult Committee in ranked order.

After kowtowing at the altar, each worshipper proceeded to both small shrines where he bowed from the waist, and then he kowtowed before all five altars in the sanctuary. For the offerings, the village was represented by the finance secretary, police agent, and civil status secretary. Unassisted by the young men as they had been at the Cau An rituals, they poured glasses of rice alcohol, offered them to Ong Than Nong, and then placed them on the altar. After this the ritual master read an invocation to the deity and the usual list of Cult Committee members. After the second offering of rice alcohol, the ritual master burned the invocation and list on the ground before the altar as the final act of the Ha Dien. The participants then repaired to the Council House where a meal was served.

The Ascent from the Fields ritual has the same form; it also was performed at the altar to the rear of the dinh, and the worshippers paid homage at the shrines and the dinh altars as well. Offerings were the same, and the ritual master also read and burned an invocation and list of members. In order to reduce the cost of the ritual, the sacrificial pig was represented by the head and feet of a pig that had been slaughtered previously by a villager for a family celebration.

The last annual village celebration is Chap Mieu, held on the fifteenth day of the twelfth lunar month to give thanks to the guardian spirits of the village for their protection during the year. In form this celebration resembles the Cau An, although it is briefer and less elaborate. Only two pigs are sacrificed, and the sorcerer's ritual is not included. For the 1958 Chap Mieu celebration, however, the village hired a troupe of players to perform Cai Luong, a type of popular Vietnamese theater, when the rituals were over.

The ritual homage to the deceased members of the Cult Committee took place in the Council House as it did in the Cau An with the ritual assistants in their mandarin robes, the offerings of sandalwood, rice alcohol, and tea, as well as the kowtowing in ranked order. This was followed by the procession to obtain the imperial decree from the shrine of Marshal Duc, after which there was a large meal for which a steer had been slaughtered. The major ritual honoring the Guardian Spirit of the Village began around midnight, and it did not vary from this ritual in the Cau An celebration. The following morning there was a brief ritual in the dinh before the procession formed to return the decree, and at the shrine another brief ritual marked the end of the celebration. Many of the participants returned to the dinh where the theater group performed for the rest of the day.

The High Venerables

The Ke Hien is an official advisor to the Village Council, and from time to time the council or hamlet chiefs also seek the advice of other high venerables—particularly the Tien Bai, Chanh Bai, Boi Bai, and Pho Bai of either committee—on proposed projects, administrative problems, and other difficulties facing the community. They are elderly men who enjoy the respect given to the wisdom of age in this society. Also, all had served as village chief, which gave them administrative experience, and they are among the well-to-do in village society.

Of all the high venerables, the Ke Hien is most revered as a man of sagacity and good character. In addition to sharing the qualities characteristic of high venerables, he enjoys the reputation of being the most adept farmer in the village (credited with having introduced chemical fertilizer). His contributions to village projects and to welfare have won him acclaim as a generous man—a good Buddhist—and devoutness was added when he financed construction of the Ap Cau pagoda.

CHAPTER 9

Socioeconomic Differentiation

HISTORICAL WORKS on Vietnam often ascribe to traditional Vietnamese society four social "classes"—part of the Chinese heritage. These are intellectuals, farmers, artisans, and tradesmen and merchants. Le Thanh Khoi[1] points out that this explicitly is an occupational classification ("elle est basée sur la profession et non sur la fortune"). While these distinctions may have been meaningful in the traditional Vietnamese society of northern and central Vietnam, there is nothing to indicate they ever existed in the south. Older villagers in Khanh Hau are likely to use the term *si* (intellectual) when referring to those versed in Chinese calligraphy and the ritual forms associated with traditional cults. At the present time, however, there are only ten villagers who can claim this esoteric knowledge and in the past the number apparently never was very large. Finally, si does not indicate an occupational specialization—the si are and were farmers.

There are relatively few artisans in Khanh Hau, and most of them are engaged also in agriculture. Merchants include rice merchants, rice millers, shopkeepers, and those in petty commerce. All rice merchants and millers own paddy land which they cultivate with hired help and/or rent to tenants. Practically all the vendors are wives of laborers or farmers. In the final analysis, therefore, while there are intellectuals, artisans, and tradesmen, all would primarily or secondarily be farmers—even the Buddhist monks and nuns and the medical practitioners.

The fact that practically everyone is directly engaged in agricultural activities indicates the homogeneity of the village life. Social expectations are that an individual marry, have children, and provide well for them. Bachelors and spinsters are fringe people, childless couples are viewed with pity (usually they adopt a son), and poor providers are scorned. A deeply

1. *Le Viet-Nam,* p. 354.

233

rooted desire among villagers is to own land and, with the exception of a small group of Catholics, villagers share many religious beliefs and practices.

Homogeneity, however, does not preclude some distinctions. Villagers themselves often make references to the well-to-do, those not-rich-not-poor, and the poor.[2] These three socioeconomic levels provide a heuristic device for describing variations resulting from relative economic means. These are variations on the village way of life—manifest in behavior and in patterns of consumption, but they do not amount to social classes as they are defined by Weber[3] and more recently by Lynch.[4]

Relating the situation in Khanh Hau to Weber's concept, there are no peculiar styles of life but rather, as already indicated, variations on a common style which is the village way of life. With the exception of the direct patrilineal descendants of Marshal Duc, none in the village can claim "charisma of prestige by virtue of birth"; and "appropriation of political or hierocratic authority as a monopoly by socially distinct groups" cannot be said to exist in Khanh Hau, even in the case of the sociopolitical elite (which actually is not entrenched). While there is social inequality in the rich-middle-poor ranking, there are neither discontinuities nor "strata culturally recognized as qualitatively distinct," which Lynch considers diagnostic of social stratification, the essence of social class.

The three levels, fusing one into the other, form a vertical socioeconomic structure. Within them there are more specific status positions (which will be seen in the profiles in Chapter 10 of individual villagers), but the aim

2. In Viet Minh, Viet Cong, and North Vietnamese literature a similar distinction is made, using the literary designations rich peasant, in-between peasant, and poor peasant, although the implication is social class in the Marxist sense.

3. The most important sources, in order, of the development of distinct strata are: (a) the development of a peculiar style of life, including, particularly, the type of occupation pursued; (b) hereditary charisma arising from a position of prestige by virtue of birth; (c) the appropriation of political or hierocratic authority as a monopoly by socially distinct groups. (Weber, *The Theory of Social and Economic Organization*, p. 428.)

4. But I do not see that they differ from the majority of students . . . who consider social stratification a system of social inequality. While accepting this formula I prefer, in view of the findings of this study, to distinguish systems of stratification from systems of ranking. Systems of social stratification are characterized by the presence of breaks, interruptions, discontinuities, disjunctions by virtue of what is at least partially a qualitative difference between the two strata so separated. Where the social inequality is not manifested in strata of this kind, one has a social ranking system, a system of social status, but not one of social stratification. Hence I would revise slightly the common definition of social stratification and call it a *system of social inequality featuring strata culturally recognized as qualitatively distinct.* [Lynch, *Social Class in a Bikol Town*, p. 6.]

of this description is more to present broad variations among the three levels than to pinpoint social statuses in the village. The latter would require more finely chiseled techniques and a more explicitly focused study. The present work is simply an attempt to indicate the activities of people of given means within the confines of village society—the distinctions among the rich, the poor, and those in between.

Socioeconomic ranking in village society is measured primarily by subsistence activities. Whether one is a landowner, tenant (and by the same token how much land he owns or rents), laborer, or shopkeeper determines relative position in the vertical structure. By and large, an upper level can be identified among farmers who own more than 4 hectares of paddy land and those who rent more than 5 hectares. Anyone owning or renting land in those amounts is considered well-to-do by the villagers. A middle level would include those who own between 2 and 4 hectares or rent between 2.5 and 5 hectares. The lower level encompasses farmers who own 2 hectares or less or rent 2.5 hectares or less. This level also includes laborers (most of whom are farm laborers), those engaged in petty commerce, shopkeepers, some artisans, and the unemployed (see Table 17).

TABLE 17. Socioeconomic Levels by Household, 1958

	Lower	Middle	Upper	Total
Resident landowners	46 (46.5)*	24 (24.2)	29 (29.3)	99 (100.0)
Resident tenants	175 (65.5)	60 (22.5)	32 (12.0)	267 (100.0)
Nonfarming	224 (100.0)			224 (100.0)
Total in each level	445 (75.5)	84 (14.2)	61 (10.3)	590 (100.0)

* (Per cent.)

It is difficult if not impossible to place some villagers in the socioeconomic structure. The Duc family, specifically members directly descended from Marshal Nguyen Huynh Duc in the male line, have a unique place. According to the criteria outlined above they are mixed—some are prosperous and some are not. Collectively, however, they have something of Weber's charisma of prestige by virtue of birth, and consequently must be treated apart.

Others who do not fit into the structure tend to be marginal to village society. The Chinese shopkeeper and the Chinese pharmacist did not participate in village affairs and are considered outsiders. The primary school teachers, with one exception, live in Tan An, and they, like the staff and students of the UNESCO School of Fundamental Education, remain apart from village society.

UPPER LEVEL

The socioeconomic upper level of village society is composed of the wealthy—the gentry. While most of them rarely if ever work in the fields, and many are busily engaged in entrepreneurial activities, they continue to consider themselves farmers. They usually oversee important phases of the planting cycle—sowing, transplanting, irrigating, and harvesting—and are sure to be present when the paddy is being measured and poured into sacks. Their ties to the village are strong, and even those who were forced out of the village by Viet Cong activities return when possible to visit kin and friends. Wealth, in most instances, makes the villager a more responsible member of the society by virtue of the noblesse oblige associated with high status.

As their landholdings increase, upper-level villagers are able to lease or sublease larger portions, which removes them more and more from direct agricultural responsibility. As their incomes rise, some lend money with interest to fellow villagers, and in recent years a growing number of gentry have become entrepreneurs. Several have invested in rice milling—a good, sound business in the minds of villagers. Some are active in rice merchandising, and at one point three relatively wealthy brothers had a rice and lumber business, traveling as far as Ban Me Thuot in the highlands. The village chief recently invested in a new gasoline station near the bridge in Tan An.

The type of house in which one lives is strongly indicative of status. Wood-tile and masonry-tile houses are associated with the upper level of the socioeconomic structure. The Viet Cong in their nocturnal tax collections use this criterion as does the local administration when a quick measure of relative wealth is needed for such things as collecting funds to implement the Strategic Hamlet Program.[5]

For the Vietnamese villager, the house is more than a home; it contains the altars honoring the ancestors, and consequently it is important to have a house that will endure. Such a house is the symbol of lineage longevity and is a prestige symbol as well. Finally, from a practical point of view, the well-constructed house is a good investment.

Two new features of houses recently constructed by well-to-do villagers are concrete water tanks and brick ovens using rice husks as fuel. Although

5. The close correlation of percentages of villagers in the three socioeconomic levels in Table 17 and percentages of house types for Ap Dinh A–B and Ap Moi in Figure 2 support the efficacy of this criterion.

the initial cost of these installations is high, both have been gaining in favor among wealthy villagers, and they also have become prestige symbols.

Farmsteads of upper-level villagers characteristically are large and usually have very decorative Chinese gardens, with dwarfed trees and flowering bushes set in ceramic pots. Polychrome pots are relatively expensive and must be purchased in the Tan An or My Tho markets. Uncommon varieties of flowers are likely to be cultivated in these gardens, and the dwarfed trees are costly, obtainable only in a few places in southern Vietnam.

Furnishings in the houses of the gentry vary somewhat. In older, more traditional houses, furnishings have a faded elegance. They retain traces of good workmanship, and the wood is of high quality, but they are weathered —unavoidable in the dampness of the delta. In all village houses, regardless of means, it is *de rigueur* to have a table with benches or chairs before the altar of the ancestors, and in older houses of the well-to-do these are of carved wood, sometimes inlaid with mother-of-pearl. Pearl inlay also is found in the ceremonial cabinet and the serving tray.

As in other village houses, the main room of a prosperous villager's house is likely to contain several beds (low, table-like platforms) but of polished hardwood rather than ordinary wood. They are intended to serve the family for many generations, and they have a variety of uses. Mats are placed on them for sleeping, and in the daytime they provide a work area for the women of the house. Female visitors and guests at weddings, funerals, and other family events remove their shoes and gather on the beds where they are served betel leaves, lime, and areca nuts. Another item commonly found in older houses is a marble-top table, usually placed in the center of the main room.

In the more recently constructed masonry houses, furniture usually is of light-colored, highly polished wood, and the styling tends to be more modern (i.e. Western). A style of furniture influenced by French *art moderne* developed in Saigon before World War II and since has diffused to the market towns and villages of the delta. Most wealthy families have a pendulum clock, perhaps two, and several families have battery-operated radios. In the main room of the house a mirror usually hangs from the wall or graces the front of the French armoires which villagers favor. Framed, gaily colored prints decorate the walls of the main room, and there invariably is a photographic collection of near and distant kin.

Among the well-to-do, the large and elaborate altars honoring the ancestors dominate the main room of the house. Altar accouterment is of fine quality. An incense burner of polished brass stands in the center of the altar, flanked by two candlesticks either of brass or turned wood. An offering stand of pearl-inlaid carved wood is to one side, and the offering plate on which fruit is placed each day very likely will be of blue and white china. A large vase, also of blue and white china, contains the flowers which are part of the daily offerings.

Guests are served tea from a decorated pot covered with a brightly colored, padded tea cozy, and the affluent pride themselves on having tea cups and saucers of French manufacture, which they use only when there are guests. Candied fruit, fresh fruit, and dry cookies usually are served. Another material luxury found in these houses is the pressure lamp that burns white gas and throws a glaring fluorescent-like light. The only motor scooters, motorcycles, and motor bicycles in Khanh Hau are owned by villagers of the upper socioeconomic level.

Only a small group of villagers can be distinguished by their dress. Men in public office, particularly members of the Village Council (all affluent villagers) usually wear Western-style white shirts, trousers of light material, and Western shoes when they are in the Council House. This attire marks them as men of official standing, and when the province chief or other high officials visit the village, this group, wearing suits and ties, is expected to greet them. Western clothes are extremely costly and, in the context of village life, continue to be foreign. In a sense, the council members in these clothes represent the village's face to the outside world—the symbolic link between the traditionally rooted village society and the Western-influenced world of Vietnamese officialdom.

When the gentry are relaxing in their own homes or taking their leisure with friends, they prefer comfortable, loose-fitting, white collarless shirts, cotton trousers, and wooden clogs—the common leisure-time dress for male villagers, regardless of economic means. For special occasions all adult males wear the traditional black tunic and tight-fitting turban. Quality of material, however, reflects one's socioeconomic status, and wealthy villagers prefer finer materials (silk or satin) purchased in Saigon or in the market towns. While some of these villagers might wear black cotton shorts and shirt around their own farmsteads, they never would do so in public.

Elderly wealthy villagers tend to be almost indistinguishable from other males of their age group. Most have retained the traditional practice of wearing their hair long, tied in a bun at the nape of the neck, and they usually have the wispy goatee—a sign of wisdom. They never wear Western clothes. When visiting in the village or in neighboring towns, elderly men wear the traditional loose-fitting white clothes and wooden clogs. The preferred headgear is an adaptation of the white jungle hat introduced by early French administrators, and they also carry large black umbrellas to protect themselves from rain and sun.

Women of wealthy families are little set apart in dress and appearance from other village women. Style is not a determinant of female social status in Khanh Hau. The Vietnamese women's costume varies little, if at all, from year to year; in Saigon there may be periodic variations such as the height of the collar, but these *haute couture* innovations never reach the village. Around the house women wear a simple cotton blouse and black pantaloons of cotton or calico. For visiting a nearby shop or another house in the hamlet, they usually wear conical hats or checked cloths wrapped around and draped over the head. For more formal occasions—family celebrations or rituals at the dinh or the pagoda—women wear black or white tunics, and some women of wealthy families have these made from fine material purchased in My Tho or Saigon.

Single girls attempt to be more individual in their dress, preferring pastel colors and light material. They also wear more jewelry than do married women. Girls of well-to-do families generally have gold necklaces and thin gold bracelets which they wear to weddings. In the village it is customary for girls to wear their hair long and loose until they reach the age of 15 or 16 when they arrange it in a long chignon. Older women favor a tight chignon at the back of the head. Hairdressing is done in the home, although occasionally wealthy families have their young daughters' hair curled at the one beauty parlor in Tan An.

The affluent are very active in the political life of Khanh Hau. They have reached the stage where they can afford the considerable time and the cost of participating in village affairs. He who holds office in the Village Council must be relatively free from farm responsibilities, and he also must have an outside income to permit periodic outlays of his own money. Public figures are expected to make impressive personal cash and food contributions to village celebrations and village projects and they also must be able to support themselves during the recurring periods when there are insufficient funds for village officials' salaries.

Education ranks high in village values, and children of the well-to-do are currently expected to receive at least a primary education. In the past, some sons of wealthy families were sent to schools in Saigon or Cholon to follow a course in traditional Vietnamese studies and learn Chinese calligraphy.

At the present time, however, the pattern is for children to attend the secondary school in Tan An (which recently has been expanded), and a few village children have been students at the secondary school in My Tho.

The prosperous also can provide better medical care for their families. They consult the sorcerer and use traditional Vietnamese medicine, as do other villagers but, having the means, they also make more use of Western medicine.

The sociopolitical elite of Khanh Hau includes Ong Khai, truong toc of the Duc family, and his younger brother who served as civil status secretary, eventually being appointed village chief. Those with the greatest prestige and power, however, are the Ke Hien, Tien Bai, and Chanh Bai, the last two from both cult committees. The Ke Hien's son serves as village secretary, and the village chief's father was Chanh Bai in the Ap Dinh-A committee. A son of the Tien Bai in the Ap Dinh-A committee is deputy chief, and a son of the Tien Bai in the Ap Nhon Hau was, until his recent slaying by the Viet Cong, police agent. It is this group who have wealth and prestige, as well as being the most active in village affairs. They decide who will be recommended to the provincial officials for the Village Council, and they decide who will be admitted and advanced in the cult committees.

Celebrations of well-to-do families tend to be large and elaborate, in some instances sumptuous. Ong Ke Hien, one of the wealthiest villagers, invites more than a hundred guests to the six death anniversaries he observes each year. Weddings, particularly, are joyous occasions—a wedding marks the beginning of a new family and symbolizes lineage continuity. Food is carefully prepared, and some families have hired chefs from Tan An to supervise preparation of the many dishes. Ice, a costly item in the village, is brought by the carload from Tan An for these occasions. One wealthy villager rented several Citroen and Peugeot taxis in addition to several buses to transport guests to the bride's village.

Funerals of the gentry are lavish, even when death comes unexpectedly. The vigil and feasting often last three days or longer so that kin may gather from distant places. In addition to having burial plots, wealthy villagers retain the services of a geomancer to select auspicious sites for the family tombs. During the funeral vigil they summon the Buddhist monk to pray before the bier (in return they are expected to make a donation to the pagoda), and they are the only villagers to hire the funeral trappings, musicians, and coffin bearers from a professional service in Tan An. Finally, after the burial there is a series of prescribed but not obligatory rituals, which, because of expense, are observed only by the well-to-do.

Having more free time and the means to travel, wealthy villagers tend to be more mobile than other villagers. Both business and pleasure take them to the towns and villages of the surrounding area. Most visits to nearby villages are to attend family celebrations and, in the case of the women, to visit parents or siblings. A trip to Saigon still is considered an adventure. One exceptional (and wealthy) villager, who is reputed to be something of a bon vivant, has a motor scooter on which he makes weekly visits to Saigon where he attends the cinema and visits bars in the Khanh Hoi port section. Several wealthy families have been to Dalat and Cap St. Jacques for holidays, and some villagers have visited Ban Be Thuot in the highlands on business.

Many upper-level villagers spend a great deal of time at public and private rituals and feasts. Those in the Cult Committee and the Village Council are expected to attend all village celebrations as well as many of the Buddhist rituals, and they are invited to many weddings, funerals, and death anniversaries. Wives attend fewer of these affairs, primarily because of household responsibilities but also because women are not expected to attend many social gatherings. Members of the Village Council divide their days between the Council House and their farms. Time at the Council House, however, is not spent entirely on official matters; being conveniently located, the Council House is a gathering place, and the ever-changing group found there spends much time chatting, reading newspapers, and drinking tea.

Leisure time in the village is passed in much the same way regardless of one's financial means. During the dry season the young men play soccer in a cleared paddy field; volley ball is a favorite rainy-season sport. Another popular pastime among young men is gathering in a house to play musical instruments and sing. Proficiency in such traditional instruments as the long, semitubular *don tranh* with its sixteen chords, the round, banjo-shaped *don kim* with two chords, or the stringed *don co* which is played with a bow, is highly regarded. A few of the young men have Western-style guitars on which they play traditional southern Vietnamese airs. Love songs, very plaintive and sentimental, are most popular, but the mood of these haunting melodies is apt to be suddenly broken by one of the fast, rhythmic, more recently composed popular songs.

Older men usually gather in the shops or in the house of a neighbor where they sit in the soft golden light of the oil lamps drinking tea, rice alcohol, or beer and discussing crops, weather, and local news or exchanging village gossip. Writing and reciting poetry is a favorite pastime among men, and the good poet enjoys high prestige in the village. At weddings, funerals, and other celebrations the accomplished poet invariably is called upon to compose a verse commemorating the occasion. A few of the older men are able to recite long passages from epic Vietnamese poems, which is considered an admirable achievement. Women and girls have no specific leisure time for such gatherings. Normally their leisure is spent gossiping in the local shops with other women of the hamlet, and visiting during the daytime is common, particularly among those who live close together.

There is little in the way of organized amusements in Khanh Hau. Occasionally the Vietnamese Information Service of the Ministry of Information sponsors a film (usually propaganda) and recently a group of village young men organized a concert of classical music which was well received. Periodically there are visits by traveling theater troupes that perform *hat boi*, classical Chinese plays, or relatively modern Vietnamese plays. There usually are hat boi performances after the Cau An rituals at both dinh. Young and old, male and female, attend these performances which often last six or seven continuous hours.

Organized entertainment usually is presented in the Ap Dinh-A dinh, making it difficult for those in the more distant hamlets to attend. In any event, such entertainment is infrequent, and villagers are accustomed to providing their own amusements after the sun goes down. When the subject of leisure time activities was being discussed with a group of farmers over rice alcohol and beer, one man, noted for his wit, summed up the situation: "When the village is darkened, there is nothing to do but go to bed and amuse ourselves with our wives." Then he added reflectively, "That's why we have so many children."

MIDDLE LEVEL

One outstanding characteristic of the middle-level villagers—those who own between 2 and 4 hectares or rent between 2.5 and 5 hectares—is that they usually are engaged almost exclusively in agricultural activities. Several have additional trades but they tend to be ancillary. Unlike most of the well-to-do, farmers of the middle level do not have the means to indulge in entrepreneurial ventures. On the other hand, unlike landowners and tenant farmers with smaller holdings, they are not forced to seek dry-season employment. Their farms sustain them, and their farms are the focal centers of their lives. They spend more time in the fields or overseeing laborers and transplanting teams than do the wealthy. Also, they own more farm implements and stock than the other villagers.

Villagers of the middle level are less explicitly associated with particular house types than are the wealthy. Although many of them live in wood-thatch or wood-tile houses, some live in masonry-tile houses or completely thatched houses. New, modern furniture would be a rare sight in their houses. A few have radios, and there are the usual photos and colored prints. Ancestral altars commonly are arranged on carved wooden cabinets, and altar accouterment is likely to be of good quality, but characteristically modest. Mother-of-pearl is less in evidence. As in the houses of the wealthy, guests are seated at a table before the altar of the ancestors and served tea, but in Vietnamese cups.

Bicycles are the common means of transportation for villagers of the middle level, although in recent years several have purchased motor bicycles. In general they tend to be less mobile than wealthy villagers; they stay close to farm and home, and few can afford frequent or extensive travel. Agricultural needs do necessitate periodic trips to Tan An and, less frequently, My Tho, and there are the weddings, funerals, and celebrations of ancestors' deaths in neighboring villages. Rarely, however, do they travel to distant towns or to Saigon.

While working in the fields or overseeing the hired help, middle-level farmers wear black cotton shorts and shirts and a conical hat. They go barefoot in the fields and around the farmstead—a practical solution to the problem of walking in the slippery mud of the fields, farmyards, and bundings. Black cotton also is worn during informal leisure time spent at home or visiting friends, but for visiting the Council House, attending meetings, or leaving the village, the loose-fitting white cotton clothing and wooden clogs are worn. The women dress alike regardless of socioeconomic level, but single girls of middle-level families wear fewer pieces of jewelry than do girls of well-to-do families.

With the gentry dominating the Cult Committee and the Village Council, villagers of the middle level tend to be peripheral in the political life of the village. A few serve as hamlet chiefs—a position without much political authority, but it requires that a man be known by his neighbors and have their respect; most hold lower-echelon titles in the Cult Committee. In middle-level families it is desirable that children receive a primary education. If a son is not going to be a farmer he should learn a trade, and it is well for a girl to learn sewing whether she becomes a seamstress for profit or not. Among villagers, the dressmaking trade has high prestige—it reflects skill, and it can be carried on at home. In upper and middle families, sewing and perhaps some mat weaving are the only respectable gainful pastimes for women.

With the exception of marriages, family rituals and feasting are considerably less elaborate among middle-level villagers than among the upper level. Funerals are relatively simple, and although some families summon the Buddhist monks to pray before the bier, no middle families hire the Tan An funeral service, nor are they likely to observe all the post-burial rituals. Well-to-do families often celebrate death anniversaries for several days, but middle-level families have only one-day celebrations, and the number of guests usually depends on the yearly fortune of the family; if the harvest has been abundant, from 25 to 30 kin and friends are invited, but in lean years the number is reduced to 10 or 12.

Lower Level

The lower socioeconomic level in village society encompasses the widest range of occupations. In addition to farmers who own less than 2 hectares and tenant farmers who rent less than 2.5 hectares, this category includes laborers, barbers, tailors, and most of the shopkeepers.

Farmers of this level rely a great deal on mutual aid in preparing the fields, transplanting, irrigating, and harvesting. Kin and close neighbors assist one another in these tasks, and only those who almost qualify for the middle-level category are likely to hire transplanting and irrigation labor. Most male laborers have one or two farmers for whom they work, and their employment usually is seasonal—from the time the rains begin until the end of the harvest—and even during this period they do not work every day. To subsist, most laborers must seek additional employment in the village, in the brick factory on the main highway, or in Tan An. The labor pool also is swelled by farmers who do not cultivate a sufficient amount of land to maintain themselves and their families and are forced to seek dry-season employment. Occasionally the province recruits labor in the village to work on a highway or bridge project, and they often hire female as well as male laborers. In the village female laborers are normally found only on the transplanting and harvesting teams.

Included in the lower social level is that odd scattering of women who eke out their subsistence in small commerce—selling food near the school and along the roads or peddling sticks of sugar cane, coconuts, and other locally available fruits and vegetables, and sometimes they weave mats ordered by other villagers. Women engaged in petty commerce are for the most part widows, women abandoned by their husbands, or women whose husbands are unable to work. Their activities require only several hours each day, leaving them ample time to care for their homes and families.

This class also includes the unemployed, particularly those solitary elderly people living on money provided by children and other kin. They live alone and often cultivate gardens, selling most of the produce, and some of the elderly men have cattle or buffalo which they may rent for plowing.

One common characteristic of lower-level families is that all members are expected to make some direct contribution to the sustenance of the group.[6] Because of this, it is not possible for many of their children to attend school, and among those who do, few complete a primary school education. Parents would like their children to be literate and they, more than middle-level villagers, are eager to have children learn a trade. A boy may become a carpenter's apprentice, and a young man or girl may be fortunate enough to be accepted as a tailor's apprentice. In both instances, however, they would have to be exempted from contributing to the family larder for several years, but a more insuperable barrier for most lower-level families is the cost of purchasing tools or a machine with which to practice the metier.

With rare exceptions, families of the lower level live in thatched houses, such as those described in Chapter 2, which are associated with villagers who exist at a subsistence level; these are constructed by the residents, assisted by kin and friends. The larger thatched house is apt to require some specialization in preparing wood for the frame, but construction is also a mutual-aid effort, as are repairs and replacement of thatch. Many of the small thatched houses provide minimal protection against the elements; lashing winds send rain through the countless openings, and once the pounded-earth floor becomes wet, it is likely to remain so for a long period. Although thatched houses are cooler than other houses in the heat of the dry season, they are damp.

Furnishings in these houses usually are simple—a wooden table or two, some chairs, and perhaps a cabinet for storing clothes. Lower-level families seem to have a wider variety of beds than the other villagers—the traditional Vietnamese beds (simply planks set on a frame), and there are hammocks as well as collapsible canvas beds or cots. Ancestral altars usually are arranged on wooden tables or cabinets. The altar accouterment varies from the brass incense burners, candleholders, and china vases to simple containers filled with sand to hold joss sticks and tumblers for the flowers. Decorations are equally modest; colored pictures from magazines or calendars are very popular; only a few have family photographs. Most thatched houses are illuminated by small oil lamps.

Most lower-level farmers make their own threshing sledges, harrows, and the small tools used in rice cultivation and gardening. Few own plows and

6. Division of labor in the family is discussed in Chapter 5.

teams, but rent them when needed. Most raise some chickens, some have
pigs, and although duck raising is considered a profitable activity, the initial
cost is too high for most families. Personal possessions are few and simple.
Women's wardrobes usually consist of several black or white cotton blouses,
some black cotton pantaloons for daily wear, and one black or white tunic
of cotton or calico for dress occasions. A few of the young women have tunics
in pastel shades of pink or blue. Very few women of the lower level have
jewelry.

Men generally wear black cotton shorts and a long-sleeved collarless shirt
of the same color and material. For visiting other parts of the village or
traveling into Tan An, they wear the usual loose-fitting white cotton garb
already described. Many villagers of this category do not possess the traditional black tunic and turban required for attendance at rituals and feasts,
so when the need arises they borrow them from kin or friends. In order to
conserve their one pair of wooden clogs, they go barefoot most of the time.

The hospitality pattern described for other villagers extends to those of
the lower level. In a thatched house the visitor is seated at a table before
the altar of the ancestors where tea is served in small glasses. Often, even
among the very poor, one of the children is sent to the nearest shop to
purchase some dried cookies for the guests. The tea cozy will more than
likely be a hollowed-out coconut shell, sometimes painted bright green.
Villagers of the lower level do not travel much. Their need for manufactured goods is not great, and the market in neighboring Tan Huong has
most of the things they require. Only infrequently do they travel to Tan
An (with the exception of those seeking employment); most cannot afford
the amusements available in the town, and few villagers of this economic
level have been to Saigon. Like other villagers, however, they attend family
celebrations outside Khanh Hau, although the cost of travel restricts them
to villages in the vicinity.

Villagers of the lower level do not participate very much in the political
life of the village. Some have received titles in the Cult Committee, but
these are low-echelon offices that carry minimal responsibilities—small contributions and participation at the four annual rituals in the dinh. Those
engaged in agricultural activities usually attend general meetings to decide
the course of such village projects as the canal construction, and all male
villagers are obliged to attend periodic Communist Denunciation meetings.
Only those who farm have benefited from government-sponsored agricultural programs (agricultural credit or agricultural extension) and a few
tenants of this level were helped by the Agricultural Reform Program.

Family celebrations among these villagers are modest. Money is set aside for weddings so that as many kin and friends as possible can be invited and served a good meal with meat dishes and some alcoholic beverages. Funerals, even when they are anticipated, are simple. The minimal rituals are observed in the minimal time, and the fare is vegetarian (in keeping with Buddhist tradition in the village, a family can choose whether or not to serve meat at funeral repasts). In some middle-level families the celebration of ancestors' deaths varies in elaboration with yearly fortunes; for the poor, however, there is no variation. The relatively simple prescribed ceremony is followed by a meal that resembles the main daily meal—fish, a vegetable or two, soup, rice, and the usual condiments. Tea is apt to be the only beverage served to the five or six guests.

Among the lower-level villagers two types of free time can be distinguished —voluntary leisure when one seeks relaxation and amusement after a period of work, and involuntary leisure due to unemployment or underemployment, which most generally occurs between the harvest and the beginning of the planting season. This is the hot, dry time of the year when those at occupational loose ends gather in the small shops and barber shops to chat or visit with neighbors. The laborers spend their voluntary leisure in much the same way as do the other villagers.

CHAPTER 10

Socioeconomic Profiles and Social Mobility

The Duc Family: Khanh Hau Aristocracy

IN KHANH HAU, if there is anything approaching an aristocracy—a group to whom high prestige is ascribed regardless of relative wealth—it is the Duc family, particularly the patrilineal descendants of Marshal Nguyen Huynh Duc. Although none of them has distinguished himself in any way and only a few would qualify for the upper level, direct-line descendants have high status in village society by virtue of birth. A number of nonpatrilineal kin, some of whom have married women of the family, have settled in Ap Dinh-B, attracted by rent-free farmstead sites, but they are accorded no special status because of this relationship.

In spite of his being a national hero and one of the early settlers in Khanh Hau, Marshal Duc did not own a great deal of land. This is probably because he was absent from the village most of his adult life. He was born in Khanh Hau and spent his last years there, but the intervening years of adulthood were passed in the army. He never held office in the village, nor did he engage in agricultural activities. The 15 hectares of patrimony which his paternal grandfather declared is now the trust of Ong Khai, the present head of the patrilineage, a son of the previous head. Part of this land is occupied by family tombs, including the large tomb of the hero, and a portion is the site of 18 farmsteads in Ap Dinh-B belonging to patrilineal and nonpatrilineal kin.

The paternal grandfather of Ong Khau purchased 15 hectares in a neighboring village, declaring them huong hoa patrimony. Ong Khai holds title to this land, and most of it is rented to kin. His elder brother and younger brother (the civil status secretary) each rent three hectares, two younger sisters each rent one hectare, and kin related through Ong Khai's father's mother rent a total of three hectares. Two hectares are rented by natives of the village where the land is located, and an additional two are farmstead sites in the same village.

According to an imperial decree signed by Emperor Gia Long, which the Duc family possesses, Marshal Duc was in his later years granted revenues from 100 hectares of land in Mau Tai village, Huong Tra district, in Thua Thien province of central Vietnam. This was a reward for his loyal services, and the decree specified that the privilege be extended to his descendants. During the reign of Emperor Minh Mang the amount of land was reduced to 60 hectares, but the revenues continued to be paid to the Duc family until the death of Emperor Khai Dinh in 1925. The succeeding emperor, Bao Dai, resided in France, which prevented the family from making a direct appeal to have the revenues restored.

In 1932 Ong Khai's father, Ong Tan, wrote to a number of government officials concerning the family claim, and when their responses indicated no interest in considering the matter, he decided to journey to Hue and speak with high officials at the Royal Court. As he was preparing for the trip, Ong Tan was summoned to Can Tho by a group of Cao Daists who advised him that they felt there would be a message of great importance for him in their forthcoming seance. One spirit message informed him that the tombs of Marshal Nguyen Huynh Duc's parents were located near Hue, and this was followed by a message that his trip to Hue would not bring favorable results. Ong Tan refused to heed the warning, and he went, as planned, to Hue. He was granted a meeting with the Minister of the Interior at the Royal Court, and this official regretfully informed him that there was no record of the decree in the royal archives.

Discouraged, but very much awakened to the possible efficacy of Cao Daism, Ong Tan returned to Khanh Hau where he embraced this new religion. Nothing more was done about the claim until 1959 when, on the advice of legal counselors, Ong Khai had the imperial decree photographed and sent a copy of it along with a formal appeal to the Ministry of the Interior in Saigon. To indicate the prestige of Marshal Duc, Ong Khai pointed out in the accompanying letter that each year the province of Long An contributed 50$ VN for upkeep of the Marshal's tomb, and the Province Chief had donated 2,000$ in the drive to raise funds for the construction of a shrine honoring the hero. In March 1959 the Ministry of the Interior responded, stating that the family's claim to the revenues could not be recognized; the family had no title to the land, and since the Royal Archives were destroyed in fighting that took place within the walled city during the Indochina War, there was no means of ascertaining which land was involved.

Ong Khai, however, does not consider the matter ended, and when representatives of the Bureau of Historical Research visited Khanh Hau in May 1959 to photograph the Marshal's tomb, he enlisted their aid in the family's cause.

As head of the Duc family, Ong Khai's primary responsibilities are in maintaining the Marshal's tomb and ancestral house. The weathered gray stone tomb is the largest in the vicinity, a small version of the imperial tombs in Hue, and nearby is the large, rambling house, set in a garden in the middle of which is a delicate tea pavilion. The section of the house facing the garden contains the shrine and museum. An imposing altar, almost hidden by brightly colored hangings, dominates the main room, and in front of it is a glass case filled with the Marshal's personal effects and imperial awards. There are several small altars, and the walls of the room are covered with photos of visitors.

The other section of the house, reached by narrow, dark passages on either side of the main altar, resembles the larger traditional wood-tile houses of the village. The main room is cavernous, and the central section is occupied by a large Cao Daist altar. Smaller altars, dedicated to other ancestors and Buddhist deities, are scattered about the room. There are the usual hardwood beds, tables, and a number of chairs to accommodate the visitors to the shrine, who are received in this room; when Cult Committee members come to remove the Guardian Spirit decree from the main altar, they are served refreshments here. It also is the meeting place for leaders of the Tien Thien Cao Daist congregation.

With the severance of revenues in 1925, the Duc family entered a period of financial difficulties. Rents from various landholdings did not amount to much, and since most of this income was from huong hoa patrimony, it had to be expended on rituals and feasting associated with the Cult of the Ancestors. Income from visitors' contributions diminished considerably when in the early 1930s a large pagoda honoring General Le Van Duyet was constructed on the edge of Saigon, which became the primary tourist attraction in southern Vietnam. Also, travel became difficult with the outbreak of World War II. The Duc family recalls this as a period of poverty for them, and they feared their ancestor would become a forgotten hero. Some of the nonpatrilineal kin quit the village; for example, Ong Khai's younger brother, unable to rent land in the village, was forced to migrate to Saigon (where he now operates a transport service).

With the end of the Indochina War in 1954, however, the fortunes of the Duc family began to rise—primarily due to nationalism and southern

Vietnamese regionalism. Southern Vietnamese culture heroes became popular, and local officials, particularly the province chief and the village chief proposed that a shrine honoring the Marshal be constructed in the village near his tomb. The Duc family agreed and donated a plot of land.

Restored to his place among the national heroes, Marshal Nguyen Huynh Duc was rapidly attaining the role of a deity. In addition to his undeclared status as a guardian spirit of the village, he was increasingly being considered a Cao Daist saint by the local Tien Thien congregation. In 1959 they dedicated an altar to him, and some of the leaders expressed the desire to have him officially included in the sect pantheon, although the holy see in Soc Sai had not given its approval. All of these events have served to reinforce the high prestige position of the Duc family. In 1958, Ong Khai's younger brother was appointed civil status secretary in the Village Council, ascending to the role of village chief in December 1961. The peak of prestige was reached, however, when early in 1960 the new shrine honoring Marshal Nguyen Huynh Duc was completed, and members of the family officiated at the dedication.

VILLAGERS OF THE UPPER ECONOMIC LEVEL

Ong Xa Khanh: Wealthy Landowner

To meet this wealthy farmer and moneylender walking on the road in Ap Dinh-B with his face hidden under a battered conical hat, one might easily mistake him for a farmer or laborer of the poorest type. He is a tall, gaunt, and somewhat taut man of sixty years who, like most older men, favors the traditional long hair tied in a bun at the nape of the neck and the wispy beard; his daily attire consists of the black cotton shorts and shirt associated with work in the fields. For visiting in the hamlet or at the Council House (which he rarely does), Ong Xa Khanh wears the usual loose-fitting white cotton outfit. At village and family celebrations, his traditional tunic and turban are of ordinary material, and his only footgear is a pair of wooden clogs.

In curious contrast, his house reflects his wealth, and the house of his father which stands nearby, reflects the wealth of the preceding generation. Ong Xa Khanh's house is the newest and most elegant masonry residence in Khanh Hau (see Fig. 13). It has a wide veranda, a sizable concrete water tank, and its floor plan represents a departure from the traditional in having a separate dining room; the thatched kitchen has been retained. The furniture is modern—of highly polished light-colored wood done in styles popular

in Saigon—and there are brightly colored prints as well as several large
mirrors on the walls. A guest in the house of Ong Xa Khanh is served tea
in Western-style cups of thin china together with candied fruit, a delicacy
usually reserved for special occasions.

Ong Xa Khanh's splendid house (almost hidden by arbors covered with
flowering vines), his father's house, and the simple thatched residences of
his two quiet and unassuming sons form a group of farmsteads near the spur
road in Ap Dinh-B. The ancestral house, constructed some fifty years ago,
is a large wood-tile structure with traditional lines, which serves primarily
as a sanctuary. The cavernous main room where the altars stand is opened
only for rituals honoring the ancestors. The rear rooms of the house are put
to practical use—some are storerooms for tools, and one large room contains
large reed-mat paddy granaries.

According to Ong Xa Khanh's family history, passed down verbally, his
paternal grandparents migrated to the delta from central Vietnam during
the interdynastic wars of the nineteenth century.[1] They settled in Tuong
Khanh, present-day Ap Dinh A–B, clearing an unspecified amount of land
for paddy cultivation. Their son served as a minor official in the village, and
through inheritance and successful farming, he accumulated ten hectares of
paddy land. He also was admitted to the Cult Committee, achieving the
position of Chanh Bai, one of the high venerables. Each of his five children
received two hectares, and his youngest son Ong Xa Khanh inherited title
to the paternal house. The eldest son assumed the role of patrilineage head
until he became a Roman Catholic when a council of the other siblings
elected Ong Xa Khanh to the role.

Ong Xa Khanh's financial rise was due to his being rental agent for Ong
Hue, formerly the largest landowner in Khanh Hau (although a resident
of Saigon), and of litigation with the present village chief. In the village
there are strong sanctions against squabbling over inheritance, and this
affair was a rare exception. Ong Xa Khanh's aunt was married to the village
chief's uncle, and the couple held joint title to ten hectares of paddy land.
The wife survived her husband, and prior to her death she made an arrangement whereby her kin and her husband's kin could by mutual agreement
have either her large wood-tile house or 1,000 pre-World War II piasters, the
estimated value of the house. For some unknown reason she did nothing
about the ten hectares of paddy land. After her death both families agreed

1. This probably refers to the wars between the Trinh of the north and the Nguyen
of the south, which began in 1620 and lasted into the nineteenth century.

that Ong Xa Khanh's eldest brother would receive the house and the village chief and his siblings would divide the thousand piasters. Soon after, Ong Xa Khanh filed a claim for the land with the district tribunal, and the village chief countered with a similar claim. The tribunal, after considerable deliberation, decided that the land was huong hoa of the alienable type and divided it between the contesting parties.

Ong Xa Khanh became the rental agent of Ong Hue when the present highest venerable in the village resigned the position. Since Ong Hue rarely visited the village, his agents had a great deal of autonomy, and a number of villagers, particularly tenants and former tenants, continue to harbor resentment against Ong Xa Khanh for his actions during this period. They accused him of overcharging on rents and keeping the difference. Villagers also claim that since Ong Hue was more interested in cash than paddy at harvest, Ong Xa Khanh paid him the rents in cash, but demanded the rents in paddy which he then stored for later sale at higher prices. This angered the tenants who would have preferred to pay rent in cash, saving paddy which they could store for later sale themselves. When he had accumulated sixty hectares of paddy land, Ong Xa Khanh resigned his position to devote full time to his own interests. He and his sons cultivate the unrented portion of his land, doing most of the field labor themselves. In addition to being an important landowner, Ong Xa Khanh is reputed to be the biggest money-lender in the village.

Despite his wealth, however, Ong Xa Khanh never has achieved a position in the Village Council higher than finance secretary. Even this proved unsuccessful; he had so many difficulties with other members that the council was disbanded and was reformed without him. Also, he refused a position in the Cult Committee, on the ground that he was too busy with his land and farming responsibilities. When there are rituals at the dinh, Ong Xa Khanh puts in only brief appearances, and he refused to donate funds for the construction of the Marshal's shrine (which provoked the village chief to comment, "Xa Khanh has big pockets without bottoms").

He is clearly an outlander (recently his son married the daughter of Ong Lam,[2] another outlander). He is in conflict with the village chief and others currently in power, and many villagers consider him crafty and miserly. Nonetheless, he is treated with deference. Since Vietnamese have strong sanctions against public rudeness, criticisms against Ong Xa Khanh are not made openly. Further, in the long run villagers have respect for the fact that

2. A profile of Ong Lam and his brothers begins on p. 260.

he has been successful in acquiring land and wealth and, more importantly, he has provided well for his family. He also has maintained scrupulously the ancestral house and the Cult of the Ancestors.

Ong Chan: Village Chief

Ong Chan is referred to and addressed as Ong Ca, an informal designation for village chief. He is 48 years old, rather stout, and generally very affable. By village standards, he has done well; he has two wives, several good houses, land, many children, and a position of respect. His rise in the socioeconomic structure of village society has come about through many circumstances. Family history records that his paternal grandfather settled in Khanh Hau and accumulated six hectares of paddy land, all of which he declared inalienable patrimony. Ong Ca's father, the succeeding head of the patrilineage, held several positions in the Cult Committee, ascending to the position of Chanh Bai before he died. Since his father placed great emphasis on education, his sons were sent to secondary school in Tan An where they learned, among other things, to speak French.

When Ong Ca was 21 years old, he was admitted into the Cult Committee and given the title of Thu Bo, the lowest rank, usually reserved for the sons of those in the high ranks. He assisted his father and brothers with farming and soon became involved in rice merchandising. This proved profitable, enabling him to purchase several hectares of paddy land in the village. Ong Ca, atypically, was over 30 years old when he married, and the alliance enhanced his economic position—his wife had some land and title to her parents' large wood-tile house. Soon after, his litigation with Ong Xa Khanh brought him an additional five hectares of paddy land.

On the death of his father, the family elected Ong Ca as head of the patrilineage, and all agreed, since he was wealthy, that his two brothers should divide the income from the patrimony rather than use it for the Cult of the Ancestors as prescribed. The elder brother took two hectares, and his younger brother received four hectares. Ong Ca's elder brother is considerably older than he, and although he had been village chief for one term and also had held several high titles in the Cult Committee, he has completely withdrawn from village affairs, even avoiding rituals in the dinh (although he does attend performances of the classical theater faithfully). He had several hectares in addition to the patrimony, and when he reached the age of 67 he transferred the titles to his sons. After his wife died, he moved out of his house, leaving it to his daughter and her family, and he constructed a small, very rudimentary thatched hut on the edge of Ap Dinh-A. An independent and philosophical old man, he says he prefers the simple life, tending his garden and watching his two head of cattle.[3]

Ong Ca's younger brother also engaged in rice merchandising, but he contends he found it too dishonest so he returned to farming. He, like his older brother, has no title in the Cult Committee, claiming he is too busy, and he is the only resident of Khanh Hau who adheres to the esoteric Chon Ly sect of Cao Daism.[4] At one time Ong Ca had been a member of the Tien Thien sect, joining in response to a spirit message received during a village seance. Subsequently, however, he fell ill, and local sect leaders interpreted it as a sign that his conversion was premature and advised him to withdraw.

Ten years after his first marriage, Ong Ca took a second wife, a prosperous widow with several houses and some land. One of the houses was converted to a granary to accommodate the ever-increasing store of paddy from Ong Ca's ever-increasing land, part of which was rented and part cultivated with hired labor. Ong Ca regretted that his farm responsibilities forced him to abandon merchandising, but when the opportunity arose, he invested 100,-000$ VN in a new gasoline station in Tan An.

As his wealth increased, Ong Ca became more active in the political life of the village. In 1954 he was named public works secretary; in 1956 he was appointed village chief, and this position has occupied most of his time since. He has the explicit goal of making Khanh Hau into a "model village," and to this end he cooperated closely with Mr. Nguyen Van Mung, the first director of the UNESCO School of Fundamental Education, who lived and worked in the village when the school was being built. They successfully launched the canal-building project, latrine construction, and a poultry-raising program. Ong Ca also was very active in organizing the campaign to construct the pagoda honoring Marshal Duc.[5]

Ong Van Tan: Prosperous Tenant Farmer

Prior to rituals in the dinh, an observer cannot fail to notice a small, wiry man with close-cropped white hair, busily preparing the altar. During the rituals he seems omnipresent—whispering the proper incantations to the boys flanking the altar and telling them when to announce the names

3. Ong Ca's elder brother died in 1961, and the family erected an elaborate concrete tomb in which he is buried.

4. This sect is described in Chapter 3.

5. Late in 1961 Ong Ca resigned as village chief and was replaced by the younger brother of Ong Khai, truong toc of the Duc family. Because of Viet Cong activities in Khanh Hau, Ong Ca moved to Tan An, returning to the village only in the daytime to oversee his land and houses.

of the next worshippers. Toward the end of the rituals, he is the venerable who reads the list of those being honored, the same list which he later ceremoniously burns on the altar. This is Ong Van Tan, who holds the high title of Ca Le in the Cult Committee, making him responsible for proper form and performance of all village rituals.

Ong Van Tan is 60 years old, and he lives in a large wood-tile house on the edge of Ap Thu Tuu, near the farmsteads of his two married sons. He rents 15 hectares from Ong Xa Khanh, which makes him wealthy by village standards. Ong Van Tan's paternal grandfather settled in Ap Thu Tuu where he rented some land; in 1904 he and his family suffered greatly from a great storm that struck the delta, destroying crops. Ong Van Tan's father also was a tenant farmer and was Huong Hao in the Village Council—responsible for expediting orders of the village chief and arranging village rituals. This undoubtedly had something to do with his enrolling his son in a School of Ritual Studies newly founded in Khanh Hau by a retired employee of the Saigon–My Tho railroad, a scholar of the traditional ritual forms and Chinese calligraphy. Sixteen young men met in classes arranged to permit them time to continue their farm duties. The curriculum was centered on traditional ritual forms, chants, symbolism, Chinese calligraphy, and Vietnamese history.

Ong Van Tan remained a student in the school until he was 23, when the master died. He was granted the title of Ca Le in the Cult Committee, but after three years, farm and family responsibilities forced him to relinquish this honor. Ong Dan, the villager who later won 1,000,000$ in the national lottery, was his only remaining confrere from the School of Ritual Studies, so he became Ca Le until 1956 when Ong Van Tan took the position again. The role of Ca Le demands considerable time, but since he now uses hired laborers to work his fields, he has the time to give. He recently instituted a course in ritual forms and prayers for young men of the village, fulfilling a long-standing desire to perpetuate the traditional knowledge he had acquired. Ong Van Tan has one final desire—to own land for his sons, and he has been saving money for this end.

Ong Dan: Wealth by Chance

The people of Khanh Hau have an implicit faith in predisposition to good or bad fortune, and occurrences periodically reinforce this belief. One of these was the good fortune that visited Ong Dan in 1952 when he won 1,000,000$ in the national lottery. Before 1952 Ong Dan lived with his wife and six sons in a large thatched house on the edge of Ap Thu Tuu. His younger brother was hamlet chief of Ap Thu Tuu, and his older brother, the head of the patrilineage, lived nearby. According to the family geneal- ogy book, one of the few in Khanh Hau, Ong Dan's paternal grandfather had come from central Vietnam in the nineteenth century, a refugee from the dynastic wars. He remained a tenant farmer as did Ong Dan's father. In spite of their relative poverty, Ong Dan's father insisted that his sons learn to read and write, and he managed to send them to the School of Ritual Studies.

Gambling is a traditional activity in Vietnam, and since the 1955 ban on gambling as one of the "four vices," [6] the only legal outlets are the national lottery and the government-controlled race track at Phu Tho, near Saigon. Villagers of all economic levels eagerly look for the lottery tickets having their "lucky numbers," and newspaper sales increase markedly when lottery results are published. When Ong Dan won, his way of life changed immedi- ately. He purchased twenty hectares of good land, seven of which he culti- vates himself; he rents the remainder, and seven of these were declared huong hoa. He then constructed a masonry house which cost 130,000$ and, knowing that masonry houses were a special target in Viet Minh raids on the village, he selected a site in Ap Dinh-A, close to the military stockade. Large hardwood beds, carved chairs, a marble-topped table, and a magnifi- cent cabinet inlaid with mother-of-pearl (on which to arrange the altar of the ancestors) were purchased for the main room of the new house. A wood- carver was hired to make a decorative frame for the altar, and draperies were bought in Saigon to grace it. Ong Dan's new house was the first in Khanh Hau to have a brick floor, and it also had the distinction of being the first house with a wide veranda—a feature which since has become the mode for masonry houses. Finally, Ong Dan donated 200,000$ to the village for the expansion of the primary school. This gesture elicited great praise from his fellow villagers who considered that this was the act of "a good Buddhist."

As a consequence of his new wealth, Ong Dan became more active in village affairs. He was awarded a high place in the Cult Committee, and for several years his home has been the headquarters of the National Revolu- tionary Party, and meetings of the Agricultural Cooperative have been held there. He also found more free time, most of which he spent in the Council House assisting with the organization of village celebrations. While his eldest son prefers farming, the other sons, with their father's encouragement, have continued their schooling. The second eldest attends a secondary school in Saigon, and Ong Dan is particularly proud of his ability to speak some

6. The other three are prostitution, opium smoking, and alcohol.

English. Recently Ong Dan has been suffering from a respiratory ailment which has not responded to medical treatment. Some villagers contend this is the result of his new life—an abrupt change that has put him out of harmony with the elements; others pessimistically point out that it is inevitable that good fortune be followed by ill fortune.[7]

Ong Hiep: The Highest Venerable

Known to all by his title, Ong Ke Hien, he has the highest position on the Cult Committee and is the wealthiest resident of Khanh Hau. With his white hair tied in a bun in traditional fashion, his goatee and lined face, he is the perfect picture of a Vietnamese village venerable. He was born 75 years ago in Ap Nhon Hau where his father was hamlet chief. Their ancestors were early settlers in the neighboring village of Tan Huong, where Ong Ke Hien's paternal grandfather farmed two hectares of paddy land, and his maternal grandfather inherited title to ten hectares, some of which was passed on to Ong Ke Hien's mother. In addition, Ong Ke Hien's father accumulated ten hectares in Tan Huong, which he later declared patrimony, and when he married a girl from Ap Nhon Hau and moved there, he purchased another ten hectares in Khanh Hau.

Before he inherited any land, Ong Ke Hien's fortunes rose when he secured the position of agent for Ong Hue and his brother (absentee landlords). Being agent under these circumstances is profitable—the salary is high and the agent has considerable autonomy. As in the case of Ong Xa Khanh, there continues to be some criticism leveled against Ong Ke Hien for alleged sharp practices while he was agent, although generally it is mild compared to accusations made against Ong Xa Khanh.

With accumulated capital, Ong Ke Hien began purchasing paddy land from his employers. He also received ten hectares when his father died, and the family elected him head of the patrilineage, giving him title in trust to ten hectares of land in Tan Huong. Although he was relatively young, Ong Ke Hien was gaining his reputation as the most successful man in the village as well as one of the most adept farmers. His decisions when to plant, transplant, and harvest were awaited by other farmers, and he was the first in the village to use chemical fertilizer. Having achieved the status of a wealthy landowner, he became more active in village affairs and was named village secretary, a position he held for almost fifty years; he was also awarded a high title in the Cult Committee.

---

7. Ong Dan died early in 1962.

Ong Ke Hien eventually acquired close to 100 hectares in Khanh Hau and considerable holdings in the surrounding area. On the edge of the river in Ap Cau he constructed the most palatial house in Khanh Hau. All his children received primary school educations, and his only sons, identical twins, were sent to a private secondary school in Cholon where they received a "traditional education," emphasizing Vietnamese history, literature, fine arts, and Chinese calligraphy.

The Indochina War brought terror and destruction to Ong Ke Hien as it did to many villagers. On one of their nocturnal raids, a band of Viet Minh approached his house and demanded a large sum of money, making it clear they would kill him if he did not comply. He refused and, with the help of his sons and some weapons hidden in the house, fought off the raiders. Hearing gunfire, guards from the watchtower near the bridge on the main highway came to the rescue, dispersing the remaining Viet Minh. The next day Ong Ke Hien moved his family into a house he had purchased in Tan An. Not long after, the Viet Minh again raided the village, plundering and burning his house. Ruins of the veranda, the rusting wrought-iron fence, and the dried-up fish pond overgrown with weeds are all that remain.

With the end of the Indochina War, Ong Ke Hien found himself even more involved in entrepreneurial and philanthropic activities. He had achieved the highest rank in the Cult Committee, and being Ke Hien demanded contributions to village projects and celebrations as well as donations to the needy from time to time. In addition, Ong Ke Hien financed the reconstruction of his brother's pagoda and became the pagoda's sponsor, contributing one hectare of paddy land and a yearly allotment of rice for its upkeep.[8] In keeping with the postwar trend of investing in enterprises, Ong Ke Hien purchased a large rice mill in the neighboring village of Ba Ly (where his daughter's husband was village chief), and he also actively engaged in rice merchandising. He continued to expand his landholdings and began purchasing uncleared land in the Plaine des Joncs area recently opened for settlement.

One of the twins assumed operation of the rice mill in Ba Ly where he constructed a modern masonry house.[9] The other twin has remained in Ap Cau, living in a masonry house near the highway. He is his father's rental agent, and for several years he has served as village secretary. He also holds a relatively high title in the Cult Committee. One of Ong Ke Hien's daugh-

8. This pagoda is described more in detail in Chapter 3.
9. In 1962 Viet Cong activities forced him to move into Tan An.

ters is married to Ong Chi, a brother of Ong Lam, a prominent resident of
Ap Dinh-A (whose profile follows), and they operate a large general store
near the market in Tan Huong.

Because of Viet Cong activities in 1958 and 1959, Ong Ke Hien has continued to reside in Tan An, visiting the village frequently, particularly for
the celebrations in which he officiates. With most of his financial affairs in
the hands of his children, he spends a great deal of his time in village and
philanthropic efforts, the latest of which is a Buddhist nunnery organized
by one of his nieces in My Tho. The Village Council constantly seeks his
advice and as Ke Hien he organizes and participates in rituals at both dinh.
In addition to giving six annual death-anniversary celebrations, he is invited
to a great many given by other families in the vicinity. Ong Ke Hien now is
preparing to die, and when he visits Khanh Hau, he invariably stops in Ap
Cau to oversee work on the elaborate concrete tombs being constructed for
him and his wife near the pagoda.

Ong Lam and His Brothers: Entrepreneurial Farmers

On the western edge of Ap Dinh-A where the coconut palms, areca palms,
and other tropical growths abound, there is a clearing, usually cluttered
with coconut shells, paddy husks, and firewood, in the middle of which
stands the house of Ong Lam. In some respects the structure resembles an
elaborate shelter more than a house—it is of mixed old and new wood with
a tile roof, and one end is practically open. Thin latticework forms a partial
wall (no barrier to weather, insects, and animals) giving the structure an
unfinished appearance. Along the path leading from the house to the spur
road, there is a large, substantially constructed wood-tile house, built by
Ong Lam's father and, in keeping with southern Vietnamese custom, it
belongs to the youngest son, Ong Nam.[10] Ong Chi, the second eldest son,
is married to the daughter of Ong Ke Hien, and they are proprietors of a
general store near the market in the neighboring village of Tan Huong.
Since he owns land in Khanh Hau and spends a good deal of time there,
Ong Chi is considered a village resident.

The brothers Ong Lam and Ong Chi resemble each other—they are thick-
set and have round, ruddy faces that break into easy smiles. Ong Nam, on
the other hand, is thin, quiet, and furtive. Ong Lam and his brothers have
many kin in the village, and they are well-known figures in the surrounding

10. In Chapter 4 the residence pattern of this part of the hamlet is described in detail,
indicating the network of kin which includes Ong Lam and Ong Nam.

area. Their paternal grandfather was landless, but their father had amassed twenty hectares. On his death, Ong Lam, his two brothers, and one sister each received five hectares. Ong Lam became head of the patrilineage, although his father's younger brother assumed responsibility for cult rituals honoring the paternal great grandparents and grandparents, leaving Ong Lam and his brothers to share ritual responsibility for their parents. The brothers and their paternal uncle also share the cost of a general ritual for all ancestors, to which over 100 guests are invited.

The family has had a tradition of political participation. In addition to their father who was deputy village chief, their mother's younger brother served several terms as village chief and currently holds a high position in the Cult Committee. In 1944 Ong Lam was appointed village secretary, and when the Japanese quit Vietnam after their surrender in August 1945, he assumed the position of Viet Minh village chief and named Ong Nam village secretary.[11] The Viet Minh administration was short-lived, however, and when the French restored the colonial administration several months later, the pre-Viet Minh Village Council was re-established, forcing Ong Lam and his brother to return to farming. Since then they have remained relatively aloof from the political life of the village.[12]

At the end of the Indochina War, Ong Lam and his brothers pooled their resources to invest in various enterprises, the most adventurous of which was a lumber and rice business. Since they realized sizable harvests from their combined 15 hectares, they planned to transport rice to the highland town of Ban Me Thuot where there is a constant demand for it (particularly since the great influx of Vietnamese settlers since 1957), and purchase lumber which is plentiful (and hence relatively cheap). The lumber then would be carried to Tan An and sold at high prices. Ong Lam went to make the necessary contacts in Ban Me Thuot while his brothers bought a truck and loaded it with milled rice. The plan was successful and the business thrived until Ong Nam had an accident when he was transporting lumber over the sinuous road from Ban Me Thuot. The brakes failed on a steep hill and the truck careened off the road, tipping over in a ravine. Ong Nam almost lost his life, the truck was a total loss, the cost of salvaging the lumber was prohibitive, and the business venture ended.

11. Understandably, villagers now speak with reluctance about events of this era, some noting, however, that it was the time the village-built school was burned, leaving them without a primary school for several years.

12. After the police chief was killed by the Viet Cong in 1961, Ong Nam replaced him, and in 1962 he continued to hold this position.

This ill-fated enterprise, however, has not dampened their spirit. Ong Nam made several unsuccessful attempts at rice merchandising—his method of contracting for unharvested crops proved too precarious—and in 1959 he turned to rice milling, collaborating with a Khanh Hau resident who operates a rice mill in Tan Huong. Ong Lam has made more of a success of his rice merchandising, purchasing milled rice on the Cholon market and selling it at Moc Hoa in the Plaine des Joncs area where rice is in demand. Ong Chi divides his time between his general goods store and his farm.

Although they have been political outsiders, Ong Lam and his brothers are regarded highly by fellow villagers. Ong Lam holds a high title in the Cult Committee and faithfully assists at rituals in the dinh as does Ong Chi, although he does not have a title. Ong Nam, on the other hand, scorns the rituals and refuses to wear traditional clothes. Although their family celebrations are elaborate, the brothers live modestly. Neither their clothes nor their houses are ostentatious. Unlike his brothers, however, Ong Chi spends more time and money on entertainment; with one of the few motor scooters in Khanh Hau, he travels to neighboring market towns and to Saigon where he attends the cinema (particularly when American films are playing) and visits the bars in the lively port section of the city.

VILLAGERS OF THE MIDDLE ECONOMIC LEVEL

Ong Ca Duoc: Middle-Level Landowner

Ong Ca Duoc lives on a farmstead apart from any of the clusters that form Ap Moi. His house is substantially constructed with a masonry roof and large masonry veranda, although the rest of the structure is of wood. The main room is large, dominated by a splendid ancestral altar with gleaming brass accouterment. There is carved wood around the altar, and the dark hardwood pillars supporting the frame of the house are hidden by large tablets of black wood on which gold Chinese characters spell out invocations. The furnishings, however, are very simple.

To one side of the house there is a stable in which several head of cattle, a horse, and a cart are kept—the only draft horse and cart in the village. With them, Ong Ca Duoc's son operates a transport service between the village and Tan An. A kitchen garden flourishes next to the house, and there is a delightful flower garden in the middle of which Ong Ca Duoc arranged a small polychrome shrine honoring Ong Than Nong, the Spirit of Agriculture. The open front of the shrine faces the veranda, enabling the spirit to watch the inhabitants of the house. "We try to be good people," says Ong Ca Duoc; "Ong Than Nong can indeed give a favorable account of our conduct to the Emperor of Jade."

Ong Ca Duoc's father came from the neighboring village of Tan Hiep, settling in Ap Moi where his wife had many kin, some of whom were willing to rent him land.[13] Ong Ca Duoc attended primary school for several years and assisted his father with farming. After his marriage he was able to rent some land from kinfolk, eventually saving enough money to purchase one hectare. When he had 3.5 hectares, he began to take a more active part in village affairs and, although he never held a position in the Village Council, Ong Ca Duoc was given a high title in the Cult Committee. Because he was not considered sympathetic to the Viet Minh, he had to quit Khanh Hau for most of the Indochina War, and during one of their raids on the village the Viet Minh burned his house. When the war ended Ong Ca Duoc returned to Ap Moi, constructed a new house, and resumed his place in village society.

Currently, Ong Ca Duoc spends most of his time tending his farm and helping his son with the transport business. He continues to hold a title in the Cult Committee, actively assisting with the organization of village projects and celebrations. Although he is not a particularly wealthy man, Ong Ca Duoc is considered one of the most prominent citizens of Ap Moi, a reputation enhanced by the fact that he has many kin in the hamlet, many of them women without husbands, and they look to him for counsel and aid. His only son is married, and Ong Ca Duoc is making plans to give him some land, and also to acquire additional land to be declared huong hoa patrimony.

Ong Hai: Hamlet Chief and Landowner

The hamlet chief of Ap Moi is 55 years old, has the reputation of being very independent, and prefers to remain in the privacy of his farmstead on the southern edge of Ap Moi. He appears at the Council House only when some official duty requires his presence, and then he goes about his business quietly and swiftly. When it is over he may briefly chat with those present before he puts up his large black umbrella and departs.

Ong Hai's paternal grandfather owned the four-cong farmstead on which the ancestral house stands. Since both Ong Hai and his father were youngest sons, they inherited the farmstead and the house, a rambling wood-tile

13. In Chapter 4 the residence pattern of Ap Moi was analyzed, and one of the larger kin groupings includes Ong Ca Duoc.

structure over 60 years old, solidly constructed with a hardwood frame and polished hardwood pillars. Its former elegance, however, has all but disappeared, and currently the main room is piled high with tools and farm implements (including an unused hand-operated husking machine), and it serves as the paddy granary. There scarcely is room to receive visitors, and the family spends most of its time in a ramshackle addition.

"A bit of land can pass through 10,000 hands in 1,000 years," is the proverb Ong Hai delights in quoting when he recalls his acquisition of land. His paternal grandfather had been a landowner with 1.5 hectares of good paddy land. Financial difficulties, however, forced him to sell it to his neighbor, Ong Tien Bai Tri. With no land other than the four-cong farmsteads, Ong Hai's father remained a tenant farmer, unable to save money because of unfortunate circumstances. Ong Hai rented 1.5 hectares, and he cultivated a vegetable cash crop on the farmstead. In 1957 Ong Tien Bai Tri, because of pressing financial obligations, put the 1.5 hectares purchased from Ong Hai's grandfather up for sale. When the news reached him, Ong Hai quickly sold the expensive inlaid cabinet on which his ancestral altar was arranged, unearthed his savings, and purchased the land.

With the aid of hired laborers, Ong Hai works his own fields. In addition to farm responsibilities, he has demanding family and administrative duties. Since his eldest brother, the head of the patrilineage, is a poor tenant farmer, and his other brother, the secretary for the district chief in Thu Thua, does not live in the village, Ong Hai has assumed responsibility for six annual death-anniversary celebrations. As hamlet chief he visits families throughout the hamlet, assisting those who have difficulties with administrative matters—registration of births, marriages, deaths, and land transfers—and he attends many of the residents' family celebrations. If a resident of the hamlet is in need of funds or medicine, Ong Hai usually approaches the well-to-do for contributions. Finally, he holds a title in the Cult Committee of the Ap Dinh-A dinh.

Ong Hai values education greatly and has sent his children to primary and secondary schools. He believes that this is more important than expending money on house, clothes, furnishings, or tomb. His eldest son, who now works in the control tower at Tan Son Nhut airport near Saigon, received a secondary education in My Tho and also studied in a government technical school in Saigon. This son periodically visits Khanh Hau on his motor bicycle, although his father insists he leave the village before the sun goes down. Security in the remote parts of Ap Moi cannot be guaranteed, and Ong Hai has had sufficient trouble during the Indochina War to make him cautious. Several times during the war he was forced to quit the village for short periods, and during one of these periods the French troops from the stockade in Ap Dinh-A entered Ap Moi to raid a reported Viet Minh meeting in Ong Hai's house. They surrounded the farmstead and opened fire on the house, killing the sole occupant, Ong Hai's twelve-year-old daughter.

Ong Tan: Middle-Level Tenant Farmer

Ong Tan is a big man with a heavy red face that some of his friends laughingly attribute to his drinking habits. He is envied by fellow tenant farmers. In addition to having a sizable wood-tile house in Ap Cau, with a large garden and fruit grove, Ong Tan rents 4.5 hectares from his father's older brother, Ong Ke Hien. It is considered choice land—within the bounds of Ap Cau, an area of ample water sources and relatively low fields which retain available water. As a result, in the droughts of 1957 and 1958 Ong Tan suffered less than other farmers and, being a kinsman of the landlord, he was assured of a rent reduction because of the drought. Further, Ong Ke Hien, in the course of putting his material affairs in order after his seventy-fifth year, suggested to Ong Tan that he begin processing a title for the land he is cultivating. This relieved him of the need to save money for the eventual purchase of land. Finally, to add to Ong Tan's good fortune, his wife expects to inherit some of her father's land.

Ong Tan is considered something of a sybarite by his fellow villagers, particularly the group of males who periodically gather to drink and talk in a shop by the path in Ap Cau. He can drink more alcohol than any of them, and he says he has a second wife with her own house in Ap Dinh-A (where she sells fruits and vegetables to support herself) in addition to a third wife in neighboring Tan Huong. Further, Ong Tan claims to have many "girl friends" in surrounding villages as well as in Tan An. His Falstaffian air makes him a popular figure in the hamlet, and his kinship to Ong Ke Hien gives him some prestige. He holds a title in the Cult Committee of the Ap Nhon Hau dinh, faithfully attending the rituals held there.

His brothers have the reputation of being more responsible than Ong Tan. His elder brother was once village chief, and his younger brother currently is hamlet chief of Ap Cau. Like Ong Tan, the younger brother was a tenant farmer, but he saved money and purchased five hectares of paddy land. He also rents three hectares from Ong Hue, the absentee landlord. His house, occupied by Wife Number One and her children, is a large masonry-tile structure on the banks of the stream in Ap Cau. Deeper in the hamlet, Wife Number Two lives in a small thatched house.

Villagers of the Lower Economic Level

Ong Kim Tai: A Small Tenant Farmer

Ong Kim Tai was first encountered squatting amid the tombs which are numerous in one part of Ap Dinh-B, scooping muddy water from a drying pool into his nearby seedbed. It was the worst period of the 1958 drought, and frantic efforts to save wilting seedlings were common throughout Khanh Hau. The afternoon sun beat down, and Ong Kim Tai in black shorts and shirt, a frayed conical hat on his head, worked steadily until there was more mud than water at the bottom of the pool. He is an old man with a leathery, lined thin face and bright smiling eyes, and seems the typical Vietnamese peasant of books and pictures. His house, a plain thatched structure with one large room and a small kitchen addition, is near the spur road and is completely obscured by thick greenery.

Ong Kim Tai is a widower, and he lives with his 16-year-old son. They divide the task of maintaining the house and farm, and are occasionally helped by a visit from one of his three daughters who temporarily does the cooking, cleaning, and washing. In keeping with Ong Kim Tai's way of life, his house is simply furnished—plain plank beds, a table, several chairs, and a small altar of the ancestors. He rents three cong of land from which he ekes a living, but bad years like 1958 are likely to plunge small tenant farmers into debt. In the dry season he works as a laborer, and although his son assists with the farming, Ong Kim Tai has insisted that he complete his primary education.

Ong Kim Tai's father was a tenant farmer as was his paternal grandfather who had come from central Vietnam in the nineteenth century. Since the family has been long established in the village, he has many kin in Ap Dinh A–B, and he has a great deal of contact with them. His only extravagances are his three annual celebrations of ancestors' deaths, to which he invites about 15 guests, mostly kin. He does not hold a title in the Cult Committee, but he faithfully attends rituals at the dinh and at the Buddhist pagoda, and he participates in numerous celebrations given by kin and neighbors. Now that his son has a basic education, Ong Kim Tai desires to find land for him to rent, and for himself he only hopes to be able to obtain for a grave a small corner of ground from some wealthy villager.

Ong Canh: Small Landowner

Near the family tombs of a well-to-do civil servant from Tan An, there were, until 1959, three thatched houses which belonged to Ong Canh and his wife and her elder brothers Ong Tin and Ong Tu and their families. At the present time only the house of Ong Tin remains—death has dispersed the other two families.

Ong Canh's paternal great grandfather was an early settler in Khanh Hau where he owned 2.5 hectares of paddy land and eventually constructed an elaborate masonry house. He married a woman from the village of Duong Hoa, some 30 kilometers from Khanh Hau and subsequently she inherited 5 hectares and a masonry house from her parents. They had only one son who inherited both houses and all 7.5 hectares. He, in turn, had four children—two sons, the elder of whom was Ong Canh's father, and two daughters. The two sisters married in Khanh Hau, and the younger brother went to live in the Duong Hoa house, later becoming a schoolteacher there. Ong Canh's father remained in Khanh Hau and assisted his father with farming. On the death of their father, each of the children received an equal share of the land—approximately 1.9 hectares. The elder son received the Khanh Hau house; his brother inherited the house in Duong Hoa.

Both Ong Canh's paternal great grandfather and grandfather had been members of the Village Council, and both had been sorcerers. Ong Canh's father learned the sorcerous secrets from his father, but unlike his ancestors he took no part in village affairs. Older villagers recall that he was rather a shiftless man, content to live on the rent from his land without attempting to increase his holdings. In his later years he fell ill with a lung ailment, and there were several years of very poor harvests. Faced with bankruptcy, he dismantled his masonry house and sold the materials, rather than sell his land. The family moved into a thatched house, and when Ong Canh's father died soon after, each of his four children received almost half a hectare.

Ong Canh had been married four times when he took the sister of Ong Tin and Ong Tu as his wife. All four wives had died as had three daughters by one wife. After his marriage he constructed a small thatched house near the two houses of his wife's brothers. The three families formed a small community, and they relied on one another for aid in house repairs and agricultural tasks. In 1958 Ong Tinh's wife fell ill with a respiratory ailment which grew steadily worse in spite of the various medicines provided by her husband and their kin. Not long after, Ong Tu began complaining of general weakness, and his abdomen began to swell. As his symptoms increased, he was unable to work in the fields, so his brother and other kin gathered his harvest. The hamlet chief collected contributions of food and cash to aid Ong Tu and his family, but all medical treatment failed to arrest the swelling.

Ong Tu clearly was going to die, and suddenly his sister, Ong Canh's wife, began to manifest the same symptoms. In the face of such difficulties, aid diminished as kin and neighbors concluded it was fate that he should die. In the shop near Ong Canh's house, one woman expressed a widely held opinion that the ill fortune plaguing Ong Canh was inevitable because of the long tradition of sorcery in his family: "Those who deal with the spirits may just as easily be their victims, and those related to them might also be affected." Ong Tu slowly died, and his wife took their son to live with her kin in another hamlet. Their house was dismantled and the thatch was used on Ong Tin's house. Since Ong Tin now became the head of the family, he moved Ong Tu's altar into his own house. Within months, Ong Canh's wife died, and he dismantled his house, selling the material. Reluctant to remarry, Ong Canh went to live with his younger brother in the rambling paternal house. He was converted to Cao Daism and has become an active member of the Ban Chin Dao committee in the village.

Ong Ngoc: Hamlet Chief

Ong Ngoc is a relatively young man to be hamlet chief of Ap Dinh-A, but the Village Council has confidence in him, and his neighbors highly praise his honesty and conscientiousness. He also manifests a genuine concern for the well-being of the people of his hamlet and has taken an active interest in organizing sports and clubs for the young people.

Ong Ngoc's father also had been hamlet chief in Ap Dinh-A and, like his son, enjoyed a good reputation; he rented seven hectares and was well-to-do. He constructed a substantial hardwood house with tile roof and filled it with costly furnishings—finely carved furniture and an imposing ancestral altar arranged on an elegant cabinet intricately inlaid with mother-of-pearl. After his death, however, the landlord refused to rent any of the land to Ong Ngoc and his brothers. Being the youngest son, Ong Ngoc inherited the paternal house as well as his father's two buffalo. He was able to rent several cong of paddy land and supplement his income by renting the buffalo. His brothers were less fortunate. Unable to rent land in the village, one went to Saigon where eventually he found employment at the post office in the Dakao section of the city; the other settled in another village where he was able to rent half a hectare of land.

Soon after he was named hamlet chief, Ong Ngoc lost the lease on his land, but being a village official he was permitted to rent one hectare of village communal land. In 1958, however, the amount of this land available for rental diminished when seven hectares were turned over to the School of Fundamental Education and, since military veterans were given priority, Ong Ngoc was again without land. In spite of his poverty, he has refused to sell his house or any of the furnishings, but not being able to afford new roof tiles or the services of a carpenter, he has let the house fall into a state of disrepair. Not discouraged by his ill fortune, Ong Ngoc began working as a laborer, and his wife with equal courage began selling some of their garden vegetables.[14]

Ong Nha: Barber and Tailor

Near the spur road in Ap Dinh-A there is a small thatched structure with a large window cut in the front wall. A weathered sign announces that it is a barber and tailor shop and that Ong Nha is the proprietor. The barbershop occupies the section of the room near the window. A mirror, a high chair, and a table on which scissors, a clipper, a razor, and a comb are kept are the equipment of the barbering trade. When Ong Nha is not cutting hair, he moves to the other side of the room where a young man and girl sit at foot-powered sewing machines performing the simple tasks entrusted to apprentices. Ong Nha inspects their work, perhaps replacing one of them at the machine to demonstrate some fine point, or he may take up some material lying on a nearby table to hand-stitch a seam. Finished products —shirts, tunics, and trousers—hang from the ceiling. In the rear of the shop are several beds, and a thatched abutment serves as kitchen and living quarters for Ong Nha's wife and five children.

Ong Nha was born in central Vietnam where he learned these trades. In 1940, seeking better opportunities in the south, he settled in Khanh Hau and married a village girl. There is a constant demand for barbers in the village and, although shorts, work shirts, and children's garments can be made at home, tunics and clothes for more formal occasions as well as Western-style shirts require the specialized skills of a tailor. Ong Nha complains, however, that living and operating costs are too high for him to realize much profit. He must purchase rice and other food, and with a large family there is need for medicine which is costly. The cost of cloth is high, and when the shop needs repairs or a new roof he must hire someone to do the work.

14. By 1962 Ong Ngoc's lot had improved somewhat when he was able to rent one hectare of paddy land in the village.

In 1959, a young man came to work as his apprentice, and the girl, Co Sao, Ong Nha's younger sister, is the latest of several siblings who have come from Tourane to learn sewing. One young brother has gone into the tailoring business in Saigon, and another brother is a tailor in Phan Thiet. A cousin of Ong Nha's wife learned from him, and she now has a thriving embroidery business in Cap St. Jacques. Periodically Ong Nha expresses a desire to establish a business in Saigon where he feels his children would have more opportunities, but the cost of leaving Khanh Hau and the initial cost of getting settled in the city are prohibitive.

Ong Nha's shop is a gathering place, particularly for young men of the area, many of whom are attracted by the presence of Co Sao. Members of the village soccer team spend their free time in the shop, and older men getting their hair cut offer them advice and joke with them. In spite of his having been in Khanh Hau for over twenty years, Ong Nha remains a marginal member of village society. He is not active in village affairs and has never been offered a title in the Cult Committee. Ong Nha himself points out that he is essentially an outsider—he has no kin in the village, no land, no tombs, and he is not a farmer.

Co Bay: Shopkeeper

In the middle of the Ap Dinh A–B agglomeration, at a point in the spur road where there usually is a great deal of activity before and after the midday heat, Co Bay has a small shop, simply constructed of gnarled logs and odd pieces of wood salvaged from houses being dismantled in the vicinity; the roof is thatched. A small addition to the rear houses Co Bay's aunt and her children; to one side of the structure, she maintains a large kitchen garden ample with green vegetables and arbors hung with melon-like vegetables.

Co Bay is a girl of 17, plump and attractive, and very popular with the residents of the area. She is the daughter of small tenant farmers who live nearby and rent one hectare from Ong Xa Khanh. The shop actually belongs to Co Bay's father who built the structure and purchased the stock, but Co Bay volunteered to run it, and it generally is referred to as hers. The stock is relatively limited: several types of nonalcoholic beverages bottled in Saigon, some fresh fruits and vegetables, a small collection of canned goods, several jars of hard candy and dry cookies, jugs of fish sauce, a container of fermented shrimp, some dried fish, and some school supplies. The shop, however, is a favorite meeting place for the women of the area, particularly the widows and the elderly, and a few young men converge on the shop in the late afternoon to talk with Co Bay.

Co Bay's brother lives near the shop and he spends a great deal of time there, often tending it in his sister's absence. He is a young man of 25 years, a veteran of the Vietnamese army, which makes him eligible to rent half a hectare of village communal land. The women who gather in the shop consider him a very amusing individual, and since he traveled while in the army, he is envied by the young men of the village. His friend Anh Teo is about the same age and is also an army veteran; he lives with his small family in a thatched house near the Ban Chin Dao temple and, like Co Bay's brother, he rented communal land which he had to relinquish (with a promise of alternative land) when the school was granted seven hectares. Anh Teo currently works as a laborer to support his family. In his leisure time he also plays on the soccer team, and he meets with other young men at Co Bay's brother's house to play traditional musical instruments and sing.

Among the many women who gather in Co Bay's shop, Ba Luc is the most frequent visitor, probably because she lives alone in a very small thatched house next to the shop. She is a relatively tall woman, extremely thin but very erect, and her lined brown face is framed with soft white hair. Ba Luc was born 78 years ago in Rach Gia, a coastal town on the Gulf of Siam; her parents died when she was a child, and she lived with poor kin. While she was still quite young she married a man who worked as a food vendor on a coastal ship, and subsequently they came to Khanh Hau where he was able to rent a small amount of paddy land. Their daughter married a tenant farmer in a neighboring village, but they were able to send their son to the village primary school, after which, with scholarships, he was able to complete secondary school, eventually obtaining the brevet for teaching. Currently he is a schoolmaster in a village close to Saigon.

After her husband's death, Ba Luc elected to remain in Khanh Hau rather than live with either of her children. Although her daughter is too poor, particularly since the drought years of 1957 and 1958, to contribute much to her mother's support, Ba Luc's son periodically brings her money. She lives simply, requiring little food, and she cultivates her own kitchen garden. She contributes 20$ VN to the major rituals held in the dinh, and as one of the respected widows of the village she is invited to participate in the feasts served at the Council House during the celebrations. Many woman of the hamlet rely on Ba Luc for advice and assistance with births or ailing children, and when she feels the need for company, she can always go to Co Bay's shop.

SOCIAL MOBILITY

In general, but not always, those born into very well-to-do families or very poor families remain in the same status. Children who are born into the upper socioeconomic level will inherit sizable tracts of land and perhaps some enterprise, and (barring unforeseen misfortune) they will remain in the upper level. Children of the lower socioeconomic level have little opportunity to move upward; most will not be able to complete a primary education, and the cost of learning a trade is prohibitive. Rental land is not usually available, and land prices in the village are now relatively high. Most people of this category live on or near a subsistence level—their primary concerns are to survive and stay out of debt. Upward mobility is good fortune and downward mobility is bad fortune, and villagers are likely to attribute changes in status to destiny; but this does not imply fatalism—one can still strive to improve one's lot or make it possible for children to improve theirs (e.g. through education).

As a relatively entrenched aristocracy in Khanh Hau, Marshal Duc's patrilineal descendants, particularly those of the senior line, are socially immobile—their unique status is crystallized. The villagers experience a certain amount of prestige in being associated with the hero of southern Vietnam, and the Duc family is the living symbol of this association. Rituals honoring the Marshal reiterate his ties to the village, and these rituals must be performed by the truong toc of the Duc family.

An increase in landholding, preferably by purchase than rental, is essential to upward mobility. The big tenant is in a precarious position—he has no guarantee that he will be able to retain his lease for a long period, nor does he have anything to pass on to his children. Ownership of land, on the other hand, represents security, and land is the most valuable thing a man can will to his children. Land declared huong hoa guarantees a cult and with it, bliss in the afterlife. Further, huong hoa helps generate lineage solidarity in providing a means to hold large family celebrations where members of the family can gather and reconfirm their bonds of kinship.

Once a villager has acquired some land by inheritance or purchase, he is motivated to accumulate more—an amount sufficient for the succeeding generation to maintain the status of the family. Given the fragmentation of land when both male and female children inherit, this is not easy; for example, a well-to-do farmer with ten hectares will pass on only two hectares to each of his five children, perhaps precipitating a process of downward mobility as in the Ong Canh family.

Fragmentation of family land is inevitable, but the sketches of some of the upper-level villagers illustrate ways of increasing one's landholding. Others have invested in enterprises, illustrating an emerging pattern in village society: an increasing number of upper-level villagers have turned to business as a means of gaining wealth.

In Khanh Hau, the well-to-do and those in the process of gaining wealth never live in thatched houses. Having acquired a sufficient amount of land to elevate his status, an upwardly mobile villager usually constructs a substantial house as a primary prestige symbol. Prior to its destruction, the grand house of Ong Ke Hien was a fitting monument to his status as the wealthiest resident and highest venerable.

Villagers striving for upward mobility must also have fine furnishings— carved wooden chairs, marble-top tables, and pendulum clocks are items of prestige. It is important to have good hardwood beds that will remain in the family many generations, and more important to have an impressive altar of the ancestors. While Ong Hai could with impunity sell the costly cabinet on which his altar was arranged, it would have been a desecration to sell any of the accouterment. Clothes, however, are not particularly indicative of status in village society.

An upwardly mobile villager is expected to have more elaborate family celebrations as his status rises. Villagers of means perform all prescribed rituals in an elegant manner, inviting many guests and properly entertaining them. Abundance of food reflects the affluence of the family. Among the many dishes, it is important to have meat, particularly pork and beef, both of which have more prestige than chicken. Alcoholic beverages—cognac, beer, and rice alcohol (in that order of prestige)—are requisite. As one moves upward it also is necessary to make more sizable contributions to such things as the construction of the pagoda honoring Marshal Duc, and the size of every villager's donation is public knowledge.

Literacy is essential to upward mobility. A villager must be able to read and write in order to have the respect of his fellow villagers, and it also is necessary to carry on economic activities. In the past a primary school education was not prerequisite to improvement of status, but with the expansion of educational facilities in the village it promises to become so. Even at the present time it would be unusual for a middle- or upper-level family to take a child out of school before his primary education was complete.

In Chapter 8 the structure and functions of the Cult Committee were described, the pattern of upward mobility in the ranking order of the committee was analyzed, and the collective role of those in the higher echelons as the sociopolitical elite of village society was pointed out. Relative ranking in the Cult Committee indicates a great deal about statuses within the upper socioeconomic level. The highest venerable is the first to kowtow at the rituals and has the highest status in the village either from a socio-political or socioeconomic point of view. The lower titles, however, do not reflect a great deal about status within either the middle or lower socio-economic levels.

For the upwardly mobile villager who aims at the Olympian heights of the high venerables, political status becomes as important as economic status when he reaches the upper level of village society. In the past the pattern has been for villagers to serve on the Village Council before being made a venerable, and while the council positions have become appointive, they continue to be held by upper-level villagers who have both the time and means to participate actively in the political life of the village. There is a political in-group which more or less controls council positions, and not every well-to-do villager is accepted into it.

In addition to being accepted into the Village Council, the upwardly mobile villager currently would be obliged to join the National Revolu-tionary Party, the only official political party in the village. He also would have to participate in village affairs—assist in organizing the rituals and other village celebrations, and attend all the meetings held, whether for anti-Communist propaganda or proposed village projects. If he should suc-ceed in gaining a high venerable title, wealth and age would become the primary factors in continued mobility. Prescribed cash contributions and those expected from the incumbent require that a venerable be wealthy. Finally, should the villager of venerable status outlive the other venerables, he will become Ong Ke Hien.

In Khanh Hau society, as in any society, the fortunes of families fall as often as they rise, because of fragmentation of landholdings, illnesses, or unwise investments; irresponsible heads of households have also been known to gamble or drink away the family fortune. Downward mobility is a process that can occur in practically any family in the village. A well-to-do family can lose its land, house, and high status, and those living on a subsistence level can sink to destitution.

The profile of Ong Ngoc illustrates the precariousness of gaining upper-level status by renting a large amount of land. On the death of the father, Ong Ngoc and his brothers were without land and the family was forced to disperse—a terrible fate for villagers. Reduced to poverty, Ong Ngoc continues to scratch out an existence in the village, retaining his position as hamlet chief, the one remaining trace of higher status. In this case, land fragmentation in three generations plunged the family from upper to lower level.

An additional example of downward mobility, not recorded in the profiles, is an impoverished Ap Moi family that continues to live in their large, ramshackle wood-tile house—the bleak monument of better days. The paternal grandfather had accumulated large landholdings in the village and constructed the house. When he died, his son inherited house and land and, according to villagers, he squandered his wealth on gambling and opium. To meet his growing debts he sold land, retaining only a small plot which he declared huong hoa before his death. His son, the present head of the household, was an active Viet Minh cadreman, and when the Indochina War ended, the family found itself in disrepute as well as poverty stricken.

CHAPTER 11

Conclusions

THE OLD PROVERB "Phep vua thua le lang" (The laws of the emperor
yield to the customs of the village) is known by all Vietnamese, and in
many respects it characterizes the village in Vietnam as a self-contained
homogeneous community, jealously guarding its way of life—a little world
that is autonomous and disregards (if not disdains) the outside world. This
image contains many elements of Durkheim's social segment—a mechanical
solidarity arising from subjecting the members to uniform conditions which
give them uniform and strong consciences. It implies as well the corporateness contained in Tönnies' concept of *Gemeinschaft* society and elements
of Redfield's recently articulated little-community model with its four outstanding characteristics: distinctness, smallness, all-providing self-sufficiency,
and homogeneity.[1]

Redfield finds that these qualities are clearly marked in such societies as
simple bands, but they diminish as societal complexity increases until they
are scarcely traceable in little communities of industrial Europe or Amer-
ica. In southern Vietnam, historical events since the end of the nineteenth
century have rendered the image implicit in the proverb less and less applicable to the village. The isolation of the village has steadily grown less, and
the ways of the village have been more and more encroached upon by the
ways of the world. This situation is very much reflected in Khanh Hau
where the little-community qualities exist but are perceptibly dwindling.

There is, for example, homogeneity in the attitudes and values of many
of the Khanh Hau villagers. They share a cosmological view deeply rooted
in the Buddhist–Taoist–Confucianist ideology of the Chinese Great Tradi-

---

1. Durkheim, *De la Division du Travail Social.* Tönnies, *Gemeinschaft und Gesellschaft.* Redfield, *The Little Community.*

276

tion, with Vietnamese alterations and additions, which underlies the amalgam of beliefs and practices that make up village religion, and it influences
all other aspects of village society as well. Adherence to it is manifest almost
daily in behavior—even in the behavior of Catholics, followers of the Minh
Chon Ly sect (who consider themselves emancipated from the traditional
religious beliefs), and villagers who for whatever reason have rejected some
of the traditional ways. Belief in universal order, and the related concepts
of harmony with this order and human destiny within it, are reflected in
the conformity of all villagers to guidance by the lunar calendar and reliance
on individual horoscopy, and in the respect of most villagers for the principles of geomancy. The notion of harmony is involved in many practices
and rituals—observance of taboos, use of amulets or talismans, preparation
of medicines, consultation with healers, propitiation or expulsion of spirits,
invocations to deities, and veneration of ancestors. The aim of these is to
preserve or restore harmony and, with it, well-being.

Before the advent of Cao Daism, and with the exception of a small group
of Catholics, all villagers identified themselves as Buddhists. Although the
homogeneity of formal affiliation (or expressed association) consequently
has diminished as several hundred villagers became Cao Daists, homogeneity
of belief in Buddhist doctrine and deities (all incorporated in Cao Daism)
has continued. This also is true of popular beliefs and practices which are
admitted by all Cao Daist sects except the Minh Chon Ly (some twenty
adherents in Khanh Hau). Veneration of ancestors (Catholics specify that
they honor rather than venerate ancestors) is almost universal in the village.
The altars are the same and rituals are performed according to prescribed
form.

There also is homogeneity in the social expectation. The drive to provide
well for one's family combined with some of the basic beliefs associated with
the Cult of the Ancestors contributes to the strong motivation for economic
gain that characterizes the Vietnamese peasant (which in turn has contributed
to the expansionism that marks Vietnamese history).

It is the desire of most villagers to improve their lot, which means having
land, a fine house, material comfort, and education for one's children. One
of the dreads of poverty is that the family may disintegrate as members quit
the village to seek a livelihood elsewhere. For the villager it is extremely
important that the family remain together: in addition to the comfort of
having kinfolk about, immortality lies in an undying lineage.

There is homogeneity in the villagers' style of life. Variations are not great enough to warrant stratification into social classes. Rather, they are variations on a common theme which amount more to elaborations than to substantive differences.

There also is a great deal of homogeneity in livelihood activities, with practically everyone in the village directly or indirectly engaged in rice cultivation. All farmers cultivate rice, and all laborers are farm laborers. Village leaders—those in the sociopolitical elite and/or the Village Council —as well as rice millers and rice merchants own paddy land and describe themselves as farmers and most specialists also are farmers. Khanh Hau farmers use the same planting techniques. They agree what methods are best suited for the different varieties of rice planted in the village and for relative elevation of one's fields. All use chemical fertilizer, all share the myths concerning its effect on the soil, and there is a common tool complex. Some variation exists in garden cultivation, although it is not great, and there is a common collection of vegetables grown in all gardens.

The homogeneity of values, style of life, and some behavior patterns, as well as the functional interrelationships that exist among the various aspects of village society, implies communal personal associations such as are contained in the conceptual models of Durkheim, Tönnies, and Redfield. These communal personal associations, however, cannot be said to exist for the whole of Khanh Hau society. Cultural values and social behavioral patterns are shared because the inhabitants have a common tradition, which in this case is the Vietnamese tradition as it exists in southern Vietnam. It does not necessarily follow that members of village society have strong social bonds or a sense of social solidarity. These qualities are found within the village but cannot be attributed to the village.

Several outstanding factors relating to this lack of communal personal association can be isolated. First, the settlements that make up Khanh Hau are widely dispersed; sections of Ap Cau and Ap Nhon Hau are 5 kilometers from the northern part of Ap Dinh-B and, unless he has kin or acquaintances in such a distant place, a villager is not likely to visit there. Villagers often remark that they do not know fellow villagers from other hamlets— they may know them by sight, but they have never spoken. On the other hand, those living in the string settlements of Ap Cau and Ap Nhon Hau literally are a stone's throw from string hamlets along the opposite banks of the streams separating Khanh Hau from the neighboring villages of Tan Huong and An Vinh Ngai (see Fig. 1).

The effect of this dispersion is compounded by the fact that there are no real focal centers to attract sizable segments of the village population, giving them the opportunity for social interaction. The dinh often is described as the social and religious center of the Vietnamese village, but this is true in only a limited sense in villages of southern Vietnam. There are four rituals held at the dinh in the course of the lunar year, but participation is expected only of the cult committee members. Although attendance is compulsory for all male household heads, there is very little interaction among the audience either before, during, or after the meetings. Undoubtedly, having two dinh and two cult committees diminishes the importance of each, but had the village only one, its primary importance would still be that of ritual center for some of the village men.

The Council House does not function as a focal center. Most villagers visit there only occasionally to take care of some administrative necessity. The Buddhist pagoda in Ap Moi (the village pagoda) and that in Ap Cau draw a relatively small attendance at rituals, and their active congregations are from the locale rather than from the whole village. Although both the Tien Thien and Ban Chin Dao Cao Daist sects have sizable congregations, their temples actually function as social centers more for the residential groups surrounding them than for any significant segment of the village. These limitations also apply to the group-sponsored cult of Quan Cong which largely is supported by residents of Ap Nhon Hau.

One might speculate that if Khanh Hau had a market it would serve as a center for social intercourse in the village. Marketing, however, is done by the women, and the proximity of the Tan Huong market to the southern portion of the village, combined with the attraction of the large Tan An market 4 kilometers from the northern edge, would reduce the significance of any market within Khanh Hau. Finally, the political events of the past several decades have greatly disrupted village life. Whereas war may have the effect of generating solidarity among a people, the guerrilla type of hostilities characteristic of the Indochina War bred only conflict and suspicion. Without battle lines, without an identifiable enemy, the war was everywhere. Pro-Viet Minh and pro-French factions existed in the village, and although most villagers did not take sides actively, accusations of being on one side or the other were rampant. This pattern continued as the Viet Cong movement against the national government reached Khanh Hau, and the effect has been to turn many villagers inward. They now are primarily concerned with survival for themselves and their families.

The lack at village level of communal personal association was manifest in the unsuccessful village cooperative. This represented the first attempt at a village-wide effort, and although it was limited to those who farm, membership was drawn from all hamlets. The trust and cooperation needed to make a success of the organization clearly was lacking. In their last meeting before it disbanded, some members openly admitted reluctance to entrust money to the group, and there was a great deal of dissension. Lamenting it afterward, some villagers pointed out that many members did not know one another very well and several of the leaders had opposing sympathies during the Indochina War. There is greater solidarity at the hamlet level, whose residents usually identify themselves as such and associate others with the hamlet in which they live.

In Khanh Hau, property relations, locality, and the beliefs and practices associated with the Cult of the Ancestors are intrinsic to the solidarity of the patrilineage. Huong hoa, the ancestral house, and the tombs are material symbols of the patrilineage, and it is around them that kin sentiments rally. Although the members (often including some very poor) receive no greater material benefit than several elegant meals during the year, they have the prestige of belonging to a toc with land. Furthermore, collective ownership of the patrimony and having a voice in the selection of the truong toc give members a sense of participation which periodically is reinforced by gatherings for celebrations associated with the Cult of the Ancestors. Members also have the consolation of knowing that a cult will be maintained for them after death.[2]

Close to the situation in Vietnam, Freedman (*Lineage Organization*, pp. 128–29) emphasizes the importance of common property in maintaining the solidarity of lineages in southeastern China:

> In order to explain why some lineages rather than others managed to hold their members together I have adduced the factor of common property. We may well wonder why rich individuals should place their wealth at the disposal of their lineage or one of its segments instead of leaving it to be enjoyed by their immediate descendants. Chen Han-seng assures us that "the sense of family responsibility" is such in China, and especially Kwangtung, that while "the individual family likes to enjoy the prestige of a big land owner, it considers it just as

2. In his study of Pul Eliya, Leach focuses on what he considers to be two important aspects of kinship in that village—locality and property relations. The former generates corporateness: "Pul Eliya is a society in which locality and not descent forms the basis of corporate grouping." Although it is in property relations that kinship emerges, "kinship systems have no 'reality' at all except in relation to land and property. What the social anthropologist calls kinship structure is just a way of talking about property relations which can also be talked about in other ways." (Pp. 296–306.)

important to strengthen the economic status of the main stem of the family, that is the clan, as to bolster up the security of the direct descendants." [Chen Han-seng, *The Present Agrarian Problems in China*, China Institute of Pacific Relations, Shanghai, 1933, p. 30.]

Hu also includes common property as well as the Cult of the Ancestors among those institutions that lend cohesiveness to the *tsu*, the Chinese patrilineage:

> All *tsu* institutions—the establishment of the common property, benefits for education and public welfare, the laying down of rules of behavior, the assumption of judicial powers—have a common aim: the consolidation of the group for the security and advancement of its members. The security offered is twofold; religious, in that the *tsu* assures the individual that the rites in his honor will be continued indefinitely; and social-economic, by assuring each member of assistance in case of need, both from the group and from individual fellow-members. [Hsien Chin Hu, *The Common Descent Group in China*, p. 95.]

Only a few patrilineages in Khanh Hau have the corporate character noted above and since, with the exception of the Duc family, most patrilineages have been established in the village only three or four generations, they are small and young compared to those described by Hu and Freedman for China and by Gourou[3] for the delta of the Red River. Nor do they have the secular functions of the well-to-do Chinese and northern Vietnamese patrilineages. While the patrilineage of the Duc family has an aristocratic aura, it cannot be said to have political power, nor does it have the wealth to guarantee welfare for its members. Rent-free farmstead sites are about the only outstanding material benefit, and they are given to nonpatrilineal kin as well. The only patrilineage in Khanh Hau which has political power and wealth is that of Ong Ke Hien.

Most families in Khanh Hau are without land, their homes do not endure long enough to become ancestral houses, and their graves are earth mounds. There is a tendency for patrilineages comprised of such families to fission. Economic necessity forces members to quit the village, and eventually they lose contact. Although there is an effort to observe the rituals associated with the Cult of the Ancestors, the group that gathers is small, usually composed of those within walking distance. Segments that fail to come together

3. *Les Paysans du Delta Tonkinois,* pp. 114–21.

for rituals honoring common ancestors usually designate their own truong toc, and consequently there is apt to be duplication of rituals honoring the common ancestors. In fissioned patrilineages, cohesiveness is found in lineage segments. In such instances, property relation would not be important (indeed, they may not exist) whereas proximity and veneration of common ancestors generate kin solidarity.

While the household group is the most basic social unit of village society, the small kin clusters (most of which are parts of patrilineages) share the same primary group characteristics. It is at this level that one finds face-to-face relationships, unqualified mutual aid, and common participation in celebrations. There also are non-kin households in some of the clusters, and consequently proximity sometimes supersedes kin ties as a basis for strong social bonds.

In addition to a predominance of kin-linked households, some residence groups have strong religious bonds. The Catholic families in the village are largely concentrated in the northernmost section of Ap Dinh-B, and many of the households are tied affinally and consanguineally. The Catholic group also has its own leader. Although the Catholics have definite in-group feelings, they are not isolated from the rest of the village, and relations between Catholics and other villagers are very close. Cao Daists have the same in-group solidarity which, in the Tien Thien and Ban Chin Dao sects, is reinforced by having their temples serving as focal centers, particularly for members living around them.

Khanh Hau's relationship with the outside world, particularly the urban world of Saigon, is reflected in the changes that have occurred in village society since the end of the nineteenth century. The most traceable of these are changes in the structure and functions of the Village Council initiated by legislation in 1904 intended to standardize the councils throughout the colony of Cochinchina. This legislation clearly defined the prerogatives and responsibilities of all councils: it delineated the secular functions and eliminated sacred functions related to the Cult of the Guardian Spirit of the Village, precipitating the formation of Cult Committees in all villages. Since that time the trend has been toward smaller councils; in Khanh Hau the pre-World War II council of twelve was reduced to five members by legislation in 1956, and by 1961 it had dwindled to three members. This reduction in size has been accompanied by a steady increase in paper work and a continued sapping of council prerogatives as outside governmental agencies have assumed greater responsibility in village affairs. The customs of the village have been yielding not to the emperor, but to the French colonial administration and subsequently to the central republican government.

Through its provincial and district administrative arms, the ministries in Saigon have had an increasing role in village education, public works, agricultural programs, financial affairs, judicial matters, and civil order. In the case of Khanh Hau, the provincial and district officials also have played an important part in the development of the Marshal Duc cult. Further, since the establishment of the republic in 1955, there has been a growing number of village organizations and associations.

In the past the village leaders emerged from the older segment of the sociopolitical elite, receiving at best only modest salaries (the prestige was more important than salary); council members now are appointed by provincial authorities. They are younger than their predecessors, and they receive fixed salaries as civil servants. In general the village is being more and more integrated into the national network centered in Saigon and, as this proceeds, the traditional administrative autonomy steadily decreases.

Changes in the area of religion also have resulted in more ties with the outside world. The arrival in 1958 of the Buddhist nuns at the Ap Cau pagoda marked for the first time contact and control by Buddhist hierarchy. The advent of Cao Daism and the establishment of the Tien Thien and Ban Chin Dao temples created new religious centers in Khanh Hau, and these sects have generated a new wave of solidarity among the villagers who have joined. This change also has been in the direction of putting Khanh Hau more in touch with the outside world, although in the case of Cao Daism, not with Saigon but with the delta towns to the south.

Khanh Hau villagers generally display a readiness to accept innovation when it is shown to be useful. Traditions are strong and the taboos and sanctions are rigidly observed. Nonetheless, there is in them a certain flexibility which allows a freedom to choose.

Many of the technological and material innovations in the village can be attributed to villagers of the upper economic level who, since they are relatively mobile, have contact with the outside and have the means and willingness to take some risk. The lower economic level manifests a considerable self-sufficiency in being able to satisfy most of their basic needs within the bounds of the village. They exploit the physical surroundings, constructing their houses of available logs, bamboo, and thatching, and they sustain themselves for the most part on village produce—rice, vegetables, fruit, and fish (as well as occasional meat). They make their own tools and furnishings, and aside from such things as clothes, kitchenware, altar accouterment, lamps, oil, and fish sauce, they have no need for goods manufactured beyond the village. As one ascends the socioeconomic structure of village society, however, dependence on the outside increases. Upper-level villagers have houses constructed by specialists (some from outside Khanh Hau), using material brought into the village. Their furnishings are manufactured in Saigon or one of the large market towns, and they consume a good deal of food from the Tan An market (occasionally even canned French food). Many have either a motor scooter or motor bicycle, and since all are farmers, they must purchase chemical fertilizers as well as pesticides.

One of the outstanding innovations since 1950 in Khanh Hau livelihood patterns has been the emergence of the entrepreneur. Some villagers were engaged in entrepreneurial activities before that year, but the predominant pattern was for those with available capital to lend it to fellow villagers or merchants in nearby towns. Within a short period of time, well-to-do villagers began investing in rice merchandising and then rice milling; now hand-operated home rice mills have all but disappeared from the village. Also, the effect of both rice merchandising and milling has been to create more local rice marketing and price fluctuations. The effect of the Cholon market on the village consequently has been somewhat lessened.

Educational facilities have increased in Khanh Hau, precipitating some changes. More villagers are becoming literate, and are thus becoming better acquainted with the outside world at an early age. There also has been an increase in contact between the boys and girls from Khanh Hau and surrounding villages. Most changes in kinship practices have been in relation to marriage. Arranged marriages are now less common, and there is more likelihood that the engaged couple already will be acquainted. Also it is possible to marry someone with the same surname when it has been reasonably well established that there are no consanguineal ties, and the hamlet exogamy of the pre-World War II period no longer is rigidly observed. The service period of a fiancé to the girl's family is now not required by many families, and since the end of the Indochina War there has been a reduction in the bride price.

These are the identifiable changes that have taken place in Khanh Hau society, and many of them have come from Saigon—the doorway to the world beyond Vietnam. Under the French, numerous administrative alterations had been effected in village government, and since the village has become part of the Republic of South Vietnam, administrative changes have been even more sweeping. These new concepts are essentially more Western than Eastern, and although they were intended to transform the village government, they really have succeeded only in bringing about a number of procedural innovations and giving new tasks to the Village Council, at the same time sapping the power and prestige of the village officials.

Nevertheless, many of the old ways have survived the sweep of Saigon legislation. Most decisions concerning village society, such as village projects, welfare, response to crisis situations (such as the drought), and justice, continue to be dealt with in ways traditional to the village. The Village Council also has retained its sacred functions, none of which is sanctioned by legislation. The councillors continue to have an important role in the Cult of the Guardian Spirit. In the Council House there is an altar honoring ancestors of the village, and the council is responsible for administering Buddhist pagoda land as well as dinh land. These are part of the village way, and they remain.

Although in many respects the well-to-do are responsible for most technological and material innovations, they are at the same time the guardians of many Vietnamese traditions. The gentry constitute the clientele of the geomancers, and they are the most active supporters of the Cult of the Guardian Spirit of the Village.

The villagers feel that the old ways are good, especially when they are expressed in rituals, but they also feel that new ways are acceptable when proven of value. The people of Khanh Hau are not descendants of ancestors who have lived in this place a thousand years, perpetuating a parochial village world. Their ancestors were migrant people—pioneers who left their natal places in the narrow coastal plain of central Vietnam about a century ago (as, indeed, *their* ancestors had quit their places of origin in the past) to settle in the strange new surroundings of the vast delta of the Mekong River. Khanh Hau people are of a tradition in which one guards the old ways while adopting the new ways necessary to changed surroundings.

In spite of the changes in some aspects of village society, the essential characteristics of the village way of life have persisted. The traditional values, practices, and rituals continue to be honored and observed, and they are being transmitted to the younger generation as they were in the past. The ordinary villager clings to the familiar. His primary concerns are his family and perhaps his farm, and in his war-weary world, his will is the will to survive.

Appendices

Appendix A

GENEALOGY OF THE DUC FAMILY

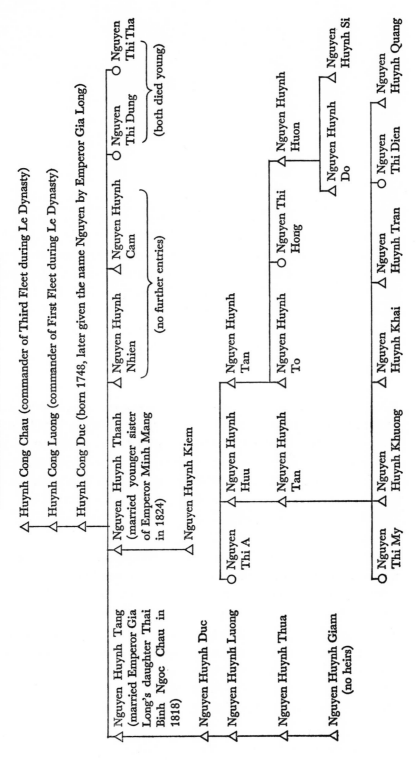

Appendix B

A Brief History of Cao Daism

Cao Daism first appeared as an identifiable religious movement in 1925,[1] founded by Ngo Van Chieu, a civil servant in the Department of Criminal Investigation (a bureau of the colonial government in Cochinchina). Long an advocate of spiritualism, Ngo Van Chieu spent much of his leisure time organizing seances with fellow civil servants. During a seance held in 1919 while serving at the District Headquarters on the island of Phu Quoc in the Gulf of Siam, he made contact with a spirit that identified itself as Cao Dai (which could be translated Supreme Palace or High Throne). At a later seance the same spirit revealed that Cao Dai was the symbolic designation for the "Supreme Being."

After his transfer to Saigon, Ngo Van Chieu continued communication with the Cao Dai in seances held with a group of civil servants in a small house in a back street of the Cho Gao quarter of Cholon. In the course of these seances, the Cao Dai directed the group to symbolize him visually with a large eye emitting bright rays of light, and it also advised them to use the beaked basket which, when held by the medium (preferably a youth aged 12 to 15), spells out the spirit message. At a seance held late in 1925 the Cao Dai directed those present to become his first disciples and organize a new religion bearing his name. At this time seances were popular among younger civil servants, and news of what had occurred spread rapidly through the bureaus. Although there was no semblance of formal organization, Ngo Van Chieu was looked upon as the head of the religious movement. Other groups then reported that they also had communicated with Cao Dai, and at a seance in a Cholon restaurant the spirit had directed one of the guests, Le Van Trung, a well-to-do businessman, to join the new religion. The message also implied that Le Van Trung was destined to have an important role in the religious movement; he therefore joined Ngo Van Chieu's group, and his life changed. Previously he had been an "impenitent

1. Gobron, *Histoire du Caodaïsme*, p. 19. Anonymous, *Le Caodaïsme*. Direction des Affaires Politiques et de la Sûreté, *Le Caodaïsme: 1926–1934*, p. 29.

materialist," but now Le Van Trung refrained from eating meat, smoking opium, and other pleasures. Eventually he gave up his business to devote himself completely to Cao Daism.

In 1926 Le Van Trung replaced Ngo Van Chieu as head of the Cao Daist movement. Membership swelled, the first cadres of leaders were formed, and the first propaganda centers were established. On October 7, 1926, an official declaration that Cao Daism was a formal religion was signed by 28 leaders and 247 adherents and filed with the Governor of Cochinchina.[2] By March of the next year the Cao Daists had acquired a sizable tract of land in Long Than village, Tay Ninh province. Here, near the sacred Black Lady mountain close to the Cambodian border, they established their headquarters or Holy See.

In the period that followed, Cao Daist doctrine and organization crystallized and some of the basic tenets of the new religion were made known: Cao Dai is the Supreme Being who for the third time is revealing himself in the orient. Owing to lack of communication in former times, the five branches of Dai Dao, the Great Way—Confucianism (Nhon Dao), Worship of Spirits (Than Dao or Khuong Thai Cong), Christianity (Thanh Dao), Taoism (Tien Dao), and Buddhism (Phat Dao)—were established in different parts of the world but failed to converge. The primary aim of Cao Daism is to bring together these great religions.

Spirit messages dictated both doctrinal and organizational structure of the Cao Daist movement. Officially known as Reformed Buddhism, much of Cao Daist doctrine is drawn from Buddhism of the Mahayana tradition, and mixed with it are concepts of Taoist and Confucianist origin. The Buddhist ideal of "the good man" provides the basis for Cao Daist ethics, and the whole complex of little-tradition Vietnamese taboos and sanctions is incorporated into their ideal behavioral scheme. In the pantheon, Cao Dai, symbolized by the eye emanating radiant light, is the Supreme Being. Below him are the three great saints, Confucius, Buddha, and Lao T'se. Having appeared at a later date, Christ is ranked below them. The high category of saints includes Quang Am, the Buddhist Goddess of Mercy (who, according to Cao Daist interpretation, also embodies the Christian Blessed Virgin), the Chinese warrior Quan Cong, and Moses. The general rank of saints incorporates all those of the Theravada and Mahayana religions, and eventually Sun Yat Sen, Jeanne d'Arc, Victor Hugo, and the French admiral Duclos were added. Ritual forms are traditional Vietnamese (kowtowing while

2. Direction des Affaires Politiques . . . , *Le Caodiaïsme*, pp. 30–32.

holding burning joss; food offerings) as are the decorations and altar accouterment (gongs, vases of flowers, incense burners, offering plates, and joss-stands).[3]

By 1930 the Tam Ky Pho Do (as the sect officially was known) had expanded considerably, and a definite hierarchical structure had emerged which is very similar to that of the Roman Catholic Church but differs notably in having a female hierarchy including cardinals, archbishops, and other high dignitaries. During this period in Tay Ninh at the Holy See there was a great deal of construction, culminating in a colorful and architecturally bizarre cathedral designed to incorporate great motifs of the past.

The French viewed the Tam Ky sect favorably and allowed them to organize their own army (with the assistance of French military advisors), and the hierarchy also was given the right to collect taxes in a large area surrounding the Holy See. This period of expansion also was a period of dissension within the hierarchy. Although Cao Daists refer to it as a period of schisms, one French source[4] points out that the differences were not doctrinal but personal. Quarrels developed over questions of power and the Pope's right to form an army as well, and dissension ensued because individual leaders acquired followers, splitting off from the Tam Ky. The result was an exodus from Tay Ninh, and of the eleven Cao Daist sects that emerged, eight survive.

The first to leave was Ngo Van Chieu, the founder of Cao Daism, and he founded the Chieu Minh Danh sect at Can Tho. In an attempt to restore order among the leaders, Pope Ly Van Trung resigned, requesting Nguyen Ngoc Tuong to replace him. The new pope began to reorganize the sect, but after several troubled years he also stepped down, leaving the leadership temporarily in the hands of a committee. Taking a group of followers, Nguyen Ngoc Tuong quit Tay Ninh to settle in the delta town of Ben Tre where in 1934 they organized the Ban Chin Dao sect, along the doctrinal and organizational lines of the Tam Ky sect. By 1940 they had numerous followers so they established their Holy See on the outskirts of Ben Tre.

During a seance at Tay Ninh in 1931 Nguyen Hao Ca, a high-ranking member of the hierarchy, received a message advising him to leave the Holy See and organize his own sect at Rach Gia, a city on the Gulf of Siam. After

3. One Cao Daist leader of the Tien Thien sect pointed out that in addition to the fact that it is not necessary for the typical Vietnamese to change any of his existing religious beliefs when he converts to Cao Daism, he enlarges his pantheon to include deities of the Judeo–Christian tradition as well as deities of other religions. Further, the ritual form is so close to the traditional that it is not alien.

4. Direction des Affaires Politiques, p. 87.

his arrival at Rach Gia, another spirit message directed him to My Tho, and there he established the Holy See for his new sect, the Minh Chon Ly. Between 1932 and 1938 this new sect gained a large following, and it diverged both in doctrine and structure from the other Cao Daist sects. Initially the Minh Chon Ly gave special veneration to Tam Tran, the Three Deities, Quan Cong, and Ly Thai Bach, described as the Supreme Spirit. Eventually they also included Thich Ca, a reincarnation of Buddha, Christ, Lao T'se, Confucius, and Ngoc Hoang Thuong De, the Emperor of Jade. Their most striking innovation, however, was the adoption of a new symbol, the "Eye in the Heart," which is an eye set in a large red heart from which rays of light emanate. Nguyen Hao Ca decided on this in the belief that while the eye simply records what is seen, the heart has full realization. True knowledge, therefore, is found in the heart.

Also, unlike other Cao Daist sects, the Minh Chon Ly rejects many traditional Vietnamese beliefs and practices—such things as the Thien cult, the Cult of Ong Tao, and beliefs in the numerous spirits (the *ma, qui,* and *than*) are not tolerated. Nor do they observe some of the usual Cao Daist food taboos such as not eating food derived from living creatures. The only traditional Vietnamese cult allowed is the Cult of the Ancestors.

The hierarchical structure of the Minh Chon Ly is symbolized in their My Tho cathedral by a pyramid of oil lamps below a large representation of the Nhan Tam, the "eye in the heart." The Committee of Three Great Heads is the highest ruling body, and within it, Nguyen Hao Ca, the founder, occupies the position of Thai Dau Su or Central Head. Below this is the Committee of Nine which is divided into the Tu Buu or Four Treasures, functioning as the secretariat, and the Ngu Hanh or Five Elements which is responsible for the five administrative regions in Vietnam. There also is a female hierarchy whose major functions are to proselytize among women and see to the religious instruction of female members of the sect. All the hierarchy reside at the Holy See, but the women have special altars at which they worship.

Another sect was founded in 1934 when, because of personal difficulties with the hierarchy of the Tam Ky, Nguyen Huu Chin left Tay Ninh with a group of fourteen followers known as the Seven Saints and Seven Sages. They remained briefly in a nearby village where they agreed to found a new sect, the Tien Thien, and they dispersed to gain followers in different parts of the delta. Their beliefs and organization resemble those of the Tam Ky and Ban Chin Dao sects and, although they claimed to have 72 temples by the eve of World War II, they still lacked a Holy See.

During the period of dissension, three relatively small and little known sects made their appearance. The Bach Y Lien Doan organized its headquarters in Tay Ninh Province some time during the early 1930s, and in 1931 the Minh Chon Dao established its Holy See in the southern city of Bac Lieu. In 1933 a small group broke away from the Minh Chon Ly, and under the leadership of Nguyen Van Kien organized in Tan An the Chon Ly Tam Nguyen, the smallest of the Cao Daist sects and also the most divergent in doctrine.

Although the French administration viewed the Tam Ky with favor, most other Cao Daist sects, associated as they were with nationalist movements, were regarded with suspicion. The Tien Thien was outlawed in 1940. During World War II and the Indochina War, Nguyen Ngoc Tuong, head of the Ban Chin Dao, and Nguyen Buu Tai, future leader of the Tien Thien, together with other members of Cao Daist hierarchies were investigated by the French authorities, and some were sent to penal colonies on the islands of Phu Quoc and Poulo Condor. During the Indochina War, French troops requisitioned the house of Nguyen Hao Ca, leader of the Minh Chon Ly, and in a battle between French and Viet Minh troops the Minh Chon Ly cathedral in My Tho was destroyed. With the exception of the Tam Ky sect, the Cao Daists were reduced to clandestine activities.

With the end of the Indochina War in 1954, the Cao Daists began to function more openly. The prisoners were released, and Nguyen Buu Tai organized the dispersed hierarchy of the Tien Thien sect. They established a Holy See at Soc Sai, a small town in the midst of the coconut estates 18 kilometers west of Ben Tre, and began construction of a cathedral which was completed in 1957. The Minh Chon Ly leaders began to reconstruct their Holy See and completed the cathedral in 1958. In 1955 the fortunes of the Tam Ky sect took an adverse turn. The leaders chose to join the Hoa Hao and Binh Xuyen[5] in their struggle against the newly formed government of Ngo Dinh Diem, and when they were defeated the Tam Ky sect lost its army and its right to collect taxes in the area surrounding the Holy See at Tay Ninh.

5. "The Binh Xuyen, a group of former river pirates who at one time cooperated with the Vietminh, were given the right to run Saigon's lucrative gambling houses and vice rackets, and later even put in control of the Saigon police." (Buttinger, p. 462.)

Appendix C

LUNAR CALENDAR

Twelve Lunar Year Cycle

Ty	Mouse
Suu	Buffalo
Dan	Tiger
Meo	Cat
Thin	Dragon
Ty	Snake
Ngo	Horse
Mui	Goat
Than	Monkey
Dau	Cock
Tuat	Dog
Hoi	Pig

Lunar Year Months[1]

Thang Gieng	Dan	Tiger
Thang Hai	Meo	Cat
Thang Ba	Thin	Dragon
Thang Tu	Ty	Snake
Thang Nam	Ngo	Horse
Thang Sau	Mui	Goat
Thang Bay	Than	Monkey
Thang Tam	Dau	Cock
Thang Chin	Tuat	Dog
Thang Muoi	Hoi	Pig
Thang Muoi Mot	Ty	Mouse
Thang Chap	Suu	Buffalo

1. The designations in the left-hand column also are used in the Gregorian calendar. In the lunar calendar the "complete months" have 30 days, the "incomplete months" have 29.

295

Hours of the Day

		A.M.
Ty	Mouse	1:00 to 2:00
Suu	Buffalo	2:00 to 4:00
Dan	Tiger	4:00 to 6:00
Meo	Cat	6:00 to 8:00
Thin	Dragon	8:00 to 10:00
Ty	Snake	10:00 to 12:00
		P.M.
Ngo	Horse	12:00 to 2:00
Mui	Goat	2:00 to 4:00
Than	Monkey	4:00 to 6:00
Dau	Cock	6:00 to 8:00
Tuat	Dog	8:00 to 10:00
Hoi	Pig	10:00 to 12:00

Seven Sample Days in the Lunar Calendar

9th day (Truc Mang) Day of the Cock, 6th lunar month (incomplete)
   Predominant element, Fire
   Predominant star, Chuy
   Unfavorable for marriage, burials
   Favorable for construction, ritual offerings, commercial dealings, to open a
      shop, long voyages
   Auspicious hours, Horse, Mouse, Goat
   Favorable ages,[2] Dragon, Snake, Buffalo
   Unfavorable ages, Cat, Mouse, Dog

10th day (Truc Binh) Day of the Dog, 6th lunar month (incomplete)
   Predominant element, Fire
   Predominant star, Sam
   Celebrate anniversary of spirit Vu Lan Bon
   Unfavorable for rituals and gatherings with guests
   Favorable for large projects and welfare endeavors
   Auspicious hours, Monkey, Pig
   Favorable ages, Cat, Mouse, Horse
   Unfavorable ages, Dragon, Goat, Buffalo, Snake

2. This refers to those born in a particular year, such as the Year of the Dragon or
Snake.

11th day (the Truc Dinh) Day of the Pig, 6th lunar month (incomplete)
  Predominant element, Wood
  Predominant star, Tinh
  Unfavorable for marriage, house construction
  Favorable for cult rituals, entering school, gatherings with invited guests,
    great voyages, tailoring clothes, cutting hair
  Auspicious hours, Horse, Goat
  Favorable ages, Tiger, Cat, Horse
  Unfavorable ages, Snake, Monkey, Mouse

12th day (Truc Chap) Day of the Mouse, 6th lunar month (incomplete)
  Predominant element, Earth
  Predominant star, Quy
  Unfavorable for long voyages, marriage
  Favorable for rituals, gatherings with guests, burials, signing contracts,
    commerce
  Auspicious hours, Buffalo, Cock
  Favorable ages, Buffalo, Monkey, Dragon
  Unfavorable ages, Horse, Cat, Pig

13th day (Truc Pha), Day of the Buffalo, 6th month (incomplete)
  Predominant element, Earth
  Predominant star, Lieu
  Unfavorable for marriage, great voyages
  Favorable for entering school, gatherings with friends, commercial rela-
    tions
  Auspicious hours, Tiger, Monkey, Pig
  Favorable ages, Mouse, Cock, Snake
  Unfavorable ages, Goat, Cock, Pig

14th day (Truc Nguy), Day of the Tiger, 6th month (incomplete)
  Predominant element, Metal
  Predominant star, Tinh
  Unfavorable for long voyages, burials
  Favorable for rituals, opening the market, commercial relations
  Auspicious hours, Buffalo, Goat
  Favorable ages, Pig, Dragon
  Unfavorable ages, Cat, Mouse

15th day (Truc Thanh), Day of the Cat, 6th month (incomplete)
  Season, Little hot season

Predominant element, Metal
Predominant star, Truong
Unfavorable for cult rituals, long voyages
Favorable for dealing with affairs of great importance
Auspicious hours, Cat, Horse
Favorable ages, Dog, Tiger, Buffalo, Mouse
Unfavorable ages, Cock, Snake, Horse

Appendix D

A MODEL HUI

DESIROUS of borrowing 4,000$ VN, Mrs. A (most participants in hui are women) organizes a hui with four other members, Mrs. B, Mrs. C, and Messrs. D and E. With five in the group, the hui will last five sessions, and at each one a participant will receive money. At the first session, the *chu hui* (the organizer), will receive a loan from the other members, and at subsequent sessions those who have not yet received money will bid on the basis of interest they are willing to pay for a loan. The maximal interest bid wins the loan for that session, and the amount of interest is deducted from the amount each participant in the bidding turns over to the winner. Those who already have received money, however, will pay the stated maximal contribution.

As hui leader Mrs. A is hostess, and at the first session she serves a large dinner. The maximal contribution has been set at 1,000$, and each of the participants gives her that amount (thus she realizes the 4,000$ she wanted). At the second meeting refreshments (no meal) are served, and on this occasion the other participants have an opportunity to bid for a loan. The bids, containing the amount of interest each is willing to pay, are written on slips of paper and passed to the leader. Mr. D wins, bidding 350$, and although Mrs. A as the nonbidder must give him 1,000$, the others pay him 650$ (350$ interest subtracted from the 1,000$ maximum). At the third meeting, Mrs. B wins, bidding 200$; both Mrs. A and Mr. D must give her 1,000$ each, the others give only 800$.

At the fourth meeting, Mrs. C wins with a bid of 150$, and she receives 850$ from Mr. E as well as 1,000$ from A, B, and D, giving her a total of 3,850$. At the last meeting Mr. E receives a total of 4,000$, or 1,000$ each from the other four participants. The result is that Mrs. A has received an interest-free loan of 4,000$, whereas Mrs. B and Mr. D pay interest of 50$ and 1,050$, respectively, for loans received. Mrs. C gains 400$ and Mr. E 700$ for their participation. The assumption in the hui is that early in the bidding those with the greatest need for loans will bid high while those who can wait, bid low, standing a chance to gain later.

Appendix E

TYPES OF RICE CULTIVATED IN KHANH HAU
(according to villagers' ranking)

I. *Oryza sativa*

A. Early or hasty rice (harvested some 90 days after transplanting)
  Tung xa
  Bangnon
  Samo
  Xiem
  Nang quot
B. Late rice (harvested some 120 days after transplanting)
  Rang chon
  Nang thom
  Ve vang (thanh tra)
  Tao huong
  Soc nau
  Trang nho
  Nang cho
  Nang ra
  Nang ray

II. *Oryza glutinosa*

Nep ruoi $\begin{cases} \text{moc, yellow grain} \\ \text{den, black grain} \end{cases}$
Nep bung
Nep sao tien
Nep ngong
Nep cang cuong

300

Vegetables Cultivated in Khanh Hau

VIETNAMESE	LATIN	ENGLISH
Bap (ngo)		Maize or corn
Bau dai	*Aegle marmelos,* Correa	Long gourd
Bau ngan	*Aegle marmelos,* Correa	Short gourd
Bi dao	*Benincasa hispida,* Cogn.	Variety of squash or gourd
Bi do	*Cucurbita maxima,* Duch.	Variety of squash
Bi xanh	*Benincasa hispida,* Cogn.	Variety of squash or gourd
Ca nau	*Solanum melongena,* Linn.	Eggplant
Ca tomat	*Solanum lycopersicum,* Linn.	Tomato
Cai bap	*Brassica oleracea,* Linn.	Cabbage
Cai be trang		Chinese white cabbage
Cai cu		
Cai sa-lat	*Lactuca sativa,* Linn.	Lettuce
Cai xanh	*Brassica juncea,* Hook. et Thunb.	Cole, kale
Dau bap	*Hibiscus esculentus,* Linn.	Okra
Dau haricot trang	*Dolichos catjang,* Linn.	White French bean
Dau haricot ve (dau mong chim)	*Phaseolus lunatus,* Linn.	Sieva bean
Dau haricot ve (dau que)	*Phaseolus vulgaris,* Linn.	Green bean
Dau phung	*Arachis hypogea,* Linn.	Peanut
Dua gang	*Cucumis melo,* Linn.	Melon
Dua hau	*Citrullus vulgaris,* Schrad.	Watermelon
Dua leo xanh	*Cucumis sativus,* Linn.	Gherkin
Hanh	(?)	Onion
He	*Allium angulosum,* Linn.	Welsh onion
Khoai lang	*Ipomoea batatas,* Lamk.	Sweet potato
Khoai mi (san)	*Manihot utilissima,* Pohl	Manioc
Khoai mo	*Dioscorea alata,* Linn.	Red yam
Khoai mon	*Colocasia esculentum,* Schott	Taro
Khoai tay	*Solanum tuberosum,* Linn.	Irish potato

Khoai tu	*Dioscorea esculenta,* Lour.	Variety of yam
Muop dang (kho qua)	*Momordica charantia,* Linn.	Bitter melon, balsam pear
Muop khia	*Luffa acutangula,* Roxbg.	Varieties of gourd related to Italian
Muop ngot	*Luffa cylindrica,* Roem.	squash or zucchini
Ot		Red chili pepper
Rau can	*Oenanthe stolonifera,* Wall.	Celery
Rau can nuoc	*Oenanthe stolonifera,* Wall.	Water celery
Rau can tau	*Oenanthe stolonifera,* Wall.	Chinese celery
Rau den	*Amarantus gangeticus,* Linn.	Brede de Malabar
Rau hung	*Mentha aquatica,* Linn.	Variety of mint
Rau huong	*Polygonum odoratum,* Lour.	Variety of thyme
Rau mung toi	*Basella rubra,* Linn.	Basella
Rau muong	*Ipomoea aquatica,* Forsk.	Spinach or bindweed
Rau que (hung cho)	*Ocimum basilicum,* Linn.	Variety of thyme
Rau rap	*Houttuynia cordata,* Thunb.	
Rau rut (nhut)	*Neptunia oleracea,* Linn.	
Thom (dua)	*Ananassa sativa,* Lindl.	Pineapple
Xu hao	*Brassica oleracea,* Caulo-Rapa	Turnip cabbage
Xu xu	*Sechium edule,* Swartz	Chayote

Fruit Cultivated in Khanh Hau

VIETNAMESE	LATIN	ENGLISH
Buoi	*Citrus grandis,* Osbeck	Grapefruit tree Pomelo tree
Cam	*Atalantia monophylla,* Correa	Orange tree
Cau	*Areca catechu,* Linn.	Areca nut tree
Chanh	*Citrus medica,* Linn. Subspecies *digitata,* Auct.	Lime tree
Chuoi	Musa	Banana tree
Dao	*Eugenia jambos,* Linn.	Peach tree
Dau	*Baccaurea sapida,* Muell-Arg.	Mulberry
Du du	*Carica papaya,* Linn.	Papaya tree (papaw tree)

Dua	*Cocos nucifera,* Linn.	Coconut tree
Khe	*Averrhoa carambola,* Linn.	Carambole tree
Long nhan	*Euphoria longana,* Lamk.	Longan tree
Man (roi)	*Prunus triflora,* Roxbg.	Jambose tree
Mia	*Saccharum officinarum,* Linn.	Sugarcane
Mit	*Artocarpus integrifolia,* Linn.	Jack tree
Oi	*Psidium guajava,* Linn.	Guava tree
Quyt	*Citrus nobilis,* Lour.	Tangerine tree
Tam duoc	*Phyllanthus distichus,* Muell.	Gooseberry
Tra hue		Variety of tea
Trau	*Piper bètle,* Linn.	Betel vine
Vu sua	*Chrysophyllum cainito,* Linn.	Milk apple
Xoai	Mangifera	Mango

Wild Fruits and Vegetables

Fruits

VIETNAMESE	LATIN	ENGLISH
Binh linh		
Le ki ma	*Lucuma mammosa,* Gaertn.	Mamey aspodilla or Mamey sapote
Mang cau (na)	*Anona squamosa,* Linn.	Anona or custard apple
Me chua	*Tamarindus indica,* Linn.	Tamarind
O-moi		Wild black fruit
Trai keo (keo tay)		
Trung ca		

Vegetables

Den den gai		
Rau cang cua		
Rau dang ruong		
Rau ma	Hydrocotyle	Marsh pennywort
Rau mo		
Rau muong	Convolvulus	Bindweed

Appendix F

Kin Groupings in Ap Moi and the Temple Sections of Ap Dinh A–B

PATRILINEAL kin groupings predominate in Ap Moi (Charts 1–4) but there are some exceptions. In Chart 1, Group d, the senior member of the group is an elderly widow who returned to her native village with her children. She resides in 12/5, her son is next door in 12/2, and her married daughter and her family live on the other side in 12/1. The daughter's husband came to Khanh Hau from the village of Cu Chi in the neighboring province of My Tho in 1940, and after his marriage he elected to remain in Ap Moi. The widow's elder brother's two sons live nearby in 13/1 and 13/2, a single structure divided into two separate units, and her younger brother's son lives in 10/3.

In Chart 1, Group e, there is also a mixture of patrilineal and non-patrilineal kin. The oldest member is an amiable man who holds the title Ca Truong in the Cult Committee. He resides in 12/4 with several widowed sisters and other kin. Two widowed sisters who periodically are visited by children and grandchildren live nearby in 13/3 and 13/4. One of the old man's sons lives in 12/3 (another son lives in 3/5 in Section D of the hamlet with his wife's kin grouping). This grouping is linked affinally to the group in 1f, on the edge of this section. The old man's wife's father's brother's eldest son is hamlet chief of Ap Moi and resides in 15/3. The hamlet chief's father's brother's son and daughter live close by in houses 15/1 and 15/2. The hamlet chief's father's sister married a man from Ap Dinh-A, and their offspring and families form part of a kin grouping around the Tien Thien temple.

Section B (Chart 2) consists of ten farmsteads scattered around the paddy fields. Group 2a is exclusively patrilineal, consisting of three brothers and their families in 10/1, 9/4, and 9/3. Group 2b also is composed of patrilineally linked households. The oldest member of the group is a villager who holds the title Ong Tien Bai, the second highest venerable in the Cult Committee. He lives in 9/5, sharing it with his youngest son's family; his eldest brother's son lives nearby in 16/2. Another brother's son lives in 5/2 in Section C. Ong. Tien Bai is a patrilineal kin of the hamlet chief, and his older son is deputy chief of the village and lives in 1/1 in Section D of the hamlet. The head of the household in 9/1 has distant kin in other hamlets of the village, but those living in numbers 10/2, 9/2, 8/4, and 8/5 (Fig. 18) have no kin in Khanh Hau.

Section C (Chart 3) has a total of 20 households, 18 of which are divided between two kin groupings. Group 3a, composed of 14 households, is a mixture of patrilineal and nonpatrilineal kin, and it simplifies explanation somewhat to identify Ego as Ong Ca Duoc (profile in Chapter 10). He is a prominent resident of Ap Moi and lives in 5/1. A large portion of this group is composed of his mother's kin. Two of her sisters returned to live with their paternal kin when their husbands died. A son of one sister lives in 5/3; the daughter of the other sister resides with her family in 6/4. Ong Ca Duoc's mother's eldest brother's son is in 8/2, and 8/1 is inhabited by his sister who is married to the brother of the man in 7/4.

Ong Ca Duoc's mother's younger brother (the only surviving sibling) lives in 6/5, which abuts the house of a daughter, number 6/7. Another daughter lives across the canal in 7/2, and a son lives next door to her in 7/3. On the other side of Section C, a son of one deceased daughter lives in 5/4. This surviving maternal uncle is married to the elder sister of Ong Ca Duoc's father's brother's wife. On his father's side, Ong Ca Duoc's father's brother's sons live in 6/2 and 6/3, and the son of the family in 6/2 lives in 6/6.

Group 3b is somewhat smaller but also has nonpatrilineal kin. Three brothers occupy houses 6/1, 7/1, and 7/5. Their father's younger sister's son lives nearby in 8/3. As indicated on Chart 2b, Ong Tien Bai's elder brother's son inhabits 5/2, a relatively isolated farmstead. House 8/6 (Fig. 18C) stands apart from the rest of the farmsteads, and its occupants have no kin in the hamlet.

Section D of the hamlet (Chart 4) has 19 households, 11 of which are part of four kin groupings. Group 4a consists of two brothers in 4/2 and 4/3, and Group 4b, located near the Buddhist pagoda, includes the monk in 2/3, his younger brother in 2/5, and their sister and her family in 3/5. The sister's husband is a son of the venerable indicated in Chart 1e for Section A, and he frankly admits he prefers living near his wife's kin than near his own kin group. Group 4c is composed of two brothers in 1/5 and 1/6, and their brother's wife's polygynous brother, a former village chief, maintains a household in 4/5, in another part of the section. House 1/1 of Group 4d is occupied by the deputy chief, and it has been pointed out that his father, Ong

Tien Bai, resides in Section B of the hamlet. Ong Tien Bai's sister's polyg-
nous son has one of his two households in 2/2. The deputy chief's wife's
mother and sister and her family live in 1/4.

Eleven households are represented in Chart 5, Group c. House 25/4 is
occupied by the leader of the sect in Khanh Hau. His youngest son and his
family live in the house, and another son lives in 23/5. The sect leader's
mother's younger brother's son lives in 26/1. Number 17 is occupied by the
sect leader's father's younger brother's son, and his father's sister's sons live
in 24/1, 22/1, and 26/3. The man in 26/3 is married to a woman from a
small kin grouping also living in this section. Her brother lives in 26/5, and
their father's younger sister's son resides in 26/2. A sister of the wife of the
man in 26/5 lives in 24/4, and this woman's husband's father lives nearby
in 24/3.

As shown in Figure 19, 27/4 is occupied by a family with kin in another
part of Ap Dinh-A. The man in 30/3 had an uncle who lived alone in the
house; after his death the man and his family came from another hamlet to
occupy the house and cultivate the extensive garden. An elderly man lives
alone in house 15, and he has kin in the hamlet. The sect provided him with
the plot of land on which his house stands, and he is aided by his kin. From
time to time grandchildren come to stay with him. Number 23/4 is an
elaborate masonry house, and although the head of the household has no kin
in the village, his wife is a distant kinswoman of the descendants of Marshal
Duc.

Six of the nine households in Chart 6 are a kin grouping of patrilineal
descendants of Marshal Duc, who live rent-free on this land owned by the
Duc family.

CHART 1. Kin Groupings in Section A, Ap Moi*

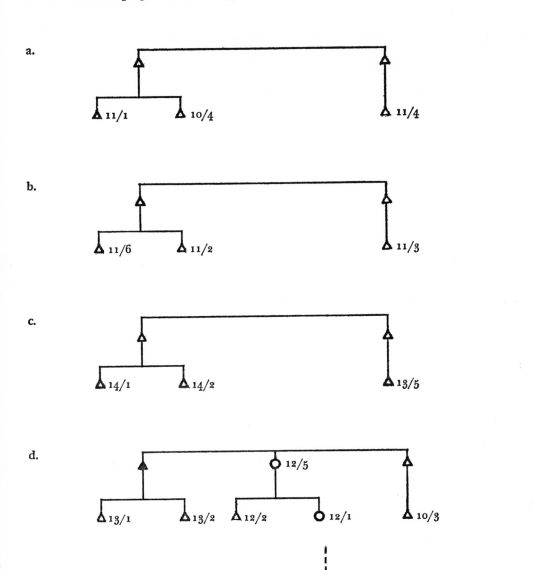

a.

11/1   10/4   11/4

b.

11/6   11/2   11/3

c.

14/1   14/2   13/5

d.

12/5

13/1   13/2   12/2   12/1   10/3

e.   f.

= 12/4   13/3   13/4
(venerable)

12/3   3/5 (Section D)   15/3 15/2   15/1
                          (hamlet chief)

* See Figure 18, p. 94. Solid symbols indicate deceased members.

CHART 2. Kin Groupings in Section B, Ap Moi*

a.

b.

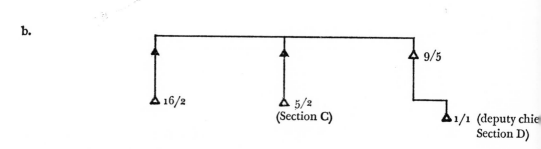

CHART 3. Kin Groupings in Section C, Ap Moi*

a.

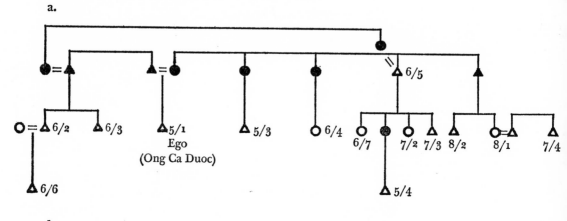

b.

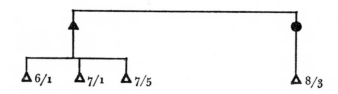

* See Figure 18, p. 94.

CHART 4. Kin Groupings in Section D, Ap Moi*

a.

△ 4/2   △ 4/3

b.

△ 2/3   △ 2/5   ○=△ 3/5 (son of venerable
                                        in 12/4, Chart 1e)

c.

△ 1/5   △ 1/6   △=○   △ 4/5

d.

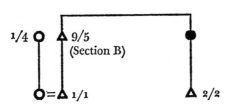

1/4 ○ △ 9/5   ●
       (Section B)

       ○=△ 1/1   △ 2/2

* See Figure 18, p. 94.

CHART 5. Kin Groupings Around the Ban Chin Dao Temple in Ap Dinh-A*

a.

b.

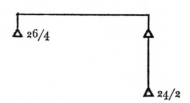

c.

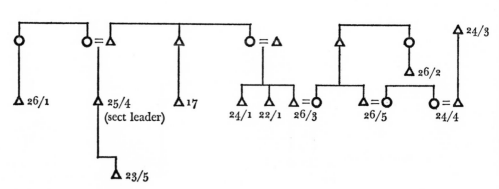

* See Figure 19, p. 97.

CHART 6. Kin Grouping Around the Tien Thien Temple in Ap Dinh-B *

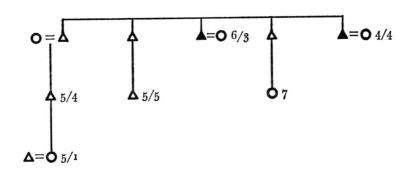

* See Figure 20, p. 98.

Glossary

Diacritical marks on all Vietnamese words have been omitted.

Cau An	an annual celebration
cong	one man-day of work
cong dien	communal paddy land
Cong Phu	Cao Daist daily prayer ritual
cu si	Buddhist lay monk
dinh	communal temple
gia pho	family genealogy book
giang do	all things needed for a funeral cortege
hat boi	classical Chinese plays
huong hoa	patrimony for upkeep of Ancestor Cult
hui	a tontine (see Appendix D)
la cham *la xe*	thatching methods
quoc ngu	romanized Vietnamese script
thien	the celestial forces
thuong luong	octagonal talisman with mirror in center
toc	patrilineage
truong toc	patrilineal head
$VN	Vietnamese dollars, 72 to U.S. dollar

MEASURES AND WEIGHTS

Traditional Vietnamese	*French*	*English*
LINEAR MEASURE		
*tac**	6 centimeters (6/100 m.)	2.36 inches
thuoc†	6 decimeters (6/10 m.)	23.62 inches
tam (truong)	no longer used	
SQUARE MEASURE		
cao (sao)	are (100 sq. m.)	about 4 poles
mau (10 cong‡)	hectare (10,000 sq. m.)	about 2.5 acres

313

FLUID AND CORN MEASURE

gia§	4 decaliters (40 liters)	8.8 gallons

WEIGHTS

ly	6 grams	
luong	60 grams	
can	600 grams	
yen	6 kilograms	13.24 pounds
ta	60 kilograms	132.24 pounds

* Four cm. in northern Vietnam.

† Forty cm. in northern Vietnam.

‡ Cong is used as a labor unit equivalent to one man-day of work; 12 cong previously equaled one mau (1 hectare, but since the introduction of chemical fertilizer this has been reduced to 10 cong.

§ In some places (not Khanh Hau), a gia equals 42 liters. Formerly the submeasure *o* was used, which equaled 1/10, 1/12, 1/16, or 1/20 of a gia, dependent on the type of grain measured and the province.

Bibliography

Anonymous, *Le Caodaïsme*, Saigon, Bao Ton, 1949.

Benedict, P., "An Analysis of Annamese Kinship Terms," *Southwest Journal of Anthropology, 3* (1947), 371–91.

Buttinger, J., *The Smaller Dragon*, New York, Praeger, 1958.

Cadière, L., *Croyances et Pratiques Religieuses des Vietnamiens, 1*, Saigon, Nouvelle Imprimerie d'Extrême Orient, 1958.

———, *Croyances et Pratiques Religieuses des Vietnamiens, 3*, Paris, École Française d'Extrême Orient, 1957.

———, "Religions Annamite et non Annamites," in G. Maspéro, *Un Empire Colonial Français, l'Indochine, 1*, Paris and Brussels, G. Van Oest (1929), 275–96.

Coquerel, A., *Paddys et Riz de Cochinchine*, Lyon, A. Rey, 1911.

Delvert, J., *Le Paysan Cambodgien*, Paris and The Hague, Mouton, 1961.

Deschaseaux, E., "Notes sur les anciens *don dien* Annamites dans la Basse-Cochinchine," *Excursions et Reconnaissances, 14*, Saigon, Coloniale (1889), 133–36.

Direction des Affaires Politiques et de la Sûreté, *Le Caodaïsme: 1926–1934, 7* (Contribution à l'Histoire des Mouvements Politiques de l'Indochine Française). Gouvernement Général de l'Indochine, 1934.

Donoghue, J. D. and Vo Hong Phuc, "My-Thuan: The Study of a Delta Village in South Viet Nam," *Provincial-Local Administration Series, 1*, Saigon, Michigan State University Vietnam Advisory Group, 1961 (mimeographed).

Durkheim, E., *De la Division du Travail Social*, 1893, trans. George Simpson and published as *The Division of Labor in Society*, Glencoe, Free Press, 1947.

Feng, Han Chi, *The Chinese Kinship System*, Cambridge, Harvard University Press, 1948.

Freedman, M., *Lineage Organization in Southeastern China*, London, Athlone Press, 1958.

Gittinger, J. P., "Communal Land Concepts in Recent Vietnamese Policy," 1963 (mimeographed).

———, ed., *Vietnamese Agricultural Statistics*, Saigon, United States Operations Mission to Vietnam, 1959.

Gobron, G., *Histoire du Caodaïsme*, Paris, Deruy, 1948.

Gourou, P., *Les Paysans du Delta Tonkinois*, Paris, Les Éditions d'Art et d'Histoire, 1936.

Hendry, J., *The Study of a Vietnamese Rural Community: Economic Activities*, Saigon, Michigan State University Vietnam Advisory Group, 1959.

Henry, Y., *Économie Agricole de l'Indochine*, Hanoi, Gouvernement Général de l'Indochine, 1932.

Hsu, F., *Under the Ancestor's Shadow*, New York, Columbia University Press, 1948.

Hu, Hsien Chin, *The Common Descent Group in China, and Its Functions,* Viking Fund Publications in Anthropology 10, New York, 1948.

Leach, E., *Pul Eliya: A Village in Ceylon,* Cambridge, University Press, 1961.

Le Thanh Khoi, *Le Viet-Nam. Histoire et Civilisation: Le Milieu et l'Histoire,* Paris, Les Éditions de Minuit, 1955.

Lynch, F., S.J., *Social Class in a Bikol Town,* Department of Anthropology, Philippine Studies Program, 1, University of Chicago, 1959.

Maspéro, H., "Études d'histoire d'Annam," *Bulletin de l'École Française d'Extrême Orient, 16* (1916) 1–55.

———, "L'Expédition de Ma Yuan," *Bulletin de l'École Française d'Extrême Orient, 18* (1918), 1–36.

Moorman, F. R., *The Soils of the Republic of Viet Nam,* Saigon, Ministry of Agriculture, 1961.

Nag, M., *Factors Affecting Human Fertility in Nonindustrial Societies: A Cross-Cultural Study,* Yale University Publications in Anthropology 96, New Haven, 1962.

Redfield, R., *The Little Community,* Chicago, University of Chicago Press, 1960.

Soothill, W. E., *The Three Religions of China,* London, Oxford University Press, 1951.

Tönnies, F., *Gemeinschaft und Gesellschaft,* 8th rev. ed., Leipzig, H. Buske, 1935.

Tran Van Giap, "Le Bouddhisme en Annam: Des origines au XIIIe siécle," *Bulletin de l'École Française d'Extrême Orient, 32* (1932), 191–268.

Weber, M., *The Theory of Social and Economic Organization,* trans. A. M. Henderson and Talcott Parsons, ed. Talcott Parsons, Glencoe, Free Press, 1947.

Woodruff, L., *The Study of a Vietnamese Rural Community—Administrative Activities,* 2 vols. Saigon, Michigan State University Vietnam Advisory Group, 1960.

Index

Adoption, 109–10; and social expectations, 223

Age grading: and kin terminology, 83, 84–86; in Cult Committee, 217. *See also* Kin (numeratives), Patrilineage

Age priority: and patrilineage head, 82, 90–91; in kin terminology, 83, 84, 85, 86; and ancestor veneration, 88, 90; in Cult Committee mobility, 217, 218. *See also* Kin (numeratives), Patrilineage

Agrarian Reform Program: promulgation, 42; implementation, 44; and tenancy, 46; and Village Council, 187; and communal land rentals, 190–91

Agricultural Credit Program (NACO): fertilizer-purchase loan program, 139–40, 176–77; repayments, reactions to, 177; and Village Council, 176–77

Agricultural Service (Service Agricole): and rice varieties, 136; pig program, 155–56; buffalo program, 157

Agriculture, Ministry of. *See* Agricultural Service, Crops, Fertilizer

American Aid Program, and Western medicine, 209

Ancestor veneration: and errant spirits, 76, 78; financial support, 82, 88, 89–90; and patrilineage, 88–91, 96, 280, 281–82; responsibility for, 88–91, 96; in engagement celebration, 101–02; in wedding, 104, 106; rituals, 128–30, 131, 132; pseudonym for deceased, 129; in Cau An celebration, 223–25; and celebrations related to socioeconomic status, 240, 243–44, 247, 254, 261, 266. *See also* Ancestry, House (ancestral), Kin (group corporateness), Patrilineage, Patrimony, Tet Nguyen Dan, Tomb, *Truong toc*

Ancestry, patrilineal: in northern and central Vietnam, 82; in Khanh Hau, 82–83, 88; of Duc family, 83, 89, 289

Animals, draft, 157–58; in rice planting, 136–37; in threshing, 144–45; taxes on, 192; sacred, in dinh, 220 n.

Asia Foundation: financial support of experimental garden, 153, of village kindergarten and maternity center, 208–09

Associations, village: Catholic, 58; funeral, 126; farmers', 175–76, 187; for younger and older men and women, 204. *See also* Village Agricultural Cooperative

Avoidance: of brothers-in-law, 107; during pregnancy, 107–08; during birth, 108–09; of real name, 109, 129; by children, 111. *See also* Taboos

Bachelors, social status, 233

Bamboo, as construction material, 28–29, 153

Bananas, varieties, uses, 151–52

Benedict, P., quoted, 5

Betel (leaves) and areca (nuts), 102–106, passim; 118, 125–26, 151, 237

Binh Xuyen, struggle with Ngo Dinh Diem, 294

Birth: rate in population pattern, 47–48; ratio to death, 50–52; preparation, 107–09; confinement 108, 109; ritual to "cleanse child," 109; new maternity center, 209–10. *See also* Pregnancy

Bride price, 102. *See also* Marriage (preliminaries), Wedding

Buddhism: Goddess of Mercy (Quang Am): protector of children, 111, 120; invoked for easy childbirth, 111

Mahayana (Chinese): introduction into Vietnam, 4; predominance in delta, 14–15, 55, 277; increasing formalization of, 59, 62–63, 283; practiced in village pagodas, 58–64; by cu si, 59, 64; rituals, 60–66; domestic deities, shrine, rituals, 120. *See also* Buddhist Studies Association, Cao Daism, *Cu si*, Hoa Hao, Monks, Nuns, Pagoda

Theravada (Indian): introduction into Vietnam, 4; persistence in delta, 14–15, 55

Buddhist Studies Association of South Vietnam, 59; and My Tho nunnery, 61–62

ricultural Cooperative, 174–75; Agricultural Service buffalo program, 157, 176

Crops: latania palm, 22–23; rice, 136, 147; commercial vegetables, fruits, 148; coconuts, 150–51; areca nuts, betel leaves, mangos, 151; bananas, 151–52; experimental, 151–52. *See also* Appendix E

Cu si: in Buddhist Association of South Vietnam, 59; in Ap Cau pagoda, 59–60; as healers, 64–65; geomancers, 65. *See also* Buddhism (Mahayana), Healers, Medicine, Therapists

Cult Committees: emergence and description, 214 ff.; membership, 215–18; mobility in, 217–18; members' participation in Cau An, Ha Dien, Thuong Dien, and Chap Mieu celebrations, 223–32; role of high venerables, 41, 232; membership and socioeconomic status, 240, 243, 246; and upward social mobility, 273–74. *See also Dinh,* Guardian Spirit, Mobility (social), Village Council

Cult of the Ancestors. *See* Ancestor veneration

Cults, private, 73–74

Dan Ve. *See* Self-Defense Guards

Death: ratio to births, 50–52; and Catholic priest, 58, 128; preparation for and registration, 123; notification, 124

Debt. *See* Credit

Deities, popular, 14, 77, 78, 79. *See also* Cholera, *and under* Spirits *as main entries*

Delvert, J., cited, 135

Descendants, Descent. *See* Patrilineage

Dien Bien Phu, battle, 9

Diet: meal schedules, 11, 115–16, 143; of Buddhist monks, nuns, and *cu si,* 61, 62, 64; and Cao Daists, 7, 293; prenatal, 107; postnatal, 109; and health, 117–19; vegetables, 148–50, 152, 301–03; fruits, 150–52, 303; meat sources, 154–56, 157–58; fish, shellfish, frogs, 158, 159, 160, 163–65; foodstands, 170; schoolchildren's lunches, 206–07

Dinh: historical function, 6; destruction during Indochina War, 9; land, 42, 221; functions 204, 205, 207, 242; description, 218–20; custodian, 218, 220–21; and Cau An rituals, 225–30; as focal center, 279. *See also* Cau An celebration, Cult Committees, Guardian Spirit

Dong Thap Muoi. *See* Plaine des Joncs

Drought: fear of cholera, 18–19, 188–89, 209; planting pattern, 139; rain-making ritual, 141; and Village Council, 188–89, 209; and land rentals, 188

Duc family: and village history, 7–8; and Cao Daism, 67, 249; ancestry, 7, 83, 89, 289; residence pattern, 97–98; and *truong toc,* 89, 250; Marshal Duc cult, 89, 212; place in village society, 234, 235, 248–50, 272; fortunes of, 248–51

Duck raising, 156, 198

Durkheim, E., cited, 276, 278

Education: literacy, 51–52, 208; preschool, 62, 208–09; expansion, 52, 206, 208–09, 284; facilities and administration, 206–09; primary school, 206–07; and celebrations, 207–08; secondary school, 208; adult, 209; and socioeconomic status, 239–40, 243, 254, 256, 257, 259, 264, 266, 271; and upward social mobility, 273. *See also* School of Ritual Studies

Elite, sociopolitical, 216; composition of, 240. *See also* Mobility (social)

Entrepreneurial activities: rice milling and merchandising, 170–73; 254, 259–60, 262; rice–lumber business, 236, 261; gas station, 236, 254; significance, 284

Errant spirits: and ancestor veneration, 76, 78, 130; placation of, 121–22, 130

Exogamy, 100. *See also* Marriage (preliminaries)

Family: kinship system, 82 ff.; nuclear, 82–83, 92; names, 109 and n.; Family Bill, 113 n.

Farmers' Association, 175–76, 187

Farmstead, 25–26. *See also* Settlement patterns

Feng, Han Chi, 5; cited, 82–83

Fertilizer: chemical, introduction, 139, 258; varieties, 139; use, 140; availability, 139–40, 176–77. *See also* Agricultural Credit Program, National Revolutionary Movement
  organic: dung, 139, 149, 158; compost, 139, 149; in gardens, 149–50, 154; buffalo hide, 154; rice bran, 171–72

Fines, and Village Council, 198–200. *See also* Punishments

Fish: dried, 158; traps, 159–61; nets, 161–62; shellfish, 159–65; ponds, 162–63; raising, 162–64; unsuccessful introductions, 164–65

Fishing: for amusement, 112; techniques, 159–62

Five-family group, 93 and n., 183, 204; head of, 195, 204; functions, 204

Food gathering: by children, 116; by rice gleaners, 147–48; fruits and vegetables, 152; mollusks, 162

Fortified village. *See* Strategic Hamlet Program

Freedman, Maurice, 5; quoted, 280–81

S